Man of
Douglas
Man of
Lincoln

Man of Douglas
Man of Lincoln

The Political Odyssey of
James Henry Lane

Ian Michael Spurgeon

University of Missouri Press   Columbia and London

Library of Congress Cataloging-in-Publication Data

Spurgeon, Ian Michael, 1976–
   Man of Douglas, man of Lincoln : the political odyssey of James Henry
Lane / Ian Michael Spurgeon.
        p. cm.
   Includes bibliographical references and index.
   Summary: "Focusing on the last twelve years of James Henry Lane's life,
Spurgeon delves into key aspects of his career such as his time as an
Indiana congressman, his role in Kansas's constitutional conventions, and
his evolving stance on slavery to challenge prevailing views on Lane's place
in history"—Provided by publisher.
   ISBN 978-0-8262-1814-8 (alk. paper)
   1. Lane, James Henry, 1814–1866.   2. Lane, James Henry, 1814–1866—
Political and social views.   3. Politicians—Kansas—Biography.
4. Kansas—Politics and government—1854–1861.   5. Indiana—Politics and
government—19th century. 6. Legislators—United States—Biography.
7. United States. Congress—Biography.   8. Slavery—Political aspects—
United States—History—19th century.   9. United States—Politics and
government—1849–1877. 10. Generals—United States—Biography.   I. Title.
   F685.L268S68 2008
   978.1'02092—dc22
   [B]

2008023295

♾ This paper meets the requirements of the
American National Standard for Permanence of Paper
for Printed Library Materials, Z39.48, 1984.

Designer: Jennifer Croppe
Typesetter: BookComp, Inc.
Printer and binder: Thomson-Shore, Inc.
Typefaces: Palatino, Adobe Garamond

For Larry and Debra Spurgeon

Contents

Acknowledgments

As a young and impressionable sophomore at Kansas State University in the mid-1990s, I remember first learning that one of my favorite history professors had written a book. I was in awe. The time, dedication, and expertise required to put together such a body of work for others to read and critique seemed monumental. While many children grow up with baseball players, police officers, or even comic book characters as their heroes, academic experts were my idols. Perhaps that made me a bit of a nerd, but it drove me all the same. This reverence for academia and the written word came from my parents, Larry and Debra Spurgeon, who encouraged me to take whatever interest I had to its highest level. For that reason, this book is dedicated to them.

Now that I have finished my own doctoral program and seen my research come together as a published book, I find my passion for research and writing, and my admiration of professional historians, just as strong. I feel honored to have the opportunity to share my work and can only hope that it offers something to historians and history enthusiasts alike.

I still see the creation of a book as a monumental task, and now understand that it can only be achieved through the help of others. I would like to thank all of my professors at Kansas State University for the wonderful education I received there. My Master's committee members, Dr. Donald Mrozek, Dr. Lou Williams, and Dr. Louise Breen, were particularly important to my maturing as a historian. During my doctoral program, the excellent historians at the University of Southern Mississippi pushed my work to a higher level. I want to thank my committee chairman Dr. Brad Bond for his support, and especially for his confidence and assurances during the dissertation process. I would also like to thank the rest of the committee, Dr. Greg O'Brien, Dr. Phyllis Jestice, Dr. Kyle Zelner, and Dr. Andrew Wiest, for their help, all of which has come together, I hope, to make me a competent historian.

Special thanks go to the archivists, librarians, and researchers (of which there are too many to name) at the Kansas State Historical Society, the Spencer Research Library at the University of Kansas, the National Archives and the Library of Congress in Washington, D.C., and the Indiana State Historical Society for their help in finding various primary materials. I would like to thank Erin Sloan and the rest of the staff at the Carl Albert Congressional Research and Studies Center at the University of Oklahoma for their extreme kindness and efforts to aid in my research. Though my visit to the center was brief, I will always remember their helpfulness and professionalism.

I must extend a special thanks to Clair Willcox, Beverly Jarrett, Jane Lago, and the rest of the staff at the University of Missouri Press. They gave this first-time author a great deal of guidance and support during the editing and publication process.

Finally, this book never could have come to fruition if not for the love and encouragement of friends and family. While my wife, Jade, has no interest in James Lane (or she hides it well), she nonetheless maintained an enthusiasm for my work that often seemed to exceed my own. Dennis and Teresa Murphy and Mark Anderson aided the completion of the study in countless ways and I will always be grateful.

Though this book would not be what it is today, or even be in print, without the contributions and influence of the people mentioned above, I take full responsibility for any errors or problems found within.

Man of
Douglas
Man of
Lincoln

Introduction

"Senators, we hear, must be politicians—and politicians must be concerned only with winning votes, not with statesmanship or courage," wrote John F. Kennedy in the introduction to his Pulitzer Prize–winning work *Profiles in Courage*.[1] No better example of this popular belief can be found than James Henry Lane of Kansas (1814–1866). Indeed, this tragic figure of territorial and Civil War Kansas has become known as one of America's most notorious nineteenth-century politicians. His fiery stump speeches and radical ideas carried him to the U.S. Senate, yet created a veritable army of critics. Furthermore, his transition from a pro-Douglas Democrat and supporter of the Kansas-Nebraska Act of 1854, to a prominent free-state leader in Kansas and associate of rabid abolitionist John Brown by 1856, to a "radical" Republican and friend of Abraham Lincoln in 1861, and finally to a "conservative" Republican and supporter of Andrew Johnson in 1866 seems to suggest a concern for votes typical among professional politicians. Yet, assumptions can be wrong. Kennedy did not defend the negative stereotypes of politicians, but challenged them. It is time someone challenged what "we hear" about James Lane.

What we read about Lane today has been heavily influenced by his unforgettable appearance and dynamic personality. Lane's mastery of western stump speaking became legendary in Kansas and across much of the nation in the years leading to the Civil War. His long, slender frame—reaching at least six feet in length—carried a sharply defined, and most often beardless, face punctuated by deep, piercing eyes. A receding hairline

1. John F. Kennedy, *Profiles in Courage,* 2.

1

exposed a smooth and prominent forehead crowned by wild shocks of hair pointing to the sky in various directions. If Lane's words electrified a crowd, they certainly seemed to electrify him as well. He could sway an audience like an orchestra director, exciting its senses and emotions. He ranged from low, guttural growls to high shrieks as he lectured fellow Americans on the most pressing matters of the day, pointing a long bony finger toward the crowd for effect, and gazing at them with those powerful eyes. As his speech warmed up, Lane was known to partially undress himself, like a man preparing for a street fight. Off came his jacket, then tie; then he would roll up his shirt sleeves, all the while holding the audience with his eyes. A speech from Lane was part political lecture, part evangelical sermon, and part theatrical production.

The forty-year-old former Mexican War colonel and politician from Indiana entered Kansas Territory in the spring of 1855, in the heart of the struggle over whether that territory would be admitted into the Union as a slave or free state. Within this environment he thrived. Quickly, Lane became a leading figure in the free-state ranks, acting as a political mover and shaker, and military commander. He experienced extreme highs and pathetic lows, as enemies within both proslavery forces and the free-state ranks made his rise difficult. Nonetheless, by the time of the Civil War, James Lane nearly dominated Kansas politics. Loved by many, but hated by many others, Lane was acknowledged by all as a force to be reckoned with.

This book is not a narrative biography of Lane. It is not the author's intent to discuss every episode or issue in Lane's life and political career. Instead, this book analyzes his larger political actions and principles during the last twelve years of his life, from 1854, when he served as a freshman congressman from Indiana, to 1866, when he died while serving as a senator from Kansas. At the heart of the matter stands the issue of consistency. Virtually no historian sees uniformity or regularity in Lane. Some historians have concluded that Lane had few if any principles, that he was a political opportunist at best or a madman at worst. Others rationalize Lane's apparent inconsistencies by emphasizing his strengths and contributions or simply acknowledging them with no explanation. Ultimately, this book argues that Lane indeed embraced democratic principles, that his larger actions were more consistent to those principles than generally believed, and that his political career consisted of a series of pragmatic responses to prevailing events.

Understanding Lane's actions, beliefs, and principles during the last twelve years of his life is complicated by the man's troubled personality, his controversial actions and words, and the chaotic events that surrounded him. As a result, historians and writers have largely failed to delve deeply enough to truly understand him. For instance, Lane's 1855 move into the Free State Party in Kansas is generally interpreted as an abandonment of the Democratic Party. On the contrary, Lane and other Free State members unmistakably maintained their traditional party affiliations even within the new organization. For months, even years, the Free State Party was intended to be a temporary interest group for people of all parties to unite with the single goal of establishing Kansas as a nonslaveholding, or free, state. Historians who have portrayed Lane's move into the Free State Party and even his eventual rejection of the Democratic Party as opportunistic or a change of principle have only looked at the surface and have taken him out of the larger political environment. They have ignored the vast political upheaval which took place across the country, and in the North particularly. Politics in Kansas proved to be far different from what the emigrants had known back east. And when sectional problems destroyed the Whig Party and depleted the Northern Democratic establishment, countless people, like Lane, abandoned traditional party identities and sought membership in new organizations dedicated to handling the volatile political climate. The Republican Party itself rose from the ashes of the Whigs and Know-Nothings, and drew in thousands of disgruntled Democrats. Lane's political realignment was not an anomaly; it is an example of the type of personal experience thousands of politically active Americans experienced in the 1850s.

Traditional views of Lane have done a disservice to the man, to Kansas history, and ultimately to the history of mid-nineteenth-century American politics. Only by investigating his interests and principles before, during, and after his transition into various political alliances can we understand his actions. Only after careful analysis of Lane within the political environment of Kansas and the North does method emerge from what so many have ascribed to madness. Lane was a man of his time, responding to events of his time. Through a more thorough analysis of Lane in his setting, historians will better understand not only his personal history but also the creation of Kansas and the breakup of the Democratic Party and formation of the Republican Party during one of the most dramatic political eras in the country's history.

Undertaking this study of Lane proved difficult for a variety of reasons. For one, Lane left little organized record of his views and work. He was a master stump speaker, who often spoke spontaneously. His personality, chaotic life, and untimely death in 1866 prevented the preservation of much of his correspondence. He moved repeatedly and also lost a great deal of personal property during William Quantrill's 1863 guerrilla raid on Lawrence, Kansas. Thus, there is no complete collection of Lane papers. His material is scattered, with partial collections located at the University of Kansas and the Kansas State Historical Society. Some sources may be found at the University of Oklahoma and at the Indiana State Library. Finally, individual letters turn up in various collections around the United States, including the Abraham Lincoln collection at the Library of Congress.

Yet, the scavenger hunt for Lane primary sources was not the greatest obstacle this writer faced—nor was the time spent trying to decipher Lane's atrocious handwriting. Instead, interpreting the wide variety of written material about Lane proved to be the biggest task. Simply put, authors have either loved James Lane or hated him. There is no consensus on what kind of a man he was. Much of the historical work on Lane was written in the years following the Civil War by people who knew him. These writers published memoirs or accounts of the struggle for Kansas to provide what they believed was the "truth," but that was really often an attempt to establish their own place in history. Lane fit into these publications as a hero or as a villain, depending upon the personal feelings of the author; and Lane had a lot of opponents. Proslavery forces vilified him as a radical who raised the "black flag" on the prairie and whose mental instability posed a threat to the nation as a whole.[2] Some free-state men—mostly New Englanders—also aligned themselves against Lane for various reasons. Furthermore, Lane was often his own worst enemy, providing ammunition for critics through his often emotionally charged words and actions.

The battle over Lane's place in history extends back to his own lifetime, but became particularly heated following the 1860s. Friends and opponents wrestled over his image in Kansas history, setting off a writing war that has heavily influenced modern interpretations of the man. Although historian Craig Miner provided a brief but excellent synopsis of the historiography of Lane in his article "Lane and Lincoln: A Mysterious Connection," and Robert Collins devotes the final chapter of his recent biography *Jim Lane: Scoundrel, Statesman, Kansan* to a discussion of various perspectives on Lane, there is as yet no established historiographical model of James Lane history.[3] Therefore, for this study, I have created a model to

2. The term "black flag" was a popular symbol (at least rhetorically) of total war. In the context of the Kansas-Missouri conflict, particularly during the Civil War, guerrilla units were said to carry the "black flag" to show they took no prisoners.
3. Craig Miner, "Lane and Lincoln: A Mysterious Connection," 186–99; Robert Collins, *Jim Lane: Scoundrel, Statesman, Kansan*, 283–304.

identify the major attitudes and perceptions of Lane and the most influential authors who espoused them. It is hoped this model may offer a basic review of Lane history and identify the common assumptions and beliefs within the field. Four basic historiographical groups can be found in the historical writing on James Lane: Critic-Contemporaries, Defender-Contemporaries, Moderates, and Critic-Consensus.

Following Lane's death in 1866, his reputation, like John Brown's, rose. Both figures were often celebrated as heroes in the late struggle to end slavery and preserve the Union. But as men and women who had lived during Kansas's territorial and wartime days began publishing memories and reminiscences, a battle over the saints and villains of Kansas history erupted. The Critic-Contemporaries and Defender-Contemporaries emerged from this literary battle.

The Critic-Contemporaries surfaced around the 1880s, but really developed in the 1890s. As the name implies, this school took a critical view of Lane. The group saw Lane as an opportunist, generally unstable, and brash to the point of being dangerous. Critic-Contemporary authors had either known Lane personally or knew his colleagues, some of whom were personal and political rivals of Lane. Two of the most important men in this school were Charles Robinson and George W. Brown. Both men worked closely with Lane as leading figures in the free-state movement in Kansas. Yet, both came to oppose Lane (and each other) shortly before the Civil War. Robinson, a New Englander, served as Kansas's first state governor. Brown (no relation to John Brown) was also from New England and edited the *Herald of Freedom*—a free-state newspaper published in Lawrence that was notorious for its outspoken denunciation of proslavery interests. Although Robinson and Brown had been personal adversaries during the late 1850s, they came to an understanding in the last decades of the nineteenth century in the interest of writing Kansas history. Sharing mutual disdain for Lane, the two men promoted each other's positive influence in Kansas history while denouncing their common enemy. Historian Craig Miner credits Robinson's book, *The Kansas Conflict*, as the genesis of the critical historical view of Lane. Robinson portrayed Lane as "destitute of principles or convictions of any kind, and of moral and physical courage."[4] Throughout the former governor's work, Lane is

4. William Elsey Connelley identified the cooperation between Robinson and Brown in his rebuttal to them, stating that in 1879 the two men had attended a meeting in Kansas that celebrated the contributions of John Brown to the Free State cause. Both men, Connelley explains, left the meeting "deeply chagrined" and "conspired to begin

condemned as selfish and reckless. Robinson did not always feel this way, at least not publicly, as he had praised Lane at various times for working to make Kansas a free state. But, by the time of the Civil War, the two men had split into separate factions of the Republican Party and clashed over military and political matters. As will be seen, the political infighting, which led to Robinson's early retirement from public office, heavily influenced his portrayal of Lane in later writings.

Brown's treatment of Lane was equally harsh. At times during Lane's life, Brown had turned the pages of his *Herald of Freedom* into an anti-Lane organ, and his distaste for Lane never waned. Apart from his newspaper articles, Brown never wrote in much depth about Lane—his proposed book on the subject was never finished. Nonetheless, the editor's late published works include some very direct criticisms of Lane. George Brown attempted to break down the celebration of John Brown in Kansas history and memory, a figure who was often associated with Lane in both deed and memorial, in his not-so-subtly titled work *False Claims of Kansas Historians Truthfully Corrected*. He decried the attempt of some Kansans to celebrate John Brown and Lane at the expense of other significant individuals—including himself. "Is it not wonderful that a person reared from early youth in free Kansas," Brown wrote, "and enjoying all the bounties of institutions secured to the State by its first pioneers, sees proper to make Eli Thayer, Andrew H. Reeder, Charles Robinson, and G. W. Brown subjects for his severest criticisms, and exalts into heroes, yea, almost gods, John Brown and James H. Lane, the authors and projectors of disorder and violence on the Free State side?"[5] In 1902, during the finalization of *False Claims,* Brown described his plans to write a similar treatise on Lane, explaining, "It is very probable as soon as my present book in press is completed I shall take up Jim Lane, and tell what I *know* about him." He saw little difference between Lane and the fanatical John Brown.

---

a systematic course of blackening the characters of those from whom Robinson had dissented in his erratic career in Kansas." Connelley further described a published letter from Robinson to Brown calling on him to write a history of Kansas; Connelley, *An Appeal to the Record,* 4–7. Brown described some communication with Robinson in a 1900 letter, explaining that Robinson had "invited me to write of Lane." In the same letter, Brown compliments Robinson's own publication as among the best treatises of Kansas history; George W. Brown to M. L. Fields, October 27, 1900, George W. Brown Collection, Kansas State Historical Society, Topeka. Miner, "Lane and Lincoln," 189; Charles Robinson, *The Kansas Conflict,* 377.

5. Brown specifically refers to Kansas historian William Elsey Connelley; George W. Brown, *False Claims of Kansas Historians Truthfully Corrected,* 13.

"Both were detriments to the Free State cause," he declared, and predicted that "so the future historian will write."[6]

The chief academic voice of the Critic-Contemporary school was Leverett Spring. Unlike Brown and Robinson, Spring had not personally taken part in the struggle over Kansas. His book *Kansas: The Prelude to the War for the Union*, published in 1885, was among the first comprehensive historical studies of the fight for Kansas statehood. His coverage of Lane was brief, but included direct references to undocumented rumors used by Lane's political opponents. In 1898, Spring's article "The Career of a Kansas Politician" expounded upon many of the rumors and assumptions that had circulated in Kansas for decades. He dismissed a few negative rumors as unreliable or exaggerated, yet his work not only accepted but helped legitimize for the historical field the image of James Lane as the absolute opportunist, void of principle and driven only by personal ambition.[7] Spring did not paint Lane simply as a con artist, for the author, like many others of the time, recognized Lane's value to the free-state cause and the Union during the Civil War. Nonetheless, for Spring, Lane's faults outweighed all else. "The personal magnetism of Lane, his enormous energy, his remarkable gifts of stump-oratory, and his impulsive patriotism," Spring wrote, "were accompanied by qualities of rashness, demagogism and moral obliquity, which made him, in spite of all that belongs to his credit, and the sum of it is not inconsiderable, a dangerous man."[8]

Opposing the Critic-Contemporary school of thought stood the Defender-Contemporaries. This group also consisted of individuals who had personally known Lane or relied upon information of those who had, but portrayed Lane in a favorable light. Lane's eccentricities and his faults were not ignored or covered up. Instead his sincerity, good works, and dedication to antislavery principles and the Union served as the primary focus for authors within the Defender-Contemporary camp. John Speer stood out among this group. Running his own newspaper in Lawrence, Kansas, during Lane's political career, Speer became one of Lane's closest friends and associates. In 1897 he published a massive treatise of Lane, which mainly

6. George W. Brown to Maria, October 23, 1902, George W. Brown Collection, Kansas State Historical Society, Topeka.

7. Spring wrote of the popular rumor that Lane had joined the Free State ranks in Kansas because the proslavery territorial government denied him a divorce, but explained that "It must be considered merely as an incident—unexpected, significant, possibly prophetic of evil—not as a capital event." Spring, "The Career of a Kansas Politician," 82.

8. Ibid., 104.

provided personal sketches, reminiscences, and stories, and offered comparatively little analysis. Speer recognized the growing critical view toward Lane, and provided a response to arguments that Lane was contradictory on the slavery question and a mere political opportunist. He described a man sincerely reacting to dangerous political and social events, rather than lustily taking advantage of the chaos. Speer not only identified with Lane's antislavery cause, for Brown and Robinson had been instrumental figures for the free-state cause as well, but also celebrated Lane as the great leader against proslavery forces: "It was in the initiatory effort to resist this tyranny that he literally broke loose in all his power, fury and energy. Thence onward he was indomitable and unconquerable."[9]

Speer's work, like all of the Defender-Contemporary camp, was heavily steeped in the Bancroft nationalist school of thought, which interpreted American history with romantic ideals. A strong tone of celebration wafts from the work, and Lane jumps from the pages not merely as a successful leader during a difficult period of American history, but as an honorable man, a hero, fighting for right against evil forces—whether it was black slavery, slaveocratic oppression, or intemperance. Speer writes glowingly that "this man, the child of the frontier of civilization, the advance herald of two wars, the leader in the Kansas Conflict against Slavery, was one of the most abstemious men I ever saw."[10]

William Elsey Connelley carried the Defender-Contemporary school well into the twentieth century. Serving as the Kansas Historical Society's secretary at the turn of the century, Connelley became one of the most prominent writers on Kansas history. His interest in Kansas not only helped build an enormous personal library of material but also contributed to the Kansas Historical Society's impressive collection. Connelley was a firm adherent of the nationalist-style approach to Kansas history. He championed Lane and many other Kansas figures as heroes of American history. The first line of the first chapter in his book *James Henry Lane: The "Grim Chieftain" of Kansas,* published in 1899, declared, "The genius and indomitable will of Lane liberated a land."[11] His romantic views on the subject flow throughout the book.

Great men leave the impress of their genius upon the institutions they help to found. To rightly understand the institutions of our State, it is necessary that we should have some knowledge of the men who builded

9. John Speer, *Life of Gen. James H. Lane,* 12.
10. Ibid., 9.
11. William Elsey Connelley, *James Henry Lane: The "Grim Chieftain" of Kansas,* 11.

[*sic*] it. In this view the study of the life of the late Senator James Henry Lane becomes to us a duty. That Senator Lane did service so valiant, so vital in the noble cause of freedom that he should be accorded the gratitude and love not only of this but of all the coming generations in Kansas and the nation, has long been the almost unanimous opinion of the people of this State.[12]

Connelley emerged as George W. Brown's chief opponent in the battle over writing Kansas history. Brown's *False Claims of Kansas Historians Truthfully Corrected* specifically challenged Connelley's *John Brown*—Connelley being the primary "Kansas Historian" referred to in the title. Not to be outdone, Connelley responded with his own publication, entitled *An Appeal to the Record.*[13] The competing interpretations of these two writers shows a split along the lines of Frederick Jackson Turner's thesis of frontier advancement. Brown championed the contributions of the refined East, especially the New England Emigrant Aid Company with its figures. The rough western characters, among whom James Lane was an extreme example, appalled many New England emigrants during Kansas's territorial days—a distaste carried into later years by Brown. Connelley, on the other hand, celebrated western and frontier imagery. He downplayed the role of New England in making Kansas a free state, much to the chagrin of Brown. "To make any appreciable impression in Kansas, the New Englanders were too far from pioneer conditions," Connelley wrote in 1929. "They had lost the pioneer instinct. And the political structure of Kansas bore scant portions of New England thought and tendencies. It was Western to the core and in some features radical, new and revolutionary." Summing up his position, in true Turnerian style, Connelley stated, "But your true Westerner carried with him the genius of the American people and the destiny of the republic."[14] The figure of James Lane became caught in the middle of this ideological battle, as a hero to one side and villain to the other.

The last remnants of the Defender-Contemporary school may be found in the words of Lloyd Lewis's address to the Kansas State Historical

---

12. Ibid., 8–9.

13. The full title listed on the cover page of the book is *An Appeal to the Record Being Quotations from Historical Documents and the Kansas Territorial Press, Refuting "False Claims" and other things written for and at the instance of Charles Robinson by G. W. Brown. And Some portions of the Public Records of Charles Robinson and G. W. Brown, taken from the Archives of the State Historical Society. Also Many Authorities and Documents relating to the New England Emigrant Aid Company, and its Transactions in Kansas.*

14. Connelley, "Introduction," in Wendell Holmes Stephenson, *The Political Career of General James H. Lane*, 5.

Society in 1939. Lewis, a playwright and journalist, called Lane "The Man the Historians Forgot," and lamented the passing of Lane's image from Kansas, and national, memory. Like Connelley, Lewis saw the battle over Kansas history as a struggle between New England and the West. "New England never liked Kansas' most influential citizen of the 1850's and 1860's," he told his audience. "That is one of the reasons—there are others—why the schoolbooks of America either have no mention at all of Jim Lane, or merely dismiss him with a few sneering phrases." Lane was a westerner, and as such "was not to be understood by the elegant authors of New England—the Brahmins who in that day decreed what was good taste in literature."[15] Like other Defender-Contemporaries, Lewis painted a romantic image of James Lane, that of a tragic figure whose charisma helped lead Kansas to freedom. Even Lane's death by suicide in 1866— usually seen as the culmination of his decline in political standing and his recurring bouts of depression—was described in quixotic terms: "He was the pioneer, the adventurer, the restless hunter for new horizons, and the glories of that time had vanished. He was a revolutionist, and the revolution had been won. . . . He was a fighter, and the war was over." His suicide, explained Lewis, was a journey into "a place often mentioned in the religious litanies of his Calvinistic boyhood, a strange dreaded region in which the fuel was promised to be everlasting. This might be the place for him now." Lewis concluded: "He would go and see."[16]

Lewis's address to the Kansas State Historical Society entertained and inspired members dedicated to preserving Kansas's historical significance. But its romantic idealism was giving way. First, since many of the authors were contemporaries of Lane, their historical writing careers began very late in life. Robinson, Brown, and Speer wrote of Kansas events they had experienced decades earlier. The personal crusades to influence the historical record ended as the generation passed away. Second, the historical field as a whole changed as the new scientific approach to history took shape in the latter part of the nineteenth century. The relationship between amateur and professional historians began to crumble. The romantic and celebratory tone of the nationalist school no longer found as welcome a reception within the increasingly methodical field of history.[17] Within this general trend, a new study of Lane emerged. It served as the

15. Lloyd Lewis, "The Man the Historians Forgot," 85–86.
16. Ibid., 102–3.
17. For a good review of this general shift in American historiography see Ernst Breisach, *Historiography: Ancient, Medieval, and Modern*, 2nd ed., 287–90.

foundation of what will be referred to as the Moderate school of Lane historiography. Wendell H. Stephenson produced the most comprehensive study of Lane to date with *The Political Career of General James H. Lane.* Written during his masters and then doctoral work at Indiana University and the University of Michigan respectively, Stephenson provided the first truly academic book-length study of Lane. The author stands at the heart of the Moderate school for what may be called a comparatively literal approach to history. Relying upon meticulous research, the author generally shied away from the rumors, stories, and personal opinions so important to the previous historiographical groups.

There is another reason why Stephenson's work may be classified as "moderate": it is largely noncontroversial. While he states in his preface that his study "seeks to explain Lane's transition from Indiana conservatism to Kansas radicalism, to reveal him as a leader of the 'intense radical loyalty' of the United States during the Civil War, and to explain his motives for reverting to conservatism," the explanation Stephenson gives is primarily simple narrative.[18] The text provides little analysis or interpretation—a fact recognized and even complimented by William Connelley, who wrote the introduction for the book: "So it is fine of Doctor Stephenson that he has given us here this balanced biography of Lane. He has avoided the controversies of Lane's day and has even ignored the bitter malice with which he was constantly attacked in life and in death. He found these themes unnecessary to his purpose. A plain statement of fact was all that the establishment of Lane's position and power required. This statement he has made in a masterful way."[19] Stephenson's "plain statement of fact" offers readers a good narrative description of Lane's life and actions, but little guidance on how to interpret it. The author's most significant attempt at analysis is left to the last chapter, entitled "Character and Leadership," which focuses mostly on the power of Lane's reputation and image among his contemporaries.

Completely departing from the conflict between the Critic-Contemporaries and Defender-Contemporaries, Stephenson made no value judgments about leading Kansas figures. Of the rivalry between Lane and Robinson (both during their lives and in later imagery) he wrote that "it would be useless to speculate upon the relative contributions of the two men. Indeed it was fortunate for the free-state cause that the party

18. Stephenson, *Political Career of Lane,* 7.
19. Ibid., 6.

contained diversity of leadership."[20] However, not even Stephenson's moderate approach to Lane's life left his work completely objective. Stephenson leaned toward the "Defender" side—an association strengthened by chief historical "Defender" Connelley's praise of the work. Within Stephenson's pages, Lane does not appear callous, unprincipled, or cold. He is a tragic figure, whose extreme energy and ambition brought him fame and success, but in turn limited any rise to greatness and became a weapon for his enemies.

Stephenson's book remains the most balanced and thoroughly researched publication on Lane to date. The author moreover refused to step far into the minefield of interpreting Lane's actions.[21] Some authors have followed Stephenson's work with a more moderate, noncontroversial assessment of Lane in their larger studies of Kansas historical topics. William Zornow, in *Kansas: A History of the Jayhawk State,* provides one example. The author related one of the most contentious parts of Lane's life, his entry into the free-state ranks in Kansas, in a matter-of-fact way: "Lane, a former Democratic congressman from Indiana, joined the free-staters, but many antislavery Democrats did not follow him."[22] While such generic description may seem hardly suited to a historiographical categorization, when compared to the final school of thought, the degree of difference becomes apparent. The Critic-Consensus provides the dominant perception—a consensus among many historians—of Lane in modern Kansas historiography. Heavily influenced by the Critic-Contemporaries, this school largely portrays Lane according to his popular faults. The authors within this class range from mildly critical of Lane to unapologetically condemnatory. W. G. Clugston was among the first historians of this school. His description of Lane in *Rascals in Democracy* stands at the extreme critical end of the school:

> The truth of the matter is that Lane had no honest convictions about any-
> thing—religion, politics, personal honor, or public trust. Apparently he

20. Ibid., 160.
21. Historian Craig Miner credits Lloyd Lewis's "The Man Historians Forgot" as doing "more to establish a balanced view of Lane in a style to the public" than any other historian and that it did "more to interpret the real Lane than anything written before or since." Lewis's work is well balanced, but the author's professed admiration of Lane and the heavy denunciation of Lane's critics edges him away from standing as a true balance between the two early historiographical schools. Miner, "Lane and Lincoln," 191.
22. William Frank Zornow, *Kansas: A History of the Jayhawk State,* 70–71.

considered life just a gigantic fraud, and that there was no purpose in living except to satisfy appetites and vanities of the flesh by whatever hook
or crook he could do so. There can be no question about his turning to
Kansas with no purpose in mind other than to get on the winning side
and promote himself to a position of power and prestige.[23]

The image of Lane as a man with no principles and no interests beyond
self-promotion has taken firm hold among many, if not most, historians of
Kansas. Allan Nevins, in his award-winning series *Ordeal of the Union*,
described Lane as "unprincipled and often unscrupulous, a selfish opportunist and a political turncoat." Nevins believed that "the chief objects of
this histrionic manipulator, full of stock tricks, but of unresting industry in
building up his political following, were simply prestige, power, and
money."[24] Albert Castel, one of the most influential historians of Civil War
Kansas, followed suit. "In an era of opportunism," Castel wrote, "Jim Lane
was a supreme opportunist. Among the demagogues of his time—and few
periods had more—he was pre-eminent in energy, persistence, and sheer
gall. Moreover, until the very end, and despite occasional setbacks, few
were more successful. To describe his stormy career is to offer a study in
demagoguery, American Civil War style."[25] And for Kenneth Davis, author
of a comprehensive work on Kansas history published in 1976, Lane was
"aided, too, in his pursuit of power by his freedom from scruple and principled commitment."[26]

The Critic-Consensus school continues to grow, as some of the most
recent publications on Kansas territorial history echo the description of
Lane as shallow and unprincipled. Historian Nicole Etcheson, in her 2004
publication *Bleeding Kansas: Contested Liberty in the Civil War Era*, interpreted Lane's early actions in Kansas as a "chameleon-like change of political principle,"[27] while Donald Gilmore, author of a recent, self-proclaimed
revision of the Missouri guerrilla image, provided one of the most condemning descriptions of the Kansas figure, even questioning the character of men who supported Lane:

He had extraordinary, albeit eccentric, oratorical skills when his audience was naïve, politically polarized, and easily moved by emotional

23. W. G. Clugston, *Rascals in Democracy,* 64.
24. Allan Nevins, *Ordeal of the Union,* vol. 2: *A House Dividing, 1852–1857,* 391–92.
25. Albert Castel, "Jim Lane of Kansas," 23.
26. Kenneth Davis, *Kansas: A History,* 49.
27. Nicole Etcheson, *Bleeding Kansas: Contested Liberty in the Civil War Era,* 71.

appeals and demagoguery. His speeches were often harangues delivered in a bizarre, rasping, affected voice, punctuated throughout by
audible gasps for air and resembling nothing so much as a crazed, back-
woods preacher gone mad. But even men of his own party fell under his
charismatic sway, and their sanction of him must be considered an
indictment against their own characters. . . . Lane was amoral, totally
pragmatic, and shifted his political sails to suit the time, place, and his
need for money and political support. He was pugnacious, ruthless—
both politically and personally—sometimes crooked, and indifferent to
human life and suffering.[28]

The Critic-Consensus school of thought does not simply include historians who blatantly call Lane amoral or unprincipled. The strength of this
historiographical camp has been enlarged by the prevalence of its more
subtle interpretations of Lane's actions. The portrayal of Lane as unprincipled, easily swayed by popular opinion, and contradictory has led many
historians to misread his real stance on important issues. The range of
these misperceptions and the information behind them are too complex to
elaborate here, but throughout this study, arguments by historians within
the Critic-Consensus school will be challenged in light of Lane's words, his
actions, and the environment in which he worked.

Very recently some writers have turned slightly away from the traditional perceptions of Lane and suggested that his actions did not quite
match the extremist interpretations offered by previous schools of
thought. It may be premature to offer a title for this infant historiographical school, for it is only now coming to light. Robert Collins's *Jim Lane:
Scoundrel, Statesman, Kansan,* published in 2007, investigates the great
divide in literature on Lane, and overall offers a more defensive view of
Lane. At various times, the author rightly suggests that Lane's critics and
his defenders failed to understand his ideas and his actions. For instance,
when abolitionist John Brown, Jr., supported Lane despite the Lane's previous comparison of blacks to mules, Collins writes that "it suggests
Lane's views on slavery were evolving, or that his remarks on the issue
had been misinterpreted by friends and foes alike."[29] Unfortunately, the
author offers little analysis of Lane's deeper political ideologies or principles to back this and other suggestions. As a result, many of these important points remain conjecture. Furthermore, Collins embraces the image of

28. Donald Gilmore, *Civil War on the Missouri-Kansas Border,* 63–64.
29. Collins, *Jim Lane,* 47.

Lane as an opportunist. At one point, he argues that "as much as his enemies wanted to portray Jim Lane as a radical, it should be remembered that he was always a politician first. As a politician, Lane used the threat of radicalism to obtain political compromises. When compromise was achieved, however, the radicals were left behind."[30] While Collins generally takes a positive approach to Lane's political maneuvering (he sees Lane's political skill as something almost admirable), the author fails to note the consistency and sincerity behind much of Lane's work.

Nicole Etcheson's essay "James H. Lane: Radical Conservative, Conservative Radical," in *John Brown to Bob Dole: Movers and Shakers in Kansas History,* edited by Virgil Dean, also makes an important conclusion about Lane's political actions. Regarding some of Lane's more notable and radical positions, such as the use of black soldiers during the Civil War, Etcheson correctly argues that "he often supported the radical position for conservative reasons."[31] While her overall work portrays Lane's changing political allegiances as "chameleonlike" and does not reflect much consistency in Lane's political career, her discussion of Lane as a product of his political and social environment is extremely important, and tackles an element of Lane's life and career ignored for far too long.

This study expands upon and pushes past some of these new views of James H. Lane and sets out to challenge the writers of the Critic-Consensus school in particular, but nearly all previous studies of James Lane. Readers will find a "defensive" tint to this work, and this author admittedly identifies more with the Defender-Contemporary and Moderate schools of thought than with the critics. Because Lane led free-state forces in Kansas, more emphasis is placed on antislavery and free-state ideas than on their proslavery counterparts. Yet, I have avoided the celebratory, traditionalist approach. The free-state and antislavery settlers in Kansas are not seen as fighters for the side of right, but simply as men and women who struggled for what they believed was right. Consequently, Lane should not be seen as a champion of good or right, but as a man who labored in his own way for a free state of Kansas and the stability of the Union, and as a man who promoted his own political career.

This book is not intended to be an apology for, or justification of, James Lane. While it defends his larger political actions as consistent to firmly set

30. Ibid., 141.
31. Nicole Etcheson, "James H. Lane: Radical Conservative, Conservative Radical," 44.

principles, it should not be taken as a defense of his controversial personality or his habits. His means of protecting those principles often appear shocking. Some of his behavior suggests that he may have suffered from occasional bouts of an emotional or mental affliction. Yet, acknowledging those controversial traits does not preclude an examination of his greater interests and objectives. This study attempts to explain *why* he took the positions he did and to trace his political transition—his political odyssey—and show consistency where others have seen only change. Lane is presented as a three-dimensional character: talented and flawed, radical and conservative, compassionate and ruthless. This book shows how these contradictions came together in a unique blend, each element emerging in response to certain events and each promoting his cause.

Challenging most historical conclusions about a man or a subject is a daunting task. I admit, when I began this book I did not expect to take such a bold stance. I expected to find great change in Lane's life and career. How could a man of Stephen Douglas's ideology become a man of Abraham Lincoln's party? It seemed obvious that a politician who left Indiana in 1854 a pro-Pierce, pro-Douglas, pro–Kansas-Nebraska Act Democrat and became a pro-Lincoln, self-proclaimed radical Republican by 1861 must have undergone a monumental transformation, or even changed sides and affiliations to suit fleeting interests. I originally hoped to provide a new and better account of how and why Lane went through this transformation. After collecting most of my primary material, I created a chronological list of his words and actions. Details and stories from contemporary newspapers made up the biggest part of this list. I believed that if there was any rhyme or reason to Lane's transformation, only following it as it happened could bring it to light. If the man was as contradictory and opportunistic as his critics have alleged, I expected to find a jumble of thoughts and actions, with little consistency except that which would advance his personal career.

The chronological list proved to be a useful tool, and immediately brought important details into perspective. For instance, I paid special attention to Lane's political affiliations, listing by date when he first openly attended a Free State meeting in Kansas, when he called himself (or was referred to by others as) a Democrat, and when he officially joined the Republicans. Through this I came to find his consistent association with the Democrats (and his defense of Franklin Pierce and Stephen Douglas) after his entrance into the Free State Party blatantly obvious. This meshed perfectly with the Free State resolution that all traditional party affiliations were to be maintained and only sidelined temporarily for the sake of free

Kansas statehood. His Democratic identity can be easily followed in the primary sources until the spring of 1856 when he and Douglas had a falling out.

As my research continued, I became increasingly convinced that previous discussions of Lane failed to understand the overall meaning of his words and actions. Those who played him off as an amoral opportunist and consummate politician did not explain his stubborn defense of democratic principles and his habit of going against popular will or authority. Those who championed him as a radical convert to Republican ideas of freedom and liberty failed to acknowledge his consistent and conservative dedication to the same old-line Democratic principles, including popular sovereignty. Gradually, I questioned the whole idea of a change or transformation. By looking beyond his wild appearance and reputation, his personal rivalries, and even his quest for political advancement, I found underlying consistency and reason. This study does not deny that Lane was opportunistic to a degree. Lane was ambitious; he loved politics and thrived in backroom wheeling and dealing. He kept his finger on the pulse of his constituency, and his ultimate goal was to reach the U.S. Senate. Nonetheless, he endeavored to lead Kansans as well as follow their guidance—and he often proved to be a very strong, enterprising, and even prophetic leader.

The idea that Lane maintained a dedication to democratic principles, a dedication to political party, and a constant interest in protecting the Union, may seem too far-fetched to some. It is my hope that this study will challenge others to reconsider Lane, to look past the wild rhetoric and disheveled appearance, to look past the old and tired laments of his critics, and find more about this fascinating and tragic man.

1

Lane in Indiana, 1854–1855

"I am no advocate of slavery."

Historians of territorial and Civil War Kansas have largely ignored James Lane's work and words in his native Indiana, before his more public career in Kansas began. He is generally characterized as an ambitious politician who, after falling out of favor with voters in his native state, moved to Kansas with hopes of attaining power in any way—and with whatever group—he could.[1] This simplistic approach fails to appreciate his embrace of the Democratic Party and the Union, as well as his distaste for the institution of slavery. Without an understanding of his early career in Indiana, historians cannot accurately interpret his actions in Kansas.

He was born on June 22, 1814, in Lawrenceburg, Indiana, a town near the banks of the Ohio River on the Kentucky border.[2] He was the third of

1. For instance, see Albert Castel, *Civil War Kansas: Reaping the Whirlwind*, 20.
2. There are conflicting reports of Lane's birthplace. Most historians agree he was indeed born in Lawrenceburg, but during Lane's lifetime it was sometimes recorded as Kentucky. Lane himself was apparently responsible for the confusion, as he listed Indiana as his birthplace while a member of the U.S. House of Representatives, but claimed Kentucky heritage on the roll of the Topeka constitutional convention; *Congressional Globe*, 33rd Cong., 1st sess., pt. 1, 611; *Kansas Historical Collections*, vol. 13, 163.

seven children. James's father, Amos Lane, a native of New York, became a prominent public figure and U.S. congressman in Indiana, while his mother, Mary, came from Connecticut. Though from eastern parentage, Lane grew up and thrived in the rougher, western environment of young Indiana. His education was fairly limited by eastern standards—it is sometimes described as similar to that of his later associate Abraham Lincoln.[3] But his mother served as a public school teacher for many years, giving James a more substantial foundation of learning than many of his opponents and later historians have assumed.

Unfortunately, we have little knowledge of Lane's personality as a young man. We know that he dabbled in commercial business, opening a dry goods store, and engaged in "packing pork, slaughtering hogs, selling goods, building, speculating and forwarding produce down the [Mississippi] river."[4] But he did not find commercial pursuits appealing, and turned to the study of law in his father's office.

In 1841, Lane married Mary Baldridge, a member of a fairly prestigious family. Relatively little is known of Mary—she kept a low profile, especially compared to her husband. Over the course of their marriage, the couple had four children. Though a very capable attorney, Lane practiced law only intermittently throughout his life, for shortly after pursuing a legal education he followed his father into politics and, more specifically, the Democratic Party. Lane made his first political speech in 1832 in support of Andrew Jackson.[5] But it was not until the 1840s that he became an active player in local politics. In 1845, Lane ran for, and nearly won, a state congressional seat. Despite the loss, his name and reputation in Democratic circles grew.

The outbreak of the Mexican War in 1846 temporarily halted Lane's political activities, but thrust him into an even bigger spotlight. When Indiana Governor James Whitcomb called for the organization of military regiments for federal service in May of that year, Lane energetically responded by equipping a company in his home county of Dearborn.[6] The lean thirty-two-year-old Lane—who was described as over six feet tall—was unanimously elected captain. The Dearborn volunteers were attached to the Third Indiana Volunteer Regiment and Lane was elected colonel. Although

3. A comparison is made between the frontier upbringing of both Lane and Lincoln in Stephenson, *Political Career of Lane,* 17, and Miner, "Lane and Lincoln," 187.

4. *Crusader of Freedom,* February 3, 1858.

5. Stephenson, *Political Career of Lane,* 28.

6. Ibid., 20.

unschooled in military affairs, he worked hard to promote discipline among the ranks and to train his men and officers, and himself, in drill and contemporary tactics. The work paid off in the battle of Buena Vista, when the Third Indiana withstood and broke a Mexican attack. Earning the nickname the "Steadfast Third," Lane and his men were celebrated as heroes by their family and friends at home. But controversy erupted when their commanding general, Zachary Taylor, criticized the conduct of the neighboring Second Indiana Regiment, which had begun to crumble in the fight, and virtually ignored the contributions of the Third Indiana. Taylor lauded the bravery of Mississippi troops—commanded by his son-in-law, Jefferson Davis—that had stood next to the Indianans.[7] Despite numerous efforts by Indiana officials to have Taylor amend his reports and give credit to Lane's men, the general stood by his words. The rift between Taylor and the Indiana men held little military significance but would become an important political issue in the 1848 presidential election. A majority of the state voted for Lewis Cass rather than Taylor.[8]

After the Third Indiana disbanded, Lane helped organize the Fifth Indiana Volunteer Regiment. Serving as colonel of the unit, he again returned to Mexico. The regiment did not see combat, but was noted for its excellent discipline and drill. While stationed in Mexico City after hostilities had ceased, Lane was appointed provost marshal during the American occupation. According to historian William Connelley, Lane excelled in this position, maintaining order and protection for Mexican residents. Grateful women in Mexico City presented him with a finely made banner of black cloth decorated with yellow silk.[9] The Fifth Indiana also awarded their young colonel with a richly decorated sword. Lane's popularity in Indiana skyrocketed from his military exploits. Though the Mexican War postponed his political career, Lane was nonetheless kept up to date on political matters by his father. Amos Lane impressed upon his son a deep passion for the Democratic Party and an equally distasteful view of the Whigs. "The leading Whigs are the blackest Traitors to this country and ought to be hung in preference to the most murderous Guerillas in Mexico," Amos wrote James in early 1848. "[Henry] Clay is now in Washington making speeches and using his influence with his friends to disgrace

7. Jefferson Davis was a graduate of West Point. He later served as secretary of war under Franklin Pierce and, more notably, as president of the Confederacy during the Civil War.

8. Stephenson, *Political Career of Lane*, 25.

9. See note by William E. Connelley in ibid., 27.

and starve the army and dishonor his country in the eyes of all the world."[10]

A letter from Lane to his wife during the Mexican War does offer a tantalizing view of his personality, including a self-awareness of his public image. "I had you know some reputation as a fighting man & to have remained at home during the progress of this war would have ruined me forever."[11] Exactly what Lane meant by the term "fighting man" is unclear. It might refer to his support of the Mexican War, which was vehemently opposed by the Whig Party. Lane likely spoke in support of the war, and felt that his military service was proof of his sincerity and commitment to that event. He may have also been talking about a personal reputation for action and conflict. During the war, and afterwards, Lane was involved in a few disputes (some nearly resulting in duels) with various individuals.

For instance, before the battle of Buena Vista, tension developed between Lane and a fellow Indianan, General Joseph Lane (no relation). The circumstances of the dispute are unclear, but at one point a verbal argument turned violent. James Lane had formed his regiment on a parade ground, when General Lane approached and expressed a few unpleasant remarks. The colonel approached him and the two exchanged sharp words, before Joseph Lane threw a punch. James dodged the blow and immediately slammed his fist into the superior officer's face. As other officers intervened, the general reportedly called on his rival to prepare for a duel and pushed his way to his tent. Colonel Lane approached his regiment, which had watched the whole affair, and asked them to not get involved. But, as General Lane reappeared with a musket and headed toward James, some soldiers in the Third Indiana prepared their own weapons to protect their colonel. Before the confrontation went any further, a military guard arrived and escorted the general away.[12] This event, and others, suggests James Lane was not adverse to facing confrontation. He may have developed a reputation in his local area as a fighter—which may not have been a particularly negative image in the rough and often dangerous western culture. Honorable military service would cement his image as a brave man willing to face any challenge.

10. Amos Lane to James H. Lane, January 24, 1848, James H. Lane Papers, Kansas Collection, Spencer Research Library, University of Kansas Libraries.

11. James H. Lane to Dear Wife, Encero, Mexico, June 21, 1848, James H. Lane Papers, Kansas Collection, Spencer Research Library, University of Kansas. Libraries

12. David Lavender, *Climax at Buena Vista: The American Campaigns in Northeastern Mexico, 1846–47*, 168–69. For other examples of Lane's personal disputes see Thomas Gibson letter to *Daily Commercial*, March 2, 1845, James H. Lane Papers, Spencer

In his letter to Mary, Lane professed a desire to back his reputation, so as not to seem inconsistent or untrue to his stated beliefs. Referring to his service with the Fifth Indiana, he declared, "I came out the second time because I was committed before I left Mexico—& consistency required my return." Yet, Lane struggled to balance love for his family with a pull toward public service—or at least toward a prominent role in public life. He assured Mary that his safe return home meant that "duty to my country and party [have been] discharged" and that he would never leave them. But Lane would not keep that promise—and later it would lead to a divorce. Though he declared that his family's "happiness & their comfort will be my moving principle," he eagerly jumped back into Democratic politics and an active political career upon returning to Indiana. Larger interests and principles drove James Lane.[13]

In 1849, Lane was elected lieutenant governor of Indiana. His time in this position was relatively uneventful—his service as the official host of Hungary's exiled revolutionary leader Louis Kossuth during an 1851 visit to Indiana stood as one of the most significant events. By 1852, the former colonel looked to more politically active fields with his bid for Indiana's Fourth District congressional seat. That same year, the Democratic Party in Indiana appointed Lane as a presidential elector. Throughout the late summer of 1852, Lane traveled across southern Indiana stumping for his own election and that of Democratic presidential candidate Franklin Pierce. His work paid off, as both men won their respective elections. For Lane, the victory was particularly sweet, since Democrats had only narrowly won his district congressional election two years earlier by a meager 68 votes. He managed to garner a 944-vote majority.[14] Thus began his political career on the national stage.

Like many freshman congressmen, he rarely spoke on the House floor, and when his name does appear in the *Congressional Globe* the discussions often focused on technical or procedural matters unrelated to the great issues of the day. On one occasion he did voice his opposition to legislation that aided the construction of a railroad in Minnesota. He argued that the proposal conflicted with the homestead bill (something he supported) and with his personal and party principles by denying land to common

Research Library, University of Kansas Libraries; Charles Robinson, *The Kansas Conflict*, 178–79.

13. James H. Lane to Dear Wife, Encero, Mexico, June 21, 1848, James H. Lane Papers, Kansas Collection, Spencer Research Library, University of Kansas Libraries.

14. Stephenson, *Political Career of Lane*, 34. Stephenson notes that the Indiana congressional districts changed during this time.

settlers for the sake of railroad owners. "Now," he told his colleagues in the House, "my first lesson in Democracy was, that we should legislate for the whole people, and not exclusively for the rich and well born. The doctrine of legislating for the rich, and trusting to them to take care of the poor, has always been opposed by me, and by the party to which I belong."[15]

Beyond a handful of Lane's speeches or letters, historians have had relatively little to analyze from this period in his life. However, a small spat between Lane and a few of his colleagues in Congress in early 1854 provides a valuable look—a small gold mine of information—at his opinions and perceptions of slavery and the Union. The disagreement began simply enough when Lane interrupted Maryland representative Augustus Sollers's speech on the paying of personal claims during a House committee discussion on March 10, 1854. Lane's request for a clarification for some reason irritated the Marylander, who sarcastically retorted that young Lane spoke out only to have "his name in print in connection with my own." The remark drew laughter from the floor. Chastising Lane further, Sollers offered "a lesson of wisdom," suggesting that the Indianan "had better undertake to control the sentiments of his constituents, than to be controlled by them."[16]

Humiliated at the personal slight, Lane charged that if Sollers believed that the interruption was designed to gain notoriety, "it exists wholly in his own imagination, and that there is not the slightest foundation for it in truth." As for the matter of constituent representation, Lane turned the tables and challenged Sollers: "I understand the gentleman from Maryland to say that he moulded [sic] the opinions of his constituents." Sollers immediately denied the characterization.[17] Undeterred, Lane took a jab at Southern slaveholding interests, suggesting that Sollers meant to "mould the opinions of that portion of his constituents, five of whom, under the provisions of the Constitution, can only count as three." Lane referred to the Three-Fifths Compromise—the constitutional provision that determined that slaves would count as three-fifths of a person for representational or statistical purposes. When Sollers again demurred, Lane repeated his charge, stating that he had no doubt "that the gentleman from Maryland has the ability to mould the opinions of that portion of his constituency that

15. *Congressional Globe*, 33rd Cong., 1st sess., 574.
16. Ibid., 603, 604.
17. Ibid., 604–5; Sollers' denial is a bit surprising, for during his original response to Lane he stated: "I would not assume the privilege of controlling my constituents, and not be controlled by them. I would mould public opinion, that public opinion might not mould me."

requires five men to count as three." In comparison, Lane continued, "I am thankful that I represent no such constituency. I am here representing an independent constituency whose opinions cannot be moulded by any influences."[18]

While Sollers did not appear to take any further insult from Lane's comments, Theodore Hunt of Louisiana certainly did. Hunt asked the presiding member if Lane was out of order "in reflecting upon gentlemen representing a slaveholding constituency?" Lane, perhaps sensing an escalation of sectional tension among the other members, quickly denied any broad meaning to his statements. But the spark had been lit. Grumbling rippled across the floor as Hunt and Sollers rose to respond to Lane. The Southerners were somewhat stymied by Representative Alfred Edgerton of Ohio, who struggled to silence the matter by calling on the question of order. When the chairman attempted to end the brewing conflict, the members engaged in a brief debate on the point of order. A vote was taken upon whether "the decision of the Chair [shall] stand as the judgment of the committee?" The chairman's decision was overturned by five votes and Hunt claimed it a symbolic victory, somehow equating the technical rules vote as a successful response to Lane. "I consider the Constitution vindicated," Hunt announced, "and that this action is a rebuke of the gentleman who has used expressions in the way of disparagement of members upon this floor representing slaveholding territory." Over the cries of "Order," Lane rose and delivered a final retort for the day, stating that if Hunt "intends to apply the term rebuked to me for any sentiment I have uttered, I laugh it to scorn!" He concluded with a final assurance that he had "uttered no expression intended to disparage members upon this floor representing bond or free territory."[19]

What had begun as a mere interruption by Lane to clarify a minor matter had degraded into personal jabs and quickly spiraled into a small sectional spat. When challenged, Lane insisted that his thinly veiled criticism of the Three-Fifths Compromise was not meant to disparage slaveholding states and their representatives. Such efforts to soothe the ruffled feathers of Southern representatives failed to appease anyone. Three days later,

18. Ibid. There is evidence that Lane's actual remark was: "The gentleman may mould the sentiments of his curly-heads; but thank God I represent a constituency that does not require five men to count as three." This version was quoted by Representative Hunt on the House floor three days later, saying that the *Congressional Globe* account had incorrectly reported Lane's words in a way that softened the insult. Ibid., 610.
19. Ibid., 605, 606.

Louisiana representative Hunt again brought the matter up on the House floor as part of a "personal explanation." He felt compelled to correct the *Congressional Globe*'s coverage of the previous discussion, stating that the reporter had softened Lane's language. In reality, Hunt argued, Lane had spoken in a manner and with words "offensive to me, and to every Representative on this floor of a slaveholding constituency." The Louisianan then called upon Lane to clarify "whether he used the language of scorn and defiance personally and to me."[20]

Lane's response to Hunt provides invaluable insight to his views on slavery and the Union. "I am no advocate of slavery," Lane explained. "I am no slavery propagandist; and yet my history will prove that I have gone as far, and will go as far . . . to maintain the constitutional rights of gentlemen representing slave States upon this floor and maintaining the rights of their constituents." He called upon others to check his personal history to find a defense of Southern rights "and the rights of every State of this Union." Looking at his colleagues there in Congress, Lane boomed that he knew "no difference between northern and southern States. I shall know no difference. Brethren all—all interested in perpetuating the harmony and integrity of this Union." Finally, the loyal Democrat who favored union over sectional partisanship announced, "I shall go as far as any of you in trampling out agitation in the North, and as far as any of you in trampling out agitation in the South, which is calculated to disturb the harmony of the Union."[21]

Following this short declaration, Lane attempted to justify his comments to Sollers on March 10 as "playful" in nature, and not meant to insult any member. He had taken Sollers's comments as good-natured, and, Lane now argued, simply returned the lighthearted sarcasm. Hunt stood dumbfounded. "Sir, upon my word, I never was more astounded since I was born," the Louisianan confessed. "It was considered in quite a contrary light by every gentleman around me. The offense was general, and there was a general indignation." Lane, according to Hunt, had acted in a scornful and biting manner, with a "sardonic play of his features." Hunt lectured Lane on behavior and ideas of honor, and the matter was finally dropped.[22]

Lane's row with Sollers and Hunt illuminates his effort to balance personal views with the need to preserve party and national unity during an

20. Ibid., 610.
21. Ibid., 611.
22. Ibid.

increasingly tense period. The *Congressional Globe* provides transcription of a speech, but it does not relate the tone or mannerism of the speaker. We know that Hunt took personal offense to Lane's comments, in both substance and in tone. Perhaps Lane truly intended to be playful as he threw the barb at slaveholding representatives. If so, he severely underestimated the sensitivity surrounding sectional differences—a mistake that would suggest that Lane was extremely naive about significant national issues. Instead, Lane likely referred to the Three-Fifths Compromise out of frustration. Sollers first charged Lane with trying to get his name in print, and then offered some "wisdom" in dealing with constituents. These sarcastic comments inflamed Lane's well-known sensibilities and were perceived as an insult. Thus, he responded with an intentional low blow to the Maryland representative. When challenged by Hunt to explain his remarks, Lane stepped back and attempted to soothe the congressman. He had embraced the Democratic interest of minimizing sectional conflict, and when faced with an increasingly irate Southern member, he cooled down. Lane may not have wished his comments to stir up a sectional fight in Congress—hence, his repeated attempts to disclaim any insult to the South—but he had identified an important ideological difference between representatives of slaveholding and free states, and he used it against a Southern opponent.

Overall, the argument of whether Lane was playful or spiteful is unimportant. Lane clearly separated himself from the institution of slavery and slaveholding interests. His declaration that he was "no advocate of slavery" was a strong, defiant expression of his personal sentiments even in the midst of minimizing his sectional loyalties. He did not identify himself as proslavery. In fact, he did not leave the matter ambiguous—Lane was not a friend to the institution. But Lane cherished the Union, its integrity, and its laws and wished to protect it from radical forces. Protecting and preserving the Union meant recognizing Southern rights and interests.

Lane's dedication to the Democratic Party and peace within the Union would be tested further when one of the most important and explosive pieces of legislation in American history made its way through Congress. In early 1854, Illinois Senator Stephen Douglas introduced his plan to organize the territories of Kansas and Nebraska in a manner he expected both Northern and Southern Democrats would ultimately approve. He hoped to provide an issue that would help unify the Democratic Party, which had begun losing support at the grass-roots level.[23] Instead, the bill

---

23. Michael F. Holt, *The Political Crisis of the 1850s*, 144.

agitated sectional tension and placed Northern Democrats, such as Lane, in a delicate balancing act between personal principle and party loyalty.

Known as the "Little Giant," Douglas was becoming a powerhouse in U.S. politics during the 1850s. Voicing a personal dislike of slavery, Douglas nonetheless labored to soothe Southern politicians within the Democratic Party in order to promote his own rise to power as well as his desire to construct a transcontinental railroad through the western territories. The railroad project met opposition from Southerners on both principled and practical grounds. Western railroad development required territorial organization, which in turn opened the door to the creation of new states. Americans had attempted to balance the power between slave and free states in the Union since the early national period. Various legislative arrangements, most notably the Missouri Compromise of 1820, had provided temporary solutions as new territories organized. Yet, by the 1850s, some Southerners saw the Missouri Compromise, which restricted slavery in territory of the Louisiana Purchase above the geographical line of 36 degrees 30 minutes, and other federal laws that restricted slaveholding property rights, as unconstitutional. As a practical matter, slaveholding Missourians were particularly wary of a new free state opening up along their border.[24]

In 1853, Douglas and his fellow Illinois representative William A. Richardson chaired the Senate and House committees on the territories. In the spring of that year, their efforts to organize the territories north of 36°30" had succeeded in the House, but failed in the Senate because of Southern opposition. Missouri Senator David Atchison was a particularly vociferous defender of slaveholding interests and shared the fears of his constituents being surrounded by free states. Douglas received word from Atchison and other leading Southern senators that passage of his Nebraska bill in the Senate required the elimination of the slavery ban from the territories; it would require a repeal of the thirty-year-old Missouri Compromise.[25]

After a couple of failed attempts to weave his legislation around the Missouri Compromise, Douglas at last drew up his Kansas-Nebraska Bill.[26] It contained a direct repeal of the 36°30' ban on slavery. The legislation further divided the contested area into two potential states: Kansas

24. Nevins, *Ordeal of the Union*, vol. 2, 88.

25. Michael F. Holt, *Political Parties and American Political Development from the Age of Jackson to the Age of Lincoln*, 74.

26. Robert R. Russel, "The Issues in the Congressional Struggle over the Kansas-Nebraska Bill, 1854," 196–98.

and Nebraska. Nebraska territory stood directly west of Iowa, while Kansas territory neighbored Missouri. This division appeared to offer a state for each section, with Kansas intended for Missouri emigrants and other Southern slaveholders.[27] Still, the slaveholding status of the territories under this bill, even Kansas, remained officially undecided. Instead, Douglas built his legislation upon the principle of popular sovereignty, which held that the slaveholding status of the territories and future states would be decided by the settlers themselves, rather than by Congress.[28]

The bill drew an explosion of protest from Northern Whigs and Free Soilers who opposed the repeal of the Missouri Compromise. Douglas expected such a response from opposing political interests. According to historian Michael Holt, Douglas actually counted upon his bill to spark an interparty struggle. Democratic and Whig leaders, including Douglas and New York Senator William H. Seward, worried about the breakdown of the old two-party system in the Union. Holt argues that these men "saw the bill as a chance to revive the flagging Second Party System by creating a new issue that Whigs and Democrats could once again fight about on party lines."[29] The Kansas-Nebraska issue was supposed to pit Democrats versus Whigs, rather than North against South. But the shock and dismay emanating from Northern Democratic ranks sent tremors through the party as a whole. Douglas defended his bill on the grounds that the Compromise of 1850 had already overturned portions of the Missouri Compromise by instilling popular sovereignty in territory gained as a result of the Mexican War. His greatest weapon was the very principle of popular sovereignty. Ignoring the moral arguments about slavery (Douglas declared that it was "no part of my purpose to discuss the merits of slavery as a domestic or political institution"), the "Little Giant" championed the power of the people in deciding their own institutions.[30] Nonetheless, his defense found little sympathy in the Northern states, and only one state legislature in session in the spring of 1854 endorsed the bill, Douglas's own state of Illinois. Four other Democratic state legislatures refused

27. James McPherson, *Battle Cry of Freedom*, 122–23.

28. Ideas about "popular sovereignty" can be traced to various officials in the 1840s and 1850s, but the doctrine formally emerged in an 1847 letter from Michigan Senator Lewis Cass to A. O. P. Nicholson of Tennessee. Cass argued against congressional authority over slavery in the territories, writing that only territorial governments could introduce or exclude the institution within their borders. Allan Nevins, *Ordeal of the Union*, vol. 1, *Fruits of Manifest Destiny, 1847–1852*, 29–30.

29. Holt, *Political Crisis of the 1850s*, 147.

30. Robert W. Johannsen, *Stephen A. Douglas*, 446.

to approve the measure, while five Whig-controlled states officially denounced it.[31]

Determined to push the measure through despite growing resistance, Douglas enlisted the help of Secretary of War Jefferson Davis of Mississippi to coerce President Franklin Pierce's endorsement of popular sovereignty and the repeal of the Missouri Compromise. If the president refused, the two men warned Pierce, he would lose the South. Pierce gave in to the pressure, and further moved to make the Kansas-Nebraska Bill "a test of party orthodoxy."[32]

Douglas had placed Lane and his fellow Indiana Democrats in an agonizing position. Personal opposition to slavery and its expansion now competed with the principle of popular sovereignty and national party unity. When Douglas first proposed to repeal the Missouri Compromise, only one of ten Indiana Democratic congressmen favored the plan—Smith Miller of the First District.[33] Mixed public response to Douglas's legislation further complicated consideration of the bill. Numerous Democratic newspapers in Indiana denounced the Kansas Nebraska Bill, while the party's most powerful publication in the state, the *Indianapolis Sentinel*, stood behind it.[34] Much of Indiana's Democratic electorate also opposed the bill, but those who answered the call for Democratic unity and met Douglas's party test pressed their congressmen to support the measure. As a result, the Indiana delegation was divided on the matter. A Washington correspondent to the *Indianapolis Morning Journal* wrote during the congressional debates that four legislators supported the Kansas-Nebraska Bill, five opposed it, while two more were "Doubtful, but rather inclined to vote for the bill." Lane's name was among those against the bill.[35]

Despite early predictions and accounts, the Indiana Democratic delegation, including Lane, overwhelmingly stood behind the Kansas-Nebraska Bill. At the bill's final House vote, only two Indiana Democratic representatives opposed it.[36] According to an 1879 account by James Rodgers,

31. McPherson, *Battle Cry of Freedom*, 124.

32. Ibid., 123. For a good, brief discussion of Pierce's concern about Northern interests see Larry Gara, *The Presidency of Franklin Pierce*, 88–96.

33. Charles Zimmerman, "The Origin and Rise of the Republican Party in Indiana from 1854 to 1860," 224.

34. Emma Lou Thornbrough, *Indiana in the Civil War Era, 1850–1880*, 55.

35. *Indianapolis Morning Journal*, March 15, 1854; apparently there were conflicting reports of Lane's position, as he was said to support the bill in the March 13 issue of the *Weekly Indiana State Sentinel*.

36. Thornbrough, *Indiana in the Civil War Era*, 56. Charles Zimmerman states that three Democrats in the state opposed the bill at its passage. Yet, the official vote shows

public pressure drove Lane's vote. Rodgers recalled being in Washington, D.C., and on intimate terms with a number of Democratic congressmen during the Kansas-Nebraska debate. He explained that Lane had at first stood against the legislation, but "the friends of the bill procured strong petitions from Lane's constituents in Indiana, asking him to favor the bill." As a result, Rodgers explained, Lane changed his stance and backed Douglas. Rodgers described Lane as uncomfortable with the change and noted that he "worried about the matter of his inconsistency and the probable effect of his changing his position." Despite this concern, Rodgers stated, Lane "pushed on strongly for the bill and seemed to aspire to become the leader of the movement."[37]

Rodgers's late account of Lane's position is telling. Almost the entire Indiana congressional delegation appeared to change positions in regard to Douglas's bill, strongly suggesting that some kind of pressure had been brought to bear against the Indiana representatives. While no correspondence pressing Lane to support the bill has been found, evidence of public pressure on Lane's colleagues to stand behind Douglas's legislation is plentiful. One Indianan wrote to Congressman William English of the Second District that "the masses of all parties (abolitionist excepted) are in favor of the principles of self government,—They believe that the bill should pass and that under the Constitution of the U.S. the people should be permitted to govern themselves. There can be no wrong in this." He continued, "For myself I will say to you, and to the Indiana delegation, pass the bill, and trust the result to the sound intelligence of the people."[38] It is likely that Lane received similar messages of support for the bill from his constituents and peers.

Still, public correspondence in support of the bill alone probably did not secure Lane's support for Douglas's legislation or change the minds of his fellow Indiana representatives. Even letters in support of the bill show evidence of party tension, and many correspondents tried to reassure nervous representatives—particularly those up for reelection in the fall. A letter to Congressman John Davis of the Seventh District highlighted the matter

---

that two Democrats and one Whig voted against the bill. He includes Democratic Representative E. M. Chamberlain among those opposed, although Chamberlain was not present to vote due to family sickness. Zimmerman, "The Origin and Rise of the Republican Party in Indiana," 224.

37. James Rodgers to F. G. Adams, December 20, 1879, Rodgers Collection, Kansas State Historical Society, Topeka.

38. R. Schoonover to William H. English, April 3, 1854, William H. English Collection, Indiana Historical Society, Indianapolis.

perfectly. "You say some think your favoring the Nebraska bill will be your political grave," the constituent wrote. "I think gentle-men that talk that way are not well posted and know very little about the sentiments of the people upon that subject. I know there was some opposition to it at first. I do not know that there is any at this time."[39] But some powerful people disagreed. The editor of the *Morning Journal,* John Defrees, prophesied the political future of those politicians who supported the Kansas-Nebraska Bill in Congress: "It will never get out of the committee and the conspirators who advocated it will retire from political life just as fast as the people can reach them."[40]

Indiana historian Charles Zimmerman suggested that the political weight of Indiana's Democratic Party leader Senator Jesse Bright may have been responsible for Indiana's congressional support of the bill.[41] Bright had direct ties to Southern slaveholding interests; he owned a plantation in Kentucky. Historian Eric Foner calls Bright a "party dictator" who used more than just political influence to garner support for Douglas. Bright had Democratic opponents of the Kansas Nebraska Bill kicked out of the state convention and from local Democratic groups.[42] Indiana's other senator, John Pettit, also came out in favor of the bill early on.[43] The influence or pressure from these two men undoubtedly weighed upon the minds of the Democratic representatives. This must have been especially true for Lane, who as a freshman congressman stood in a particularly vulnerable position. Some historians have reported that Lane's vote was due to specific political pressure—particularly from Douglas. William Connelley wrote that Lane "afterwards reported that he voted for the bill because he had been instructed to do so."[44] Unfortunately, Connelley provides no source for this information.

The idea that Douglas essentially bought Lane's vote with the promise of patronage has also been suggested. Kenneth Davis's 1984 general history of Kansas promoted a more conspiratorial theory. Though "representing a district with a large antislavery majority," Davis explained, "[Lane] had made speeches in Congress attacking the slave power in the

39. B. H. Commill to John G. Davis, April 14, 1854, John G. Davis Collection, Indiana Historical Society, Indianapolis.

40. *Indianapolis Morning Journal,* March 24, 1854.

41. Zimmerman, "The Origin and Rise of the Republican Party in Indiana," 221.

42. Eric Foner, *Free Soil, Free Labor, Free Men: The Ideology of the Republican Party before the Civil War,* 158.

43. Zimmerman, "The Origin and Rise of the Republican Party in Indiana," 221.

44. Connelley, *Lane: The "Grim Chieftain,"* 43.

strongest terms, yet voted for the Kansas-Nebraska Bill, thereby destroying his chance for reelection. Why? Because, according to rumor, he and
Douglas made a secret bargain: Lane's vote for Kansas-Nebraska and his
emigration to Kansas, there to do battle for popular sovereignty doctrine,
was to be paid for by Douglas's support, and the administration's support, of his bid to become U.S. senator from Kansas when the new state
was admitted."[45] As Davis admits, the idea that Lane voted for the bill as
part of an agreement with Douglas was a rumor. No evidence has ever
been found of a Douglas-Lane agreement. While possible, the rumor circulated among Lane's political rivals during his rise in the antislavery
ranks in Kansas. It was strengthened, no doubt, by Lane's early references
to his personal connections with Douglas and Pierce—something probably exaggerated, although not completely untrue, in order to gain some
legitimacy in Kansas circles.

Historians who have relied upon a conspiratorial explanation of Lane's
vote have assumed that he was a complete opportunist, devoid of any larger
principles. This is in part due to the failure of most writers to analyze Lane's
recorded words before he moved to Kansas and a failure to compare his
actions to those of others within his political environment. Ironically, these
historians project greater power and authority onto Lane than he actually
had. Lane has been seen as a man pulling the strings, rather than as a man
struggling to retain his position in a shifting political environment.

Stephen Douglas, Franklin Pierce, and Indiana Senator Jesse Bright—all
major Democratic figures directly above Lane—threw their political
weight behind the bill. Lane had been a dedicated Democrat for his entire
adult life. With national Democratic leaders making support for the bill a
test of party loyalty, and with state party leaders pressing their juniors,
Lane began to stand behind the Kansas-Nebraska effort. Still, even during
his shift to support the bill, Lane held reservations about the legislation—
evidence that he had not become a convert overnight, as rumors of his bargain with Douglas suggest. In a letter to the *Weekly Indiana State Sentinel* on
March 30, Lane attempted to clarify his concern with the Senate's version
of the bill. He announced his objection to an amendment to the Kansas-
Nebraska Bill offered by Delaware Senator John Clayton. Clayton's
amendment excluded recent foreign immigrants from voting or holding
office in the territories. Clayton intended to limit the antislavery voice of
many German and British settlers.[46] Lane vehemently opposed the mea-

45. Davis, *Kansas: A History*, 49.
46. Nevins, *Ordeal of the Union*, vol. 2, 128.

sure, stating that it stood against the right of suffrage approved by the Indiana constitution. With the amendment, the bill stood "in direct conflict with my former course of action and the course of policy adopted by the Democratic party of the State" he represented.[47]

While Lane's letter to the *Sentinel* did not show strong support for the Kansas-Nebraska Bill as a whole, it does suggest that Lane had at least resigned himself to its success. "If Clayton's amendment can be voted down in the House, the original provision in Douglas's bill restored," he wrote, "the Senate concurring therein, and if this body will pass the Homestead bill sent to them some weeks since by our House, giving to every white person male or female, over 21 years of age 160 acres of land, my fears of slavery being extended into the territories of Nebraska and Kansas, would, to a considerable extent, be removed."[48] These words are not from a man determined to fight for the bill. But Lane did not stand in opposition to it as a whole. More importantly, he specifically identified his fear of slavery extending into the territories. His list of qualifications seems to imply a justification for the Kansas-Nebraska Bill, including the Homestead Bill, which Lane believed would promote free Northern white settlement in the territories and guarantee antislavery success with popular sovereignty. In short, Lane accepted the Kansas-Nebraska Bill and its doctrine of popular sovereignty as long as it appeared that Northern white settlers would constitute a majority in the territories.

Before closing his letter, Lane provided one last cryptic quip regarding the Kansas-Nebraska matter. He wrote: "The question then will resolve itself into this, how far shall we go to humor our Southern friends, and what effect will the repeal of the Missouri compromise restriction have upon the slavery agitation?" The remark shows an abandonment, if only temporarily, of his previous dismissal of sectional identity. While he emphasized Democratic and national unity during his debate with Congressman Sollers, here Lane clearly identified a sectional rift—in which Southerners appear as the antagonists. There is a simple explanation for the discrepancy. The repeal of the Missouri Compromise marked an important change in Lane's approach to the sectional conflict. While he had always identified with Northern interests, his dedication to party unity had previously led him to downplay the conflict over slavery—even after his emotions had gotten the better of him with Sollers. With the passage of the Kansas-Nebraska Act, sectional differences could not be

47. *Weekly Indiana State Sentinel,* March 30, 1854.
48. Ibid.

ignored so easily. James Lane began showing signs of frustration in balancing party unity with his own anti-Southern bias.

The effect of the repeal of the Missouri Compromise upon Lane cannot be overemphasized. Like his colleagues, he had to decide between opposition to slavery—more specifically, to its extension—and a new party line that potentially opened the territories to slavery through popular sovereignty. While Douglas had hoped the Democratic Party's embrace of the Kansas-Nebraska Act would reinvigorate the old second party system and his own party, the bill accomplished the opposite. It reshaped the American political party environment by leading to the formation of the anti-Southern and antislavery Republican Party and tearing holes in the Democratic establishment.[49] Even for many Democrat loyalists who did not bolt from the party, like Lane, the bill ultimately changed their party's direction. The repeal of the Missouri Compromise seemed to counter such things as the Indiana State Democratic resolutions of 1849, which had declared that "the institution of slavery ought not to be introduced into any territory where it does not now exist."[50] Lane took a middle ground. He voted with his party leaders for the bill, but qualified his support along the line that true popular sovereignty in the Kansas and Nebraska territories, through the protection of free white Northern immigration and suffrage, would result in free states. His position was founded on the Democratic Party's concentration on democratic principle, rather than morality. The *State Sentinel* outlined the principle as such: "We do not believe that there is a Democrat within the State, who, if he were a citizen of Nebraska, or Kansas, would vote to incorporate slavery among its elements. But we view the question as one involving the constitutional right of a people to make their own laws and regulate their own domestic institutions."[51]

Ultimately, the call to support the party under the banner of democratic principle struck the heart of a man like James Lane, who had championed the voice of the people during his brief time in Congress. During his debate with Congressman Sollers over the representation of constituents, Lane announced, "I represent a constituency that have opinions of their own. I came here to represent their opinions as their servant; and I do not envy

49. Michael F. Holt, *The Fate of Their Country: Politicians, Slavery Extension, and the Coming of the Civil War*, 114.

50. *Weekly State Journal*, June 3, 1854, quoted in Zimmerman, "The Origin and Rise of the Republican Party in Indiana," 229.

51. *State Sentinel*, September 8, 1854, quoted in Zimmerman, "The Origin and Rise of the Republican Party in Indiana," 219.

any man who comes here to dictate to his constituents, or to mould, or endeavor to mould their opinions."[52] With such standards, Lane could understand Douglas's claim that popular sovereignty would simply allow the people to decide the status of their own territory and state.

Lane did not see himself as a puppet of the people or the party. In the same response to Sollers mentioned above, Lane charged that "by the close of this session [Mr. Sollers] will admit that I adhere as strictly and strongly to my own opinions as the gentleman himself, or any other gentleman upon this floor; and I not only will adhere to them, but I will press them upon this House with as much energy as any other member upon this floor."[53] And with this point he was consistent. He was not comfortable with leaving the territories open for whatever result should occur. His acceptance of popular sovereignty hinged on the protection of Northern white interests and Northern antislavery influence in the territories.

Lane's vote for the Kansas-Nebraska Act may have proven his loyalty in the eyes of the Democratic leadership, but it jeopardized his reelection. The Democratic Party in Indiana split in 1854, leading to the creation of a fusion ticket. The Kansas-Nebraska problem was not solely responsible for the Democratic rift, as some party members divided over a controversial opposition to alcohol. But the combined force of these two issues, as well as political rivalry among leaders (particularly Indiana Governor Joseph Wright and Senator Jesse Bright), came to a head in 1854 and fractured the party. The fusionists, made up of Democrats opposed to the Kansas-Nebraska Act, Know Nothings, Whigs, and Free Soilers, took the name "People's party" and won a smashing victory in the 1854 election in Indiana.[54] They took nine of eleven congressional seats; only two Democrats who had voted for Douglas's bill won their reelections in Indiana—both of whom were in southern districts near Lane's.[55] Whether the Kansas-Nebraska Act and the party split would have actually thwarted Lane's reelection is unclear, for he declined to run for another term. Officially, Lane cited health problems as the reason for this decision.[56] In fact, Lane did occasionally suffer from recurring bouts of diarrhea contracted during the Mexican War.[57] His subsequent move to Kansas and energetic

52. *Congressional Globe*, 33rd Cong., 1st sess., 605.
53. Ibid.
54. Thornbrough, *Indiana in the Civil War Era*, 63.
55. Ibid., 67.
56. *Daily Indiana State Sentinel*, July 3, 1854.
57. Stephenson, *Political Career of Lane*, 39.

entrance into the political arena there weakens his claim, though. Instead, his withdrawal from the 1854 race suggests he likely foresaw defeat at the polls.[58] In any case, soon after the end of his term, Lane set out for Kansas with hopes of new political opportunities in that territory.

Coverage of Lane during his time in Congress often ranges from woefully inadequate to misleading. In 1879, Kansan James Legate told a gathering of fellow "Old Settlers of Kansas" that Lane "came here as near a pro-slavery man as a man could come from a northern State," and that he believed "all that portion of the country in which rice, cotton, tobacco and hemp could be raised, and which he regarded as only products of slave labor . . . rightfully belonged to slavery."[59] Yet the most influential characterization of Lane as proslavery was first made by historian Leverett Spring in 1885. Spring wrote that Lane "betook himself to the fresh fields of Kansas, pro-slavery in sentiment," and stated in 1899 that "Lane was a pro-slavery Democrat when he came to Kansas in 1855."[60] Exactly how Spring came to this conclusion is unclear, although a reliance upon characterizations made by Lane's critics is no doubt partly responsible. Further, Spring spent virtually no time discussing Lane's background in Indiana, and completely ignored Lane's comments and writings on slavery while in Congress. However Spring developed his position, his influence has been significant as numerous historians have continued to portray Lane as a friend to slavery.

Even historians who have not labeled Lane proslavery have firmly denied or ignored Lane's opposition to the extension of the institution. Eric Corder argued that "Slavery in Kansas Territory was not a question of ethics to Jim Lane but merely a matter of climate. If the weather was suitable for slaves, then he had no objections to slavery in the territory."[61] Thomas Goodrich echoed these sentiments: "A Democrat who had voted for the Kansas-Nebraska Bill, Lane was initially indifferent to slavery."[62] These statements were, like those of Spring, largely based on rumors that

58. Lane later denied leaving Indiana because of political failure. In August 1855, he spoke before a Free State meeting in Kansas, explaining: "It is represented that I came to Kansas to retrieve my political fortunes; but gentlemen should know that I was urgently solicited to be a candidate for another term to Congress, but I positively declined." *Herald of Freedom*, August 18, 1855.

59. "Address by Hon. Jas. F. Legate," 60.

60. Leverett W. Spring, *Kansas: The Prelude to the War for the Union*, 63; Spring, "The Career of a Kansas Politician," 100.

61. Eric Corder, *Prelude to Civil War: Kansas-Missouri, 1854–1861*, 35.

62. Thomas Goodrich, *War to the Knife: Bleeding Kansas, 1854–1861*, 50.

circulated in Kansas, chiefly among Lane's opponents. Further, they appear to be part of a larger trend by historians who have summed up Lane's two years as an Indiana congressman into one event—his vote for the Kansas-Nebraska Bill. His overall support for the bill was, undoubtedly, the most significant part of his term in the House. However, his specific perceptions of the bill and popular sovereignty, and his position on slavery and its extension, have been largely ignored, or, more commonly, have been assumed given the simple fact that he voted for the bill.

Early Kansas historian William Connelley wrote admirably about Lane in the late nineteenth century and championed him as a great leader for the cause of freedom. But Connelley also portrayed Lane as originally indifferent to the institution, saying, "Lane afterwards admitted that when he came to Kansas he cared nothing about the great question of slavery."[63] Unfortunately, Connelley gives no citation for Lane's "afterwards" comments. Further, his portrayal of Lane's apathy toward slavery is consistent with a common perception of the Kansas-Nebraska Act. Connelley, although an excellent historian, was steeped in the Traditionalist school of thought, and apparently was highly influenced by the thoughts of men like Frederick Jackson Turner. His writings on Kansas history are often celebratory in tone, portraying the struggle for Kansas statehood as a battle between good and evil. Antislavery settlers and leaders were seen as the forces of good struggling against the proslavery minions. The approach found its roots among the partisan ideologies of the sectional conflict and the Civil War. Within this period, most antislavery settlers in Kansas viewed the Kansas-Nebraska Act as a proslavery maneuver.[64] Thus, Connelley and many others perceived a vote for the bill in Congress to be a vote of confidence or support for the institution. Connelley's portrayal of Lane as disinterested in slavery appears to be, at least partially, a means of actually defending the man from the general criticism he received from opponents of the bill during Lane's life and afterwards; it was an effort to separate Lane from the proslavery image the Kansas-Nebraska Bill had generated.

63. Connelley, *Lane: The "Grim Chieftain,"* 37–48.
64. The Kansas-Nebraska bill intensified sectional hostility, particularly within the national parties: Whigs in Congress were directly split according to the slaveholding status of their respective states, while Northern Democrats struggled to maintain party integrity in the face of sectional interests; further, many Northern Democrats who did vote for the bill were denied reelection or, like Lane, chose not to run again due to the unpopular nature of the bill. For more information see McPherson, *Battle Cry of Freedom,* 125, and Nevins, *Ordeal of the Union,* vol. 2, 316–23.

Connelley's assessment of Lane was not baseless. Lane's position on slavery did include a professed apathy toward the institution in the same vein as Stephen Douglas. The supposed unconcern was not a true ideological indifference to the institution (although Lane initially cared little about black people). Instead, it was a personal opposition to the institution of slavery tempered by a pragmatic concern for the Union and, thus, a respect for Southern interests. Lane did in fact "care" about slavery before he came to Kansas, even if that care was to keep the territory free for Northern white settlers with little humanitarian concern for blacks. But the fact that he voted for the Kansas-Nebraska Act and was said to have publicly stated an indifference toward slavery has led many historians to unfairly deny him *any* element of antislavery ideology.

Reviewing Lane's political career in Indiana, and particularly his single congressional term, some important details emerge about the man, his views on national issues, and his principles. Lane was, by all contemporary accounts, a dedicated Democrat. He adhered to party ideology as well as party identity. As a representative from a free state, Lane separated himself from proslavery ideology in the few instances he became involved in the sectional controversy. But as a Democrat interested in party and sectional unity, Lane sidelined his personal prejudices for the larger cause. His debate with Sollers offers a fascinating glimpse into this struggle, as he provided a quick jab against slaveholding identity and pride, only to back down and deny any ill will to agitated Southerners. When Sollers challenged Lane's personal dignity, Lane reacted emotionally. When faced with the political problem of sectional tension, Lane drew upon the calm, reasoned approach of Democratic principle, proclaiming no sectional loyalty.

Stephen Douglas's Kansas-Nebraska Bill and its repeal of the Missouri Compromise placed the freshman congressman in an extremely difficult political position. Torn between his personal opposition to the extension of slavery into previously protected territories and a Democratic leadership pushing a new party line under the blanket of traditional principles— not to mention a fiercely divided electorate—Lane stuck with his party. But his dedication showed signs of wear. His public letter about the bill qualified his support upon grounds that protected free white Northern interests, and illustrated his frustration with sectionalism. Lane was still a party man, but he was not entirely happy with the direction in which the national organization was headed.

2

Lane Goes to Kansas, 1855

"Moderation, moderation, moderation, gentlemen!"

James Lane arrived in the Kansas Territory in late April 1855. His decision to leave his native state was no doubt prompted by the Kansas-Nebraska Act and the Democratic split in Indiana. Still, he looked forward to political advancement in a new territory through the establishment of his beloved Democratic Party. Instead, Lane found Kansas territorial politics far different than politics anywhere else in the nation. In Kansas, the traditional two-party balance gave way to a proslavery versus free-state tug-of-war. During his first year in the territory, Lane quickly adjusted to this new political environment—as did many other immigrants—all the while holding on to basic tenets of the Democratic Party and popular sovereignty.

Lane settled in the antislavery town of Lawrence.[1] His arrival drew little attention, the only public mention being in the Lawrence newspaper the *Kansas Free State,* which reported, "Col. James H. Lane, late member of congress from Indiana, arrived in our place on the 22d inst., with his family all in good health and spirits. He is comfortably ensconced in a log

---

1. Lawrence was established by abolitionist and antislavery immigrants from New England. The town was named after Amos Lawrence, wealthy financier of the New England Emigrant Aid Company. Etcheson, *Bleeding Kansas,* 37.

cabin, and will in all probability remain permanently with us. His design is to live in the territory."[2] For his first few weeks in Kansas, Lane kept a low profile, likely investigating the political atmosphere. James McClure, a military and political friend from Indiana who migrated to Kansas in 1854, wrote of conversing with Lane during the latter's move to the territory. McClure stated that the turmoil in Kansas had attracted Lane as a means "to gratify his irrepressible desire of notoriety and leadership." He further explained that "Lane had always been a Democrat, and I think intended at that time to support the side of slavery, but was willing to espouse either cause that he found was most likely to advance his political interests."[3] McClure's account is important, but, like virtually all commentary on Lane's arrival in Kansas, it was written long after the fact.[4] Why McClure thought Lane intended to support slavery in the territory remains a mystery, particularly since Lane had been on record stating his opposition to slavery's extension into the territories only months before.

Most information on Lane's trip to Kansas comes from sources that were unfavorable toward him. For instance, one rumor circulated that, upon arrival, Lane had mentioned to friends that his "action in regard to the institutions of the territory depended upon the adaptation of the soil and climate to the growing of hemp. If it was a good hemp-growing country, he was in favor of making Kansas a slave state; if it was not adapted to the growing of hemp, he was in favor of making it a free state."[5] One of the earliest published versions of this account appeared in an 1858 issue of the *Herald of Freedom*, three years after Lane's arrival in Kansas. George W. Brown, the editor of the *Herald,* was an increasingly vocal opponent of Lane, and by 1858 regularly criticized him. Further, no reference to Lane taking a proslavery stand appears within the pages of the *Herald of Freedom* in the three years before the story. In fact, Brown's commentary on Lane in 1855 and much of 1856 was rather positive, and only questioned his stance as a Democrat and pro-Nebraska man, as Brown was a Republican.

One rumor claimed that Lane attempted to buy a slave girl in Missouri, but was denied the purchase due to poor credit.[6] The *Herald of Freedom* relayed the rumor in 1858, and editor Brown attempted to validate the

2. *Kansas Free State,* April 30, 1855.
3. James R. McClure, "Taking the Census and Other Incidents in 1855," 242.
4. It is unclear when McClure wrote this account of Lane. It was part of a manuscript, written as a memoir, found among his papers, presumably after his death in 1903.
5. *Herald of Freedom,* May 8, 1858.
6. Charles Robinson, *The Kansas Conflict,* 143; *Herald of Freedom,* May 8, 1858.

claim by crediting the information to "one of our citizens, whose affidavit to that effect can be procured, if desired."[7] Another rumor credited Lane with stating that "he knew no difference between a negro and a mule."[8] Historian William Connelley explained that this comparison was quite popular in some circles, and had been attributed to many different people at different times.[9] In 1886, John Brown, Jr., wrote of directly confronting Lane in the 1850s about his comparison of blacks to mules. When Lane approached Brown for political support, the latter voiced his opposition to Lane's comment that "so far as the rights of property are concerned, I know of no difference between a negro and a mule." Lane, according to Brown, replied, "Well, Brown, I've felt like kicking myself ever since."[10] While this account was also recorded many years after Lane's death, Brown was a friend of Lane and his letter was not designed to paint a negative image. Indeed, Brown's account concludes that he supported Lane's political aspirations.

Lane's reported comparison of blacks to mules should be viewed with care. While it is possible, perhaps even likely, that Lane made the comparison during an impromptu speech, all records of it are secondhand accounts, related well after the event and without context. In any case, the statement itself is not inconsistent with a Northern Democratic acknowledgment of slaveholding rights.[11] Like most white Americans in the Midwest before the Civil War, Lane was not only antislavery but antiblack. This opposition to the institution of slavery focused more on the protection of white interests rather than any great concern over the humanity or treatment of blacks. White supremacist ideology dominated midwestern culture, leading to laws in midwestern states banning the immigration of free blacks—a measure endorsed by Lane and many other antislavery settlers in Kansas Territory.[12] Some contemporary New Englanders and later

7. *Herald of Freedom*, May 8, 1858.

8. Spring, "The Career of a Kansas Politician," 82.

9. William Connelley reports that Lane was rumored to have said "he would as soon buy a negro as a mule." Connelley, *Lane: The "Grim Chieftain,"* 46.

10. "Letter from John Brown, Jr., to the Committee of Quarter-Centennial Celebration, January 25, 1886," 463–64.

11. Lane presided over a Democratic meeting in Lawrence on June 27, 1855, which resolved that "we can appreciate the rights of the citizens of the different States of this Union, both of the North and the South, and that by no act of ours will we trample upon those rights, or interfere in anywise with their domestic Institutions." *Kansas Free State*, July 2, 1855. This meeting is covered in more detail later in the chapter.

12. Eugene H. Berwanger, "Negrophobia in Northern Proslavery and Antislavery Thought," 271.

observers failed to recognize this discrepancy, equating his antiblack position and recognition of slave property rights to support of slavery.

The most prevalent claim regarding Lane's initial support of slavery described him as eagerly meeting with proslavery legislators in Kansas shortly after arriving in the territory. He supposedly petitioned the legislature for divorce, but was rebuffed. Outraged, Lane vowed to oppose the proslavery government and immediately joined the free-state side.[13] In 1929, *Tyler's Quarterly Historical and Genealogical Magazine,* an avowedly anti-Republican (and anti-Lincoln) journal, printed the "Reminiscence of Col. Joseph C. Anderson." Anderson, described in the publication as the Speaker of the Lower House of the First Legislature of Kansas, recounted that Lane approached him about granting a divorce. When Anderson refused to support Lane's request, Lane then attempted to bribe the official. Anderson again refused. "Well, said he," Anderson recalled, "if my life is to be wrecked, it matters to me but little what becomes of me. I will make you another proposition, grant me the divorce, and I will aid you in the execution of your laws." Lane then supposedly offered a remarkably radical (and prophetic) proclamation: "If you do not, I will go North, work upon the fanaticism that exists, raise an army and overturn the country, and set at defiance the laws and the constituted authorities. I will make Kansas a free state." Anderson claimed to call Lane on his boast: "I replied, Colonel, crack your whip, and he did crack it."[14]

The accuracy of the account is questionable, particularly Lane's alleged vow to "work upon the fanaticism" and "overturn the country." Lane's entrance into the free-state ranks was punctuated by his conservative stance and calls for moderation. Further, no evidence of a divorce petition has been found. Biographer Wendell Stephenson noted that he had "searched both the House Journal and the Council Journal for 1855, but found no mention of Lane's petition for a divorce in either. This cannot be construed to mean, however, that Lane did not attempt to petition for a divorce. A concurrent resolution was passed declaring that the legislature would not entertain petitions for, nor grant divorces, in any case." Lane and his wife did divorce. However, it was Mary Lane who filed for

13. *Kansas Weekly Herald,* February 23, 1856; *Herald of Freedom,* May 8, 1858; *Kansas Herald,* January 18, 1884, in *Kansas Biographical Scrapbook* 98: 184; Spring, "The Career of a Kansas Politician," 81–82; see also George W. Brown to M. L. Fields, October 27, 1900, in George Washington Brown Papers, 1855–1914, Kansas State Historical Society, Topeka.
14. *Tyler's Quarterly Historical and Genealogical Magazine* 11, no. 2 (October 1929): 110–11.

divorce—in Indiana rather than Kansas. Despite James's promise in 1848 that he would never leave his family again, Mary came to believe he had abandoned his family for a political career in Kansas in 1855. The couple, however, remarried in 1857.[15]

While the divorce issue retained prominence among Lane's early critics, few historians have argued that Lane's opposition to the proslavery legislature stemmed from his encounter with Anderson.[16] Historian and Lane critic Leverett Spring, who recounted this rumor and others in his work, brushed aside the divorce issue "merely as an incident—unexpected, significant, possibly prophetic of evil—not as a capital event."[17] Indeed, Mary documented reason for filing for divorce, Lane's abandonment of the family, illustrates her husband's extreme political drive. But it does not prove he was without political principle, nor does it prove he was willing to betray those political principles for office. It proves that Lane was ambitious, and that his political drive, at least at times, could interfere with his personal and family life. The divorce issue may reflect upon Lane's private life, but it should not carry much weight in determining his political stance in Kansas.

Overall, historians are left with apparent contradictions of Lane's in 1855. In Indiana, he went on record separating himself from the institution of slavery and declaring his personal opposition to its extension. Within months of entering Kansas, Lane actively sided with antislavery settlers and labored for a free state. Yet, various accounts of the time in between, basically spring 1855, portray Lane on the fence, even leaning toward the proslavery side. Critics have concluded that Lane was an absolute opportunist, void of any real principle in relation to slavery. His defenders grudgingly acknowledged apparent contradictions, but emphasized his later work. While it is possible that Lane was contradictory on the slave issue upon arrival in Kansas, as of yet, no primary source from Lane showing support of slavery or its extension into the territory has surfaced. Every source describing Lane as favorable to slavery during this short period of time is secondhand, often penned by his political opponents, and written months or years after the fact. The possibility that the above claims are true cannot be ignored. But the weight of these claims in the historiography of Lane far outreaches their proved merit.

15. Stephenson, *Political Career of Lane*, 44; *Lecompton Union*, August 30, 1856.
16. For one example of a contemporary historian who accepts the divorce refusal as a reason for Lane's entrance into the Free State ranks, see Castel, *Civil War Kansas*, 20.
17. Spring, "The Career of a Kansas Politician," 82.

Lane's first documented political activity in Kansas came on June 27, 1855, when he presided over a meeting to organize the territory's Democratic Party. The small gathering in Lawrence passed a series of resolutions that echoed principles Lane had voiced in Indiana. First, the Democratic Party was to be established "upon truly National grounds." Second, the group endorsed the Kansas-Nebraska Act and its principle of popular sovereignty. Citizens from all parts of the country were welcome to settle in Kansas. The party resolved that "we can appreciate the rights of the citizens of the different States of this Union, both of the North and the South, and that by no act of ours will we trample upon those rights, or interfere in anywise with their domestic Institutions." More importantly, the group emphasized territorial autonomy in popular sovereignty, stating that "we feel we are fully capable of managing our own affairs—and kindly request the citizens of Northern and Southern districts and adjoining States, to let us alone." Following that resolution came a very specific warning, aimed at the center of controversy in Kansas: fair voting practices. "Resolved, That while making this request, we wish it distinctly understood, that we appreciate the rights of suffrage as the most important privilege guaranteed to us by the framers of our Institutions—and, that we regard the ballot box as the palladium of our liberty and will not if in our power to prevent—permit the privilege to be rested from us or permit the ballot box to be polluted by outsiders or illegal voting from any quarter."[18]

Outside interference in Kansas voting had been a problem from the beginning. During the territory's congressional election in November 1854, numerous settlers reported Missourians flooding into Kansas to vote and to chase free-state voters away from the polls. The proslavery candidate, J. W. Whitfield, received more than two thousand votes, while the next two men on the ballot combined for fewer than six hundred. Andrew Reeder, the appointed territorial governor, did not challenge the results—though a congressional investigation later concluded that as many as seventeen hundred votes were fraudulent. The territorial legislature election in March 1855 proved equally problematic, as only one free-state man won a seat throughout the territory. Again Missourians had entered Kansas, encouraged by the fiercely proslavery Missouri Senator David Atchison, and by Dr. J. H. Stringfellow, editor of the proslavery newspaper *Squatter Sovereign*. Many people in the South lauded the Missouri "invasion,"

18. *Kansas Free State,* July 2, 1855; *Herald of Freedom,* June 30, 1855; William Elsey Connelley, *A Standard History of Kansas and Kansans,* 425.

including Alabama's *Jacksonville Republican*, which announced that "Missourians have nobly defended *our* rights." Yet, even some people sympathetic to slaveholding interests were put off by the blatant interference, including Kansas Governor Reeder, who appealed to the president for help. But the presidential administration was friendly to Southern interests and Franklin Pierce had no desire to become personally involved in Kansas affairs. Reeder faced threats from proslavery forces within Kansas to accept all ballot returns, and attempted a compromise by ordering a new round of elections in districts with the most suspicious returns. Although free-state candidates nearly swept the new election, the proslavery legislature refused to recognize them. Instead, the original proslavery victors were welcomed into the territorial government.[19] While some Missourians argued that their participation in the Kansas elections merely equaled the influx of New England voters, the proslavery landslide proved anything but a balance. Further, while some New England settlers returned east after voting, most attempted to live in the territory.[20] Many Missourians also stayed in Kansas, but thousands traveled to the territory simply for the election, with no intention of settling.

Lane and fellow Democrats met in Lawrence in the midst of the conflict over elections in Kansas and the legitimacy of the territorial legislature. The Lawrence Democratic resolution generally denounced outside interference in Kansas elections, and certainly condemned the actions of Missourians. The Democratic meeting also illustrates another important point concerning Lane's perceptions of the proslavery territorial government. That body had the support of Southern Democrats and President Franklin Pierce. Lane labored to build a separate National Democratic Party in Kansas. The Democrats meeting in Lawrence did not embrace the Southern Democratic Party and activity in the territory.

The resolutions passed at the meeting did not specifically favor one section or one interest over the other. And because of this, Lane's hopes of establishing a National Democratic presence failed. The Lawrence meeting

19. Etcheson, *Bleeding Kansas*, 54; Jay Monaghan, *Civil War on the Western Border, 1854–1865*, 20; *Jacksonville Republican*, quoted in James A. Rawley, *Race and Politics: "Bleeding Kansas" and the Coming of the Civil War*, 89; Tony R. Mullis, *Peacekeeping on the Plains: Army Operations in Bleeding Kansas*, 54–55; McPherson, *Battle Cry of Freedom*, 147.

20. Many proslavery advocates reported eastern voters leaving after the election; however, upon cross-examination, many of these proslavery sources admitted that the easterners had voiced their frustration with the settlement and employment opportunities in the territory; Samuel A. Johnson, *The Battle Cry of Freedom: The New England Emigrant Aid Company in the Kansas Crusade*, 102.

generated little support. Kansas territory was too polarized by June 1855 to accept a peaceful, fair handling of popular sovereignty.[21] Antislavery and proslavery newspapers ridiculed the traditional party interests. The *Kansas Free State* argued that antislavery settlers were "sick of all political organizations and rallies around standards that float over no great and eternal principles of right and justice. The Whig and Democratic parties have arrived at that point where the popular will no longer entertains their obsolete and unneccessary [*sic*] ideas."[22]

While the National Democratic Party did not materialize in Kansas, Lane did not abandon its banner. Finding the political party system in the territory far different than that in Washington and the Midwest, Lane began scouting out the developing Free State Party. On July 17 he quietly attended a small Free State meeting in Lawrence at which a general convention in September for antislavery interests was discussed. On August 14, free-state advocates in Lawrence met again. Lane attended, this time openly, even taking the floor to speak. Far from working upon Northern fanaticism, as Anderson's account had claimed, Lane preached moderation. "I say it as a citizen of Kansas, I wish we had wisdom to-day," Lane said. "There is the existence of a nation hanging upon the action of the citizens of Kansas. Moderation, moderation, moderation, gentlemen! I believe it is the duty of each of us to define our position. I am here as anxious as any of you to secure a free constitution to Kansas."[23]

His participation in the Free State convention did not mark any change in principle or philosophy. Embracing his Democratic identity, Lane explained that he was not a man without a party, struggling for power. "It is represented that I came to Kansas to retrieve my political fortunes," he acknowledged; "but gentlemen should know that I was urgently solicited to be a candidate for another term to Congress, but I positively declined. I would vote for the Kansas-Nebraska bill again." He made clear that his endorsement of the Kansas-Nebraska Act did not mean he supported slavery or its extension into the territory, assuring the audience, "I desire Kansas to be a free State." Finally, he related his concern for the peace and stability of the Union, explaining that he wanted "to act with my brethren, but not in a manner to arouse the passions of the people of other States. I

21. Connelley, *Lane: The "Grim Chieftain,"* 47–48.

22. *Kansas Free State*, July 2, 1855; see also the *Kansas Weekly Herald* (proslavery), September 29, 1855, for commentary on proslavery repudiation of efforts to establish the National Democratic Party in Kansas.

23. Lane's speech was quoted in the *Herald of Freedom*, August 18, 1855.

would not repudiate the Legislature, but the *acts* of that Legislature which contravene the right of popular sovereignty."[24]

Many people within the free-state ranks denounced the Kansas-Nebraska Act with its repeal of the Missouri Compromise, and looked upon Lane suspiciously. Rather than downplay or ignore his role in supporting the controversial legislation, Lane defended it. He stood before a group of politically motivated opponents of slavery in Lawrence—the heart of antislavery activism in Kansas—and reiterated his support for an unpopular bill that potentially paved the way for a new slave state. He did not abandon his principles, nor did he use this event as an opportunity for personal gain by telling the audience what it wanted to hear. James Lane believed in the principle of popular sovereignty.

A rumor circulated that Lane personally worked under the watchful eyes of Stephen Douglas. It was believed that Lane had opposed the Kansas-Nebraska Bill as a congressman from Indiana until Douglas persuaded him of the long-term political benefits of its success. Douglas hoped that his legislation would lead him to the presidency. Lane, the rumor continued, would then enjoy federal patronage as he helped set up a Democratic presence in the territory and future state of Kansas. Such support would then lead to Lane's own election as senator.[25] While no evidence has been found to validate these rumors, Lane did profess to know the interests of Douglas and Pierce. He used these claims to help boost his own role in the growing free-state movement. During the August 14 meeting, Lane announced that "Frank Pierce would give his right arm to-day, to insure freedom to this Territory."[26] Lane believed that the president, like himself, wanted Kansas to be free, and saw the means of achieving that goal peacefully through the democratic process—if only both sides would work fairly.[27]

Following the August 14 meeting, an election took place for representatives to attend the territorial convention at Big Springs. Lane ran for and won a seat as part of the Lawrence delegation. The Big Springs convention opened on September 5 and delegates from across the territory attended, including former governor Andrew Reeder. Having found proslavery activity in Kansas incompatible with a fair democratic process, and losing his office when President Pierce succumbed to pressure from Senator

24. *Herald of Freedom*, August 18, 1855.
25. Connelley, *Lane: The "Grim Chieftain,"* 43.
26. *Herald of Freedom*, August 18, 1855.
27. *Kansas Free State*, August 20, 1855.

Atchison, Reeder became an important voice and representative for the new Free State Party.[28] The main agenda for the delegates was to create a solid, competent free-state political force. Lane took an active part in the proceedings and reported the platform resolutions at the convention. The Committee on a Platform announced the organization of the party for the protection of constitutional rights that were threatened "by superior force." It declared the future of Kansas as the great question of the day, and that a concerted effort from all proponents of free labor was necessary to secure a free state. It further resolved, "That setting aside all the minor issues of partisan politics, it is incumbent upon us to proffer an organization calculated to recover our dearest rights, and into which Democrats and Whigs, Native and Naturalized citizens may freely enter without any sacrifice of their respective political creeds, but without forcing them as a test upon others."[29] In very clear language, the new Free State Party described itself as inclusive of all other parties. Traditional party membership for free-state Kansans remained intact and unaffected. The Free State platform was also fairly conservative. It specifically denounced attempts by opponents to label its members as abolitionists. The party denounced "any attempt to encroach upon the Constitutional rights of the people of any State, or to interfere with their slaves, conceding to their citizens the right to regulate their own institutions and to hold and recover their slaves, without any molestation or obstruction from the people of Kansas."[30] Like the Democratic resolutions Lane had presided over in June, the Free State platform contained a resolution opposing all outside interference in Kansas elections, "whether from Missouri or elsewhere." The Free State Party platform Lane helped create did not depart from the principles of the Democratic Party to which he still maintained allegiance.

Certain resolutions presented at the convention were more harsh toward the territorial government and the presidential administration. Lane went on record as objecting to, or distancing himself from, these more radical positions on at least two occasions. When the Committee on the Legislature provided a list of resolutions condemning the acts of the proslavery territorial government, Lane objected to a part that impeached the action of the Territorial Supreme Court. Opposition to the acts of a fraudulently elected legislature was one thing, but Lane did not wish to condemn all portions of the established territorial authority. Later, when

28. McPherson, *Battle Cry of Freedom,* 147; Gara, *Presidency of Franklin Pierce,* 115–16.
29. *Herald of Freedom,* September 8, 1855.
30. Ibid.

the Committee on Miscellaneous Business introduced resolutions condemning President Pierce for his dismissal of Governor Reeder, Lane
stated that he was unwilling to take sides in the matter.[31] Again, Lane's
entrance into the blossoming Free State Party did not mean an abandonment of his old party or his old affiliates.[32]

The Free State organization, however, rolled in a radical direction. While
Lane hesitated to repudiate *in toto* the territorial government, the Big
Springs convention paved the way for an independent state movement.
The body scheduled another Free State convention in Topeka to draw up
a Free State constitution in opposition to the proslavery government. By
the following month, Lane had joined the movement, and even took a
leadership position during the constitutional proceedings. Historian
Nicole Etcheson described Lane's adoption of the Free State constitutional
effort as a "chameleon-like change of political principle."[33] Her interpretation is common among historians who see Lane's increasingly active role
in Free State politics as opportunistic, rather than practical or principled.
In fact, two simple but important events preceded the Topeka convention,
which may have influenced his opposition to the territorial government
and helped push him into the independent state movement. Around September 15, shortly after the Big Springs convention, the new territorial
governor, Wilson Shannon, passed through Lawrence. Lane served as
head of a delegation that met the governor and asked him to meet the people of Lawrence to address some concerns. Shannon's recent speeches to a
proslavery crowd in Westport, Missouri, solidly backing the territorial legislature had worried free-state settlers. Shannon declined to make a public appearance in Lawrence, despite the assurances by Lane that the entire
matter would take only a few minutes. When the governor stated that he
was anxious to travel with his companions to the town of Franklin, a short
distance away, Lane apparently offered to personally provide a carriage
for Shannon's use following the meeting. Shannon rejected the offer. A
crowd gathered to see the governor hop into his carriage and ride out of
town, some voicing their frustration by "groaning rather loudly." The *Herald of Freedom* reported the incident, stating that "our citizens felt that Gov.
Shannon had grossly insulted them, as well as the people of the Territory

31. Ibid.; *Kansas Free State*, September 10, 1855.

32. Historian Wendell Stephenson wrote that "Lane, Marcus J. Parrott, and other
moderate men sought to modify the resolutions, but without success." Stephenson,
"The Transitional Period in the Career of General James H. Lane," 84.

33. Etcheson, *Bleeding Kansas*, 71.

at large, in accepting a public demonstration from an adjoining State, and refusing it at the hands of those he was sent to govern."[34]

The incident, although seemingly minor, was splashed across antislavery and proslavery newspapers. The proslavery *Leavenworth Herald* described the governor as "assailed with a torrent of hisses, yells, and groans, from a motley crowd of polluted fanatics who were gathered together listening to a flaming book on ABOLITIONISM and HIGHER LAWISM from an itinerant Abolition lecturer named Lane."[35] The antislavery *Kansas Tribune* responded that citizens had "assembled to see the Governor, and they thought he did not show them proper respect, and they 'groaned him.'"[36] During a time of increased tension and distrust between proslavery territorial officials and the growing majority of free-state settlers, the governor's dismissal of the Lawrence population generated a strong reaction.

The second event leading to Lane's falling out with the territorial government struck much more personally. On September 17, Lane and fellow attorney J. S. Emery applied for admission into the District Court of the United States for Kansas Territory. Though meeting all of the requirements to practice law in the territory, including an oath to support the Constitution and laws of the nation, the two refused to pledge to sustain the laws of the proslavery legislature. As a result, Samuel Lecompte, the presiding judge and proslavery advocate, rejected both applicants.[37] Lane requested the opportunity to appear in court as a "regular practice attorney in the Supreme Court of Indiana, as also in the Supreme Court of the United States." Lecompte promptly banned Lane from the Kansas courts, according to the *Herald of Freedom*, "in violation of all precedent, and in a manner unheard of by the legal profession."[38]

Twice within a week Lane saw firsthand the territorial government's rejection of free-state people and interests. These two events coincide with the period in which Lane joined the call for an independent statehood

34. *Herald of Freedom*, September 22, 1855.
35. Quoted in *Kansas Tribune*, October 17, 1855. The term "Higher Lawism" referred to the abolitionist justification of appealing to a "higher law," such as that of God or of human rights, while resisting and disobeying federal slave laws, such as the Fugitive Slave Act. Jane H. Pease and William H. Pease, "Confrontation and Abolition in the 1850s," 926–27.
36. *Kansas Tribune*, October 17, 1855.
37. The proslavery capital of Kansas Territory, Lecompton, was named after Samuel Lecompte.
38. *Herald of Freedom*, September 22, 1855; *National Era*, October 4, 1855, in Webb Scrapbook, Kansas State Historical Society, Topeka, 6:12 (hereafter referred to as Webb Scrapbook).

movement. While no primary sources detailing Lane's thoughts on the events have surfaced, antislavery journals recorded general outrage over these slights. The new governor's casual disregard for the Lawrence population sent a clear signal to Lane and the town's citizens that the territorial authorities were not sympathetic, and most likely hostile, to antislavery interests. Lane's deference to the territorial courts, as demonstrated at the Big Springs convention, was likely tarnished by his ostracism by the territory's leading proslavery judicial figure.

The shift toward an independent state movement was also a matter of political expediency. Abolitionist and Free State leader Charles Robinson later wrote, "When it became evident that the Legislature would be endorsed by the territorial judiciary and the President, and that there would be no escape by election for at least two years, it was equally evident that some means must be devised to keep the settlers from abandoning the fight." The Free State Party relied upon not only settlers with true antislavery convictions but also those people—like former governor Reeder—who had come to oppose the actions of the proslavery territorial government. "Such a movement," Robinson explained, "would serve to occupy the minds of the people, attract the attention of ambitious politicians, become a rallying point for all opposed to the usurpation, and, in case of necessity, when all other means of self-preservation should fail, be used as a de facto government, even though not recognized by Congress."[39] While Lane fits the description of "ambitious politician," the interests and activities of the growing free-state movement did not conflict with his democratic principles, nor with his allegiance to the National Democratic Party.

By October 1855, James Lane had not only heard about proslavery oppression of free-state interests, but had personally experienced it. His willingness to bypass the territorial legislature and to appeal directly to national authorities for Kansas statehood is not surprising, nor was it very radical. James Lane's work in the free-state movement was reactive to the Kansas political environment and the established state authorities. Antislavery settlers and those disgusted with proslavery control of territorial power drew together in the Free State Party and the new statehood movement.

A convention of Free State men gathered in Topeka on October 23 to draw up a new constitution. Lane attended as a Democrat as well as a Free State man. In fact, Democrats provided more delegates than all other party affiliations combined. The convention roster lists Lane among twenty "former"

39. Charles Robinson, *The Kansas Conflict*, 169.

Democratic delegates.[40] The rest of the delegation included nine Whigs, four Republicans, two independents, and one Free Soil Democrat.[41] Lane actively labored to secure a leading role. A savvy politician, he reportedly used promises, flattery, and threats to have himself elected president, despite the fact, one newspaper correspondent believed, that few delegates favored his election.[42] His supposed relationship with President Pierce also played an important role in his rise to power. As he had done in previous meetings, Lane claimed to know the sentiments of Douglas and Pierce. He told Free State men that "Douglas would make any sacrifice to secure the immediate admission of Kansas to the Union as a free state," and, a newspaper reported, he "occasionally drops precious morsels, such as that *he knows* that the application of Kansas, if in this shape, will receive favor at Washington."[43] Lane's reference to the interests of Douglas and Pierce worried some free-state people. The *Kansas Free State* warned of the "conquest" of the Free State Party by the administration through a mass entrance of proslavery Democrats into party ranks.[44] Lane, at least, was not a proslavery Democrat, but cautious Whigs and Free-Soilers failed to appreciate that fact given his support of the Kansas-Nebraska Act. However, the realization that national support would be necessary to obtain Kansas's admission as a free state helped bring Lane into power.

Upon his election to president of the convention, Lane gave an inspirational speech, painting a glorious picture of Kansas's future. The men assembled there, he explained, had a great task. "Your first business will be to guard the ballot box in such a manner as to prevent a repetition of the greatest crime that can be perpetrated in a representative Government like ours." He again defended the Kansas-Nebraska Act, stating that when the bill was before Congress, "no one of its supporters claimed that Kansas could ever become a Slave State; all, from the highest to the lowest, discarded the idea that Slavery could ever be extended within her borders. Our Southern friends were among the most prominent impressing this

40. For some unknown reason Lane recorded his birth state as Kentucky and his age as thirty-three. In October 1855, James Lane was forty-one years old. "The Topeka Movement," 164.

41. Ibid., 165; Wendell Stephenson states that there were fifty-one delegates sent to the convention. However, only thirty-six are accounted for in the Kansas Historical Collection roster. Stephenson, "The Transitional Period," 85.

42. *New York Daily Times,* November 5, 1855, in Webb Scrapbook, 6:158.

43. *National Era,* October 5, 1855, in Webb Scrapbook, 6:12; *New York Daily Tribune,* November 18, 1855, quoted in Stephenson, "The Transitional Period," 86.

44. *Kansas Free State,* October 29, 1855.

position before the country." The present effort forcing slavery upon the territory was "an afterthought for sinister purposes."[45]

Lane's political progression was careful and measured. He had not abandoned his principles, even with his new leadership role in the Free State Party. Popular sovereignty could work, and it would work, he believed, as long as the true, honest settlers in Kansas were free to voice their interests and vote in their territorial government. As before, Lane urged moderation:

> The people you represent, although excited beyond measure by the fraudulent and violent course pursued by those citizens of an adjoining State, who were, by falsehood and misrepresentation, induced to join in the crusade to force Slavery upon them contrary to their wishes, and destructive of their best interests, nevertheless expect you in the final settlement of that question to pursue a fair and liberal course toward the holders of that species of property within and without our borders.[46]

In other words, Lane argued that despite the great conflict and hatred between antislavery and proslavery forces in and around Kansas, the free state movement must legislate fairly and recognize the interests of slaveholders and not unjustly harm their rights or interests.

Because the convention included a variety of free-state and antislavery representatives, factionalism became a problem. Two specific elements emerged, one conservative, the other radical. Lane, along with other Democrats, formed the conservative or administration group, which stood opposed to the "radical" men who held stronger antislavery, even abolitionist, views. The conservatives backed the Kansas-Nebraska Act. A resolution that endorsed popular sovereignty passed through the convention, aided by "much persuasion on the part of Col. Lane and others, and the assurance that its passage would secure the friendly cooperation of Douglas."[47]

The "black law," which excluded any black person from entering Kansas, became another contentious issue during the convention. While some delegates opposed the measure, particularly those from New England holding sincere abolitionist ideologies, a large, conservative midwestern element led by Lane had no interest in sharing Kansas with either

---

45. *New York Daily Times,* November 5, 1855, in Webb Scrapbook, 6:158.
46. Ibid.
47. *Vermont Phoenix,* December 1, 1855, in Webb Scrapbook, 7:71.

free or enslaved blacks.[48] A correspondent to the *New York Tribune* explained that many settlers "who are known as Free-State men are not anti-Slavery in our Northern acceptation of the word. They are more properly negro haters who vote Free-State to keep negroes out, free or slave."[49] As a compromise, the convention decided to place the "black law" before Kansas voters, separate from the constitution. Some easterners voiced their frustration with the compromise. "It is true a different state of facts surround us now," wrote George W. Brown in the *Herald of Freedom*, "and here we are willing our neighbors, who agree with us in the main, but differ on this question—and who we have conceded are in the majority—shall fix the matter up to suit themselves; but we do object to their placing us in a position which will require us to stultify ourself [*sic*], or give the lie to our entire past history." Nonetheless, Brown and other opponents of the black law were satisfied with achieving a united front for making Kansas free. "A determination was apparent with every delegate to the convention that the Free State party should unite. Division, it was evident, was defeat. A united front was victory."[50]

On November 11, the Topeka convention concluded with a free-state constitution, scheduled for voter ratification on December 15. On that date, free-state voters turned out in force, and recorded 1,731 votes in its favor. Officials counted only 46 votes in opposition. The referendum on the "black law" also passed, 1,287 to 453.[51] Free-state voters had chosen a state not only without black slavery but also without any blacks at all. The free-state movement and its Topeka Constitution seemed to move along smoothly. An independent statehood effort was underway, boldly (but peacefully) challenging the established territorial government for national approval. The conflict between free-state and proslavery forces may have remained solely political in nature had not a proslavery settler killed a free-state man on November 21, 1855, sparking a "war" around Lawrence. The homicide was the culmination of a land dispute between Franklin Coleman and Jacob Branson near Hickory Point, a small settlement outside of Lawrence. Coleman, a proslavery settler, shot and killed Charles Dow, a free-state settler who had settled on the controversial claim by Branson. Afraid of retaliation from free-state settlers, Coleman fled to Mis-

48. See Eugene H. Berwanger, *The Frontier against Slavery: Western Anti-Negro Prejudice and the Slavery Extension Controversy,* 97–118.

49. *New York Tribune,* July 12, 1855.

50. *Herald of Freedom,* September 8, 1855.

51. Rawley, *Race and Politics,* 95; Etcheson, *Bleeding Kansas,* 75.

souri. On November 26, Branson and the local free-state militia responded violently, burning numerous proslavery households, including Coleman's abandoned home. In response, Douglas County Sheriff Samuel Jones arrested Branson that same night for disturbing the peace. As Jones and his posse escorted their prisoner on a dark road to Lecompton, a band of fifteen free-state men confronted the group and demanded the release of Branson. After a tense standoff, Jones watched his prisoner flee with the free-state men toward Lawrence.[52]

The sheriff immediately sent word to Governor Shannon that a group of men around Lawrence had defied territorial law and forcibly released his prisoner. The governor called out the territorial militia and requested assistance from nearby federal forces.[53] The local military commander refused to get involved until ordered by the president.[54] But President Pierce's response to the governor seemed promising, reassuring Shannon that all efforts would be made to maintain peace. Rumors that antislavery men were congregating in Lawrence preparing for war circulated among proslavery communities.[55] Shannon called upon "all well-disposed citizens of this territory to rally to the support of the laws of their country" and for civil and military officers and citizens "to be aiding and assisting, by all means in their power, in quelling this armed organization."[56] Shannon's words and Sheriff Jones's correspondence to supporters in Westport, Missouri, drew a great response from the neighboring slaveholding state. As many as twelve hundred Missourians flooded into Kansas to help Jones confront the free-state force at Lawrence. The Missouri contingent dwarfed the approximately three hundred Kansas settlers who responded

52. *Herald of Freedom*, December 15, 1855; "Narrative, the Murder of Charles Dow, by Isaac Goodnow," Isaac Goodnow Collection, Kansas State Historical Society, Topeka; Charles Robinson, *The Kansas Conflict*, 184–86; Etcheson, *Bleeding Kansas*, 79–80; Zornow, *Kansas*, 71, 72.

53. Copies of the correspondence between Jones, Shannon, and Major-General William P. Richardson of the territorial militia can be found in *Personal Recollections of Pardee Butler*, 85.

54. Marvin Ewy, "The United States Army in the Kansas Border Troubles, 1855–1856," 386.

55. For example, the proslavery publication *Kansas Weekly Herald* reported that "Letters and papers were found on E. C. K. Garvey of Topeka, and a Mr. Dunn, going to show the organization of the secret order called the Kansas Legion, and a preparation for war, and the resisting the laws by force." *Kansas Weekly Herald*, December 15, 1855.

56. Governor Wilson Shannon's "Proclamation," November 29, 1855, copied in William Phillips, *The Conquest of Kansas by Missouri and Her Allies: A History of the Troubles in Kansas, from the Passage of the Organic Act until the Close of July, 1856*, 169.

to the governor's request. The hodgepodge military force gathered on the Wakarusa River, outside of Lawrence.[57]

While Lawrence residents officially denounced the Branson rescue party and sent them out of town shortly after the incident, free-state men quickly prepared military defenses for the expected proslavery retaliation. Groups of armed free-state settlers arrived in town, some from as far away as Topeka, to help combat the Missouri presence.[58] The town's defenders elected Charles Robinson as commander-in-chief, while Lane was placed second in command. As one of the few men in Lawrence with military leadership experience, Lane set about organizing the town's physical defenses as well as drilling the citizen soldiers. Author Donald Gilmore argues that Lane's secondary role behind Robinson was due to his radical nature. "The belief was that if the more experienced Lane were placed in command at this 'critical juncture,' it might offer an 'unballasted leadership,'" Gilmore wrote. "Lane, despite his elevation in Free State ranks, was justly considered intemperate, to say the least."[59] There is little evidence to support this claim. Although Lane's enthusiastic stump speaking drew attention, he had largely made a name for himself within free-state ranks as a conservative, calling for moderation in the previous Free State conventions. Regardless of the division of power, free-state minister Pardee Butler credited Lane as "the principal figure in the enterprise. He alone had military experience, and he alone had the daring, the genius and personal magnetism of a real leader."[60]

With the tension between proslavery and free-state forces growing to a new and potentially explosive level, Lane thrived. He commanded around six hundred citizen soldiers, training them in basic military drill. The men erected rough fortifications in key defensive locations. Lane's energy was boundless. He shouted out orders and occasionally gave inspirational speeches. Under a direct proslavery threat, Lane took a more aggressive tone, giving speeches to prepare the citizens for a fight. Robinson, on the other hand, appeared restrained, laboring to keep the citizens calm.[61]

C. H. Dickson later recalled Lane's excited behavior, and explained at least one reason for it. Numerous free-state men in Lawrence grew frustrated that the standoff kept them away from their families, many of whom waited in

---

57. Rawley, *Race and Politics*, 97.
58. *Herald of Freedom*, December 18, 1855.
59. Gilmore, *Civil War on the Missouri-Kansas Border*, 69.
60. *Personal Recollections of Pardee Butler*, 87.
61. Stephenson, *Political Career of Lane*, 56.

isolated cabins across the prairie. Dickson watched as one group of men complained to Lane that they "all had better be at home fixing up for winter, than fooling our time away here." Lane, Dickson remembered, "made some good-natured and smiling reply." Nonetheless, discontent quickly spread and many voiced their desire to leave Lawrence. "With the instinct of a born leader," Dickson wrote, "Lane took in the situation and recognized its gravity. Instead of remaining on a level with the men and wrangling or arguing with them, where he would most certainly have been out-talked, he sprang upon the embankment and commenced making a speech. By this shrewd move he obtained 'the floor,' and silenced his opponents."[62]

According to Dickson, Lane spoke smoothly, taking care not to instigate further discontent. More people soon gathered, thinking Lane shared some valuable bit of news. As the audience grew, Lane's speech intensified. "He comprehended the magnitude of the occasion," Dickson explained. "The army must be held together; the words he must now utter must accomplish that end." Here Lane's oratorical mastery emerged. "He became afire with eloquence. Off went his large, circular military cloak, next his hat, soon his coat, as he saw his appeal telling; then his vest followed." The audience loved it. As Lane finished his speech, cheers erupted from the crowd and, according to Dickson, "General Lane knew, as he came down from his perch and put on his discarded clothing, that he had won an important, although bloodless victory."[63]

Governor Shannon arrived in Lawrence on December 7 and met with Robinson and Lane to end the "Wakarusa War," as it became known, before fighting commenced. Free-state forces agreed to obey territorial laws but refused to surrender their arms. The governor traveled back to the proslavery lines to find the Missourians riled up, ready to invade Lawrence. Worried about the impending action, Shannon finally arranged a treaty with Lane and Robinson. In the treaty the free-state leaders explained that the rescue of Branson was "made without our knowledge or consent, but that if any of our citizens in the Town of Lawrence were engaged in said rescue, we pledge ourselves to aid in the execution of any legal process against them."[64] In turn, Shannon declared that he would aid in the compensation of damages caused by Sheriff Jones's posse, and that he had not called upon residents of any other state to help enforce Kansas laws. As a final statement,

---

62. C. H. Dickson, "The 'Boy's' Story: Reminiscences of 1855," 83.
63. Ibid., 84.
64. *Kansas Free State,* January 7, 1856, *Kansas Weekly Herald,* January 12, 1856; Charles Robinson, *The Kansas Conflict,* 202–3.

however, Lane and Robinson clarified that "we wish it understood that we do not herein express any opinion as to the validity of the enactments of the Territorial Legislature."[65] While not specifically denouncing the proslavery legislature, the free-state leaders wanted to leave no doubt that the treaty did not justify or recognize the body.

With the carefully worded treaty in hand, which ignored larger political matters, Lane, Robinson, and Shannon met with a group of proslavery leaders in Franklin.[66] After three hours of discussion, the Wakarusa War came to an end. Decades later, Charles Robinson described the meeting, taking nearly sole credit for convincing the Missourians to go home. Lane, Robinson explained, nearly sabotaged the conference by offending proslavery leaders who threatened to leave. Robinson quickly focused their attention and stated that no authority had come to Lawrence to demand the surrender of Branson. Thus, the people of Lawrence were unwitting victims of circumstance. When the Missourians questioned Sheriff Jones and found this to be true, one called out, "We have been damnably deceived."[67] And so the meeting ended.

Lawrence residents generally welcomed the end of the standoff, except for at least one soon-to-be famous figure, John Brown. Brown stood before a crowd and warned of some hidden concession. Before he could finish, free-state leaders assured the residents that the town and the cause were safe.[68] Lane and Robinson gave their own speeches in Lawrence, congratulating the residents and praising each other. "You have won a glorious victory by your industry, skill, courage and forebearance [sic]," Lane stated. "In these fortifications, wrought if by magic, you took your position, there determined never to surrender while a man was left alive to pull a trigger; with a desperate foe almost in your very midst, you restrained your fire—determined to continue them in the wrong and compel them to commence hostilities—to take all the responsibility of a battle which you believed would shake the Union to its very basis." Turning toward Robinson, Lane announced, "From Major General Robinson I received that council and advice which characterizes him as a clear-headed, cool and trust-worthy commander. He is entitled to your confidence and esteem."[69] Robinson in turn credited Lane with "the thorough

65. Ibid.
66. Goodrich, *War to the Knife*, 85.
67. Charles Robinson, *The Kansas Conflict*, 204–5.
68. Stephenson, *Political Career of Lane*, 57.
69. *Herald of Freedom*, December 15, 1855.

discipline of our forces, and the complete and extensive preparations for defense. His services cannot be overrated, and long may he live to wear the laurels so bravely won."[70] Whatever differences these men may have had before or in the midst of the standoff on the Wakarusa, they publicly praised each other during the celebration.

Descriptions of Lane during the Wakarusa War generally paint a radical picture. C. H. Dickson recalled that Lane "paced, like some wild animal, rapidly back and forth on the embankment, with the perspiration standing in great beads upon his face," as he rallied frustrated Lawrence defenders. For men like Dickson, this radical action was not negative, but necessary for the free-state cause, and demonstrated Lane's "rare tact and marvelous magnetic power." Lane's motivational oration renewed the town's spirit, and as he stepped down from the embankment, men around him "were in a perfect frenzy; yelling and cheering, jumping about, shaking hands, slapping one another on the back, and acting in a ridiculous manner generally." Dickson recalled that Lane had "poured forth a stream of eloquence, the like of which have never heard, although I am now an old man and have listened to many of America's most-noted orators."[71]

Lane's excited behavior unnerved others. When free-state man Thomas Barber was shot and killed by a proslavery man on his way home from Lawrence before the Wakarusa War had ended, his body was brought back to the Free State Hotel in Lawrence on December 7, inciting a great deal of anger among town residents.[72] New England settler Hannah Ropes overheard Lane speaking in the hotel, and wrote a scathing report of the man:

Col. Lane's voice could be heard in different rooms, detailing to eager listeners the most painful circumstances of poor Barbour's death, and, with wonderful ingeniousness, keeping up the wicked spirit of vengeance among those over whom he exercised any power. What on earth he was driving at by such a course, it seemed to my stupid self quite impossible to understand; while, at the same time, I knew very well that he aimed at something he could not otherwise attain so well. Any reader of human faces can never study his without a sensation very much like that with which one stands at the edge of a slimy, sedgy [sic], uncertain morass. If there is any good in him, I never, with all my industry in culling something pleasant from the most unpropitious characters, have been able to make the discovery. And he has not, in lieu of

70. Ibid.
71. Dickson, "The 'Boy's' Story," 83, 84.
72. For an account of Barber's death, see Goodrich, *War to the Knife*, 80–82.

anything better, that agreeable fascination of manner which so often gives currency in society to men as hollow-hearted as he.[73]

While Hannah Ropes portrayed a man bent on vengeance and extremism, decades later Charles Robinson questioned Lane's sincerity to the free-state cause as a whole, again suggesting that Lane was, deep-down, proslavery:

> There has always been a question as to the motive that actuated Lane. It was well known to the leading Free-State men that at heart he preferred a slave State. . . . He was always on intimate terms with some of the proslavery leaders, and during the "war" had General Richardson and staff dine with him by invitation, when their forces were laying siege to the town and killed Barber. Whether he designed to change the position from one of defense to one of offense, and thus bring ruin upon the Free-State cause, or whether he wanted to court favor with inconsiderate and exasperated men to secure a little political prestige, may never be known. Fortunately for the Free-State cause he was so well understood, and his loyalty so questioned, that he was never implicitly trusted, and hence could not betray the cause if he should attempt it.[74]

Ironically, while Robinson's account portrays Lane as an absolute opportunist, it also suggests that he was not radical at all. Still, Robinson and Ropes described Lane as a dangerous man, whose handling of the Wakarusa War could have been disastrous if not for the levelheaded leadership of a New Englander.

Even biographer Wendell Stephenson accepted the view that Lane proactively took an aggressive stance during the standoff and "wanted to take the offensive."[75] But one account suggests that Lane resisted free-state aggression. James Redpath, abolitionist reporter and early biographer of John Brown, credits Lane with stopping an offensive move against the Missourians. When John Brown set out to skirmish with the proslavery besiegers, Lane convinced him otherwise. "Lane sent for [Brown] to attend a council of war," Redpath wrote. Disgusted at talk taking the place of action, Brown supposedly replied, "Tell the General, that when he wants me to fight, to say so; but that is the only order I will ever obey."[76] Accord-

---

73. Hannah Ropes, *Six Months in Kansas: By a Lady*, 144–45.
74. Charles Robinson, *The Kansas Conflict*, 217.
75. Stephenson, *Political Career of Lane*, 56.
76. James Redpath, *The Public Life of Capt. John Brown*, 87.

ing to Redpath, Brown saw both Lane and Robinson as he did most politicians, mostly talk with little action. But the account is important, for it offers a description of Lane from the opposite spectrum of the free-state side. While Robinson and Ropes were among the New England contingent, which came to despise Lane and the rough western characters who made up such a large proportion of the free-state group, Brown represented the ultra-radical faction. Robinson and Ropes saw Lane as dangerous; Brown felt Lane was not aggressive enough. Thus, Lane seems to fall somewhat in the middle.

Biographer Wendell Stephenson described the Wakarusa War as a "turning point" in Lane's career in Kansas. "He was essentially a conservative until that crisis presented a proper background for radical leadership," the author wrote. "For in battle array the belligerent Lane was in his element, and the hysteria of exciting events intensified his fiery and impulsive nature."[77] Stephenson rightly saw the Wakarusa conflict ignite Lane's fiery nature. But calling the event a "turning point" in Lane's career may be too much. Such a term conjures up imagery of Lane changing direction. In fact, Lane's aggressive behavior in the defense of Lawrence was not atypical of the man who helped raise men to fight in the Mexican War and then commanded them. Nor was his behavior at this point a radical departure from his work or interests in Kansas Territory. His time and behavior in Kansas was a progression. As he studied the political environment, Lane adjusted, associating himself with people and organizations that, while not affiliated with his traditional party, nonetheless shared the same basic interest of establishing a free state. When confronted with blatant prejudice or oppression from proslavery officials, as in the case of his failed law application and then the Wakarusa War, Lane increasingly adopted more aggressive tactics in achieving a free state. His basic principles, however, remained the same.

Following the Wakarusa War treaty, the Topeka movement continued smoothly. Voters adopted the Topeka Constitution days afterwards, and at the end of December Lane participated in a meeting to schedule a January election of "state" officials. In January, Free State men held a convention in Lawrence that passed a resolution pledging noninterference with slavery where it existed, but general opposition to its extension.[78] This development prompted some in Kansas to celebrate the spread of "Republicanism"

77. Stephenson, *Political Career of Lane*, 58.
78. *Herald of Freedom*, March 1, 1856; Stephenson, *Political Career of Lane*, 58.

in the territory. George W. Brown of the *Herald of Freedom* stood proud among them. In a story titled "Republicanism in Kansas," Brown described the convention as the origin of the Republican Party in the territory, and rejoiced in the fact that Lane and a number of other National Democrats endorsed a resolution recognizing the right of Congress to interfere with slavery in the territories. The *Herald of Freedom* explained that Lane was moving along in his views by admitting "what he has hitherto denied—that he was deceived in imagining that squatterophobia is a symptom of good health."[79]

While some celebrated Lane's apparent change, others criticized his inconsistency in party principle.[80] However, the trend toward Republicanism did not signal a party switch among Lane or other National Democrats within Free State Party ranks. Historian Wendell Stephenson states that the Free State convention should not be understood as the formation of the Republican Party in Kansas. Not until 1859 did the Republicans formally replace the Free State Party.[81] While the resolutions passed by the convention may have been similar to some of the Republican platform, the delegates did not all adopt a Republican identity. A copy of the resolutions printed more than a month later includes Lane's endorsement and labels him a pro–Kansas-Nebraska Act Democrat.[82] Even Brown of the *Herald* admitted that Lane had not yet adopted the Republican creed. But the fiery editor warned that the ambitious Free State leader had better adopt the Republican platform "if he wishes to preserve a character of consistency."[83]

Lane's continued place within Democratic ranks during this period is well documented. The *Kansas Free State* reported that Lane had been selected as a delegate to the National Democratic convention in Cincinnati by the Democratic element of the Free State Party.[84] While no evidence that Lane attended the convention has surfaced, his active role and recognized leadership among Democrats within Kansas and the Free State Party during the first few months of 1856 cannot be denied.[85] James Lane, while learning a hard lesson about the failure of popular sovereignty in the territory, was still a Democrat.

79. Popular sovereignty was often called "squatter sovereignty" by its critics. *Herald of Freedom,* January 19, 1856.
80. *Kansas Freeman,* February 2, 1856.
81. Stephenson, *Political Career of Lane,* 59.
82. *Herald of Freedom,* March 1, 1856.
83. Ibid., January 19, 1856.
84. *Kansas Free State,* March 24, 1856.
85. Stephenson, *Political Career of Lane,* 61.

Throughout January and February, Lane helped lead the Topeka movement toward statehood. Agents were sent by the committee across the country to draw support for the free-state cause. Fears of another Missouri invasion surfaced. As chairman of the executive committee, Lane wrote to President Pierce warning of "an overwhelming force of the citizens of Missouri" on the verge of marching into Kansas Territory. Taking a very firm stance, Lane "respectfully demand[ed]" military assistance in preventing such aggression.[86] Free State officials appointed Lane "2nd Major General" and authorized him to organize free-state defenses under the commander-in-chief, Charles Robinson. While the feared invasion never took place, the energy and drive for protecting free-state rights continued.

In March, the Free State legislature elected Lane and former governor Reeder senators of Kansas upon admission into the Union. Lane had already been selected to travel to Washington with three others to help secure statehood; now he held the expectation of shortly taking a seat in the upper house of Congress. Within days of the legislature's votes, Lane traveled east with a memorial from the free-state leadership to Congress. He carried the hopes of free-state Kansans as he rushed to meet with Northern Democrats, particularly Douglas. He had gone to Kansas Territory to set up the Democratic Party and with the interest of it becoming a free state. While a formal Democratic presence had not materialized, he had worked diligently to defend Democratic principles in the face of Republican and Whig opposition. More brutal had been the Missouri resistance, which had, in his eyes, made a mockery of popular sovereignty. His support of the Kansas-Nebraska Act's chief principle had wavered— he realized popular sovereignty did not work under the current territorial government and with Missouri interference. But, he remained confident that the free-state movement, with support from a majority of settlers, would succeed under the democratic principle of popular sovereignty if he could personally see their cause presented in Congress.

86. "The Topeka Movement," 153.

3

Lane and the Kansas Memorial, 1856

"Senator Douglas cajoled me into an undeserved trust of his sincerity."

As James Henry Lane arrived in Washington, D.C., around the end of March 1856, he carried the hopes and expectations of many in Kansas and across the Northern states. In his hands rested the Kansas Memorial—a petition by free-state Kansans to Congress for the acceptance of the Topeka Constitution. If accepted by Congress, Kansas would enter the Union as a free state and Lane would take his seat as a U.S. senator. He entered Washington confident that the Democratic leadership would support free-state Kansans, for, he rightly believed, a majority of settlers wanted a free state. By the time he left, the Senate's reception of the Kansas Memorial had destroyed his confidence in the National Democratic Party.

When Lane left Kansas for Washington in March, the free-state effort for statehood was a gamble. Lane's rise within free-state ranks had been aided by his repeated assurances that President Franklin Pierce and Senator Stephen Douglas wanted Kansas admitted as a free state, and that his influence with these men would help the success of their cause.[1] Unfortunately, the president's message to Congress in January 1856 did not bode well for

1. *New York Daily Tribune*, November 20, 1855, Webb Scrapbook, 6:243.

the Topeka Constitution. Pierce described the free-state movement as "merely a party of the inhabitants" of the territory who "without law, have undertaken to summon a convention for the purpose of transforming the Territory into a State." He called these acts illegal and revolutionary.[2]

Free-state Kansans responded defiantly to Pierce's proclamation. Some of their leaders, including Lane, spoke on the subject at a public meeting in Topeka in early March. According to the *Herald of Freedom*, Lane "replied" to Pierce's portrayal of the free-state cause as "merely a party" within the territory. All inhabitants had been invited to participate in the Topeka constitutional movement. He further explained that the real minority group in the territory was the proslavery contingent, which depended upon support from outsiders.[3] He was right. Proslavery settler George Clarke wrote to Jon A. Quitman in Washington that free-state men "rely upon us submitting to a majority-rule" and he was not compelled "to submit to the rule of a majority in an unconstitutional measure."[4] Though Lane disagreed with Pierce's proclamation, there is no evidence that the matter led to any great rift between Lane and the administration. The senator-elect traveled to Washington confident that the presentation of the free-state case would still find a sympathetic audience among the National Democratic leaders.

In Washington, Lane placed the hopes of the free-state cause in the hands of one of the Democratic Party's most powerful icons, Senator Lewis Cass of Michigan. The Topeka Convention chose Cass to introduce the memorial for statehood due to his seniority in the Senate.[5] Cass had also been chiefly responsible for constructing the doctrine of popular sovereignty, a fact noted by Charles Robinson to the Free State legislature.[6] With a figure such as Cass presenting the memorial, the unauthorized free-state movement intended to gain an element of legitimacy.

On April 7, with an anxious Lane observing the proceedings, Cass introduced the memorial to the Senate, describing its authors as "composing the self-styled Legislature of Kansas."[7] Senator William H. Seward from New York asked from which of the two legislatures in Kansas the petition

2. *Congressional Globe,* 34th Cong., 1st sess., 296–98; Pierce's message may also be found in "Administration of Governor Shannon," 250–57.

3. *Herald of Freedom,* March 29, 1856.

4. George W. Clarke to Jon A. Quitman, January 29, 1856, Misc. Clarke, G. W. Collection, Kansas State Historical Society, Topeka.

5. See *Kansas Free State,* March 24, 1856.

6. Nevins, *Ordeal of the Union,* vol. 1, 30; "The Topeka Movement," 181.

7. *Congressional Globe,* 34th Cong., 1st sess., 826.

originated. Cass brushed aside the remark, inferring that Seward, as well as every senator in the chamber, understood which body in Kansas stood as the "self-styled" legislature. For months Congress had followed developments in Kansas and knew of the resistance to the territory's officially sanctioned proslavery government. Cass did not bother to rehash the interests and motives of the petition he introduced.

Opponents of the free-state movement were also familiar with the independent legislature in Kansas and ready to resist the petition. The Senate quickly agreed to Cass's motion to send the petition to the Committee on Territories, but Stephen Adams, Democrat from Mississippi, and Andrew Butler, Democrat of South Carolina, objected to its printing upon technical grounds, including the dubious nature of the Free State Party. Butler, a champion of proslavery interests in Congress, denounced the memorial, stating that he could not "recognize the source from which this comes, as one of the States of this Confederacy, or as a member of the body-politic."[8] Lane should not have been surprised at the South Carolinian's objection, as he had come to Washington specifically to resist Southern slaveholding opposition.

Cass defended the petition on principle. He did not tie himself to the free-state cause or the Topeka movement itself. Instead, he championed the right of petition and argued his wish "to see the representation which these people make of their own condition," and further warned the other senators not to draw the constitutionally guaranteed right of petition into the matter. Butler remained unconvinced, and continued to lash out at the memorial. He invoked his personal sense of honor, stating, "I do not know that I have ever felt on any occasion more sensibly an insult offered to the Senate of the United States—a Senate composed of regular authorized representatives of the States—than now, when this impudent petition comes here, and claims something like equality."[9]

While Butler's animated dismissal of the memorial no doubt served as a serious obstacle to the free-state cause, Lane had placed his hopes on support from Northern Democrats to weather the storm. Chief among those figures was Illinois Senator Stephen Douglas, the ultimate champion of popular sovereignty and the author of the Kansas-Nebraska Act. While the rumor that Lane worked specifically under Douglas's eye has never been confirmed, Lane's repeated assurances of Douglas's support of a free

8. Ibid.
9. Ibid.

state under popular sovereignty demonstrated the amount of faith the new Kansan had placed in the "Little Giant."

How Lane perceived Douglas's first reaction to the memorial on the Senate floor is unknown. He could not have been pleased as Douglas took a relatively noncommittal position. Immediately after Butler concluded his denunciation of the Topeka movement as a whole, Douglas rose. He immediately focused on potential problems within the document. "I find that the signatures are all in one handwriting," he explained, "showing that it is not an original paper." He further pointed out that portions of the document had been erased or otherwise altered. "All of these things are calculated to throw doubt on the genuineness of the document, unless there be good evidence that it is genuine."[10] Still, the Illinois senator did not abandon the petition. Despite the discrepancies, Douglas stated that he did not have any objection to the reception of the memorial and its printing. Such actions would allow the Senate to better consider the document and the free-state movement, and hopefully explain the apparent alterations to the memorial. Upon completion of Douglas's statements, the Senate moved on to other matters without voting on whether to print the petition.

The initial introduction of the Kansas Memorial was not a success, but it had not failed. In fact, it had probably achieved all that could have been realistically expected given the controversial nature of the Kansas question by the spring of 1856. In short, it survived the first round. No person had yet stepped up to defend the free-state cause, but the moderate voices of Cass and Douglas had stalled the inevitable attack by the proslavery forces in the Senate.

Round two for the memorial began two days later, on April 9, as the Senate resumed consideration of Cass's motion to print the document. Seward immediately called for a vote, but South Carolina's Butler again voiced his opposition to the printing of the petition on the grounds that the free-state organization was illegitimate. This time he focused on the signatures. Cass rose and explained that he had spoken with Lane, and that Lane told him "that it had been signed by the persons whose names are attached to it, and that it is a genuine document." Beyond that basic explanation, Cass would not commit. Butler was not impressed. He challenged the right of Lane to vouch for any document in the Senate. "I do not know who he is," Butler declared.[11] After a spirited lecture on the rules of printing petitions, the

10. Ibid., 827.
11. Ibid., 839.

South Carolinian concluded by denouncing the efforts of "creeping intruders" into the U.S. Senate.

The Senate's April 9 discussion on the memorial did produce one strong defense of the free-state cause. Republican Senator William Seward of New York took the floor soon after Butler's comments and gave a lengthy summary of the Kansas struggle from an antislavery point of view. Seward particularly criticized the Pierce administration, which he accused of oppressing the people of Kansas in a way similar to that of the king of England before and during the American Revolution.[12] While Lane and others sympathetic to antislavery interests in Kansas likely embraced Seward's remarks, he spoke more generally about the Kansas situation rather than on the specific nature of the Kansas Memorial. The New York senator's speech did not bring Lane or the Topeka Constitution any closer to success.

The Senate debate of April 10 decided the fate of the petition. Rather than revolving around the heart of the memorial—Kansas statehood—the Senate became locked in a lengthy series of speeches, arguments, and statements concerning the right of petition and the dubious nature of the Kansas Memorial. With Butler again leading the critics, it appeared as if the petition would die on a technicality. And while the debate centered on the principle of petition and constitutional rights, traditional sectional loyalties and ideologies shaped the debate—at least for the South. Senators from slaveholding states resisted even the printing of the petition. Vocal antislavery senators, such as Seward, helped provide a glimmer of hope for the free-state cause. But it would require the strong support of Northern Democrats for the memorial even to be printed, let alone have its contents considered.

Lane needed the support of Northern Democrats. He had expected it. It did not come. In fact, shortly after the debate on April 10 began, James Lane's world came crashing down. The short, stocky, and fiery Stephen Douglas took the floor. Explaining that he had previously advocated printing the petition out of courtesy to Senator Cass, Douglas now declared that the stakes had changed. Charging that "gentlemen on the other side of the Chamber" had made the petition's printing a test of principle, he had no choice but to defy them. The Topeka Convention was not a legitimate political entity possessing the rights or privileges of states or authorized governments. This being the case, he argued, the memorial had no ground on principle.[13]

12. For Seward's full speech, *Appendix to the Congressional Globe*, 34th Cong., 1st sess., 390–405.

13. *Congressional Globe*, 34th Cong., 1st sess., 851.

While Douglas's new position was bad enough for Lane and the Topeka movement, his next comments shattered any hope of Northern Democratic leadership support:

> Here we are now asked by this vote to recognize the fact, that this revolutionary proceeding in Kansas makes it a State. I am not willing to recognize that fact. We are asked to recognize the fact that these petitioners are Senators and Representatives. I am not willing to recognize that fact, because it is not true. We are asked to give countenance to these proceedings as having been legal instead of revolutionary—as having been loyal to the Constitution, instead of an act of defiance to the constituted authorities. I am not willing to give any countenance to it; and when it is presented as a question of right, I am for meeting it at the threshold. I am in favor of denying the printing; I am in favor of reconsidering the vote which referred the memorial, and raising the question of its reception, and keeping it out.[14]

Douglas not only opposed printing the petition, but wanted the entire memorial thrown out of the Senate.

For Lane, the situation only grew worse. Senator Cass stood up shortly after Douglas's comments and qualified his previous actions in regard to the petition. Explaining that he had always supported the right of petition, Cass excused his involvement as simply passing on a memorial that had been presented to him. He then clarified that "I do not believe these persons are members of the Legislature of Kansas. I believe the legal Legislature of Kansas is the Territorial Legislature, acting under the authority of the United States."[15] Still, Cass threw in a word of encouragement for the Topeka movement. He believed it was worth hearing their concerns; he believed they did have a right to present their case.

Cass's carefully couched support probably brought little comfort to Lane, who watched helplessly as the very men he hoped would champion his cause began to distance themselves or turn hostile. Even senators who challenged the proslavery arguments of men like Butler and Senator James A. Bayard of Delaware often picked on specific points not related to the Topeka Constitution. Senator Lyman Trumbull of Illinois attacked the inconsistency of those senators who on one hand denied that the Kansas Territory could be considered a state in any sense of the word, yet on the other hand vehemently supported the enforcement of the Fugitive Slave

14. Ibid.
15. Ibid., 853.

Law, whose language specifically indicated laws and commerce between two states.[16] Unfortunately for Lane, Trumbull's logic did not advance the free-state petition.

Trumbull, however, did provide an extremely illuminating condemnation of another inconsistency among the Kansas Memorial's critics. Many of these men had championed the Kansas-Nebraska Act and popular sovereignty. "It has been said by Senators here," Trumbull said, "that those who opposed the Kansas-Nebraska act opposed the great principle of self-government or popular sovereignty—the principle for which our fathers fought—the principle lying at the foundation of the Declaration of Independence." He asked why the Kansas-Nebraska Act is "held up before the people of the country as conferring on the inhabitants of a Territory the right to govern themselves" if the people do not have that right. "If you only mean that the people of the Territory may do what you permit them to do, say so. That is not self-government. It is government derived from you."[17]

Trumbull identified a crucial weakness in opposition to the free-state cause. The essence of the Kansas-Nebraska Act was the right of its people to decide the status of an incoming state. The principle of popular sovereignty had been accepted by a vote in the Senate only two years previously, and supported by many of the Kansas Memorial's critics. Yet Senate critics denounced the Topeka movement as illegal, unauthorized, and illegitimate because it was not part of the officially sanctioned territorial government. "It comes with a bad grace indeed," Trumbull told his colleagues, "from those who have instilled into the minds of the people who have gone to Kansas the idea that they would have the right to govern themselves when they got there, now to turn round and denounce the settlers as traitors for attempting to assert the very right which they themselves told them they possessed."[18]

If Trumbull's words had an effect on any person in the gallery, it was probably Lane. He had defended the Kansas-Nebraska Act and popular sovereignty against the criticisms of many free-state settlers.[19] The free-state movement in Kansas had assumed authority according to ideas and principles of self-representation. During the January 14 meeting in Lawrence, the Free State Party had passed a resolution stating that the "unoffending settlers of Kansas have endeavored by every means within

16. Ibid., 854–855.
17. Ibid., 857.
18. Ibid., 857.
19. See *New York Daily Tribune,* November 20, 1855, in Webb Scrapbook, 6:243, and *Herald of Freedom,* August 18, 1855.

their power, to cultivate relations of friendship and amity with their pro-slavery brethren in Missouri," and that these efforts "have been met by outrages the most brutal and degrading." As a result, the committee resolved that "it is our duty to unfurl our banner to the breeze, and adopt as our motto:—A Free State Government without delay, emanating from the people, and responsible to them." The first signature under this reso-lution read "J. H. Lane," followed by the words "Nebraska Dem," an indi-cation of his political status.[20]

Despite Trumbull's efforts, and an equally energetic attempt by Seward to defend free-state Kansans, Lane could only watch as the Kansas Memo-rial and its authors were picked apart on the Senate floor. Senator Judah P. Benjamin of Louisiana jumped on the matter of the memorial's discrep-ancies, but emphasized the free-state disregard for law. While many crit-ics of the petition questioned the overall validity of the Topeka Convention, Benjamin pointed out that the signers had fled from justice in the territory. Thus, the senator from Louisiana not only undermined the authenticity of the signatures but also charged that even the accuracy of the document could not overcome the illegal nature of the movement.[21]

The final blow to the Kansas Memorial in the Senate came during dis-course between Butler and Cass toward the end of the debate on April 10. Butler took the opportunity to separate Cass from the questionable nature of the memorial. The South Carolinian complimented Cass as a well-meaning and honorable senator, who no doubt presented the petition in the interest of constitutional rights. But, Butler continued, when the petition was "branded with fraud and forgery," he was shocked that it still had support-ers. Thus, Butler had politely cracked one of the memorial's strengths in the Senate—its link to Cass. Whether this effort was simply an expression of respect to Cass, or a means of trying to undermine Cass's original support for the petition, it appears to have caused the Michigan senator to reconsider his role in the matter.

20. Account of meeting and resolutions printed in *Herald of Freedom*, March 1, 1856.

21. Benjamin stated: "Mr. President, are we not aware that the men whose signatures purport to be attached to this paper are fugitives from justice? Has it not been stated in the public journals of the land that the judges and marshals of the United States have gone into the neighborhood of the place where they were practicing their treasonable maneuvers, and that they have fled before the indignant justice of the land?" *Congres-sional Globe*, 34th Cong., 1st sess., 859. Benjamin may have been referring to the Wakarusa War and other complications between Sheriff Jones and the population in Lawrence. Shortly after this debate, free-state leaders in Kansas (including Lane) were in fact charged with treason and dozens were arrested.

Thanking Butler for the kind words, Cass explained that concern for the petition's authenticity had led him to have "an interview with the gentleman who presented me with the petition," James Lane. While there is no record of that conversation, we know Cass's feelings about it. As a result of the conversation, Cass explained, "I am bound to say to the Senate, that I am not satisfied that this paper is one which ought to be acted on by the Senate. This is all that is necessary for me to say."[22] And with that, the last pillar of Democratic support in the Senate for the Kansas Memorial crumbled.

More debate took place, but the matter was essentially settled. The formality of a vote only served to seal the coffin. A motion by Virginia Senator James Mason to rescind the order referring the memorial to the Committee on Territories and that the petition be removed from consideration for printing came to a vote.[23] Of thirty-five votes taken, only three Republicans supported the memorial.[24]

The day's events were a nightmare for Lane. The Kansas Memorial had been crushed in the Senate, and its only support had not come from his own party. Horace Greeley, an influential newspaper man and Republican, observed the Senate's handling of the memorial and was furious with the failure of more Republican senators to support the petition and the free-state cause. Conferring with Lane shortly after the debate, Greeley advised Lane to get Iowa Senator James Harlan "to move a reconsideration of the question, so that the Republican senators could put themselves right on the record." Harlan had been the first to vote against Mason's motion to rescind the petition. His vote gave courage, he later learned, to Massachusetts Senator Charles Sumner to support the Kansas Memorial also.[25]

Lane followed Greeley's advice and met with Harlan on April 11. The Kansan stated that "he was mortified beyond the power of words to express over the debate of the preceding day." Harlan also expressed his frustration with the handling of the memorial and, like Greeley, with the "complete demoralization" of the Republican senators on the Kansas matter. Yet, Harlan explained, he could not move to reconsider the issue as it stood. Instead, he suggested that Lane give him a personal petition with the memorial included in it.[26]

22. Ibid., 862.
23. Ibid., 854.
24. Senators James Harlan of Iowa, William H. Seward of New York, and Charles Sumner of Massachusetts voted against Mason's resolution; *Congressional Globe*, 34th Cong., 1st sess., 864.
25. Johnson Brigham, *James Harlan*, 98, 99.
26. Ibid., 99.

Lane, never the sort of man to back down from a challenge, set to work creating this personal statement. Despite the beating the Kansas Memorial had taken in the Senate, Lane stood strong to his position, claiming, in the very first line of his petition, "to be entitled to a seat in your honorable body as a Senator from the State of Kansas, when her present application for admission into the Union shall be granted." He went on to write that in March the Topeka legislature had authorized a committee, chaired by John Hutchinson, to draft a memorial to Congress. Upon its completion, the Free State legislature approved it. Lane admitted that the memorial was "hastily prepared by Mr. Hutchinson; and although entirely correct in its relation of fact, was deemed by some crude and prolix in its phraseology." The memorial was then referred to a committee to revise and refine the text and to prepare three copies. Lane was invited to be part of the revision committee, and said that the group's examination had "determined that so much of it as was superfluous and inconsiderate in its form of expression should be omitted in the revised copies which your memorialist [Lane], who was on his way to this city as one of the United States Senators elect, was instructed to prepare and submit." Upon arriving in Washington, Lane "proceeded to discharge immediately" this duty. In short, Lane's personal petition explained that he had been authorized by the legitimate figures in the Kansas assembly to edit the text before the memorial's submission to Congress.[27]

As for the matter of the signatures, Lane stated that he had been given three separate sets of signatures by the Kansas assembly to be attached to the revised copies when completed, but "these, unfortunately, have been mislaid." As a result, Lane had copied the names of the original signers from "autographs now in possession of your memorialist."[28]

While Lane's petition concluded that he trusted this explanation of the Kansas Memorial would be "satisfactory" to the Senate, he arranged another, more formal, means of validating its authenticity. Lane appeared before Supreme Court Justice John McLean on April 14 and swore under oath that "the twenty four half sheets of paper hereto annexed contain the original draft of the memorial from the members of the General Assembly of Kansas."[29]

With Lane's personal statement and affidavit, Harlan entered the Senate chamber ready to fight the issue one more time.[30] Harlan first set out to

27. *Appendix to the Congressional Globe,* 34th Cong., 1st sess., 382.
28. Ibid.
29. Ibid., 379.
30. For a short contemporary editorial on Harlan's efforts, see *Berkshire County Eagle,* April 13, 1856, Webb Scrapbook, 11:116.

defend Lane's character as a means of legitimizing the Kansas Memorial. He immediately emphasized Lane's connection to the Democratic Party, one "not by conversion, but by conception and birth." The Iowa senator questioned the lack of support the Kansan had received from Democrats in the initial debate over the Kansas Memorial, and, with a subtle biblical reference, stated that he "desire[d] to remind the Democracy of the country—so ably represented on this floor—who had conferred on him so many distinguished honors, that when he came to his own his own knew him not."[31] These words surely echoed in the ears of Lane, who had remained loyal to Democratic leadership and principles. He had wagered not only his personal career in Kansas, and within the Free State ranks, upon Northern Democratic support, but also the success of the Topeka Constitution. Now Lane found himself standing beside a Republican, upon whom his hopes and dreams rested.

Harlan continued his comments on the Democrats' abandonment of Lane by drawing up a remarkably accurate appraisal of the Kansan's feelings. "Had I been the bearer of a petition," Harlan stated, "had these grave charges been preferred against me, and a voucher demanded, and had no one responded, I would have concluded that my friends had forgotten me, or that they were willing to contribute to my ruin."[32] Harlan's finger-wagging at the Democratic leadership only incited further denunciation of the memorial. Douglas ridiculed both Harlan and Lane on the matter. Taking the floor, Douglas dismissed Lane's new petition as a petty attempt to defend a fraud. Lane's oath, the Illinois senator argued, was "drawn in language so equivocal and evasive, as to raise a doubt in regard to the fairness of the explanation." Further, Douglas stated that he would prove that the Kansas Memorial presented to the Senate was "not a true or even substantial copy of the one which he alleges was adopted in Kansas." His analysis focused on significant differences between the original memorial and the one included in the recent petition. Douglas particularly pounced on omissions. He explained that the "first three pages of the original are not to be found at all in the paper presented by the Senator from Michigan." These three pages included a paragraph that, Douglas announced, "declared their right to form a State constitution because the Nebraska bill was unconstitutional; because, being unconstitutional, it was a nullity;

31. *Appendix to the Congressional Globe,* 34th Cong., 1st sess., 381; John 1:11 of the King James Bible reads: "He came unto his own, and his own received him not."
32. *Appendix to the Congressional Globe,* 34th Cong., 1st sess., 382.

because there were no constituted authorities in the Territory; because Congress had no power over them; and hence they would not submit to the power of Congress. That is the ground on which this memorial adopted by the Kansas Legislature puts their case." Douglas then accused Lane of excising this and other portions of the document when he found that it would not be supported by "his friends."[33]

While Douglas's attack against the memorial and its messenger was enough to incense Lane, the commentary on party loyalty must have particularly enraged him. First, Douglas acknowledged some merit in emphasizing Lane's history as a Democrat, and that his vote for the Kansas-Nebraska Bill "ought to have its full weight in his favor, and may raise the presumption that he is an honest man, and incapable of perpetrating a fraud upon the Senate." But, he asked, "are these satisfactory proofs on the point in dispute?" Douglas pointed out that "Colonel Lane now is as essentially identified with the Black Republican party as Mr. Blair himself is, or as Mr. Donelson is with the Know Nothing Party," and asked whether "the mere fact that they once belonged to the Democratic party conclusive evidence that they could not have done anything wrong since their apostasy?" Lane witnessed his personal and professional mentor compare him to political traitors. Douglas continued:

I admit the virtue, so long as they are faithful to Democratic principles; but I deny that they have a right to claim, as a saving grace, sufficient to exculpate them for subsequent sins, that they were once Democrats and apostacized from the true faith. That, sir, is all I have to say of the Democracy of Colonel Lane, and all that class of modern politicians whose chief claim to popular favor consists in the fact that they were once Democrats, and have betrayed those who reposed confidence in them, and heaped honors on them.[34]

These comments by Stephen Douglas, more than any other single event, mark the end of Lane's career as a Democrat. Lane had supported the Kansas-Nebraska Bill despite reservations, and had defended popular sovereignty and Douglas before free-state Kansans. He had come to Washington fully expecting to find support from Douglas in making Kansas free. Instead, the Little Giant rejected the Kansas Memorial as a forgery, rejected the Topeka movement as illegal, and rejected Lane as an apostate.

33. Ibid., 383.
34. Ibid.

Douglas's identification of Lane as a Black Republican was either an exaggeration or, more likely, a mistake based on the inaccurate stereotyping of people and groups during the heated Kansas struggle. While proslavery forces had tagged the free-state settlers as abolitionists and Black Republicans, Lane's actual ties to the Republican Party at this point were circumstantial. Republican Party members were associated with the Free State Party in Kansas, but the two were not identical during this period. Regardless of the accuracy of Douglas's comments, the effect they had upon Lane were enormous. To Lane, he had not abandoned the party; the party had abandoned him.

While Douglas's rejection of Lane stands as the moment when Lane truly separated from the Democratic Party, it also marks the emergence of Lane's new friends. Subsequently, Republican senators such as Benjamin Wade of Ohio and Henry Wilson of Massachusetts defended the Kansan and the free-state cause. When the Senate finally voted on Lane's petition, after several hours of debate, every Republican senator stood behind the Kansas Memorial and James Lane.[35] The eleven Republican senators were not enough to save the petition. In fact, it is unknown whether Lane really believed that this second attempt to push the Kansas Memorial through the Senate stood a chance. The Senate debates of April 7, 9, and 10 had been unpromising for the petition, and the vote on the memorial on April 10 had been an embarrassing defeat. He certainly wished to defend his image and that of the free-state cause, and hoped that his affidavit and personal petition would provide a response to the overwhelming criticism leveled by both Northern and Southern Democrats on April 10. However, one cannot assume that Lane's last-ditch effort to save the memorial in the Senate was simply a matter of saving face. Unlike the Senate, the House of Representatives had approved the Kansas Memorial.[36] That important step meant not only that Kansas statehood under the free-state constitution was past one major hurdle but also that it served as a congressional vote of confidence for the petition that could potentially sway moderate senators.

The debate of April 14 did, however, unify Senate Republicans. The Kansas Memorial had not, as Lane hoped, drawn support from Northern Democrats on principle, or validated his assumption of their support for a free state. It had instead generated a clean division between the two

35. Ibid., 395.
36. Monaghan, *Civil War on the Western Border,* 48. Monaghan also gives an excellent account of the House of Representatives investigation of the Kansas conflict following the failure of the Kansas Memorial.

major parties. The lifelong Democrat learned very bluntly during the first half of April 1856 that the Democratic Party in Washington would not stand behind him.

Still, it was the personal nature of Douglas's criticism on the Senate floor that infuriated Lane most of all. In an April 18 letter to Douglas, Lane outlined his frustration with the Illinois senator's treatment of his character, at both a professional and personal level. He stated that "I came here your friend, confidently expecting to find you on the Kansas application where you stood in '44 on the Texas question, and in '50 on the California question, in favor of recognizing the people's Government, and extending over American citizens the protecting arm of the General Government," and that he hoped and expected Douglas to give an explanation for his actions on the Senate floor.[37] While the letter to Douglas was fairly short, Lane had taken a somewhat aggressive attitude in its wording. Lane's demand for an explanation from Douglas became public, as newspapers across the nation printed the letter. After its delivery to Douglas by intermediary C. R. Watson, rumors circulated that Lane intended to challenge the Illinoisan to a duel.[38]

Douglas carefully examined the contents and asked for some time in responding. Unsure of the tone of the letter, he met with a few colleagues, including Jesse Bright, Joseph Lane, James Orr, John Weller, and Robert Toombs to formulate a proper reply. These men cautioned him not to interpret the letter as hostile.[39] Douglas's formal response came in the form of a lengthy "note" to Watson describing his perception of the event. Douglas found Lane's letter "so equivocal in terms, and portions of it so irreconcilable with other portions, that it is impossible to determine, with any certainty, whether it is intended as a hostile message or a friendly note." He admitted that "the city is full of rumors that your friend, Col. Lane, intended to challenge me, and the letter-writers for those newspapers in the eastern cities most friendly to the revolutionary movements in Kansas; and most hostile to myself, not only announced the facts, some three or four days ago, but actually fixed the time when your friend intended to send the hostile message."[40]

37. *New York Daily Tribune,* April 26, 1856, in Webb Scrapbook, 11:169; *Herald of Freedom,* May 10, 1856.

38. *Herald of Freedom,* May 3, 1856.

39. Johannsen, *Stephen Douglas,* 501; Stephenson, *Political Career of Lane,* 66; for correspondence between Douglas and these five political figures on the Lane letter, see *New York Daily Tribune,* April 26, 1856, in Webb Scrapbook, 11:169.

40. Robert Johannsen, ed., *The Letters of Stephen Douglas,* 355.

As for the Kansas Memorial, Douglas reviewed the events in the Senate and defended his actions and findings. He explained that he had not questioned Lane's integrity on April 10, although Lane had accused him of such. It was not until the memorial had proven to be a fraud on April 14, Douglas explained, and when Senator Cass, the original presenter, had himself stepped away from it that he had joined the majority and voted to rescind it from consideration. He concluded by saying that "there are no facts within my knowledge which can 'remove all imputations upon the integrity of his action or motives in connexion [sic] with that memorial.'" With a final dismissal, Douglas explained that because of Lane's actions and accusations, "I can have no correspondence with Col. Lane, and [I] therefore address this note to you."[41]

Upon learning of Douglas's response from Watson, Lane took his case even further, publishing a "card." Lane copied his original letter to Douglas and then provided a scathing condemnation of the Little Giant for his actions and subsequent reply. "Mr. Douglas and myself had long been personal and political friends," Lane wrote. "If, because in conscience I had felt moved to advocate the cause of Kansas, with every civil right trodden under foot by foreign invaders," he further explained, "while he, with fatherly love, and perhaps equal conscience, was cherishing Kansas as she is—as a child of his own begetting—a doubt had arisen in my mind respecting our future relations, it was banished on my coming to Washington." Douglas had met Lane with great kindness upon Lane's arrival in Washington. "I became his invited guest, and communicated with him in honest friendship. He thus annihilated distance between us, and baptised [sic] me his friend and equal, beneath his own roof, and before his very household gods." But this friendship was torn apart, Lane declared, by Douglas's words in the Senate. "Senator Douglas cajoled me into an undeserved trust of his sincerity," he complained. The Illinois senator had "struck his blow through me . . . with a vulgar atrocity of manner which characterized the insincerity of his friendship." This sin was amplified when, Lane continued, Douglas refused to admit his fault.[42]

Making sure that the tone of this public "card" or letter was not so ambiguous this time, Lane leveled direct insults upon Douglas, describing him as "a heroic dog, grown insolent upon fat diet, with his head out of the kennel, he growls with swollen courage, with a constitutional privilege at

41. Ibid., 360.
42. *Herald of Freedom*, May 10, 1856; *Kansas Free State*, May 19, 1856.

his back, behind which to retreat."[43] Lane wished to generate public sympathy with repeated references to "public justice." He also likely wanted to draw another, more aggressive response from Douglas. If Lane intended to challenge Douglas to a duel, or to wrangle him into some sort of confrontation, it did not work. Beyond publishing his original response to Watson, Douglas let the matter sit.[44]

The spat between the two men did fire up a great deal of conversation across the nation. Lane's actions were mostly defended by free-staters in Kansas. James Redpath, journalist and later publisher of the *Crusader of Freedom*, sent Lane a supportive letter, proclaiming, "Hurrah for J. H. L.!! Hit him again!" As for the talk about the duel, Redpath announced, "D—n the Topeka Constitution!—if you had had to fight, we would have got up another, without the disqualifying 'Dueling clause' for your special benefit!"[45] George W. Brown, the outspoken editor of the *Herald of Freedom* in Lawrence, voiced his support for his fellow Kansan in the encounter. "Whatever may have been said heretofore of the Colonel in *other* matters," Brown wrote, "in *this* it is evident that he was 'A man more sinned against than sinning.'"[46]

Still, not everyone in the free-state ranks approved of Lane's behavior. The *Kansas Free State*, another Lawrence publication, criticized his aggressive nature: "We do not understand that the Colonel was sent to Washin[g]ton with revolver in hand to demand our admission into the Union, and we do not desire that he should imperil our cause, in trying to obtain revenge for a personal insult, whether merited or unmerited."[47] The *Springfield Daily Republican* bemoaned Lane's poor handling of the original draft of the Kansas Memorial, which "gave its enemies opportunity to attack it and misrepresent it, and cover up the real issue in dust about a merely incidental matter."[48]

Lane's attempt to gather up Democratic support in Washington and push the Topeka Constitution through the Senate failed miserably. His hopes—his expectations—of Kansas shortly becoming a free state and

43. Ibid.

44. According to John Speer, biographer and personal friend of Lane, Douglas was challenged to a duel, but declined "on the ground that Lane was not his peer as a Senator." Speer, *Life of Lane*, 44.

45. James Redpath to James H. Lane, April 29, 1856, in James H. Lane Papers, Spencer Library Collection, University of Kansas.

46. *Herald of Freedom*, May 10, 1856.

47. *Kansas Free State*, May 5, 1856.

48. *Springfield Daily Republican*, April 29, 1856, in Webb Scrapbook, 11:181–82.

himself finding a seat on the Senate floor had been smashed, not by vehemently proslavery senators like Butler and Benjamin whose opposition to the free-state cause could be expected, but by the original author of the Kansas-Nebraska Act. Yet, it was the political isolation Lane experienced on April 14 that was the most significant element of his trip to Washington. The dismissal of the Kansas Memorial and the Topeka Constitution by the Senate at this point was not an end to the free-state cause. Lane's chance to obtain a seat in the Senate would come again. But the relationship between James Lane and the Democratic Party had been broken forever. Throughout his adult life, Lane had been a devoted party man, whose Democratic allegiance and identity was vouched for by all who knew him. His emigration to Kansas and subsequent entrance into Free State Party ranks had puzzled many and been mistakenly identified as a party switch. During the free-state activities in Kansas leading up to the memorial's introduction, Lane had begun to question certain planks of the Democratic platform, and had already found opposition from President Pierce. The Democratic Party in Kansas, Lane believed, had been corrupted by extreme proslavery views. Yet, he had not given up on Douglas and other Northern Democrats. He still believed in the National Democratic Party as a whole. That all changed on April 14, 1856. When Stephen Douglas branded the free-state Kansas legislature as revolutionary, the Kansas Memorial as a forgery, and James Lane as a political traitor, all of Lane's perceptions and relations with his beloved party shattered.

Surprisingly, few historians of territorial Kansas have analyzed the exciting two weeks in April 1856, or the effect of the Memorial's failure on Lane. Robert Collins spends a few pages talking about the failed petition in his recent work *Jim Lane: Scoundrel, Statesman, Kansan,* but mostly discusses how it was interpreted by newspaper editors and later historians. He does suggest that "this incident may have been a turning point in Lane's political career," and notes, "Sometime in April 1856, Lane crossed his own personal Rubicon; he changed political parties."[49] But Collins offers no further analysis of how the event affected Lane or his views toward the Democratic Party. Most other historians give the episode even less coverage, portraying it as a side note, or simply another occurrence in the long line of political and physical battles between proslavery and antislavery forces in Kansas. Jay Monaghan's 1955 publication *Civil War on the Western Border, 1854–1865* devotes only about a page's worth of descrip-

49. Collins, *Jim Lane,* 92.

tion to the Senate's consideration of the Kansas Memorial and the following war of words between Douglas and Lane. Nothing in Monaghan's book suggests that the event affected any political party alliance among Lane or other Kansans, nor does the author explain why Lane took special offense to Douglas's criticism.[50] Kenneth Davis's *Kansas: A History* refers to the Topeka Constitution, but gives no description of the Kansas Memorial or Lane's trip to Washington.

Nicole Etcheson, in her solid study of the territorial struggle, *Bleeding Kansas: Contested Liberty in the Civil War Era,* spends less than a full page on the Kansas Memorial, and describes Lane's actions as more show than substance—stating that Lane's affidavit before Justice McLean in defense of the memorial was part of "his taste for the dramatic."[51] This description illustrates one of the most persistent problems in the historiography of James Lane: an overemphasis on his personality and a lack of attention to the context of his actions. Lane's controversial behavior must not be ignored, but it cannot be a template for which to interpret all of his actions—particularly in regards to an event as significant as the failure of the Kansas Memorial. When Douglas first addressed the Kansas Memorial, he noted that it appeared suspicious unless "there be good evidence that it is genuine."[52] The personal oath Lane took before Justice McLean was not a matter of show, but a fervent attempt to provide evidence that the original memorial was genuine. His sworn affidavit and petition were fairly conservative in their language. They were designed to provide a carefully constructed explanation to the questions and problems brought up in the Senate. Etcheson's description of Lane and the event is in line with most modern perceptions of Lane. His powerful and controversial personality has in many ways drawn attention away from the influence of other figures and events of his time.

Donald Gilmore's *Civil War on the Missouri-Kansas Border* takes an even more critical approach to Lane and the memorial. After incorrectly listing the date of the lengthy April 14 Senate debate, Gilmore quotes three lines from Douglas's criticism of the petition, and concludes: "All of which was true, and Lane ignominiously withdrew the document."[53] The author's

50. Monaghan, *Civil War on the Western Border,* 47–48.
51. Etcheson, *Bleeding Kansas,* 99.
52. *Congressional Globe,* 34th Cong., 1st sess., 827.
53. Gilmore states: "Later, on April 17, 1856, when Lane presented the memorial of the Topeka legislature to Congress requesting that the state of Kansas be admitted to the Union, Senator Douglas responded." Gilmore, *Civil War on the Missouri-Kansas Border,* 66.

simplistic summary of the Kansas Memorial may be attributed to his use of only one source for the Kansas petition episode and a personal dislike of Lane.[54] Gilmore's work is a self-styled revision of the Kansas-Missouri struggle in defense of Missouri guerrillas. While proclaiming to offer a new look at the conflict, in hopes of balancing the public's perception of Kansas "Jayhawkers" and Missouri "Bushwackers," Gilmore persistently portrays notable Kansas figures—and particularly Lane—as tyrants and criminals. Little effort is taken to analyze Lane's actions in Kansas, and thus the author sees the struggle for the Kansas Memorial in the Senate as an untruthful effort to obtain statehood.

The full effect of Douglas's criticism on Lane has not been recognized even by Lane's early biographers. The first book-length biography of Lane, entitled *Life of Gen. James H. Lane*, by his friend and colleague John Speer only briefly discusses the proposed duel between Douglas and Lane, and states that Lane made great use of Douglas's insult as a campaign tool for his own Senate election.[55] There is no indication of any effect upon Lane's political or party position. William E. Connelley fails to note Lane's efforts to push the Kansas Memorial through the Senate in his *James Henry Lane: The "Grim Chieftain" of Kansas*. Lane's trip east in the spring of 1856 is portrayed simply as a "tour of principal cities of the Free States in the interest of the Free-State settlers."[56]

Wendell H. Stephenson, author of the most important and comprehensive book on Lane, does devote a chapter to the Kansas Memorial. The author's description of the Senate's rejection of the petition and Lane's standoff with Douglas is thorough, but contains virtually no analysis. Stephenson does argue that the failure of the Kansas Memorial largely rested upon Lane's shoulders. The presentation of a petition so crudely drawn up undermined an already weak free-state movement. Still, Stephenson fails to appreciate the significance for Lane of Douglas's rejection of the Kansas Memorial, namely how it affected Lane's political party standing or his interpretation of the Kansas struggle.[57]

---

54. Gilmore's sole source is Spring, *Kansas: The Prelude to the War for the Union*.

55. Speer, *Life of Lane*, 44.

56. Connelley, *Lane: The "Grim Chieftain*," 70.

57. Stephenson, *Political Career of Lane*, 60–67. Historian James Rawley also blames Lane, at least partially, for the memorial's failure, writing that Lane "with his crude methods had exposed the Topeka movement to ridicule, and had turned his cause into a personal controversy." Rawley, *Race and Politics*, 125.

The Senate's debate and dismissal of the Kansas Memorial serves as the single most important event in James Lane's political transition. It was then, in Washington, D.C., in April 1856, that the real switch in party allegiance took place. And Lane's exit from the Democratic ranks had not been opportunistic, nor was it quiet or subversive. Lane did not abandon the Democratic Party. In his eyes, Democrats had abandoned Kansas, the principles they had championed, and, perhaps most painful of all, him. The party leadership's betrayal would not go unanswered. From Washington, Lane set out on an explosive speaking tour across the North. His blood was up, his old friends were the target, and the Republican Party was the new force for Kansas.

4

Lane's Army of the North, 1856

"I went to Kansas to enjoy the privileges I supposed were guaranteed by the Kansas-Nebraska bill, and for which I voted . . . but I was denied my rights."

The rejection of the Kansas Memorial severed James Lane's bond with the Democratic leadership. He continued to consider himself a *true* Democrat, believing that men like Stephen Douglas had forsaken the party's principles. Although he did not join the Republican ranks at this time, Lane began to promote Republican candidates. During the late spring and summer of 1856, he embarked on a Northern speaking tour, led hundreds of free-state migrants toward Kansas, and by August battled proslavery forces in the territory. It was during this period, the summer of 1856, that Lane's reputation as a dangerous radical crystallized. No longer calling for moderation, Lane had come to see the struggle for Kansas statehood as a battle for democratic principles against political injustice and armed oppression.

Lane left Washington in late April 1856 for a highly publicized tour across the Old Northwest, denouncing proslavery actions in Kansas and condemning Democratic leaders.[1] In Franklin, Indiana, he was reported to

1. Stephenson, *Political Career of Lane*, 68.

be "in fine health and spirits, and entered into the subject of the rights and wrongs of Kansas with a zeal and energy truly commendable." He spoke of the promises the Kansas-Nebraska Act had given the people in the territory, and how they had been denied the right to "form their own institutions in their own way." The reporter who covered the speech for the *New York Tribune* concluded that "If Lane could traverse the whole State and have access to the people, I give it as my candid opinion that the State would be carried, as he carried this county for Lieut. Governor, by the largest majority ever given for Free Kansas and the Republican candidate for President."[2]

During his campaign across the North, events in Washington and in Kansas shocked Northern audiences and gave Lane's speeches valuable ammunition. In late April and throughout May, Sheriff Samuel Jones attempted to arrest Samuel N. Wood, a man involved in the rescue of Jacob Branson months before. Lawrence residents resisted Jones's efforts to capture Wood. After the sheriff detained six men for failing to aid in the arrest, an unknown assailant fired a pistol at the sheriff while he camped in Lawrence.[3] Jones received a wound in the back, but survived the assault. Nonetheless, proslavery newspapers in Kansas published heated reports of the attack, claiming that the sheriff had been killed. Even after the newspapers admitted that Jones was still alive, and had quickly recovered, the event proved to proslavery minds that free-state Kansans opposed territorial law with violence. Lawrence leaders denounced the attack, but the damage had been done.

On May 5, Judge Samuel Lecompte ordered a grand jury to indict free-state leaders on charges of treason. Lawrence's free-state newspapers and its Free State Hotel were also condemned as nuisances to peace in Kansas.[4] Learning of the indictments, some free-state leaders fled. Former governor Andrew Reeder gruffly shrugged off one attempt by an official to arrest him and escaped to Kansas City. From there, Reeder waited for an opportunity to travel further east and draw support for the Kansas cause. He shaved his beard and disguised himself as a common laborer to board a steamboat. His harrowing escape finally succeeded as he crossed into Illinois. Almost immediately, Reeder began a speaking tour, like Lane's,

2. *New York Daily Tribune,* May 5, 856, in Webb Scrapbook, 12:39–40.
3. James C. Malin, "Judge Lecompte and the 'Sack of Lawrence,' May 21, 1856," pt. 1, 472; Etcheson, *Bleeding Kansas,* 101.
4. Etcheson, *Bleeding Kansas,* 102.

across the Midwest.[5] Charles Robinson also headed east, but was detained in Lexington, Missouri, from where he was sent to Lecompton for confinement. Lane, still touring the Northern states, was also indicted.

With free-state leaders either imprisoned or in exile, proslavery officials turned to deal with Lawrence. On May 21, Sheriff Jones, Senator David Atchison, and local proslavery militia leader Colonel H. T. Titus led a force of seven hundred men (again, mostly Missourians) against the town. Residents did not resist, and stood back as the proslavery army, carrying banners reading "Southern Rights" and "The Supremacy of the White Race," marched into town.[6] The proprietor of the Free State Hotel was ordered to remove his belongings in preparation for the building's destruction. Proslavery forces believed the hotel was a fortress, with thick walls and firing ports made ready by pushing out loose stones from the wall.[7] Once the building had been abandoned, proslavery militia cannons fired artillery rounds into it. When that failed to destroy the structure, gunpowder was placed inside and lit. The explosion shattered windows, but, incredibly, the building remained standing. Finally the hotel was set on fire. Widespread looting ensued. Houses were raided and proslavery men unceremoniously dumped the *Herald of Freedom*'s press into the river.[8]

Reports of the "Sack of Lawrence" inflamed Northern audiences. Senator Atchison received blame as the chief instigator.[9] In fact, the Missouri senator may have attempted to prevent proslavery forces from causing damage beyond the legal orders.[10] Still, the image of Missourians led by a notable proslavery figure raiding a free-state community played well for Lane and others interested in recruiting support for the free-state cause.

This assault was not the only or the most sensationalized news item of the month. In Washington, the political debate over Kansas turned bloody. On May 19, Massachusetts Senator Charles Sumner began a two-day

5. For an account of Reeder's escape, see "Governor Reeder's Escape from Kansas," 205–23.
6. Shalor Winchell Eldridge, *Recollections of Early Days in Kansas*, 52.
7. Historian James C. Malin quotes two free-state accounts describing the hotel as a fortress. He explains that "these two independent statements by Free-State writers do not prove that the hotel was a fortress; but they do, in an absolute sense, prove that that assertion was not a Proslavery lie." Malin, "Judge Lecompte and the 'Sack of Lawrence,'" pt. 1, 479.
8. W. C. Simons, "Lawrence Newspapers in Territorial Days," 328; Rawley, *Race and Politics*, 131–32; Eldridge, *Recollections*, 53–54.
9. Monaghan, *Civil War on the Western Border*, 58.
10. Nevins, *Ordeal of the Union*, vol. 2, 436; William E. Gienapp, *The Origins of the Republican Party, 1852–1856*, 298.

speech, blasting proslavery efforts to create a slave state from Kansas Territory. His speech, entitled "The Crime Against Kansas," in particular condemned two notable Senate Democrats, South Carolina Senator Andrew Butler and Illinoisan Stephen Douglas. "As the Senator from South Carolina is the Don Quixote," Sumner declared, "so the Senator from Illinois is the squire of Slavery, its very Sancho Panza, ready to do its humiliating offices."[11] The speech drew criticism from many Democrats. But Sumner's treatment of Butler and his home state of South Carolina especially incensed Congressman Preston Brooks. Two days after Sumner's speech, Brooks entered the Senate chamber, strode up to the Massachusetts senator's desk, and began striking the surprised man on the head and shoulders with a gold-headed cane. Sumner vainly attempted to defend himself from the blows, eventually pulled his desk from its floor anchors, and collapsed with serious injuries.

The divided public response to Sumner's "caning" illustrated the radical nature of sectionalism in 1856. Northern newspapers expressed shock at the event, and even Northerners who had opposed Sumner's radical antislavery positions sympathized with him. "Has it come to this that we must speak with bated breath in the presence of our Southern masters," asked New York editorialist William Cullen Bryant; "that even their follies are too sacred a subject for ridicule; that we must not deny the consistency of their principles or the accuracy of their statements?"[12] The South, on the other hand, celebrated Brooks's self-styled justice. When the South Carolina congressman resigned his seat after being censured by the House, voters in his home state reelected him. Brooks even received new canes in the mail from admirers.[13]

As Lane and Reeder separately traveled across the Midwest speaking to crowds about the Kansas situation, reports of these events circulated through local newspapers and played a significant part in an American political realignment. Republican Party historian William Gienapp argued that the attacks against Charles Sumner and on Lawrence "galvanized northern public opinion around sectional issues and combined to give the faltering Republican cause a desperately needed boost."[14] Accounts of

11. Charles Sumner, "The Crime Against Kansas," published in *Charles Sumner: His Complete Works. With introduction by Hon. George Frisbie Hoar*, vol. 5, 149.

12. William Cullen Bryant, "The Republican Convention, September 29, 1855," quoted in William Cullen Bryant, *Power for Sanity: Selected Editorials of William Cullen Bryant, 1829–1861*, 290.

13. McPherson, *Battle Cry of Freedom*, 150–51.

14. Gienapp, *Origins of the Republican Party*, 296.

problems in Kansas had filtered east in Northern newspapers during the previous months without much of an uproar. Gienapp explains that Northerners reacted so strongly to the Kansas issue now because of the timing of the attack on Sumner. It had been difficult for many in the North, particularly conservatives, to identify with the free-state effort due to contradictory reporting and its abolitionist label. But an assault upon a U.S. senator, for making a speech in the Capitol, shook many Northerners and was seen as an attack upon the Constitution itself.[15] The invasion of Lawrence did not seem so removed or unclear. Many conservative Northerners, men and women with the same political background and principles as James Lane, reexamined the growing sectional conflict and sympathized with the Republican Party.[16] Following one of Reeder's speeches against "Border Ruffians," one Ohio Democrat wrote that he felt his "blood leap faster through my veins and an irrepressible indignation at their course filled my heart." With a firm resolve, he declared "that I have always been a democrat and had expected to act with the democracy throughout my life but the new position assumed by the party has forced me to act with the Republicans which I will do with my whole heart."[17] Like Lane, the political loyalties of many Northern Democrats changed. The sectional conflict increasingly broke traditional party affiliations.

Across the North public support for the Kansas free-state cause grew. Lane spoke at the Ohio Republican Convention in Columbus and at a large gathering in Cincinnati. In Cincinnati, he blamed the Pierce administration for the violence in Kansas. Justifying his criticism, Lane explained that he "had a right to talk as he pleased, having made more than one hundred speeches advocating [Pierce's] election, and having also, as one of the electors of Indiana, cast the vote of that state for him."[18] Lane *had* supported Pierce and the Democratic Party in Kansas. His new virulence against the administration was not mere convenience, but a response to Pierce's disregard for free-soil interests in the West, the free-state movement, and himself.

During his Cincinnati speech, Lane emphasized conservative elements of the free-state cause. He explained to the Midwest crowd that a majority of free-state settlers in Kansas were not New England abolitionists. Most were hard-working westerners—like those in his audience—interested in a good life and a peaceful country, and opposed to interference and

15. Ibid., 301.
16. Gara, *Presidency of Franklin Pierce*, 122.
17. Milton M. Powers to "Dear Friend," Cyrus K. Holliday, June 7, 1856, Cyrus Kurtz Holliday Collection, Kansas State Historical Society, Topeka.
18. *Kansas Tribune*, June 16, 1856.

oppression by slaveholding Southerners. With the sacking of Lawrence and caning of Sumner on their minds, Lane found a receptive audience. The destruction of old party lines was demonstrated in dramatic fashion when Caleb Smith, a former Whig congressman and senator from Indiana, took the stage after Lane, and echoed the exiled Democrat's sentiments. A newspaper recounted:

> [Smith] had been a Whig. Lane had been a Democrat, And they had warred over the old issues before the people of Indiana. But that was past. The old issues were buried. A new question of startling, awful importance had loomed up before the nation. On it he and Lane agreed, *and they shook hands on the platform* amid tremendous applause. Henceforth they were brethren in arms, to resist those who marched under the black banner of slavery and shed blood to extend that curse.[19]

New bonds such as this took place all across the North during this time, giving rise to the Republican Party.

Lane's Chicago speech of May 31 may have been the greatest of his tour. No transcription has been found, but numerous journals reported the event. The *Chicago Daily Tribune*'s announced "ILLINOIS ALIVE AND AWAKE!!" and "10,000 Freemen in Council!" Lane's words in Chicago echoed those from Cincinnati. He explained that Kansas settlers were "really more than nine-tenths from the northwestern States," and that those "who styled them Abolitionists lied willfully and basely." Describing the free-state settlers as the true victims of oppression, Lane held up a copy of the territorial statutes passed by the proslavery legislature and explained that portions of the U.S. Constitution and the Kansas-Nebraska Act protecting free-state rights had been repealed.[20] He further explained in detail the invasion of Kansas Territory by Missourians, and lamented the free-state men who had been killed over the previous year. But one of his more memorable points came as he denounced attempts by proslavery propagandists to label free-state settlers in Kansas "nigger worshippers." The *Chicago Daily Tribune* reported that Lane wanted to show "that these Pro-Slavery men were the most abject of nigger worshippers." Lane cited standing Kansas law which held, he said, "if a person kidnapped a white child, the utmost penalty was six months in jail—if he stole a nigger baby, the penalty was Death. Who worshipped niggers, and slave nigger babies

19. Ibid.
20. *Chicago Daily Tribune,* June 2, 1856, in Webb Scrapbook, 13:7–8.

at that?" This was a powerful message that touched upon the white interests of his midwestern audience. He emphasized his point, booming, "To kidnap a white child into slavery—six months in jail,—kidnap a nigger into Freedom—Death!"[21]

Lane explained how far proslavery efforts in Kansas had turned against Northern and Democratic interests. He read a statute from the territorial laws that made even speaking or writing against slavery illegal, punishable by two years of hard labor. Lane argued that according to Kansas law the Democratic platforms across the North would be "incendiary documents," and those who circulated them would find themselves part of a chain gang. Further, with his knack for touching an audience's deepest sentiments, Lane questioned whether the proslavery law would prevent circulation of the *Holy Bible* in Kansas. Lane reminded listeners that he was wanted for treason by the territorial government. "But were the rope about his neck," the *Chicago Daily Tribune* recorded, "he would say that as to the Kansas code, it should not be enforced—never—never."[22]

At one point in the Chicago speech, Lane spoke of suffrage for foreign immigrants. While contemplating his vote for the Kansas-Nebraska Bill in 1854, Lane had published a letter outlining his concern for the protection of immigrant voting rights.[23] Now, two years later, Lane announced that the proslavery Kansas officials had limited immigrant suffrage, in violation of the Kansas-Nebraska Act. His fears had been realized. Foreign immigrants, who were primarily antislavery, were denied voting rights until they had lived in the state for five years. At the same time, Lane announced, proslavery officials recognized Indian citizenship and voting rights—as long as these Indians adopted a single habit of white men: drinking whiskey. While this part of the speech worked upon the audience's prejudices, it also illustrated the clear link between Lane's free-state activity in Kansas and his stated principles while in Indiana.

Another, seemingly small, element of Lane's Chicago speech takes on additional significance when considering his 1854 letter to the *Weekly Indiana State Sentinel*. Lane had closed the letter with the comment, "The question then will resolve itself into this, how far shall we go to humor our Southern friends, and what effect will the repeal of the Missouri compromise restriction have upon the slavery agitation?"[24] On May 31, 1856, Lane

21. Ibid., 8.
22. Ibid.
23. See discussion of letter in chapter 1; *Weekly Indiana State Sentinel*, March 30, 1854.
24. *Weekly Indiana State Sentinel*, March 30, 1854.

announced that Kansas must be brought into the Union as a free state, for the sake of the territory's majority population and for the country's struggle against the slave power. The *Chicago Daily Tribune* reported that Lane "argued elaborately and conclusively, the right of Kansas to come into the Union as a free State now" and that it "was the only way to stop Slavery agitation." If Kansas became a slave state, "he warned the fragment of the Democratic party which clung to Pierce" would firmly establish itself in American society.[25]

Throughout his speech, Lane made a powerful case for the free-state cause in Kansas. He portrayed free-state settlers as complete victims. His speech was not meant to be an objective history or analysis of the Kansas conflict, but to generate support. And this he did very well. Other reports from Kansas Territory helped his cause. A letter to the *Chicago Daily Tribune*, published only days after Lane's speech, reinforced his leading role in the free-state effort by stating, "Every Northern man in Kansas is impatient for his arrival. He is the only man now at liberty who can command the confidence and reinstate the spirit of our harassed and worn-out squatters." The correspondent further called out for public support: "Send on men, armed and equipped for the fields of peace and war, too, as speedily as possible."[26] Some of the accounts coming from Kansas were absolute fabrications or extreme exaggerations, which, according to William Gienapp, were part of an effort among Republicans to score a great propaganda victory.[27] Lane himself had not formally stepped into the Republican fold. His efforts were designed to help his fellow free-state settlers, regardless of national political party interests. As such, his work in Chicago certainly helped the free-state cause. Chicagoans donated fifteen thousand dollars, as well as rifles, pistols, and ammunition. Further, about five hundred Illinoisans volunteered to settle in Kansas, all for the sake of a free state.[28]

Lane followed up his Chicago performance with other speaking engagements, including an appearance in Cleveland that was also a great success. Lane's words in Cleveland echoed those in Chicago and other places. But the account of his speech offers important insights into Lane's political views during this dramatic period. First, he clearly described the collapse of the Democratic Party and his reason for stepping away from it. The *Cleveland Evening Herald* reported that Lane "had been reared in the

25. *Chicago Daily Tribune,* June 2, 1856, in Webb Scrapbook, 13:8.
26. *Chicago Daily Tribune,* June 9, 1856, in Webb Scrapbook, 13:69.
27. Gienapp, *Origins of the Republican Party,* 298.
28. Stephenson, *Political Career of Lane,* 70.

belief that two things were essential—to attend the 'stated preaching' of the Gospel, and to vote an unscratched Democratic Ticket." Lane declared that "he was yet a Democrat, but could not longer sanction the action of the party that now acted under its name,—its leaders and supporters were traitors, and not Democrats."[29] He did not deny his support of popular sovereignty. "I went to Kansas to enjoy the privile[g]es I supposed were guaranteed by the Kansas-Nebraska bill, and for which I voted—great God! forgive me for that political sin!!" he explained, "but I was denied my rights."[30] Though Lane has been called a man lacking principles, as he turned against the Democratic Party and its policies he did not deny his own role in its rise to power.

Lane's repeated reference to his Democratic roots did serve a tactical purpose. By linking himself to the administration, the Kansas-Nebraska Act, and the Democratic Party, his criticism was more credible. He had not been a political opponent, but a friend of the party he now blamed for the present problems in Kansas. The failure of popular sovereignty, and, even more important in Lane's mind, the abandonment of the free-state cause by Pierce and Douglas, had led to his political transition. Reports of his speeches in Cleveland and elsewhere generate the image of an evangelical revival, where Lane's political conversion seems to mimic a religious one. Lane seemed a sinner admitting his faults and preaching his path to redemption. But this conversion imagery should not be taken too far. After all, Lane did not denounce traditional Democratic Party principles—he claimed to be a *true* Democrat still—but blasted the current Democratic leadership. To him, *they* were the sinners, *they* had strayed and consequently pulled Kansas Territory—and the nation—down with them. Lane told the crowd that he had been taught to look for his democratic principles in the letters of Washington, Jefferson, and Madison, but, he continued, "were Jefferson now in Kansas, the Administration party would hang him."[31]

"The People of Kansas sent me to Congress, but the Administration won't let me in—it won't let free Kansas in," Lane said in Cleveland. "If they want freedom in Kansas, why don't they let us in?" His answer raised an increasing suspicion among Northerners, and what would become a theme in later Republican speeches: that there was a slaveholding conspiracy within the Congress. Lane's experience in Kansas and with the

29. *Cleveland Evening Herald,* June 23, 1856, in Webb Scrapbook, 13:172.
30. Ibid.
31. Ibid.

Kansas Memorial led him to announce, "The fact is, they are pledged to slavery."[32]

As before, Lane's opposition to slavery had little moral or humanitarian basis. Instead, he championed the interests of free white Northerners. The *Cleveland Evening Herald* reported that Lane "wanted to have free labor respected, and it could not be if slavery were permitted. The laboring white man could not live in a Slave State, where the grades may be defined thus— 1st, the slaveholder; 2d, the slave; 3d, the free negro; 4th, last and lowest, the laboring white man." This was a real concern among Northerners who cared little for the plight of blacks. They believed that the institution of slavery threatened their own interests. Lane elaborated with a personal anecdote. He told the story of traveling down the Ohio River on a flatboat with a young carpenter. In Kentucky, the two men stopped at a plantation and asked the owner if he was interested in hiring the carpenter. "My dear fellow," said the planter, "I would like to hire you, but the fact is I bought two carpenters yesterday."[33] Lane looked over his Cleveland audience and asked them to imagine a group of Irishmen applying for work with a railroad only to be told, "We bought two or three hundred yesterday." Lane did not preach abolitionism, but the protection of free white labor. The Pierce administration, he argued, threatened that interest.[34]

Though Lane generally appeared before friendly audiences, in Cleveland he had at least one critic. During his speech an unidentified man yelled out that Lane's account of voting restrictions in Kansas Territory was a lie. Without missing a beat, the proud Kansan "drew himself up in manly atitude [sic] and with the true feeling of Western chivalry" called on the man to step forward. The man did not appear. Lane announced that "the man that says that what I say is not true, is a liar! I have a copy of the laws at the Hotel—meet me at 9 o'clock to-morrow, and I will prove that what I say is true."[35] The crowd excitedly looked for the heckler, as Lane

32. Ibid.

33. Historian Leverett Spring wrote that Lane repeated this story in Nebraska City, Nebraska, a few weeks after his appearance in Cleveland. According to Spring, a number of Missourians were in the crowd, "not, however, in the interest of peace and goodwill." Lane used his masterful oratorical skills to draw the crowd to his side. Telling the account of the planter denying the carpenter work, Lane cried out, "Great God! If such men are buying carpenters, machinists, engineers, how soon will they sell you and me in their marts of human merchandise!" Spring, "The Career of a Kansas Politician," 90.

34. *Cleveland Evening Herald,* June 23, 1856, in Webb Scrapbook, 13:172.

35. Ibid.

continued to challenge his manhood, but with no success. The incident illustrated Lane's mastery of western stump-speaking as well as his understanding of western perceptions of honor.

Lane concluded his speech in Cleveland with an official endorsement of the Republican ticket. He based his hopes for success in Kansas upon the election of John C. Fremont in the 1856 presidential election. Republican support of a free Kansas just when Democratic leaders had turned against it made a substantial impression on Lane. And the Republican platform that year echoed many free-state complaints, including condemnation of slaveholding aggression and a demand for the admission of Kansas under the free-state constitution.[36] Lane's support for Fremont in the summer of 1856 served as an important step in his political transition. He had not yet officially become a Republican—the party would not organize in Kansas until 1859.[37] But he had found this political vehicle vital to the success of the free-state cause. His entry into the Republican fold had begun.

As Lane wrapped up his Northern speaking tour, supporters made plans for a safe migration route into Kansas. Residents of Indiana, Illinois, and Iowa showed great interest in aiding, and settling in, the territory, inspired by Lane's speeches and by published letters from Kansans describing proslavery depredations. Vigilant proslavery men often stopped Northern migrants passing through Missouri or along traditional waterways into Kansas. In some instances, emigrants from the North were forcibly blocked and sent back east. So, on July 4, 1856, the Iowa State Central Committee announced the creation of an overland route through Iowa to Kansas. News of what came to be called the "Lane Trail" then spread from Chicago across the North.[38]

While Lane drew support and settlers from the Midwest, a new organization to aid the free-state cause met in Buffalo, New York.[39] This National Kansas Committee combined numerous local organizations into a single movement, helped raise two hundred thousand dollars, and established

36. Republican Platform of 1856 in *National Party Platforms*, vol. I, 1840–1956, compiled by Donald Bruce Johnson (Chicago: University of Illinois Press, 1978), 27–28.
37. The Republican convention in Osawatomie on May 18, 1859, is recognized as the official organization of the party in the territory; Daniel Wilder, *Annals of Kansas*, 201–4.
38. *Quincy* [Ill.] *Daily Republican*, June 13, 1856, in Webb Scrapbook, 13:105, and *Springfield* [Mass.] *Republican*, June 13, 1856, in Webb Scrapbook, 13:105–6. Peter Page to Thaddeus Hyatt, July 6, 1856, Thaddeus Hyatt Collection, Kansas State Historical Society, Topeka; Etcheson, *Bleeding Kansas*, 118–19. A copy of the announcement can be found in William Elsey Connelley, "The Lane Trail," 268–69.
39. Stephenson, *Political Career of Lane*, 73.

Chicago as its staging area for emigration to Kansas.[40] Supporters in Massachusetts did not join the national organization, but relied upon their own existing association.[41] Overall, the large-scale efforts by communities and organizations across the North helped revitalize the free-state cause in Kansas.

The first large body of Northern migrants, numbering around four hundred, did not arrive in Kansas until August.[42] Though the settlers came from across the Northern states, and had joined the cause through various organizations, Lane's high profile and commanding role for a portion of the journey led to the group being dubbed "Lane's Army of the North."[43] While in Iowa, Lane continued to speak out for the Kansas cause. He later wrote that while "passing through Iowa I addressed the citizens upon the subject of politics at every prominent point—often speaking three, and sometimes four times a day—making during the march seventy-two speeches."[44]

Shortly before the group reached the territory, doubts about Lane's leadership prompted officials of the National Kansas Committee to send investigators to Kansas to report the state of affairs.[45] The investigators described the expedition as in poor condition, lacking supplies and money. Further, they believed that Lane's presence potentially endangered the group by placing it in "a false position before the North, where men were not prepared for armed and organized emigrations, and gave to its enemies a pretext for calling it a military or filibustering expedition."[46] Many in Kansas shared this fear when reports circulated that federal troops waited to intercept the group at the border. Proslavery newspapers carried reports of Lane's actions in the North and warned of a large army coming through Iowa to help defy territorial law.[47]

40. *Albany Evening Journal*, July 22, 1856, in Webb Scrapbook, 15:72; Monaghan, *Civil War on the Western Border*, 71.

41. Stephenson, *Political Career of Lane*, 73.

42. The number varies according to different reports. William Connelley states that as many as 600 settlers were in the group. Wendell Stephenson gives a more conservative count of between 300 and 400. Various newspaper reports and personal accounts during the summer of 1856 list the number of settlers between 250 and 400. See Stephenson, *Political Career of General James H. Lane*, 74.

43. W. H. Isely, "The Sharps Rifle Episode in Kansas History," 561.

44. Lane to the editors of the *Cincinnati Gazette*, January 10, 1857, quoted in the *Indianapolis Daily Journal*, February 10, 1857, and quoted in Stephenson, *Political Career of Lane*, 74.

45. Monaghan, *Civil War on the Western Border*, 71.

46. Unidentified clipping in Webb Scrapbook, 16:3.

47. For instance, see July 5, 1856, and July 26, 1856, editions of *Kansas Weekly Herald*.

Overall, tension mounted within Kansas during the summer of 1856. Lane's friend Samuel Walker carried a letter from concerned Kansans asking Lane to leave the group so as to avoid confrontation with the U.S. Army. Finding Lane and the expedition at Civil Bend, on the opposite side of the Missouri River, Walker delivered the note and later remembered the response. With tears streaming down his face, Lane revealed a fatalistic attitude. "Walker," he said, "if you say the people of Kansas don't want me, it's all right; and I'll blow my brains out. I can never go back to the states and look the people in the face and tell them that as soon as I had got these Kansas friends of mine fairly into danger I had to abandon them." Walker replied that "the people of Kansas had rather have you than all the party at Nebraska City," and arranged for a group of fifteen men to secretly escort him back into Kansas.[48] Lane then slipped into Kansas under the alias "Joe Cook" and was back in Lawrence on August 7.[49]

In Lawrence, Lane found the free-state cause in terrible shape. The town still showed damage from the proslavery raid in May. On July 4, free-state representatives had met in Topeka to conduct legislative matters, but were dispersed by federal troops under Colonel Edwin V. Sumner. While U.S. forces had regularly observed actions in Kansas, the growing crisis during the summer of 1856 led to the army's more active role. Sumner, hesitant to get involved in local affairs, nonetheless was ordered to shut down the illegal free-state legislature. As the body opened its session, the reluctant colonel strode to the front and announced that "[u]nder the authority of the President's proclamation I am here to disperse this Legislature and therefore inform you that you cannot meet." When one free-state man asked whether "the Legislature is dispersed at the point of the bayonet," the officer replied, "I shall use the whole force under my command to carry out my orders."[50] The group disbanded. Lane also found that territorial officials had imprisoned numerous free-state leaders, including free-state governor Charles Robinson, and *Herald of Freedom* editor George W. Brown, in Lecompton on charges of treason. Finally, proslavery strongholds had been erected around Lawrence, intimidating the town's residents.

48. Quoted in Charles S. Gleed, "Samuel Walker," 267; Monaghan, *Civil War on the Western Border*, 73; and Stephenson, *Political Career of Lane*, 74–75.

49. Connelley, *Lane: The "Grim Chieftain,"* 84; a contemporary account of Lane's undercover arrival in Kansas can be found in a letter from A. D. Searl to Mr. [Thaddeus] Hyatt, August 21, 1856, Thaddeus Hyatt Collection, Kansas State Historical Society, Topeka.

50. An account of the incident was recorded in the Free State legislative minutes, published in "The Topeka Movement," 235.

Peaceful resistance seemed impossible, and already groups of militant free-state men attacked and skirmished with proslavery rivals. John Brown was among the most notable of these militants. A fanatical abolitionist, Brown had cried out for action during the Wakarusa War. Following the sack of Lawrence, he carried out his own style of vengeance, executing five proslavery settlers on the night of May 24.[51] The proslavery response was fierce, and armed men set out on the hunt for Brown. H. C. Pate, leading a group of proslavery militia men, captured two of Brown's sons and destroyed some of the family's property.[52] Brown and a group of free-state men caught up with Pate and his men near Black Jack, south of Lawrence. The proslavery force, surprised in camp, held off the attack for nearly three hours. Finally, believing they were surrounded, Pate and his men surrendered, ending the Battle of Black Jack, the first military-style engagement of "Bleeding Kansas."[53]

Lane arrived in Lawrence after open hostilities had erupted. Without any hesitation, he joined the fight. His first interest was the liberation of free-state prisoners in Lecompton. He wrote to Charles Robinson on August 10, "I am here at last, with a sufficient force and ready to rescue you." Lane suggested that the men escape and meet the rescuing party nearby. "If you cannot escape," he wrote, "I can and will attack your guard, although it were best policy, if blood is to flow, that it be shed in your defense rather than in your rescue—Decide and that quickly. Time is everything."[54]

Robinson demurred, stating that the prisoners expected congressional aid from Washington. He wrote to Lane that preempting federal support by a forcible rescue could hurt their cause. Instead, he urged Lane to turn his attention toward the warfare in the territory: "Guerrilla operations are rife now, and they should be attended to." Whether Robinson meant to endorse Lane's military actions against proslavery militias or to encourage Lane to bring order to the area is unclear. Robinson warned of an impending attack

51. Stephen B. Oates, *To Purge This Land with Blood: A Biography of John Brown*, 126–37; Oswald Garrison Villard, *John Brown, 1800–1859*, 148–88; an account of the killings by participant James Townsley is quoted in Charles Robinson, *The Kansas Conflict*, 265–67; also see Robert W. Johannsen, ed., "A Footnote to the Pottawatomie Massacre, 1856," 236–41.

52. Etcheson, *Bleeding Kansas*, 114.

53. Ibid.; Monaghan, *Civil War on the Western Border*, 63.

54. Lane to Charles Robinson, August 10, 1856, Charles and Sara Robinson Collection, Kansas State Historical Society, Topeka. It is also quoted in Charles Robinson, *The Kansas Conflict*, 300.

by Missourians, yet with another ambiguous comment explained, "but we can *sweeten them now.*" One part of Robinson's letter does appear to support some kind of military resistance. Speaking of the possible Missouri invasion, he wrote that "officers here are willing that our people should put an end to these invaders without troubling them."[55]

With a rescue operation put aside, Lane quickly assembled a free-state force to attack a proslavery stronghold outside of Lawrence. On the evening of August 12, a group of fewer than one hundred free-staters besieged a party of proslavery men in a blockhouse near Franklin. After nearly four hours of shooting, with a few men sustaining wounds, Lane's men set fire to a hay-filled wagon and pushed it up against the building. As the flames rose, the proslavery men fled before the celebrating free-state band. Lane's men gathered up a number of firearms, a large amount of provisions, and even a cannon from the abandoned outpost.[56]

Lane and the free-state forces followed up this victory with attacks against two other proslavery positions over the next few days. On August 15 he successfully captured Fort Saunders without firing a shot.[57] On August 16 a detachment of free-state men, under the command of Lane's friend Samuel Walker, assaulted Fort Titus—a reinforced building named after the owner, Colonel H. Titus, a prominent proslavery militia leader. The ensuing skirmish wounded some men—including both Walker and Titus—and killed a few others. After free-state men fired their newly acquired cannon at the "fort," and used the tried-and-true method of setting fire to a hay-filled wagon, the proslavery defenders surrendered.[58]

As hostilities around Lawrence peaked, Governor Wilson Shannon traveled to the town on August 18 to work out a treaty. Various captives were released, including Titus, and property was returned. Shortly after this last diplomatic act, he tendered his resignation—at the same time the Pierce administration had set about notifying him of his removal as governor of Kansas Territory.[59]

55. Charles Robinson to James Lane, August 11, 1856, quoted in Stephenson, *Political Career of Lane,* 76n56.

56. Stephenson, *Political Career of Lane,* 76.

57. Monaghan, *Civil War on the Western Border,* 76. The defenders fled before Lane's men arrived.

58. *St. Louis Intelligencer,* August 21, 1856, in Webb Scrapbook, vol. 16, 95; *Missouri Republican,* August 21, 1856; Speer, *Life of Lane,* 115.

59. Monaghan, *Civil War on the Western Border,* 78; *Chicago Democratic Press,* August 28, 1856, in Webb Scrapbook, vol. 16, 167.

Shannon's peace treaty did not end the conflict. Daniel Woodson temporarily stepped in as acting governor until the newly appointed official, John W. Geary, arrived.[60] Woodson strongly sided with proslavery interests, and four days after taking control issued a proclamation declaring the territory to be in a state of insurrection. He called upon patriotic men to uphold the law and punish the traitors.[61] The move was largely fueled by reports of free-state depredations within proslavery communities. On September 3, Woodson wrote of Lane leading "a large body of armed men, obtained chiefly in the Northwestern states, after canvassing those States for some time for them, avowedly for the purpose of setting at defiance our Territorial laws, and of subverting by force and violence the regularly established government of the Territory." This group, he explained, "commenced, in pursuance of threats previously made, the bloody work of exterminating or driving from the Territory such of our citizens as had sought to enforce the Territorial laws, by attacking at midnight the law-abiding citizens of the town of Franklin with an overwhelming force of armed men." He described similar attacks by Lane in other portions of the territory.[62]

A number of publications nationwide ran similar stories of Lane and his "army." The *Weekly Mississippian* reported that "Lane is already in the territory with his marauders and 2000 more are on the northern boundary waiting to enter."[63] Many of these reports with apocalyptic headlines were aimed at Missouri audiences. The *Kansas Herald Extra* ran the headline: "War and Desolation!—Lecompton taken by Lane's Men!—Col. Titus's Company Held as Prisoners!—Sheriff Jones's House Threatened by the Outlaws!—Murder and Butchery!"[64] The *Missouri Republican* printed a letter announcing that the "outrageous conflict of Lane's, Brown's and Walker's parties in Kansas has at length aroused the border counties, so that it will be impossible to keep assistance from being sent to the proper authorities in Kansas to aid in maintaining the peace of the country."[65] As a result, much like Governor Shannon's proclamation in November 1855 that led to the Wakarusa War, Woodson's words struck a responsive chord among Missourians. By August 29, hundreds of men from that state

60. Gara, *Presidency of Franklin Pierce*, 124.

61. Stephenson, *Political Career of Lane*, 79.

62. Daniel Woodson to William Hutchinson and H. Miles Moore, September 3, 1856, *Transactions of the Kansas State Historical Society*, vol. 3, 330.

63. *Weekly Mississippian*, quoted in Monaghan, *Civil War on the Western Border*, 78.

64. *Kansas Herald Extra*, quoted in Connelley, *Lane: The "Grim Chieftain,"* 88.

65. *Missouri Republican*, August 23, 1856.

marched into Kansas under the leadership, once again, of David Atchison.[66] Lane, after spending two weeks in Nebraska Territory, rounded up a band of nearly three hundred men and skirmished with the Missouri group at Bull Creek. No serious engagement took place, and the Missourians returned to Kansas City while Lane's men fell back to Lawrence.[67]

Still, reports of free-state depredations continued. The proslavery *Kansas Weekly Herald* ran an account of "Lane's men" sacking the town of Tecumseh. Every store was ransacked and goods of all kinds were stolen, the paper explained, "even down to the brooms!"[68] Lane's reputation as a threat to proslavery interests and settlers climbed even higher. On September 5, Lane led 450 men into position outside the town of Lecompton, the proslavery capital of Kansas, to force the release of free-state men still imprisoned there. The size and strength of this force prompted Governor Woodson to ask for federal reinforcements. Colonel Philip St. George Cooke, commanding officer of the U.S. dragoons, arrived on the scene and met with free-state officers. He strongly suggested that the men return home, as the proslavery militia was disbanding and the prisoners were being released.[69] Lane and his men agreed to disperse without incident. Governor Woodson and Sheriff Jones learned of Lane's presence and were in the act of writing up a warrant for his arrest when Colonel Cooke persuaded them to drop the matter.[70]

The standoff outside of Lecompton was not the final clash of the year. On September 13, Lane led an attack upon proslavery forces at Hickory Point. After a day of skirmishing, he received word that newly arrived territorial governor John Geary had issued a proclamation ordering all armed bodies to disperse.[71] Lane immediately commanded his men to stand down. Colonel J. A. Harvey, leading a smaller group of free-state men to reinforce Lane at Hickory Point, failed to receive word of the cessation of hostilities. On September 14, Harvey's men attacked the proslavery garrison. The attack failed, and he and his group of nearly one hundred free-state men were captured by U.S. soldiers.[72]

66. Monaghan, *Civil War on the Western Border,* 80.

67. Charles Robinson, *The Kansas Conflict,* 318–19; Stephenson, *Political Career of Lane,* 79; Monaghan, *Civil War on the Western Border,* 82.

68. *Kansas Weekly Herald,* September 13, 1856.

69. Colonel Cooke's report describing the incident can be found in Speer, *Life of Lane,* 119–22, and Charles Robinson, *The Kansas Conflict,* 319–20.

70. Stephenson, *Political Career of Lane,* 80.

71. Wilder, *The Annals of Kansas,* 108.

72. A good personal account of the battle can be found in Samuel James Reader, "The First Day's Battle of Hickory Point," 28–49. Wilder, *The Annals of Kansas,* 108.

Following Geary's proclamation, Lane left Kansas Territory to help migrants travel through Iowa and Nebraska. Hostilities in Kansas ceased for a time, but tension over the future of Kansas and the Union continued to simmer. The *Kansas Weekly Herald* looked forward to a (most likely violent) settlement of the great divide over slavery:

> We call upon the South to come to our assistance. Shall the people of the South, they whose homes and honor are at stake, look calmly on when Abolitionism, unabated in violence, and unyielding in spirit, bids us to yield to its demands or be destroyed, though, disunion and civil war stare it in the face. . . .
>
> If Kansas is ever rescued from Abolitionism, we are persuaded it will be, not by any aid from the Union or the Administration, but by the stout hearts and arms of her own sons. . . . We have never been of those who could see any good to be gained by postponing the struggle which every reflecting man believes to be inevitable between the North and the South. Our motto is that of PATRICK HENRY: "Let it come."[73]

A national clash between North and South was still some years away. More pressing for many in Kansas and across the nation was the upcoming presidential election. Historian William Connelley suggests that Lane's military actions in Kansas in August and September were intended to garner a great public response in the Northern states.[74] In fact, following Geary's entrance into the territory, Lane headed back east to speak again on Kansas matters, making stops in Indiana and Ohio, and stumping for Republican presidential candidate Fremont.[75] The growing tension within the country and among those who remained in the Democratic ranks led to that party's abandonment of Franklin Pierce. Like the three Kansas territorial governors appointed by Pierce, Democrats desperately looked for a figure who could appease Northerners and Southerners *and* be an effective administrator. In reality, such a combination was virtually impossible. Effective administration required a leader who could stand up to one or both sections when necessary. This, in turn, required an individual who truly understood each side and the problem at hand. The man the Democrats chose, James Buchanan, bridged the gap on paper, but—like so

73. *Kansas Weekly Herald,* September 20, 1856.
74. William Elsey Connelley, *The Life of Preston B. Plumb,* 38.
75. An account of Lane's activities in Ohio was published in the *National Eagle,* later printed in the *Lecompton Union,* November 27, 1856; also see Franklin B. Sanborn, "Some Notes on the Territorial History of Kansas," 249–50.

many American political leaders in the 1850s—did not understand the depth of the conflict, or the interests of all of the players.[76] Nonetheless, Buchanan managed to garner enough national support to carry the election and keep the executive branch in Democratic hands. Lane continued to travel across the Northern states in support of the free-state cause, not returning to the territory until March 1857.

The year 1856 stands as the most significant period in Lane's political transition. Previous events, such as the Kansas-Nebraska debates of 1854, the failure of his Democratic Party movement in Kansas Territory, and the Wakarusa War, challenged his party loyalty and views of how to achieve a free Kansas. But his humiliation at the hands of his Democratic colleagues and the proslavery aggression against free-state Kansans convinced him that more radical measures were needed. Lane maintained the same principles and objectives he had always publicly espoused, but merely adapted them to the political realities of Kansas Territory in 1855 and 1856. Numerous Democrats, in Kansas and across the North, made similar adaptations. Kansas settler Oscar Learnard wrote to his father in Vermont in the summer of 1856, chastising him and others there for supporting the Pierce administration's policies. Was this support "because they belong to the so called Democratic party?" he asked. "So does Andrew H Reeder, J. H. Lane, Wm Y Roberts and a large majority of the leading men of Kansas, but they have learned to graduate their political sympathies by a different standard than that of the bodies and souls of men."[77] The situation in Kansas, these men and others had learned, required a different approach than what they had previously assumed.

Events in Kansas had turned numerous conservative and moderate men against the proslavery party in the territory, including at least two Kansas territorial governors. Andrew Reeder, the first governor, who had entered the territory as a Northern, pro–popular sovereignty Democrat, became a leading free-state figure after the Pierce administration turned against him.[78] John Geary, the dedicated Democrat and Pierce appointee who had labored successfully to end the bloodshed of 1856, had resisted another Missouri advance upon Lawrence and struggled against the proslavery legislature in Lecompton. He too concluded that the Pierce administration had abandoned the effort to fairly settle the fate of Kansas. Geary resigned

76. Elbert B. Smith, *The Presidency of James Buchanan*, 5–9, 22.

77. O. E. Learnard to Dear Father [S. T. Learnard], July 23, 1856, Oscar E. Learnard Collection, Kansas State Historical Society, Topeka.

78. Etcheson, *Bleeding Kansas*, 53; Gara, *Presidency of Franklin Pierce*, 112.

from his position as governor, and warned President-elect James Buchanan that proslavery Democrats in Kansas did not have national party interests in mind.[79]

Countless people within the United States made a similar adjustment as the American political system underwent a fundamental reorganization, with the Whig Party crumbling and scores of Democrats migrating to the emerging Republican Party. New York journalist, and former Democrat, William Cullen Bryant noted that many faces in his state's inaugural Republican convention were those "whose names have been identified with the most memorable triumphs of the democratic party during the last quarter of a century." These men, he explained, "have been constrained to form new, and, to some extent, perhaps uncongenial associations by the course pursued by their old friends, and to take upon themselves the responsibility of commencing the dissolution of an organization which has ceased to serve the cause of freedom and justice."[80] Lane's turn against the Democratic Party was not opportunistic, nor particularly strange or uncommon. He was one of many Democrats who lost faith in the management and new direction of the party.

Historian Eric Foner estimates that former Democrats made up 25 percent of the Republican vote in the 1856 presidential election. During the 1850s, eight Republican governors and seven Republican senators, as well as a number of Republican representatives, had left the Democratic fold. Countless other Democratic voters followed. "I was educated a Democrat from my boyhood," recalled one Iowan. "Faithfully did I adhere to that party until I could no longer act with it. Many things did I condemn ere I left that party, for my love of party was strong. And when I did, at last, feel compelled to separate from my old Democratic friends, it was like tearing myself away from old home associations."[81] Lane's separation had been more traumatic: he had been embarrassed by his old friends and associates. And the cause of that separation would burn inside of him for years.

Lane's transition has been labeled opportunistic and unprincipled. The man who had voted for the Southern-backed Kansas-Nebraska Bill in 1854 led free-state men in arms against proslavery communities only two years later. The former congressman who failed to establish a National Democratic presence in Kansas worked his way into a leadership position within

79. Etcheson, *Bleeding Kansas*, 133, 140–41.
80. William Cullen Bryant, "The Republican Convention, September 29, 1855," quoted in Bryant, *Power for Sanity*, 287.
81. Foner, *Free Soil, Free Labor, Free Men*, 165, 149, 150.

a local party that included Republicans, former Whigs, and Know-Nothings. The man who had preached moderation in free-state meetings became famous for his firebrand speeches calling the president a murderer and advocating violence against territorial officials. All of these developments appear to show a man of extremes—a man of little consistency.

But such appearance is only skin deep. The man who voted for the Kansas-Nebraska Bill did so after expressing antislavery concerns. The former congressman who failed to establish a National Democratic presence in Kansas maintained his Democratic identity until its leaders ridiculed him and his cause. The man who had preached moderation in Kansas found armed Missourians standing outside his town. Lane's political transition was an understandable reaction to the events of his time.

James Henry Lane, as he appeared during the Civil War.
Photo courtesy of the Library of Congress.

Stephen A. Douglas. He was the author of the Kansas-Nebraska Act and
leading figure in the Democratic Party. His harsh rejection of the Kansas
Memorial in 1856 caused James Lane to turn against the party.
Photo courtesy of the Library of Congress.

Franklin Pierce. James Lane championed Pierce's Democratic bid for the
1852 presidential election. Events in Kansas changed Lane's mind. By 1856,
he denounced Pierce as an enemy of free-state and democratic interests.
Photo courtesy of the Library of Congress.

Gaius Jenkins. A free-state man in the New England faction, his dispute with Lane over a land claim outside of Lawrence led to a deadly confrontation in 1858. Jenkins was killed and Lane temporarily retired from public life. *Photo courtesy of the Kansas State Historical Society.*

Major General David Hunter. He called James Lane an "unscrupulous trickster" during the struggle over command of the Southern Expedition in early 1862. *Photo courtesy of the Library of Congress.*

Charles Robinson. Free-state leader and governor of Kansas, he and Lane became bitter political rivals. Robinson's speeches and writings strongly affected Lane's image as a dangerous radical and demagogue. *Photo courtesy of the Kansas State Historical Society.*

Charles Sumner. His support for the free-state cause in Kansas, and the attack upon him by a Southern congressman on the U.S. Senate floor, helped draw people like Lane into the Republican Party. At the end of the Civil War, however, Lane and Sumner split on how to handle Reconstruction. *Photo courtesy of the Library of Congress.*

5

Lane and Lecompton, 1857

"The time has come for action, and I have always believed that we should never have peace in Kansas until these hell-hounds were driven from our midst."

Kansas in 1857 was spared a recurrence of the bloodshed it had seen the previous summer. Nonetheless, the political battle over statehood illustrated an ideological divide as extreme as ever. Free-state voting power that year overwhelmed the proslavery government and seemed to place Kansas in the Free State Party's hands. A last-ditch effort by proslavery forces in Lecompton to ratify a constitution enraged free-state residents and sent James Lane into a political and oratorical frenzy. Lane was willing to declare total war in support of his cause. His calls for violent action against proslavery officials shocked some Kansans, and have understandably contributed to his reputation as a demagogue. Still, his rhetoric was a progressing reaction—albeit extreme—to proslavery events. His speeches retained the same dedication to democratic principles and a free state of Kansas.

By the time Lane returned to Kansas in March 1857, the territory had settled into a remarkable peace, considering the level of violence present only six months earlier. Word of Lane's arrival stirred up concern among settlers on both sides of the slavery question. Rumors of his arrest and even death circulated within the territory. Despite the initial excitement, no problems arose and Lane, for the time being, took up a less political interest—namely, land speculation. Purchasing property in the proslavery town of Doniphan, Lane was reported to be "over head and ears in business." Even more shocking were reports of Lane and fellow free-state figure Samuel Pomeroy associating with Dr. J. H. Stringfellow, editor of the proslavery *Squatter Sovereign* and a participant in the sacking of Lawrence. The relationship between these men during this period was cordial and business-related. Still, Lane and Pomeroy received criticism, including from correspondents to the *New York Times,* who, according to the *Herald of Freedom,* behaved "as if there was something criminal in their late transactions with the pro-slavery party." The *Herald of Freedom* admitted "that we are not an admirer of [Lane's]," but argued that his "purchase of Doniphan has conferred a lasting benefit to the Free State cause; and those who would rather see Kansas a Free State than to see a particular party in power will thank Gen. L. for his labors at Doniphan." Whether Lane's business transactions were politically motivated is unknown, but they were perceived as damaging to proslavery interests in Kansas by commentators on both sides.[1]

While business may have been good, the struggle over Kansas statehood resurfaced. The proslavery legislature in Lecompton planned a constitutional convention, and scheduled a June election for delegates. Robert J. Walker, the territory's newest governor, backed the election, but announced his intention to protect the integrity of the polls. He proclaimed that "the majority of the people of Kansas must govern; that the majority of the people of Kansas must adopt their own constitution or reject it; that the majority of the people of Kansas at the polls must decide whether they shall have a free or a slave state."[2] Lane, like many others in the Free State ranks, opposed the proceedings by the so-called "bogus legislature" in Lecompton, and spoke out against free-state participation

1. *Herald of Freedom,* April 18, 1856; *Missouri Republican,* May 19 1857. For mention of Stringfellow at attack on Lawrence, see Monaghan, *Civil War on Western Border,* 57. *Herald of Freedom,* May 30, 1857. On July 18, 1857, the *Herald of Freedom* ran another defense of Lane's and Pomeroy's actions, stating: "Our own opinion has been that Lane and Pomeroy did more in those two business transactions to close the opposition to the Free State movement from the pro-slavery party, than any other movement inaugurated for many months." The proslavery newspaper *The Constitutionalist* from Doniphan was quoted in the same article criticizing the sale of the *Squatter Sovereign* to Pomeroy: "It is to be regretted by the whole pro-slavery party. The sale of that paper has injured the cause more than the sale of every pro-slavery town in Kansas."

2. "Address of Governor Walker at Topeka," June 6, 1857, in "Governor Walker's Administration," 292.

in the election. While free-state settlers largely outnumbered their proslavery rivals, the minority power had retained official territorial authority—with or without gubernatorial support. And free-staters were unsure about the most recent executive appointee. Walker was born in Pennsylvania, but had migrated to Mississippi, where he became a slave-holder and politician. Like Buchanan, he seemed to offer the Democratic Party a suitable public official, capable of appeasing both factions. He had written an essay arguing that Kansas, due to environmental and population factors, would not become a slave state. Buchanan embraced Walker as a potential savior for the Kansas situation. Northern Democrats heartily agreed, while the South seemed split on the issue.[3]

Free-state delegates met in Topeka on June 9 to consider participation in the Lecompton-based election. Lane, serving as president of the convention, provided listeners with his "usual style of theatrical eloquence" in denouncing "every proslavery man." Turning to the Topeka Constitution, he reportedly asked, "Have we not made our Constitution? And do not the people of Freedom like it? Is there any one of the Free State party opposed to it? Can't we submit this to the people, and who wants another?"[4] Though rejected by the U.S. Senate in early 1856, the Free State Party continued to embrace the Topeka Constitution. Twice in 1857—once in January, and then again in March—Free State delegates in Kansas reaffirmed their support of it and urged Congress to accept it.[5]

The *Herald of Freedom*'s correspondent explained that Lane's speech "was one which a certain portion of the Convention delighted in, while the other portion was much displeased with the position he occupied."[6] Despite his critics, Lane's opposition to the Lecompton election carried the day as the convention first denounced the authority of the proslavery legislature as invalid, and then passed a resolution recommending "that the election for delegates, in pursuance of the law enacted by the Lecompton bogus Legislature, be disregarded and permitted to pass without any participation therein by the Free State party of Kansas."[7] The Free State convention again endorsed the Topeka Constitution.

3. Kenneth Stampp, *America in 1857*, 159–60.
4. *Herald of Freedom*, June 13, 1857.
5. Stephenson, *Political Career of Lane*, 86.
6. *Herald of Freedom*, June 13, 1857.
7. The resolution read: "Resolved, 1. That the people of Kansas now as ever, disown as invalid and of no force or effect the authority of the Territorial government as embodied in the enactments of the so-called Legislature of Kansas." Printed in the *Herald of Freedom*, June 13, 1857, and the *Kansas Weekly Herald*, June 20, 1857.

The convention's official opposition to the Lecompton convention sparked another round of tense political fighting in the territory. Governor Walker continued to back the June elections, and at a gathering in Big Springs on June 10, he declared the Topeka movement was "against the authority of the United States."[8] "What pretext is there for putting into operation a set of laws thus violating the supreme authority of the land?" Walker asked his audience. "And who is it formed this so called Topeka Constitution, and intend to impose it by force upon the people of Kansas? [W]ho but 1731 men—a mere handful?"[9]

Following Walker, Lane took to the stump. As one of the 1,731 free-state men "denounced here to-day," Lane explained that Congress had not entirely rejected the Topeka Constitution. The House of Representatives had passed the measure in the spring of 1856, though the Senate had thrown it out. He reminded the audience that "we have the right to make a revolution," but clarified that Free State members "did not revolt, but sought a peaceful solution of our difficulties, and took a perfectly legal mode of adjusting it—that of forming a State Constitution." As for the laws of the territory, Lane rejected them as oppressive rules forced upon Kansans "by a body of usurpers, who were elected by armed men, with all the munitions of war, who invaded our Territory and took possession of the polls." Lane further criticized the proslavery government and Walker's support of it, and closed by celebrating the democratic efforts and interests of his fellow free-state settlers, who "stand without sin before the people, and will maintain their integrity." He defiantly announced, "We will not obey these laws, and will not stultify our past history by voting under your Territorial enactments."[10]

On July 15 free-state delegates met in Topeka to plan an election for state offices and to schedule an official convention in August. Lane again played a central role in the proceedings. At one point, he addressed accusations of improprieties with funds sent from Northern organizations to help the free-state cause. He read an extract from the *Jeffersonian Extra,* a Democratic publication from his former district in Indiana, which charged that Lane "has FRATERNIZED with 'bloody Atchison and with the monster Stringfellow,' and that he (Lane) is investing the proceeds of his freedom-shrieking speeches in joint speculations with these pro-slavery worthies."

8. A general account of the meeting can be found in the *Lawrence Republican,* June 18, 1857.
9. *Kansas Weekly Herald,* July 4, 1857.
10. Ibid.

Lane responded that he had not taken a single dollar sent to help Kansas. His only compensation had been six hundred dollars in scrip, paid to him to cover his expenses to Washington, D.C. A Mr. Whitman then rose and defended Lane, saying that "no man received pay last fall or summer for services excepting the attendants of the hospital."[11]

The controversy surrounding Lane's business dealings with leading proslavery figures in the spring of 1857 haunted him for months, and continued to spring up in the following years from his political opponents. As late as December 5, Kansas newspapers printed a "Card" from Lane defending his handling of Northern funds and denying any financial impropriety.[12] The matter is indicative of the political environment in territorial Kansas, and helps explain the charges of opportunism critics and historians have heaped upon the man over the past century and a half. Though many free-state men in Kansas defended Lane's land speculation as beneficial to the free-state cause, and despite the fact that no evidence has been found that Lane's actions were politically motivated (certainly not in support of proslavery interests), his political opponents latched onto the image of Lane working side by side with proslavery leaders in a business deal as evidence of his lack of principle.

His comments later in the meeting are extremely significant for understanding his political transition. Kansas settlers created the Free State Party as a special-interest organization, separate from traditional political affiliations. Republicans, Democrats, Know-Nothings, Free-Soilers, and others joined the party solely according to their interest in creating a free state, and without abandoning their national parties. For many in Kansas, including Lane, the Free State association was maturing. He announced that "I have had frequent occasions to be proud of the Free State party, but never so proud as now. To-day we are a unit." While this statement referred to the history of various factions within the party, it also illustrated Lane's new approach to the Free State Party since his fallout with Democratic leadership. He explained:

> Our present State organization was sanctioned by such men as Pierce and Douglas, before I came to Kansas. I came directly from Washington here, and attempted in good faith to organize the Democratic party—hoping through that party to make Kansas free, and that the question might be settled and out of the way, before the Presidential election of

11. *Herald of Freedom,* July 25, 1857.
12. Ibid., December 5, 1857.

1856. You know that it was in a Democratic caucus that the Topeka movement was brought forward—that the adherents of Pierce and Douglas scouted that organization, and it failed. Then, and not till then, did I attach myself to the Free State party of Kansas. Pierce and his party played false; they treated you ill; they basely deserted the Democracy of Kansas.[13]

Lane's experience in Kansas and transition into the Republican fold led to his adoption of an important policy change. Convinced that the slaveholding interests had taken over the Democratic Party and threatened democratic principles and the integrity of the nation, he declared an interest in two objectives: "First, the tide of Slavery turned back, and this institution surrounded by a cordon of free States; second, the scattering to the four winds, to utter dissolution, that corrupt, old line, pro-slavery, Democratic party, which is now cursing the nation. For the accomplishment of these two objects, I enroll myself a crusader."[14] While this statement resembles Lane's free-state speeches from the summer of 1856, the two objectives in this case were not simply local issues. Here Lane endorsed national changes: slavery should not simply be kept out of Kansas, but should be "turned back" and "surrounded" by free states on a broad scale; the National Democratic Party was not only corrupt, but should be destroyed.

Though Lane adopted a change of policy, he did not abandon his personal principles. Before the Kansas Memorial's failure, Lane believed that the Democratic Party would ultimately protect democratic principles and that respect for slaveholding rights and interests would best serve the Union. His experiences in 1856 shattered that belief, and Lane concluded that only by restricting slavery expansion could slaveholding aggression be halted and the integrity of the Union preserved. The Democratic Party, he believed, not only had failed to prevent agitation but also was firmly in the pocket of proslavery interests.

Before closing, the July Topeka assembly addressed the matter of the October territorial election. Walker defended this upcoming round of elections as one "not under the act of the late Territorial Legislature, but under the laws of Congress."[15] The convention recommended an assembly at Grasshopper Falls in late August to debate the issue. The assembly received

13. Ibid., July 25, 1857.
14. Ibid.
15. "Address of Governor Walker at Topeka," "Governor Walker's Administration," 293.

information that Missourians planned to enter the state and interfere with the upcoming elections. The convention assigned Lane the duty of organizing a military defense of the ballot-boxes in the many districts.[16] He quickly issued orders calling for the organization of volunteer units across the territory.[17] Governor Walker objected to this new militarization of free-state men, fearing that conservative voters would be kept away from the polls.[18] To prevent violence the governor requested federal reinforcements.

On August 26, the Grasshopper Falls Convention opened. The Business Committee, chaired by Lane, presented a set of resolutions concerning the territorial elections in October. Arguing that the "Territorial government should be controlled by the *bona fide* citizens" of Kansas, and acknowledging that Governor Walker "has repeatedly pledged himself that the people of Kansas shall have a full and fair vote before impartial judges," the committee recommended that the people of Kansas participate in the October elections. The committee men placed their trust in Walker, resolving that "we rely upon the faithful fulfillment of the pledge of Gov. Walker, and that we, as heretofore, protest against the enactments forced upon us by the voters of Missouri."[19]

After the resolutions had been introduced, various speakers rose to recommend or discourage participation in the October polls. Martin Conway rejected the resolutions and argued that the Free State Party "will be tarnished by engaging in this election." Participation would "recognize the legality of the body prescribing the rules for that election," and would be inconsistent with the Free State position. "The man who is opposed to the Topeka Constitution can consistently go into the election, but those who sustain that Constitution cannot."[20]

As Conway concluded his remarks, Lane stood to address the crowd. He reaffirmed his stance in favor of the Topeka Constitution. He admitted that participation would be humiliating. Nonetheless, Lane urged his fellow delegates to pass the resolutions. "There are prudent men in this Territory—men with wives, and children, and property, and here are their homes and their all," he said. "They are confident they can regain their lost liberties by another effort at the ballot box. They wish to try their hand

16. *Herald of Freedom,* July 25, 1857.
17. See Lane's "General Order No. 1" and "General Order No. 2" in "Governor Walker's Administration," 364–67.
18. R. J. Walker to Lewis Cass, July 25, 1857, found in "Governor Walker's Administration," 361.
19. *Herald of Freedom,* September 5, 1857.
20. Ibid.

at this peaceful remedy, and we must concede to them the right to do so."[21] Though Lane had preferred another tactic, he acknowledged the will of the people. But, his support of election participation included two important conditions. First, if fraud once again robbed the free-state population of its rightful political authority, the people "will join us in sustaining the Topeka Constitution and Government." Second, if the convention decided to participate, it must carry out the plan completely:

> I do believe if we fail in carrying the October election, Kansas is a slave State. You must resolve to carry this election before determining to engage in it. A thousand disorganized men are said to be no stronger than a score of thoroughly organized men. If you have made up your minds to go into the election and win, you should at once join some organized company that you may be prepared with others in standing up with them, and maintaining the right. With a determined heart, and united effort the result is certain, and the victory will be complete. Then, with the aid of that Legislature we can place the Topeka Constitution in a condition that Congress will cheerfully let us into the Union.[22]

Thus, Lane took a moderate, or compromising position: try to take control of the territorial government legally; if unjustly denied, then once again set out on an independent statehood movement. Charles Robinson gave further support for participation. He voiced his dedication to the Topeka Constitution, but saw the election as an opportunity to "get the battery and spike it, so it cannot be used against us."[23] With two of the Free State Party's leading members encouraging participation, the convention passed the resolutions. Free-state Kansans looked forward to October's election as an opportunity to kill the proslavery legislature from within.

In early September a committee appointed at the Grasshopper Falls Convention and led by Lane wrote an "Address to the American People on the Affairs of Kansas." The text was carefully crafted and moderate in tone, prompting biographer Wendell Stephenson to suggest that "it did not emanate from Lane's pen."[24] Though Stephenson is to date Lane's greatest biographer, the assumption that a "well written and conservative" address could not have come from Lane fails to recognize the man's ability to read his audience and construct an appropriate message; Lane's

21. Ibid.
22. Ibid.
23. Ibid.
24. Stephenson, *Political Career of Lane*, 88.

speech before the Grasshopper Falls Convention urging participation is one example. Stephenson was part of the Moderate school of thought, and his work leans toward a defense of Lane in many instances, but he falls too heavily, in this instance, for the image of a man radical in nature and in behavior. The original author of the address is unknown, and any of the other thirteen committee members could have written the text. However, Lane's signature is listed first—as chairman of the committee—proving his endorsement of the message. In any case, the address briefly detailed the free-state version of the struggle for Kansas statehood and defended the Topeka movement and constitution. The decision to participate in the October election was a carefully considered act, intended to take control peacefully of the territorial legislature and to show Congress the true wants and power of the free-state population. However, the signers doubted the likelihood of success, declaring that although Governor Walker promised to uphold the sanctity of the election, "with our past experience, we find it difficult to indulge in any hope of justice from the agents of the Federal Administration."[25]

Overall, the address was designed not only to explain previous free-state actions and their present course but also to justify the reemergence of the independent statehood movement should the election be fraudulent. The committee called upon the people, asking that if the free-state cause were again denied justice at the polls, "will not all good men sustain us in giving effect to our State Government at all hazards?"[26] The committee further clarified relations with Missouri. Carefully explaining that "the people of Kansas do not charge the outrages to which they have been subjected upon the people of Missouri as a body," the free-state officials complimented the democratic principles of most Missourians. The two states were linked, sharing "identical" interests: farm production, railroad connections, and town building in Kansas necessarily benefited Missouri. But the committee clarified that any attempt by Missourians to interfere in Kansas politics would be resisted. And though their address separated the "invaders" from the general Missouri population, the committee's discussion of Kansas resistance turned toward the neighboring state as a whole:

> If you persist against your best interests, against all considerations of patriotism, against all manly and Christian duty, in the mad course you have marked out, a war must ensue, protracted and bloody, between

25. *Herald of Freedom,* September 12, 1857.
26. Ibid.

Missouri and Kansas; and it may be extended all along the line to the Atlantic coast. A dissolved Union and a broken government may be the result.—For the highest welfare of Kansas and Missouri; in the name of our common country and the living God; we appeal to you to refrain. Remain at home; the Kansas question will then be peacefully settled; the agitation of slavery will cease; and Kansas and Missouri will go on prospering and to prosper.[27]

To protect the ballot boxes during the October election, Lane busily engaged in military matters. He corresponded with John Brown, who had left the territory to collect supplies, including weapons, for the Kansas cause. Lane wrote to Brown that the arms were needed as quickly as possible, but due to health problems the abolitionist did not return to Kansas until after the elections.[28]

The excitement of the election, scheduled for October 5, stirred Lane's famous energy. The proslavery *Kansas Weekly Herald* reported that "Lane said with a braggart swing of the arm, that since the Grasshopper Falls Convention he had been going night and day, and had not changed his clothes." By the look of his shirt, the *Weekly Herald* continued, that claim seemed true. Further, Lane "declared that since that time he had not slept, and did not intend to sleep till after the October election. That by next morning he would be in Lawrence, and by the next at Topeka, &c. This was said to make it appear what a mighty man Jim Lane is, and what invaluable services he is rendering the party."[29] While there is little doubt that Lane thrived on the attention he received during his various speaking engagements and played up his personal sacrifices for the free-state cause as the *Weekly Herald* suggested, his tireless efforts to promote and protect a free-state election victory were invaluable.

With official Free State Party endorsement of the October 5 election, free-state voters turned out in force. Despite heightened tensions throughout the territory, no significant violence occurred, and no large-scale Missouri invasion took place. The election was not, however, free from fraud. At the small town of Oxford, near the Missouri border, sixteen hundred proslavery votes—in a district of fewer than one hundred resident voters—were recorded. A careful investigation proved that someone had copied part of

27. Ibid.
28. J. H. Lane to Sir [John Brown], September 7, 1857; J. H. Lane to Genl John Brown, September 29, 1857; John Brown to James Lane, September 30, 1857, John Brown Collection, Kansas State Historical Society, Topeka.
29. *Kansas Weekly Herald,* September 26, 1857.

the Cincinnati directory onto the polling record.[30] Governor Walker, standing firm on his promise to protect the integrity of the polls, rejected the Oxford returns, thus firmly placing the legislature in Free State hands.[31]

Although the Free State Party won the election, proslavery officials were not willing to let power shift so easily. On September 7, a month before the election, the proslavery constitutional convention (made up of delegates from the June election that the free-state settlers had boycotted) organized in Lecompton. The initial meeting was brief. John Calhoun was elected president and the convention adjourned until after the October election.[32] Still, the activity grabbed free-state attention. Lane spoke out against the Lecompton movement, reportedly warning that if that assembly, "called into existence by fraud, should frame a Constitution and submit it to the Missouri registry, or admission should be had without ratification by the *bona fide* citizens, resistance to the bitter end would inevitably be the result."[33]

With proslavery interests threatened by the majority of incoming legislators, the Lecompton convention reassembled on October 19 to draw up a constitution. Free-state men exploded in protest. On the same day the convention opened, Lane led nearly three hundred men to Lecompton and aired a fiery denunciation of proslavery officials.[34] The group held a semiofficial meeting in the town, with resolutions and informal debate between proslavery and free-state men. Lane commended the free-state resolutions, which denounced the Lecompton convention and championed the right of the majority will in Kansas. "The ballot-box is second in purity only to the alter of Deity," Lane told the crowd; "the poisoning of the sacred springs from which we draw the water of our national life; it is a

30. Allan Nevins, *The Emergence of Lincoln*, vol. 1, *Douglas, Buchanan, and Party Chaos, 1857–1859*, 173–74; Etcheson, *Bleeding Kansas*, 153.

31. Walker released an official proclamation regarding the "Oxford Frauds," published in the *Lawrence Republican*, October 22, 1857; Wilder, *The Annals of Kansas*, 151.

32. John Calhoun was originally from New England, had served in the Illinois state legislature, and was a friend of both Abraham Lincoln and Stephen Douglas before finding an appointment in Kansas as surveyor-general. Despite his Northern background, Calhoun was a notable proslavery advocate in the territory. Robert Johannsen, "The Lecompton Constitutional Convention: An Analysis of Its Membership," 237; Nevins, *The Emergence of Lincoln*, vol. 1, 173.

33. *Herald of Freedom*, September 12, 1857.

34. On October 15 Lane requested free-state military leader J. B. Abbott to bring his "Brigade" to Lecompton on the nineteenth "with all their arms (not in sight) & with four days provisions." Lane apparently prepared for a skirmish but did not intend to instigate open hostilities. J. H. Lane to J. B. Abbott, October 15, 1857, James Abbott Collection, Kansas State Historical Society, Topeka.

crime so stupendous that lawmakers grow dizzy when they approach it, and nothing but the visitation of the sovereign wrath of the people thus outraged can effect an adequate punishment."[35]

The gathering illustrated the bad blood between the opposing political sides, but no actual violence took place. Reports of the affair vary according to sentiments. A correspondent for the proslavery *Kansas Weekly Herald* wrote that Lane told the crowd "that every man engaged in the Oxford fraud should meet with summary punishment, Sheriff Jones not excepted." Sheriff Jones stood up and challenged Lane, "and dared him to attempt to put his threat then in execution, called him a liar and coward, and dared him to resent it." But, the *Weekly Herald* recorded, Lane backed down. "Lane can gas, charge and threaten, but when danger approaches, he can take the lie from such men as Sheriff Jones, with a very good grace." According to the *Weekly Herald*, Lane and the free-state men intended to forcibly disrupt the convention, but "wisely concluded it best to leave."[36]

The *National Democrat*, Lecompton's newspaper at the time, gave a slightly more moderate assessment of the event. "Gen. J. H. Lane was the orator of the occasion," the paper reported, "and delivered a lengthy harangue in his usual style of inflamatory rhetoric, though he was by no means so belligerent or infuriated as some of the ninies who preceded him." The *Democrat* also reported that free-state men in Lawrence had planned to disrupt the convention violently, "but the effort signally failed, and this result was known to our citizens as early as Sunday."[37]

Perhaps ironically, the free-state gathering's peaceful dispersal from Lecompton drew a great deal of attention. Given the reputation of political bloodshed in the territory, newspapers took special care to comment on the lack of confrontation. Like the *Weekly Herald* and *National Democrat*, the *Lexington Express* ridiculed what it perceived as the anticlimactic retreat of Lane and his followers. "[Lane] went to Lecompton, he did! And in obedience to what he had promised, gave the assembled Conventionists the opportunity of quietly disbanding before he—left the place! He asked the members to quit, and his job was finished; having 'marched up the hill' 'he marched down again.'" Taking a final shot at Lane and the free-state men, the article concluded, "The music for the occasion should have been the 'rogue's march.' Vive la humbug!"[38]

---

35. *New York Times*, October 30, 1857.
36. *Kansas Weekly Herald*, October 31, 1857.
37. *National Democrat*, October 22, 1857.
38. *Lexington Express*, printed in *Kansas Weekly Herald*, November 14, 1857.

The antislavery *Lawrence Republican,* on the other hand, celebrated the free-state assembly outside of the Lecompton constitutional convention as a great success. "For thrilling pathos, for withering invective, for crushing argument, for sublime earnestness of purpose, [Lane's] speech of yesterday stands without a parallel in his history." He had, the *Republican* reported, humbled proslavery critics. "Jim Lane the fighter is enough to scatter a panic through a legion of ruffians, but Jim Lane the orator is more an object of dread than was Cromwell to the infamous Long Parliament." The *Republican* accused Sheriff Samuel Jones and other proslavery figures of trying to instigate a fight with free-state men. But, the article continued, "the Free-State party, true to the noble impulses which have held them in all their struggle, forgave both the bullies and their insults, and 'in the midst of judgment remembered mercy.'"[39] Proslavery papers perceived the peaceful free-state dispersal as anticlimactic and cowardly, while the *Republican* portrayed it as noble.

Despite the free-state gathering and general criticism of the convention, the Lecompton constitutional effort continued through late October and into early November. When it closed on November 3, it had constructed a constitution that protected the institution of slavery in the territory. Ratification by Kansas voters was scheduled for December 21. Yet even the ratification vote was rigged against free-state voters, as Kansans had two choices: vote for the constitution with slavery or without slavery. A vote for the document without slavery did not affect the legality of the institution within Kansas Territory before statehood. Either way the Lecompton convention planned to push their constitution through. Word of the Lecompton "swindle," as it came to be known, set off a firestorm of criticism across the nation. Enraged by the proslavery officials in Lecompton and by President James Buchanan's support of the constitution, Governor Walker, the dedicated Democrat and Mississippi slave owner, resigned. Other leading Democratic voices announced their opposition to the Lecompton convention as well. "What mockery is this?" asked the *Detroit Free Press,* the chief Democratic newspaper behind Democrat Senator Lewis Cass. "The Convention did not submit the Constitution to the people because the Convention knew the people would vote it down!" "What is this," the story continued, *"but an utter denial of the right of the people recognized by the Cincinnati Democratic National Convention!"* "Are the 'Democratic' principles of 'Popular Sovereignty,' 'State Sovereignty' and 'State Rights,' as they have

---

39. *Lawrence Republican,* October 22, 1857.

been generally understood and accepted, to be overridden and crushed down, in order to quiet the fears of a handful of slaveholders in and on the border of Kansas," a Kentucky Democrat wanted to know.[40]

Even Stephen Douglas, who had crushed the Kansas Memorial and James Lane's faith in the Democratic Party in early 1856, denounced the Lecompton actions as a mockery of popular sovereignty and a fatal blow to Northern Democratic support of the administration.[41] When the senator had heard of the president's endorsement of the Lecompton Constitution, he traveled to the White House to confer with Buchanan. Douglas expressed his frustration with the situation, particularly since he was the chairman of the Senate Committee on Territories. Naturally, as a Democrat, he would be expected to act in concert with the president. This would be difficult to do, Douglas believed, since the Lecompton Constitution denied Kansans the principle of popular sovereignty. As Douglas chastised the president for standing behind Lecompton before conferring with him, Buchanan issued a threat. "Mr. Douglas, I desire you to remember that no Democrat ever yet differed from the Administration of his own choice without being crushed." This was largely true. Many Democrats who had opposed the Democratic administrations of Pierce and even Buchanan had found themselves run out of the party. That happened to James Lane, aided by none other than Douglas himself. To emphasize his point, Buchanan reminded Douglas of those Democratic senators who had stood against President Andrew Jackson: "Beware of the fate of Tallmadge and Rives." Unperturbed, Douglas shot back, "Mr. President, I wish you to remember that Gen. Jackson is dead, sir." The fight over Kansas had caused even the author of the Kansas-Nebraska Act, and a rising star in the Democratic Party, to split with the Democratic administration.[42]

On December 8, Buchanan sent a message to Congress urging the admittance of Kansas under the Lecompton Constitution. The following day, Douglas rose from his desk in the Senate to reply.[43] Anticipation of his

40. Text of the Lecompton Constitution can be found in Wilder, *The Annals of Kansas*, 134–48. The Lecompton Constitution stated, "The right of property in slaves now in the Territory shall in no manner be interfered with," and "No alteration shall be made to affect the right of property in the ownership of slaves," quoted also in Charles Robinson, *The Kansas Conflict*, 374. Davis, *Kansas: A History*, 69–70; *Detroit Free Press*, quoted in the *New York Times*, December 3, 1857; *New York Times*, November 28, 1857.
41. McPherson, *Battle Cry of Freedom*, 165–66.
42. Johannsen, *Stephen A. Douglas*, 586.
43. Douglas biographer Robert Johannsen calls this speech "probably the most significant of his career." Johannsen, *Stephen A. Douglas*, 592.

response drew a packed house. Visitors filled the galleries, reporters and other guests crowded into the chamber, and his Senate colleagues all sat at their desks awaiting his speech. So many people came for the event that the hallways and lobbies were full of those unable to find room in the Senate chamber. His speech did not disappoint, for Stephen Douglas set out to oppose the president he had helped elect.[44] He attempted to turn Buchanan's message to Congress around by declaring that the president had actually "made an argument—an unanswerable argument in my opinion—against that constitution, which shows clearly, whether intended to arrive at that result or not, that, consistently with his views and principles, he cannot accept that constitution." He then blasted the Lecompton Constitution as a violation of the rights and interests of the Kansas majority. As before, he declared an indifference to the details of a territory's constitution. "It is none of my business which way the slavery clause is decided. I care not whether it is voted down or voted up." Douglas wanted people of a territory to have the right to fairly and legally establish their own constitution. He announced that "if this constitution is to be forced down our throats, in violation of the fundamental principle of free government, under a mode of submission that is a mockery and insult, I will resist it to the last."[45] Here, in late 1857, Stephen Douglas sounded a lot like James Lane.

A few days later, Douglas expanded upon his opposition to the Lecompton Constitution. "When the broad fact stands admitted before the world that this constitution is the act of a minority, and not of the majority, the injustice becomes the more manifest and the more monstrous," he told his Senate colleagues. "The only reason for not submitting the constitution fairly is, that it would be voted down if it were submitted. This is an admission that it is the act of a minority, not a majority." Like Lane, Douglas had come to see the machinations of proslavery officials in Kansas as a denial of basic democratic principles. And instead of seeing violence in Kansas as the result of irresponsible and dangerous fanatics, Douglas acknowledged that forceful resistance would be a natural outcome of the constitution's passage. "The scheme is a scheme of civil war. It leads directly to war." If passed, the army would be needed to enforce the Lecompton Constitution, he argued, and that "means violence, or it means the subjection of the majority to the minority."[46]

44. Stampp, *America in 1857*, 301.
45. *Congressional Globe*, 35th Cong., 1st sess., 14–18.
46. Ibid., 50.

Douglas knew that his stance against the president would lead to questions of his party loyalty. During his December 9 Senate speech, he claimed he had "no fear of any party associations being severed." Nonetheless, even if his social and political bonds were broken, he declared, "I cannot act with you and preserve my faith and my honor, I will stand on the great principle of popular sovereignty." Whatever the political future held, he was determined to "follow that principle wherever its logical consequences may take me, and I will endeavor to defend it against assault from any and all quarters."[47] Indeed, Douglas's position caused many to question his future in the Democratic Party. Democrats in New York met at Tammany Hall in late December to express their support of the president. One speaker took a few shots at Douglas. Pointing to an article in the *New York Tribune*, which informed its readers of a "full and frank conference between Senator Douglas and leading Republicans, on the latest aspects of Kansas affairs," he expressed amazement. "You and I never had a conference with Republicans on any affair," he told the crowd, "least of all on this, which is so important to the Democratic Party."[48]

Douglas did meet with some Republican leaders at various times, including Congressman Schuyler Colfax of Indiana, former Speaker of the House Nathaniel Banks, and Senator Benjamin Wade of Ohio. At one point, Douglas expressed his belief that Southern extremists were intentionally trying to cause conflict. He added that he could not understand why his defense of popular sovereignty in Kansas—the right of the Kansas majority to fairly and justly create their own government—received such opposition from fellow Democrats.[49] That sentiment mirrored Lane's own complaint against Douglas and the Pierce administration only a year and a half earlier.

Despite the fact that Douglas, like Lane and his fellow free-state Kansans, had come to see the actions of the proslavery minority as a threat to the majority interest, the Illinois senator had no desire to jump on the Free State bandwagon or leave the Democratic Party. He remained careful not to criticize the Lecompton Constitution on account of its proslavery bias.[50] And he continued to argue that the Topeka Constitution was equally bogus, for "it was made by a political party, and not by the people" and because he still believed it was created in defiance of

47. Ibid., 18.
48. *New York Times*, December 24, 1857.
49. Johannsen, *Stephen A. Douglas*, 594.
50. Damon Wells, *Stephen Douglas: The Last Years, 1857–1861*, 24.

congressional authority.[51] Douglas still believed he could unite Southern and Northern Democrats on the principle of popular sovereignty, and he set about in an effort to authorize a new constitutional convention.

While Douglas tackled the new political situation in Washington, tension in Kansas continued to escalate. Lane demanded that the governor call the recently elected territorial legislature into an extra session to vote on the Lecompton Constitution. He continued his marathon speaking tour across the territory, addressing crowds as often as three times a day. One account described him traveling a total of ninety miles in one day to deliver five speeches.[52] His energy seemed boundless and his arguments were focused. In Leavenworth, on November 14, Lane gave one of his more aggressive speeches denouncing the Lecompton Convention. Kansans were not deciding whether their state should be admitted as a free state, he argued, because the Lecompton Constitution had already established it as a slaveholding one. "It is a slave State now," he declared. "It is a slave State by the body of their Constitution." Slavery in the territory was protected as it existed—the December vote merely decided whether *more* slaves could be admitted into Kansas after statehood. He announced that "Kansas is a slave State to day, and forever, unless you contrive some means to defeat this Constitution made by these bloodhounds at Lecompton."[53] Lane took on the type of threatening tone that has led historians to brand him a radical and a fanatic. "I am not going to advise war or bloodshed here to-night, for perhaps there is no need of that," he explained. But, he continued, "[w]e have now got the goats so separated from the sheep that we can easily kill them without committing crime. For I truly believe if God should show his special Providence to-night, we should see in these starry heavens his hand commanding us to exterminate these damned villains."[54]

Some in the crowd did not share Lane's extreme position. Leavenworth had been a proslavery stronghold, although it gradually shifted into a free-state community. Lane preempted his critics, challenging calls for moderation. "You may say, 'Lane you are excited.' I say; ought we not to be excited? Have we not suffered enough to excite every nerve in our body?" He continued to challenge the crowd. "Have we not labored for three years to build up Kansas a free and glorious State for ourselves and children? [A]nd after we have it within our reach to have these usurpers by fraud and violence to

51. *Congressional Globe,* 35th Cong., 1st sess., 17.
52. Speer, *Life of Lane,* 143n.
53. *Kansas Weekly Herald,* November 21, 1857.
54. Ibid.

institute a villainous project ruining our best interests? Should we not feel like taking these villains by the throats and choke their very life from them."[55] "His utterances may have been wild," Lane's friend and associate John Speer later wrote, "but nobody denied that they were convincing."[56]

Though Lane did not plan to incite his audience to immediate violence, he made it clear that he believed that proslavery aggression had to be resisted forcefully. "Take these men and give them a fair trial," he suggested, "but if you find them guilty of performing this fraud, they should suffer death." Further, he reflected upon the attitude proslavery men had toward free-state settlers and their leaders (particularly himself). He explained that proslavery newspaper editors Jack Henderson of the *Leavenworth Journal* and Lucien Eastin of the *Leavenworth Herald* "grumble because I would put them to death."[57] Looking across the audience, he declared, "Why there is not a moment for the past 2 years but what they would gladly have heralded in their papers, 'Jim Lane is dead.'" He did not wish to kill them for revenge or out of vengeance, but, he argued, to protect the future of Kansas. "I would let Jack Henderson and Eastin live alway[s] if it was not necessary to put them to death, but if it is for the peace and prosperity of Kansas, to kill them, I say cut their throats now, and I will not ask to stay away but will gladly join in the act." He told the audience that "the time has come for action, and I have always believed that we should never have peace in Kansas until these hell-hounds were driven from our midst."[58]

Henderson was in the audience at Leavenworth and at one point called out: "'Dry up Jim,' 'Dry up Jim,' 'stop that[,] you know you are lying Lane.'" Lane reportedly turned to Henderson and "in a very sarcastic manner" replied "oh, Jack, you have gone far enough, you have trampled on us too much already, and now we have got you fast, and mean to hold you, and your lives are in danger every moment you remain in this city. You are outlaws and villains every one of you."[59]

55. Ibid.

56. Speer, *Life of Lane*, 143.

57. John "Jack" Henderson later served as the official printer at the Lecompton constitutional convention. He was found guilty by an investigating committee of fraudulently adding proslavery votes to the Delaware Crossing returns during the Lecompton Constitution referendum in 1858 and left Kansas Territory for Colorado. Calvin W. Gower, "Gold Fever in Kansas Territory: Migration to the Pike's Peak Gold Fields, 1858–1860," 71–72. On the other hand, historian James Malin described Lucien Eastin as "certainly one of the ablest men in territorial Kansas journalism," who offered a conservative proslavery voice. Malin, "Judge Lecompte and the 'Sack of Lawrence,'" 474.

58. *Kansas Weekly Herald*, November 21, 1857.

59. Ibid.

Lane's concern for Kansas was deadly serious. Perhaps his inflammatory rhetoric was spurred in part by a mental condition. However, while critics have looked at Lane's words as evidence of a dangerous and unstable mind, the restraint he also showed in this episode cannot be ignored. He did not attempt to turn the crowd into an actual mob against proslavery figures, even though some of his enemies, like Henderson, were in the audience. He wanted to draw up political and moral opposition—or, more correctly, outrage—against the Lecompton Constitution. In fact, after laying out his condemnation of the Lecompton convention and its members, and advocating violence against them, Lane looked to his audience and concluded, "Others will now speak to you and will differ in my views. I thank you and hope you will listen to them as to me."[60] Even if this was an obligatory or insincere acknowledgment of his political opponents, it is compelling evidence that he nonetheless respected the forum of open political discussion and understood there were limits to his own actions.

Lane continued to urge community officials to press the governor to call the territorial legislature into session. He promised to back the Topeka movement if the governor failed in the matter.[61] On November 28, a majority of the free-state legislators met in Lawrence and sent a petition to acting governor Frederick Stanton—who had been a proslavery politician in Tennessee—asking for a special session in order to prevent violence in the territory.[62] Appended to the petition was the endorsement of George Brown, Charles Robinson, James Lane, and "upwards of one hundred other leading citizens of Kansas," who wished, with respect, to join their elected representatives in requesting a legislative session.[63]

Around the first of December, Lane attended a large gathering at Stockton Hall in Leavenworth. After one conservative free-state man denounced Lane's actions and radical speeches as dangerous to the cause, Lane rose before the crowd to respond. At that moment, John Speer pushed his way through the audience and grabbed his arm. Leaning over to his friend, Lane was told that Stanton had indeed ordered the legislature into special session.[64] With this information, Lane turned on the audience with even greater energy. "Great God!" he cried out. "I am amazed at the cowardice around me; but I have the honor to announce to the weak-

60. Ibid.
61. Stephenson, *Political Career of Lane*, 90–91.
62. Stampp, *America in 1857*, 161.
63. *Herald of Freedom*, December 5, 1857.
64. A copy of Stanton's proclamation can be found in the *Herald of Freedom*, December 5, 1857, and Speer, *Life of Lane*, 145–46.

kneed, timid Free-State men, trembling in fear of their lives and property, and to the hell-hounds of slavery, chuckling over their timidity, that STAN-TON HAS CALLED THE LEGISLATURE!" "There is no devil too vigilant," he declared, "and no hell too hot for the tyrants and oppressors of Kansas!"[65]

On December 2, Lane took part in a delegate convention in Lawrence. He served as chairman of the committee on resolutions and reported a motion that denounced the Lecompton "swindle" and declared—apparently inspired by the American Revolution—that:

> we utterly repudiate said Constitution, framed at Lecompton, that it is an instrument hostile to the popular will, and appealing to the God of Justice and humanity for the rectitude of our intentions, we do solemnly enter into a league and covenant with each other, that we shall NEVER, under any circumstances, permit the said Constitution, so passed, and NOT SUBMIT-TED, to be the organic law for the State of Kansas, but do pledge our lives, fortunes and sacred honor in ceaseless hostility to the same.[66]

Numerous voices called for Lane, and he addressed the crowd with his usual flare and passion. He described the free-state force in Kansas as fielding "18,000 stern and brave men, tried and true, who are ready to face any danger, and suffer any consequences, so they secure the great boon of freedom for which they have been so long contending." Lane also demonstrated a consistency in belief and principle that his critics have ignored. As he spoke in support of the resolutions, Lane defended the principle behind the Kansas-Nebraska Act. "By the programme contained in the resolutions, just adopted," he stated, "we propose to vindicate that distinctive principle incarnated in the Kansas-Nebraska Bill, which allows the people to govern themselves."[67] Even as Lane had officially broken from the Democratic Party, had moved toward the Republican fold, and had come to urge a greater resistance to the expansion of slavery as a whole, he maintained the respect for democracy that he had held from the beginning. He had given up on the Democratic Party's ability or willingness to protect popular sovereignty, but he had not abandoned the principle.

The legislature met on December 7 and the new free-state members quickly took control. With the governor behind them, the body rejected the December 21 ratification election and scheduled a new one for January 4, 1858—the same day representatives under the Lecompton Constitution

65. Speer, *Life of Lane*, 145.
66. *Herald of Freedom*, December 5, 1857.
67. Ibid.

were to be elected. This second vote would not merely decide whether the Lecompton Constitution would be accepted "with" or "without" slavery, but would also decide the fate of the document as a whole. Stanton wrote to the Buchanan administration explaining his decision to call the legislature into session. However, unhappy with the governor's role in scheduling a second ratification vote, the administration promptly fired him.[68] Stanton was the fifth governor in three years to fall victim to Kansas political turmoil.

On December 21, proslavery Kansans went to the polls to vote on the Lecompton Constitution. The overwhelming majority of free-state men stayed home. A total of 6,266 votes were recorded in favor of the constitution with slavery, while 569 votes accepted the constitution without slavery. Later accounts estimated that as many as 2,720 of the votes "with slavery" were fraudulent.[69]

Following the first Lecompton referendum, free-state delegates met in Lawrence to debate participation in the January 4 election of representatives under the Lecompton Constitution. The rescheduled vote on the whole constitution was the same day, and some free-state men believed that electing men under a constitution one simultaneously rejected was hypocritical and counterproductive. Lane became the leader of this faction. During the two-day assembly, word spread that Missourians again threatened the safety of Kansas. On December 16, the free-state-led legislature had passed a bill organizing the territory's militia. Lane was elected major general. Taking the field, Lane led around two hundred men into a fortified position in expectation of attack. Although no attack materialized, Lane's supporters apparently made use of the excitement and fear of proslavery aggression in Lawrence to turn the convention against the January referendum. Conservative free-state men George Brown and Charles Robinson later accused Lane of carrying out a "characteristic trick" and "artful ruse" by intensifying free-state fears in order to oppose the January legislator election. Following their failure to convince the assembly to vote for candidates under the Lecompton Constitution, the conservatives broke away and held their own meeting in the *Herald of Freedom* building. This faction urged participation in the January 4 election as well and endorsed a platform of candidates. Decades later Robinson described Lane returning to Lawrence "after his ruse" very content "thinking he had obtained a great victory." But when he learned that a majority in Lawrence endorsed the

---

68. Etcheson, *Bleeding Kansas*, 157–58; Smith, *The Presidency of James Buchanan*, 41.
69. Charles Robinson, *The Kansas Conflict*, 374; Wilder, *The Annals of Kansas*, 155.

conservative ticket, Lane acquiesced and backed the January 4 balloting. It is unclear whether Lane and his men intentionally spread rumors of a Missouri invasion to disrupt the Lawrence meeting. Although decades after the fact both Brown and Robinson were convinced Lane had masterminded the scare, contemporary editions of Brown's *Herald of Freedom* did not question the authenticity of the threat or accuse Lane of trickery. Two days after the Lawrence meeting, Brown's newspaper reported news of military action from across the territory, explaining, "Persons are marching forward from all parts of the Territory to the scene of excitement, and the danger is imminent that the contest will become general." A week later, the *Herald* reported that "our original statement two weeks ago as to the origin of the difficulties seems to be nearly correct," and that tensions surrounding claim disputes and the *"war element,* on both sides" threatened "to involve the country in a civil war."[70] In short, at the time George Brown and others believed that Missourians had indeed threatened Kansas.

In February 1858 the *Herald of Freedom* copied a story from the *Providence Post,* describing Lane's warning of an imminent attack as a "trick" to turn the Lawrence convention against the January 4 election: "He didn't want any reinforcements. He hadn't rode down four horses. He hadn't hurried and wasn't jaded. He had not seen any fighting, or any dragoons, although, before leaving Fort Scott, and as an excuse for leaving, he had heard that they were coming. . . . So the trick was exposed." Rather than give credence to the story, however, Brown's newspaper ridiculed it. The *Herald* called the *Post* "an ultra Democratic journal," which was "disposed at all times to color

---

70. Samuel Tappan complained to a friend that "Our political affairs have changed very much since you were here. Then it was a firm and manly adherence to the Topeka organization. Now it is a game of chance, a dependence upon the honesty of John Calhoun for success. . . . Having gained the control of the Functional Legislature, it is now considered necessary to take possession of the organization wh[ich] is an offshoot from that [Lecompton Constitution], and wh[ich] is threatening to take its place. So our free state party run the risk of getting it, by voting under the Lecompton voting swindle." Tappan criticized Lane and Charles Robinson for advocating this path. Lane, though supporting the referendum on the constitution, came to oppose participating in the election of Lecompton officials. Samuel F. Tappan to Gen. Thomas W. Higginson, December 14, 1857, Thomas W. Higginson Collection, Kansas State Historical Society, Topeka. Stephenson, *Political Career of Lane,* 93. *Herald of Freedom,* December 26, 1857; also see J. H. Lane to Genl. A. W. Philips, December 17, 1857, James Abbott Collection, Kansas State Historical Society, Topeka. Charles Robinson, *The Kansas Conflict,* 375–77. The *Herald of Freedom,* January 2, 1858, states: "Gen. Lane is giving the State ticket a reluctant support. He regrets the action of the Delegate Convention; thinks it was ill-advised, and would have preferred to have 'pitched in,' and is determined to do so for himself." *Herald of Freedom,* December 26, 1857, January 2, 1857.

the facts in regards to Kansas affairs." "We only publish it to let our friends at home see what Democratic journalists in the East publish at our expense," Brown wrote. "Of course the story is a gross exaggeration, but it will do at this distance from the event to laugh over."[71] George Brown may have become one of Lane's greatest critics, but many of his accusations did not appear until well after events they purport to describe.

Lane reluctantly supported participation in the January 4 election, though he had attended a meeting in Topeka on December 28 that passed resolutions opposing participation.[72] However, only two days later he urged his friends to go forward in voting, realizing that if free-state men were to go to the polls, the effort should be unanimous.

> We have concluded to go into the Election on Monday—It is confidently expected that you will have *good* and *true* men as candidates for the legislature and elect them—Men that will never qualify under the Lecompton Swindle—
>
> By pursuing this course we can strangle the infernal thing—if a corrupt Congress should accept it—
>
> It is hoped that not a single vote will be lost against the Constitution[73]

On January 4 Kansas voters overwhelmingly rejected the Lecompton Constitution; proslavery settlers for the most part boycotted the election.[74] The final tally recorded 138 votes for the constitution with slavery, 24 for the constitution without slavery, while 10,226 votes were cast against the constitution as a whole.[75] The controversial election of officers under the Lecompton Constitution also took place. The entire free-state ticket was elected, placing them firmly in charge of the territorial government.[76]

After this second referendum, no one could legitimately deny that a solid majority in Kansas opposed the Lecompton Constitution. Former governors Walker and Stanton had rejected the Lecompton effort and new governor James W. Denver, who stepped into office on December 21, urged President

71. Ibid., February 27, 1858.

72. Stephenson, *Political Career of Lane*, 92.

73. Lane to O. C. Brown, Charles A. Foster, Col. Williams, and other citizens of Osawatomie, December 30, 1857, Charles A. Foster Collection, Kansas State Historical Society, Topeka.

74. McPherson, *Battle Cry of Freedom*, 166.

75. Ibid.; David Zarefksy, *Lincoln, Douglas and Slavery: In the Crucible of Public Debate*, 12. John Speer gave the total of votes for the constitution "without slavery" as 23; Speer, *Life of Lane*, 147.

76. Stephenson, *Political Career of Lane*, 92.

Buchanan against submitting the constitution to Congress. At this point even Dr. J. H. Stringfellow, the notorious proslavery editor of the *Squatter Sovereign*, was willing to throw in the towel. In a letter to the *Washington Union*, he opposed the passage of the Lecompton Constitution, saying that the future of Kansas "is settled against the South by immigration." But Buchanan felt heavy pressure from Southern Democrats in Congress, who wanted a proslavery constitution for Kansas. South Carolina Senator James Hammond asked, "If Kansas is *driven out of the Union for being a Slave State*, can any Slave State remain in it with honor?" On February 2, Buchanan sent the constitution to Congress. He stated that Kansas "is at this moment as much a slave state as Georgia or South Carolina."[77]

James Lane's actions in 1857 directly corresponded to events in Kansas. Upon his return to the territory in the spring, he had peacefully associated with notable proslavery figures in business ventures. Only when he feared that proslavery actions threatened democratic rights did he call for blood. And the events that led to his more radical rhetoric and actions—the attempt by proslavery officials to force the ratification of the Lecompton Constitution—also drove other men of impeccable Democratic credentials, such as Stephen Douglas, into a political battle with the Democratic administration and Southern Democrats. New factions within the Free State Party ranks took shape, and though Lane often stood on the more radical side of the party, he repeatedly acquiesced to the will of the majority. Still, his words during this year have greatly contributed to his reputation as a fanatic. His recommendation that Lecompton officials should be chased away or killed certainly presents an ignoble image. Yet, his behavior is not particularly surprising, as Lane perceived the Lecompton delegates as criminals.

The fact that countless other Democrats turned against proslavery and administration policies demonstrates that his political positions, if not his means of action, were not abnormal. His calls for violence and his general extremist image have, understandably, obscured his commitment to his principles. It has caused most writers to overlook the fact that his extreme rhetoric represented not a change in values, or a selfish grab for power, but rather an escalation of tactics. Drastic measures were needed, he believed, to overcome proslavery obstruction of the democratic process.

---

77. Ibid., 93; Nevins, *The Emergence of Lincoln*, vol. 1, 269. Stringfellow is quoted in Davis, *Kansas: A History*, 70. Hammond is quoted in McPherson, *Battle Cry of Freedom*, 166. Zornow, *Kansas*, 78; Smith, *The Presidency of James Buchanan*, 42.

6

Lane and the Leavenworth Constitution, 1858

"I doubt not some plan will be adopted by which the Lecompton Constitution and Government can be laid aside, and the Leavenworth Constitution and Government substituted, without in the slightest degree disturbing the peace of the country."

In the spring of 1858, the battle over the Lecompton Constitution was for the most part transferred to the halls of the U.S. Congress. Free-state Kansans feared the possibility that the proslavery plan would be forced upon them. James Lane, though still animated against local proslavery officials, gained confidence in Free State Party control of the territory and foresaw a peaceful conclusion. His tactics to prevent a fracture of the Free State Party and to construct a new state constitution led to renewed accusations of inconsistency and opportunism. Still, as before, Lane had only crafted his words and actions in response to threats to his efforts for the admission of Kansas into the Union as a free state.

After the January elections, Lane returned to military affairs. The legislature in its 1858 session renewed its effort to organize the militia. Governor James W. Denver, who within days of entering Kansas expressed his disgust with the territory, quickly stood in opposition to what he termed the "Abolition" legislature. He immediately vetoed the militia bill, but the free-state-dominated legislature overrode him. On January 15, Lane sent a report to the legislature about problems in the southern part of the territory. It recorded his maneuvers in the field during the previous two months, including the events surrounding the scare of another Missouri invasion in December. He closed with the explanation that "the object of the organization provided for in the law of Dec. 17th was the protection of the people of Kansas, and as the action had was indispensable in that direction, it is hoped it will meet your hearty approval." Governor Denver did not meet Lane's actions with "hearty approval." When Lane ordered the organization of the Kansas militia in February, Denver issued a proclamation calling the act "illegal, without authority of law, and on the part of 'J. H. Lane' a usurpation of power." The governor warned of the trouble that would ensue "if one turbulent man is thus allowed to set up a military dictatorship over the civil authority and squander the public money at pleasure."[1]

Denver's criticism struck a nerve in Lane. He published a "Card," dated March 16, 1858, reviewing his experience with the last two presidential administrations: "By President Pierce and his myrmidons, I was denounced as a traitor and indicted for high treason. . . . By Mr. Buchanan I have been charged as a rebel and a 'military leader of most turbulent and dangerous character.'" Accusations by both presidents, Lane announced, had been refuted. He then responded to Denver's criticism of recklessness, stating that his actions had been overseen by the territorial legislature. As for the idea of a military dictatorship, Lane explained that "upon four different occasions I have been invested with the chief command of the military forces of the people of Kansas, and that immediately after the emergency ceased which called them into the field, that command was voluntarily surrendered into their hands."[2]

1. Denver was sworn in as governor on December 21, 1857. On January 4, 1858, he wrote to his wife: "The Legislature was to meet here today but there was not a quorum and did not organize. In a day or two I suppose they will be fairly under way, and then you will see how I will get along with an Abolition Legislature. I am greatly in hopes that the whole thing will be closed up in this month and let me off. If they will only let me turn over the government to some of them in four or five weeks, I will give them a pledge never to put my foot inside of their Territory again. Confound the place it seems to have been cursed of God and man." James W. Denver to My Dear Wife [Louisa Denver], January 4, 1858, James W. Denver Collection, Kansas State Historical Society, Topeka. Stephenson, *Political Career of Lane*, 93–94; "Report of Gen. J. H. Lane on the Troubles in the Southern Party of the Territory," printed in *Lawrence Republican,* January 21, 1858.

2. Lane's "Card" published in *Lawrence Republican,* March 18, 1858. Though Lane repeatedly highlighted his conflict with federal and territorial authorities during the Kansas struggle, he never resisted federal military forces. Lane separated his disdain of specific officials from the U.S. government as a whole. Colonel Daniel H. Horne recalled

Turning the tables on the governor, Lane wrote that Denver had "arrogantly usurped and ruthlessly trampled under foot the Legislative department of the government of a free people, and in violation of his official oath and duty seeks to unite in his own person, and thus control, the power of the sword and purse of the people to crush out their liberties." To make sure his point was clear, Lane scoffed at all of Denver's charges and arraigned "'J. W. DENVER' before This Country, And Do Denounce And Brand Him As A Calumniator, Perjurer And Tyrant."[3]

Lane referred to Denver's reputation as a duelist, remarking that "his hands reek[ed] with the untimely shed blood of his fellow man—having won from his friends the soubriquet of 'butcher,'—a fit appointee of the oligarchical Administration, which disgraces the nation by its criminal efforts to enslave a Free People!" Implying that Denver wished to draw him into mortal combat, Lane "respectfully demand[ed] that there may be no interference on the part of my friends."[4] Nothing came from the war of words.

Around this time, Lane appears to have led a short-lived secret society dedicated to protecting free-state interests through violence. The group, known as the "Danites," had a mysterious origin—one that many of its members could not explain.[5] Lane's political rival, Charles Robinson, later wrote of being initiated into a group that he later assumed was the Danites. He accused Lane of attempting to use the group to unjustly attack proslavery settlements, and called him a monomaniac who was, "like all timid men with arbitrary power, cruel and bloodthirsty."[6] James Redpath, an abolitionist newspaper editor and onetime supporter of Lane, turned against him after his experience with the Danites. In the spring of 1858 Redpath wrote:

> Lane organized a club of Danites in Doniphan County. I became a member of it. Although he could have attended it, and was expected to attend it, he attempted, on the second night of its meeting, to make me the agent

---

in 1879, "Some claim that Lane was opposed to Government troops, at the time the pro-slavery government employed them against Kansas. . . . That is not true. Lane always respected the Government troops. . . . I know there was not a disloyal hair in Lane's head, even when loyalty to the Government was almost a crime against Kansas." "Address by Col. Daniel H. Horne," in Charles S. Gleed, ed., *The Kansas Memorial: A Report of the Old Settlers' Meeting Held at Bismarck Grove, Kansas, September 15th and 16th, 1879*, 175.

3. *Lawrence Republican*, March 18, 1858.

4. Ibid.

5. A recent publication on the Danites credits their origins to the Wakarusa War in 1855. Lane seems to have become involved in the fall of 1857. Todd Mildfelt, *The Secret Danites: Kansas' First Jayhawkers*, 1–12.

6. Charles Robinson, *The Kansas Conflict*, 380.

to induce the club to kill Bob Kelly. . . . I never hated Lane till he asked me to do this deed. I did indeed despise him from the bottom of my soul, but did not believe him capable of a scheme as diabolical as to involve a young man, without any cause, in a criminal act of private revenge. It was so cowardly, contemptible, and hellish that I left him without saying a word.[7]

Further, Redpath accused Lane of threatening to use the Danites to assassinate Denver if the personal quarrel came to the brink of violence.[8]

Nothing seems to have resulted from these reported threats, and so far there is no evidence that Lane carried out or was involved in any secret violent acts. Surviving Danite correspondence from Lane mimicked logistic military orders he openly issued as a commanding officer under legislative authority.[9] Still, secondary accounts of Lane's supposed violent intentions do exist. Charles Robinson recalled that at his initiation into the Danites Lane rose and stated that "he had ordered General _____ to strike at Leavenworth, General _____ to strike at Atchison, General _____ to strike at Kickapoo, and other places were to be struck by other generals."[10] Lane supposedly closed his order with the words, "It now remains for Lawrence to say what shall be done with Lecompton." Robinson claimed to challenge Lane's plans by demanding to know "by whose authority this general massacre was to be made." Lane referred to the Military Board. Robinson remembered refuting Lane's explanation and giving notice "that whoever attempted to execute any such orders would have [Robinson] to fight."[11] As evidence, Robinson provided a copy of an order signed by Lane, which detailed certain plans upon proslavery communities:

7. James Repdath quoted in *Kansas Weekly Herald,* May 29, 1858, and Charles Robinson, *The Kansas Conflict,* 380–81. Redpath's sudden hatred toward Lane is a bit surprising. Apparently it was not the supposed radical or violent nature of Lane that repulsed Redpath, for the young editor wrote glowingly of John Brown and his violent attacks against proslavery interests and people in later years. Instead, it may have been the perception that Lane was advocating violence for personal means rather than on principle or for loftier goals.

8. *Kansas Weekly Herald,* May 29, 1858; *Herald of Freedom,* June 5, 1858.

9. A copy of a Danite order dated March 27, 1858, and signed by Lane reads: "Sir: There is business of the greatest importance now transpiring here and I would like it much if you would come with the utmost dispatch and bring fifty men with you. You will go to the president of the association treasury and draw as much money as you think will pay the expense, but that will not be much, as you will be traveling through thickly settled places. Bring two pieces of artillery and the ammunition and baggage wagons." Found in Mildfelt, *The Secret Danites,* 65–66.

10. Robinson omits the generals' names.

11. Charles Robinson, *The Kansas Conflict,* 379.

General: The bearers of this, Colonel Leinhart and his friend Dickinson, have some idea of colonizing Kickapoo. If you could furnish them forty or fifty hardy pioneers who could bear the exposure of such a settlement, I am clear that it would be attended with good results to Kansas and the cause of freedom. Leinhart and Dickinson are the men to put through without flinching anything they may undertake. I trust you will give this matter your earnest and immediate attention, as Kickapoo should be colonized at an early day.[12]

The order makes no mention of attacking or killing anyone. Conspiracy theorists (perhaps including Robinson, who saw everything Lane did as dangerous) may assume that the letter was written in a simple code, with "pioneers" and "settlement" meaning "soldiers" and "attack." Yet, there is little to take from such assumption—Lane had openly advocated, indeed had led, attacks against proslavery forces in the past. Not only would such a code be unnecessary, but also if Lane intended to use force against proslavery settlements, he would not have hesitated to say so.

Like much of Lane's time in Kansas, his involvement within the Danites is a complex and bitterly contested issue. His critics have pointed to it as evidence of his radical and dangerous nature. His defenders explain that it was simply another avenue of fighting for free-state interests. What seems clear is that little came about from the Danites. Free-state settler and former Danite James Legate later wrote that the society "had not much more than a year's duration, because Lane was continually calling meetings, and would invariably have a long paper of 'whereas' Bill Smith, a 'proslavery hell hound,' had been guilty of stealing free-state men's horses, or burning some one's house, or some crime of less grade, and then, 'Therefore, resolved,' that Bill Smith shall be brought before this body of men, his case investigated and adjudicated, and the decree shall be executed by one or more men appointed by the commander of this council, or of some subcouncil." Legate complained, "Lane's 'whereases' killed the society."[13]

During the period in which Lane may have associated with the "secret" society, more pressing political interests came to a head. Free State men briefly reendorsed the Topeka Constitution, but ultimately it receded into the background as leading free-state officials abandoned its fold for the recognized territorial government they now controlled.[14] The future of the Lecompton Constitution before Congress became the most pressing mat-

12. Ibid.
13. James Legate quoted in Stephenson, *Political Career of Lane*, 91–92n56.
14. Stephenson, *Political Career of Lane*, 94–95.

ter. Lane made headlines by doing an apparent about-face upon Lecompton's potential success. In Elwood the opponent of the Lecompton document was heard to say that "passage of the Lecompton Constitution . . . would not even create a ripple on the surface of Kansas affairs."[15] He further spoke in positive terms about Kansas and Missouri relations. One account reported:

> To the people of Missouri he desired to say one word. For years they had declared that Jim Lane was an abolitionist. He denied it. It was his desire to cultivate friendly intercourse with them, and claimed them as his brethren . . . .
> It was now time that unfriendly feelings between the two States should cease. They had common interests at stake and should let bygones be bygones. Missouri should take Kansas by the hand and bid her God speed; the time had passed by when there should be any difficulty between them; it was to their interest to have peace. He tendered to Missouri the olive branch of peace, and thanked her citizens for their attendance.[16]

People on both sides of the Kansas debate were shocked. The proslavery *Kansas Weekly Herald* called it Lane's "New Dodge." The *Herald of Freedom* predicted that eastern newspapers would complain that Lane had "apostacised" and "turned traitor." Yet Lane's approach was understandable, and many agreed with him. Robert Elliott, founder of the *Kansas Free State,* wrote to his sister that free-state men "regard the Lecompton Constitution as verbally defeated, and even if it pass Congress, it won't give us much trouble." Like Lane, Elliott believed that "in one month after it is attempted to be put in operation by its framers it will be scuttled and set adrift without captain, pilot, engineer or fireman." George Brown, of the *Herald of Freedom,* also defended Lane's stance as his own, writing, "We are conscious that a class of newspapers in Kansas and out of it, will give us 'fits' because we are of opinion that the passage of the Lecompton Constitution through Congress will not produce civil war. When their fury is spent on us they will annihilate Gen. Lane."[17]

The Lecompton Constitution continued to generate controversy in the U.S. Congress. Lane's comments did not support the document, but were

15. Quoted in the *Herald of Freedom,* March 20, 1858.
16. Ibid.
17. *Kansas Weekly Herald,* March 27, 1858; *Herald of Freedom,* March 20, 1858; Robert Gaston Elliott to his sister, Mary Jane Elliott, February 20, 1858, in Carolyn Berneking, ed., "A Look at Early Lawrence: Letters from Robert Gaston Elliott," 287.

meant to reassure his audience that passage of that constitution would not destroy free-state hopes or interests. Further, Lane's speech in Elwood focused on the future of railroads into the territory.[18] Months before, the "Address to the American People on the Affairs of Kansas," written by the Grasshopper Falls committee chaired by Lane, had taken a similar message, linking the interests of Kansas and Missouri and promising peace should Missourians leave Kansas political matters alone. The success of a railroad into Kansas benefited and depended upon Missouri. Political conflict between the two states would interfere with economic development. Within this context, Lane's "olive branch" toward Missouri was not remarkable—on the contrary, it was pragmatic.

Lane's confidence in the face of Lecompton's passage stood upon free-state power within the territorial legislature. In an April 29 letter to various free-state men concerning the future of Kansas statehood, Lane specifically explained this confidence. He acknowledged his steadfast opposition to the Lecompton movement, relating that "I favored the plan of breaking up the Lecompton Constitutional Convention by hanging its members, and therefore under no circumstances could I favor any movement originating from or growing out of the action of that body." But the constitution's passage through Congress would not be a problem. He advised that the people of Kansas meet immediately after the Lecompton Constitution passed, assuring free-staters that he had no doubt "some plan will be adopted by which the Lecompton Constitution and Government can be laid aside, and the Leavenworth Constitution and Government substituted, without in the slightest degree disturbing the peace of the country."[19] Thus, Lane believed that Kansas free-state legislators should simply, and quietly, replace the Lecompton Constitution after statehood.

The Leavenworth Constitution Lane referred to was the new effort in the territory to provide Congress with a document that was hoped to overcome both the Lecompton Constitution's and the Topeka Constitution's shortcomings.[20] As he had in past conventions, Lane played an instrumental part in the Leavenworth movement. His first notable role was preventing the convention from falling apart. At the first meeting in

18. The *Kansas Weekly Herald* explained: "The editor of the St. Joseph Journal recently went to hear Lane make a Railroad speech at Elwood." *Kansas Weekly Herald,* March 27, 1858.

19. Correspondence printed in the *Lawrence Republican,* May 13, 1858.

20. Most Kansans rejected the Lecompton convention as illegitimate while many in Congress rejected the Topeka movement as illegitimate.

Minneola, a dispute over the convention's location threatened to break up the effort entirely. Land speculation around Minneola—with the expectation of it becoming the capital—caused a great deal of excitement and consternation among the representatives. Considering the problem of fraud and corruption among previous territorial officials, a majority of delegates favored relocating the convention to a more neutral town.[21] Lane, serving as convention president, favored relocation. When those representatives with land interests objected, and even suggested they might bolt from the Free State Party, Lane delivered a masterful speech to maintain party unity.[22] Standing before the convention, he boomed that if "in the momentous and supreme hour of the party's struggle they were bound to leave it on account of a few paltry shares in Minneola, then let them go—and go to hell!"[23] With that, the assembly agreed to move to Leavenworth. But disagreement within the convention hardly subsided.

Upon meeting in Leavenworth, Lane retained his presidency and committees were assigned. However, he soon stepped down from his position due to "prejudice existing against him," he explained, "even among some good free-state men." Lane still served as a delegate in the convention, and weighed in on certain controversial matters. No issue was more controversial within the convention than black suffrage. As with the Topeka Constitution, slavery was outlawed. Unlike with the previous free-state movement, free black exclusion from the state—known as the "black law"—was not an issue. Isaac Goodnow wrote to a friend that the "Black Law of the Topeka Constitution, made as an offering to the Slave power, has no place in this." Though Goodnow mistakenly labeled the "black law" as part of the Topeka Constitution, the law was nonetheless a significant part of the Topeka movement. The Leavenworth movement had a decidedly more progressive tone. With a free black presence accepted in Kansas, some delegates voiced their concern over black rights and citizenship. During the final review of the constitution on April 1, a delegate from Leavenworth "moved to insert the word 'white' before the word 'male'" in the section on "Elective Franchise." Lane made a motion to send the matter to a select committee. His motion was defeated. Another

21. For a contemporary description of the "Minneola Swindle," see Isaac T. Goodnow to Friend Sherman, April 1 and 3, 1858, Isaac Goodnow Collection, Kansas State Historical Society, Topeka.

22. Connelley, *The Life of Preston B. Plumb*, 80.

23. Quoted in Etcheson, *Bleeding Kansas*, 178.

delegate moved to table the whole subject. Lane and thirty-four other delegates supported the motion to table the effort, but were defeated.[24]

Lane had been a vocal proponent of the "black law" during the Topeka movement. His apparent shift now to oppose stringent language limiting black rights in Kansas seemed out of character. Yet, some evidence of Lane's thoughts during the convention illustrates his purpose behind what appeared to be a surprising reversal. A newspaper reported that "Gen. Lane said he belonged to the Abolition wing of the Free State party, and he appealed to them not to agitate this question, which might seriously distract the party." Fearing that the convention may again divide, he suggested that "[w]hen the question came up, and any negro asked to vote, then would be time enough to agitate the suffrage question."[25]

Lane's claim to be part of the "Abolition wing" triggered a round of criticism and ridicule across Kansas. The *White Cloud Kansas Chief* announced that Lane "must consider the Free State people of Kansas an arrant set of fools, whom he can wheedle about at his pleasure." "But it does appear to us that he would secure a more substantial popularity, (for popularity and honors is all he is after,)" the story continued, "if he would pursue a straight forward course, and not profess a different set of principles for every different locality—a Pro-Slavery man on the border; a moderate man, in a moderate community; and a radical Abolitionist in a Convention of that sentiment."[26] The *Herald of Freedom* ran a satirical story on Lane, tracking his recent speeches and showing what appeared to be inconsistent views, and stating that "it will be a source of pleasure to learn that so distinguished a person as Gen. Lane has at last come up to the *Abolition* standard" and all of its more radical viewpoints.[27]

Lane's reason for claiming to be part of the "Abolition wing" of the party was practical—although it made him appear hypocritical. He had not

24. *National Era*, April 15, 1858, quoted in Stephenson, *Political Career of Lane*, 95; *Kansas Weekly Herald*, April 3, 1858; Isaac T. Goodnow to Friend Sherman, April 1 and 3, 1858, Isaac Goodnow Collection, Kansas State Historical Society, Topeka. Lane and most other midwestern settlers had supported black exclusion laws. Due to sufficient opposition within the convention, the Topeka Constitution did not include the "black law." However, a referendum on the "black law" was attached to the Topeka Constitution. "The Topeka Movement," 145. Journal, Leavenworth Constitutional Convention, April 1, 1858, Kansas State Historical Society, Topeka.

25. Quoted in the *White Cloud Kansas Chief*, reprinted in the *Herald of Freedom*, May 1, 1858.

26. *White Cloud Kansas Chief*, reprinted in the *Herald of Freedom*, May 1, 1858, and *Kansas Weekly Herald*, May 8, 1858.

27. *Herald of Freedom*, May 8, 1858.

adopted abolitionist viewpoints. Instead, fearful of the convention split-
ting along conservative and progressive lines, Lane attempted to identify
with and thus appeal to the important abolitionist contingent. His use of
the word "Abolition" was his chief mistake, for his advice following this
identification was quite conservative. He asked the radicals—those with
abolitionist interests—"not to agitate the question" of black suffrage. His
primary objective was to maintain party and convention integrity by trying to delay the suffrage issue until *after* the constitution passed.

Lane regularly used the oratorical tactic of identifying with his audience. In Chicago in the spring of 1856, as he labored to draw in support for
Kansas, Lane appealed to the Illinois audience's pride, recalling how he
fought alongside Illinoisan Colonel W. H. Bissell, a Republican gubernatorial candidate:

> I was side by side with your gallant and noble Bissell at Buena Vista and
> in Congress. I wish that I could describe to you the scene on the morn-
> ing preceeding [sic] that glorious battle. On a ridge stood Clay, Bissell,
> McKee, Hardin, and myself. Before us were twenty thousand armed ene-
> mies. It was a beautiful morning and the sun shone bright upon the pol-
> ished lances and muskets in the breeze. . . . Around us stood five ragged
> regiments of volunteers, two from Illinois, two from Indiana, and one
> from Kentucky, they were bone of your bone, blood of your blood, and
> it was only when you were near enough to look into their eyes that you
> could see the d—l was in them.[28]

Occasionally he made a stretch, or took some liberty, in linking himself
to his audience. Perhaps the most notable example regarded his birthplace. Kansas historian William Connelley explained that Lane "often
claimed Kentucky as his native State."[29] In fact, Lane mysteriously listed
Kentucky as his birthplace at the Topeka constitutional convention.[30] Connelley further states, "In the sketch of his life written by himself, he says
he was born on the bank of the Ohio river, but does not say upon which
bank."[31] The ambiguity, though frustrating to historians and some of
Lane's contemporaries, served him well as he stood before crowds—some
of which were Southern or sympathetic to the South.

28. *Chicago Daily Tribune,* June 2, 1856, in Webb Scrapbook, 13:8; also see Speer, *Life of Lane,* 103–4.
29. Connelley, *Lane: The "Grim Chieftain,"* 38.
30. A copy of the list of members can be found in "The Topeka Movement," 163–64.
31. Connelley, *Lane: The "Grim Chieftain,"* 38.

Overall, this tactic, like many others, demonstrated Lane's mastery of public speaking. Though gaining a reputation for wild, radical oratory in Kansas, Lane's speeches in Washington, D.C., and in eastern states were often marked by careful logic, a calm demeanor, and appealing wit. After attending one of Lane's speeches in Connecticut during the Civil War, one reporter noted that "great was the surprise of some present to find before them a man of fair proportions, of genteel appearance, of unobtrusive manners, instead of the rough and savage animal which the antiwar papers have seen fit to represent him." His speech "had no leading towards radicalism, [and] was well received throughout, and elicited hearty applause."[32] Lane did mold his appearance and behavior to conform to various audiences. But far from being a fault or vice, this trait helped Lane's career and his cause. Most importantly, though Lane's manner—and occasional details—may have shifted to better influence his audience, the interests and principles behind his speeches did not. It is this consistency of interest in a free state of Kansas and adherence to democratic principles that his critics have ignored.

Lane's claim of being part of the "Abolitionist wing" helps fuel the image of inconsistency, of contradiction, of a man shifting his "political sails to suit the time, place, and his need for money and political support."[33] However, the incident demonstrates Lane's interest in maintaining party unity. Lane was not a blind follower of the popular tide. In Leavenworth, as in virtually all of the free-state activities he had been involved in, Lane stepped forward as a leader. He labored to unite the Leavenworth assembly, even stepping down from its top position when he felt such an act was necessary to maintain peace. He did what he thought necessary to make the Leavenworth convention a success. His means of accomplishing this task appear contradictory, and do make Lane appear hypocritical. But the message and purpose behind his claim were practical. And they worked. The convention did not fracture. During the convention's final days, free-state delegate Isaac Goodnow wrote to a friend that "Gen. James H. Lane was the ruling spirit which directed & inspired the energies of the mass to the speedy formation of The People's Constitution, of Kansas." Rather than see Lane as a demagogue or opportunist, Goodnow explained that it was "with the greatest interest that I have carefully watched the labors, & the influence of this Wonderful Man!" He continued:

32. *Waterbury American,* quoted in Stephenson, *Political Career of Lane,* 161–62.
33. Gilmore, *Civil War on the Missouri-Kansas Border,* 65.

Sometimes, conflicting measures would throw into confusion the Convention & threaten dissolution. Then was the time for Lane to throw himself into the arena! A general appeal to the whole, with direct appeals to factious leaders rebuking one, & coaxing and this, the effect is astonishing! Explanations acknowledgements, &c, till the repulsive elements are fused & assimilated into a homogenous Mass, and all things soon found again with order & rapidity. He is the man for the boots, & fills a place in our history that no other man can. He can command any office is the gift of the People & will no doubt be sent to the U. S. Senate.[34]

The *White Cloud Kansas Chief* argued that Lane would gain more popularity by maintaining a more consistent path. The paper was both right and wrong. Lane's adaptation to audiences did leave him vulnerable to charges of hypocrisy. Yet, his adaptation served an important purpose, whether it was preventing free-state factionalism, or converting a hostile audience into supporters. This should not be construed to mean that Lane said only what his audiences wanted to hear. Instead, he carefully crafted his messages to best draw listeners to his side. In short, Lane's adaptation to audiences was a tactic designed to achieve his consistent objectives. And such adaptation was necessary, as the political minefield of Kansas Territory chewed up and destroyed a number of capable and previously successful men. By the time of the Leavenworth Constitution—less than four years after the creation of the territory—Kansas was under its fifth appointed governor.[35] Men who were unwilling or incapable of dealing with the competing interests in Kansas, through some measure of association or intimidation, had no future in the territory's political environment. Thus, as a creature both shaped by and designed for the controversy in Kansas, Lane thrived.

Though the convention did not crumble on the matter of black suffrage and the issue remained divisive, no change was made to the constitution's Election Franchise article. In fact, the Leavenworth Constitution remained silent on many racial issues. During the convention's final session on April

34. Isaac Goodnow to Friend Sherman, April 1 and 3, 1858, Issac Goodnow Collection, Kansas State Historical Society, Topeka.

35. The five appointed governors were, in order, Andrew Reeder, Wilson Shannon, John Geary, Robert Walker, and James Denver. Two other men served as acting governors in between the appointments: Daniel Woodson and Frederick Stanton. Thus, between July 1854 and April 1858 seven men had served as governor in the territory. Three more governors (one appointed and two acting) would serve before Kansas became a state in 1861. For more information, see Wilder, *The Annals of Kansas.*

3, some delegates, frustrated with the document's ambiguity on certain matters, qualified their support of the constitution. Caleb May stated that he signed the constitution "believing that it does not extend the right of suffrage to negroes." Four other delegates presented a statement that declared, "We sign this Constitution under protest for the reason that we believe a majority of our constituents are opposed to negro suffrage and the Emigration of free negroes to the State of Kansas—Believing this we feel entirely justified in our course."[36]

Far from solving the constitutional dilemma of Kansas, the Leaven-worth Constitution created more problems. First, it proved to be a failure in Congress. Many powerful men in Washington, D.C., including the pres-ident, continued to support the Lecompton Constitution. Second, the Leavenworth Constitution's ambiguity on racial matters left few satisfied. George Brown of the free-state *Herald of Freedom* predicted widespread opposition to the document because "it is neither 'fish, flesh nor fowl,' but it is all things to all men."[37] The apparent pro-black elements of the con-stitution drew opposition from voters. The proslavery *Kansas Weekly Her-ald* ridiculed any protection of black suffrage within the Leavenworth Constitution. "Let the Convention pass this clause, and attempt to enforce their Constitution upon the people," the *Herald* read, "and they will find the mass of the people are not prepared to allow a buck negro to walk up to the polls with a white man and vote."[38]

Lane struggled to defend the ambiguous nature of the constitution and to stem the negative reaction it received from various Kansans. He took a moderate position to maintain support for the constitution within the con-vention and in front of the public. He abandoned the strong support of the "black law" he had advocated during the Topeka movement. But he did not embrace black rights in Kansas. In Leavenworth, Lane, speaking in defense of the newly drafted constitution, reportedly used the Supreme Court's decision concerning the slave Dred Scott to prove that blacks were not citizens and thus could not vote.[39] Further, he referred to a letter by Sec-

36. Journal, Leavenworth Constitutional Convention, April 3, 1858, Kansas State Historical Society, Topeka.

37. *Herald of Freedom*, May 1, 1858.

38. *Kansas Weekly Herald*, April 3, 1858.

39. Ibid., April 24, 1858. Chief Justice Robert Taney delivered the Supreme Court's majority opinion on *Dred Scott v. John F. A. Sandford* in early 1857, setting off a national sensation. The plaintiff, Scott, sued for his freedom on the grounds that his master had taken him to a state designated as free by the Northwest Ordinance. Taney's decision was monumental in its handling of congressional authority over slavery in the territo-

retary of State Lewis Cass as further proof that blacks were not citizens, and as such could not vote. Cass wrote to Senator Henry Wilson that "[a] passport, being a certificate of citizenship, has never, since the formation of the Government, been granted to persons of color."[40]

Lane's arguments had little effect. Irish immigrants in Leavenworth heckled Lane and other speakers for the seemingly pro-black elements of the document. The proslavery *Kansas Weekly Herald* criticized the defense of the constitution as "a signal failure," and many strong antislavery and abolitionist settlers were similarly unimpressed. Though the Leavenworth Constitution was presented to Congress, it died quickly. Meanwhile, the Lecompton controversy continued to boil in the Senate until a compromise proposed by William English placed the Lecompton Constitution before Kansas voters in the summer. Kansans soundly rejected the measure, and the Lecompton Constitution finally passed away.[41]

The first few months of 1858 for James Lane had begun with continued excitement against leading proslavery figures, and especially the new territorial governor. Battling factionalism within Free State Party ranks, Lane had used his oratorical and political gifts to preserve the Leavenworth convention and put forth what he hoped was an acceptable plan for the people of Kansas and Congress. His efforts failed, and his actions during the convention brought further criticism of inconsistency and hypocrisy. Still some Kansans, like Isaac Goodnow, recognized Lane's commitment and value to the free-state cause. In the chaotic political environment of Kansas, Lane adjusted and adapted to new threats and new difficulties to achieve free statehood. However, his political career almost came to an early end in the early summer of 1858. In late May, Lane attended to more regular matters, and opened up a law office with James Christian in Lawrence. A newspaper advertisement for the business stated, "The Kansas struggle being

---

ries. For more information, see Don E. Fehrenbacher, *The Dred Scott Case: Its Significance in American Law and Politics.*

40. Letter quoted in *Herald of Freedom*, May 8, 1858.

41. Etcheson, *Bleeding Kansas*, 182; *Kansas Weekly Herald*, April 24, 1858; *Herald of Freedom*, May 8, 1858; Etcheson, *Bleeding Kansas*, 179; Wilder, *Annals of Kansas*, 186–88. The English Bill offered Kansas voters an incentive for voting for the Lecompton Constitution as well as providing a slight punishment for rejecting it. Kansas acceptance of the measure promised a substantial land grant as well as a percentage of government profits from an upcoming land sale. Kansas rejection of the measure meant a delay in statehood based upon a new population requirement. Critics of the bill argued that it was blackmail. Still, Kansas voters rejected the Lecompton Constitution and remained a territory for over two more years. Nevins, *The Emergence of Lincoln*, vol. 1, 297–301.

over, Mr. Lane will devote exclusively to the practice, and trusts by strict attention to business to receive a portion of the business of the people of Kansas."[42] He settled back into life in Lawrence to regroup at home and enjoy time with his family until statehood and state elections would draw him back into the public eye. But his personal life took a tragic detour on June 3, 1858, when a long-standing property dispute turned deadly.

42. *Lawrence Republican*, May 27, June 3, 1858.

7

Lane's Political Comeback, 1858–1861

"The writer seeks no leadership—asks no office, but simply desires to enjoy the right of free speech, and permission to labor as a private in the ranks of the great Jefferson Republican party of freedom."

An unfortunate personal matter nearly brought James Lane's life to an end in the summer of 1858. After a property dispute turned deadly, the backlash caused his virtual exile from public matters for almost a year. Yet the final push in Kansas for statehood and the establishment of the Republican Party in the territory drew him back with a vengeance. His embrace of the Republican Party was consistent with his previously espoused interests and principles, and clearly resulted from his experiences in Kansas. Emerging from what appeared a political grave, Lane sprang back into the political arena in time to stump for Abraham Lincoln's presidential election and push for his own election to the U.S. Senate.

The problem centered on Lane's doorstep, or at least land his home occupied. Lane and a fellow free-state Kansan, Gaius Jenkins, had become at odds over a land claim outside of Lawrence. The details and history of the property dispute are fairly confusing and Lane's friends and enemies argued for years, even after his death, over who was entitled to the land. In brief, Jenkins had claimed a portion of land west of town shortly after

Kansas was opened for settlement, and agreed to let a man named Edward Chapman settle there and begin making improvements to satisfy homestead laws. While Jenkins was away, Chapman apparently sold part of the property to the Lawrence township, without Jenkins's knowledge or approval. Jenkins protested this action, but was rebuffed by the town association. Chapman also sold a portion of the land to Lane in 1855, who, according to John Speer, was unaware of any dispute. When Lane learned that Jenkins felt cheated out of the land, he reportedly put forth a compromise and offered to sell part of his purchase to Jenkins. While Jenkins first agreed to the arrangement, he soon changed his mind. The two men took their respective cases to the General Land Office. Over the next two years, officials were unable to make a ruling. In late 1857, the land office in Lecompton directed local officials to gather more evidence. By the summer of 1858, neither Lane nor Jenkins had been awarded the claim.[1]

Tensions between the two men grew during the pending land case. In late 1856, while Lane was leading free-state militia forces around Kansas and his wife and children were in Indiana, Jenkins seized the property and planted his own set of crops. When Lane returned to Lawrence in 1857, he found that Jenkins had plowed over the grave of one of Lane's children, near the house. The small fence that had surrounded it was gone, leaving no trace of the grave. Lane, distraught, searched unsuccessfully for any sign of the coffin. He immediately suspected Jenkins of intentionally removing or plowing over his child's body, and told a friend, "Such a —— ghoul is not fit to live. If I was only certain that he dug up my child out of revenge upon me, I would kill him at first sight."[2] Jenkins may not have had anything to do with the grave's destruction, but the event heightened the animosity between the two men.

James Christian, Lane's law partner, claimed that while Jenkins was a "generous, whole-souled, warm friend," he also had a wild temper that was easily inflamed, particularly when he had been drinking, "a habit he frequently indulged in." Christian witnessed a confrontation between the two men in Lecompton that he believed demonstrated Jenkins's violent tendencies. During a discussion of the land dispute, someone made an off-the-cuff statement that Lane and Jenkins should "go out and fight it out." Jenkins immediately agreed, and suggested the men step outside and decide the case on the street. Lane stood up and fired a nasty glare toward

1. Speer, *Life of Lane*, 187–98; Collins, *Jim Lane*, 152–56.
2. Speer, *Life of Lane*, 214.

his rival. Recalling an incident in which Jenkins was detained by a slave during the summer of 1856, Lane declared, "Any man that would let a — – nigger take him prisoner need not talk to me about fighting!" Others stepped in between the two men before they came to blows.[3]

During the spring of 1858, a number of people heard Jenkins make threats against Lane.[4] The tension escalated when Jenkins began drawing water from a well on the property, inside Lane's fence. Lane locked up the gate to the property, but Jenkins found the well to be the best source of water for his own use and insisted that he had a right to it. Jenkins's hired man, Ray Greene, testified that he and Jenkins had each broken the gate down at least once before in order to draw water. On another occasion, Mary Lane confronted Jenkins when he approached the gate with an axe to force his way in. At the house alone, she took the axe from his hands and told him to return when her husband was home if he wished to press the matter. From then on, use of the well became the focus, though not the cause, of the dispute.[5]

On June 3 the ongoing conflict between Jenkins and Lane exploded. After Lane threatened and chased off Jenkins's hired man, Ray Greene, who tried to retrieve water from the well, Jenkins along with two relatives and Greene grabbed firearms, buckets, and an axe and marched off to the home. As they arrived, around one o'clock in the afternoon, Lane walked into his front yard to confront them. The group approached the gate, at which point Lane yelled at them to stop. When Jenkins began chopping down the gate, Lane ran into his house and returned with a shotgun. Again Lane yelled at Jenkins to stay out of his yard, threatening to shoot. Jenkins pushed his way through the broken fence and for a brief moment the two men stared at each other, separated by about thirty feet. Behind Jenkins, the three other men nervously readied themselves for action. The following events are unclear, but in a matter of seconds at least three gun blasts echoed across the town.[6] Lane fired his shotgun into Jenkins, killing him. Almost simultaneously, Jenkins's companions opened fire on Lane with their pistols. One bullet whizzed past Lane's head and another struck him

3. Letter from James Christian, Speer, *Life of Lane*, 212–13.
4. For instance, see testimonies of R. D. Nichols and James Walker in *Lawrence Republican*, June 24, 1858.
5. *Lawrence Republican*, June 24, 1858.
6. Lane believed that a total of five shots were exchanged—his single shotgun blast and four shots from his opponents. *Lawrence Republican*, March 17, 1859.

near the knee.[7] Frantically, he hobbled back into his house, while Jenkins's friends and family ran to the fallen man.[8]

Lane was immediately arrested and charged with murder. Jenkins's three accomplices were also detained. Local and national newspapers followed the developing reports. "No event has produced such excitement in our community," a correspondent to the *New York Times* wrote. "Some were for hanging Lane at once, and the mobocratic spirit was intense for a time."[9] A Lawrence resident on the scene wrote to his father that "some few justify Lane but the most condemn it as a foul murder." Although Jenkins's death and other recent episodes of violence cast a shadow over Kansas "which any where else would take a long time to remove," he concluded that within a few days "this will all be forgotten by the mass of the people."[10]

The trial focused on a number of factors. Was Jenkins armed? Most witnesses agreed that he did not have a firearm with him, but there was some question as to whether he still had possession of the axe as he advanced toward Lane. Another contentious point was who fired first. Lane's opponents argued that he fired the first shot. Yet, during the ensuing trial, two witnesses—including Sheriff Samuel Walker—testified that immediately after the incident Ray Greene admitted trying to shoot first. When the sheriff approached the three men after the shooting, he heard Greene say that if his pistol had gone off Lane would not have killed Jenkins—suggesting that his pistol had misfired before Lane's fatal shotgun blast. Greene denied this statement during the trial and insisted he only fired after Lane pulled the trigger.[11]

By the end of the month, the trial concluded. Lane was acquitted on grounds that he had acted in self-defense. Nonetheless, it seemed to mark an inglorious end to his political career. His acquittal meant little to his political opponents, particularly those in the New England faction of the

7. In March 1859, Lane provided his own version of how many shots were fired and their effect: "Three shots were fired by them, two of which touched my person—one passing through my garments, the other cutting the hair from my left temple; the third shot penetrated the window of my house, into the room occupied by my frightened and shrieking family; and almost simultaneously with my own shot the fourth was make, striking me in the knee." *Lawrence Republican,* March 17, 1859.

8. *Herald of Freedom,* June 5, 12, 19, 1858; *Lawrence Republican,* June 24, 1858.

9. *New York Times,* June 14, 1858.

10. P. R. Brooks to his father, June 6, 1858, James Stanley Emery Collection, Kansas State Historical Society, Topeka.

11. *Herald of Freedom,* July 3, 1858; *Lawrence Republican,* June 24, 1858.

Free State Party—of which Jenkins had been part. George Brown at the *Herald of Freedom* declared that "we never knew such a gross case of usurpation of the prerogatives of a Justice of the Peace, as that of Justice Ladd, rendered on Wednesday last, in *acquitting Gen. Lane,* and turning him loose upon community, instead of committing him, or holding him to bail for a trial before a jury of his country." The *New Albany Tribune* in Indiana explained that Lane "might have maintained his position as the leader of the Free State party of Kansas for a long time, if he could have controlled his passions, but this he never could do. His life has been one of bitterness, hatred and personal difficulties."[12] Sol Miller, editor of the *White Cloud Chief,* took an even more critical tone, noting that "with all Gen. Lane's bluster, skirmishes, marches, parade and fuss generally, in Kansas, the only blood he is known to have shed, and the only life he has taken, is Free State. He has been abused, blackguarded and dared to his face, by proslavery men, and sneaked off like a whipped dog; but because a Free State man attempts to get water—one of the necessaries of life—from a well on a disputed claim, Lane shoots him down like a beast!" Miller concluded, "Such is General Lane. That was a fatal shot for him!"[13]

Before Jenkins's death, George Brown and his *Herald of Freedom* had already mocked and criticized Lane. The paper had run what was reportedly a sarcastic string of endorsements for Lane as a presidential candidate.[14] On June 12, the *Herald* printed a story entitled "Dropped" in which Brown explained the parody of Lane he had carried out until that time:

> It is but justice to our readers to state, that it has been understood for months that Gen. Lane was an aspirant for the Presidency, and we are informed that he has been laboring with considerable energy to get his name brought forward as a candidate for that post. . . .
>
> It occurred to us that the best way to meet such a *crazy* proposition was with ridicule, hence our burlesque candidate for the Presidency; and hence the sarcastic articles which followed.
>
> While, personally, we have no controversy with Gen. Lane, yet, politically, we conceive him the most impractical politician we ever knew, and his counsels the most unsafe of any to follow. The tragical affair, which he has introduced into the politics of Kansas, is more fatal to his prospects than all else. . . . The name of *Gen. Lane,* like that of *Aaron Burr,*

12. *New Albany* (Ind.) *Tribune* printed in *Herald of Freedom,* July 3, 1858.
13. *White Cloud Chief* quoted in *Herald of Freedom,* July 17, 1858.
14. See *Herald of Freedom,* May 29, June 5, 1858.

will fill a mournful page in the history of his country. We drop it in silence and in grief.[15]

James Redpath, the editor of the antislavery *Crusader of Freedom*, provided another account of Lane seeking the presidency. According to Redpath, Lane labored to push Charles Robinson out of key leadership positions in Kansas, in order to set himself up for a presidential bid.[16] Finally, historian Leverett Spring explained that the "belief had long haunted [Lane] that some day the people of the country would call him to the highest office within their gift."[17] Though Spring provides supposed quotes from Lane on the matter, he lists no sources. Whether or not Lane actually had aspirations for the Executive Mansion, the killing of Jenkins seemed to end all hopes of a future in politics.

Nursing his own bullet wound, which nearly caused him to succumb to tetanus, Lane stepped out of the public eye for months.[18] Little mention of him can be found in the territory's newspapers throughout the rest of 1858—except for the Jenkins episode. Occasional reports arose concerning Lane's activities and future, including word that he was a candidate for a local territorial office.[19] In December a committee in Lawrence formally requested Lane to give a lecture on the "History of Kansas." He uncharacteristically declined the invitation to speak, citing a lack of sufficient time to prepare.[20] This was atypical of the man whose impromptu stump-speaking abilities were legendary. It appeared that the wind had been taken out of Lane's sails, and he preferred—for the time being—to keep a low profile.

In early 1859 things changed. Events in Kansas stirred Lane back into action. In late January, a proslavery posse captured a New York free-state man, Dr. John Doy, and his son outside Lawrence while attempting to help thirteen slaves escape from Missouri. The Doys were taken back to Missouri and detained for trial. Days later citizens in Lawrence held an "Anti-Kidnapping Meeting" to denounce the proslavery capture of the Doy party. The *Lawrence Republican* reported that after J. C. Vaughan of Leavenworth made a rousing speech to the crowd, "Gen. Lane being loudly

15. *Herald of Freedom,* June 12, 1858.
16. *Doniphan Crusader* reprinted in *Kansas Weekly Herald,* May 29, 1858.
17. Spring, "The Career of a Kansas Politician," 97.
18. *New York Times,* June 14, 1858.
19. *Herald of Freedom,* July 24, 1858.
20. *Lawrence Republican,* December 30, 1858.

called for, made an eloquent address." After resolutions were introduced, Lane gave a second speech with his legendary energy, calling for the "hanging of the traitors."[21] Not everyone was impressed with Lane's showing. A letter-writer under the moniker "A WHITE REPUBLICAN" complained that Lane had turned the assembly into a "political meeting, and denounced all as Democrats, or Pro-Slavery men, who were not in favor of hanging the whole crew." Although identifying himself as a regular Republican voter, the writer explained that if the interests and actions of Lane and his friends constituted the new Republican Party in Kansas, "you can count me *out.*"[22] The *Herald of Freedom* characterized Lane's participation as an attempt to "recover, by speechmaking and other means of notoriety, the position and influence that he held before the Jenkins affair, [and he] works day and night to accomplish this objective."[23]

The Doy affair rekindled images of previous border problems. Though it brought Lane back into the spotlight, he began to look toward more substantial political matters. Lane reportedly traveled to Leavenworth to help establish the Republican Party there.[24] Four weeks later Lane added his name to a long list of residents recommending a territorial Republican convention in May.[25] He was making his political return, and now he officially committed his future to the Republicans.

But this reemergence was complicated. Territorial officials denied him the use of a facility to "lecture to the working men of Lawrence," because his conduct "for sometime past, was not such as to justify the Representatives, fresh from the people, extending this courtesy."[26] Further, rumors regarding his return to public life circulated. In a letter to George Brown of the *Herald of Freedom,* a writer in Mt. Hope, Ohio, listed a number of popular old and new claims:

> It is asserted here that Gen. James H. Lane, the Kansas Hero, went to Kansas a Pro-Slavery man; that he tried to buy slaves; that he sided with the Pro-Slavery men; that he recognized the first bogus Legislature, by trying to get a divorce from his wife; that the Legislature refused; Lane got mad and turned Free State man; stumped the Territory, and went for a Free State because it was not a hemp growing country. It is also said

21. Ibid., February 3, 1859.
22. Printed in the *Herald of Freedom,* February 19, 1859.
23. Ibid., February 5, 1859.
24. Ibid., January 29, 1859.
25. *Lawrence Republican,* March 3, 1859.
26. Ibid., February 5, 1859.

that he seduced a woman, got drunk, joined the Temperance Society, the Church, and was elected United States Senator under the Topeka Constitution, all in one week.

It is also said, that he has recently (since the killing of Jenkins,) again joined the Temperance Society and the Methodist Church (on probation,) that he is now the most popular man in Kansas, and will probably be the Republican nominee for President in 1860, with Wm. H. Seward for Vice President, and "belongs to the Abolition wing of the Free State party.[27]

Lane's appearances at religious services and social clubs, such as the Good Templars, drew notice. His critics believed he designed to "get his name before the public in every possible shape, with the view of making himself appear to be a temperance man, a moral man, a religious man, and a patriot." But, George Brown continued, "did we not know the man and his claquers it is possible we, too, might be deceived into his support."[28] Lane's sincerity regarding religious matters has been a contentious issue. As with nearly everything about the man, his friends and critics sharply disagreed. Typical is the story of Lane attending a Methodist revival in Kansas, emotionally joining the congregation in prayer and devotion. When the minister denounced the vices of humanity, including tobacco, Lane bowed his head, removed a large piece of chewing tobacco from his vest, and handed it to the preacher. The energy among the assembly increased as the minister and the congregation saw a humbled Lane give in to faith. Rejoicing, the minister flung the tobacco into some nearby bushes. After the revival, two young men searched the area in hopes of scavenging the package, but to no avail. The next day, Lane addressed a large crowd on political matters, chewing what appeared to be the previous night's plug of tobacco.[29]

Still, others maintained confidence that Lane's acts of piety were genuine. John Speer stated that with "all his oddities, [Lane] had a firm faith in the Christian religion."[30] The Reverend Hugh Fisher later recalled, "I knew him intimately and long and well, and never knew a man who, when with good men and in refined surroundings, was so wholly and powerfully under the influence of mother's teachings."[31] Even before the

27. Ibid., February 19, 1859.
28. Ibid., January 22, 1859.
29. Speer, *Life of Lane*, 86–89.
30. Ibid., 89.
31. H. D. Fisher, *The Gun and the Gospel: Early Kansas and Chaplain Fisher*, 29.

Jenkins affair, a correspondent to the *New York Times* explained that "the General has never been even a frequent partaker of spirituous liquors, since his residence in Kansas, and is now a teetotaler and member of the order of Good Templars."[32]

Overall, it is likely that Lane was sincere in many of his religious convictions. Nonetheless, his adherence to western ideas of imagery and honor—related to perceptions of masculinity in the Old South—often put him at odds with conservative New England settlers. Sara Robinson, wife of Lane's political opponent Charles Robinson, described the puritanical view of masculinity in 1856. In her book on the Kansas struggle, she explained that the territory needed "such men, with unwearying confidence in God, and the humanity of men, with whom the love for a distressed brother is more than one's faith in creeds, and whose faith is strong."[33] Historian Kristen Tegtmeier Oertel further described this conservative attitude, stating, "In accordance with certain Christian teachings, the ideal Northern man valued nonviolence and held pacifism in high regard, especially when backed by principles of justice and liberty."[34]

While most free-state settlers from New England were not complete pacifists, the level and type of aggression demonstrated by western settlers often perplexed easterners. Charles Robinson illustrated this divergence when discussing Lane's obsession with honor and image. "No one seemed to care about such matters except himself," Robinson believed, "but he evidently thought much ado about his honor and courage was necessary to secure the confidence of the people."[35] In fact, Lane's sense of honor and imagery closely followed attitudes in his native Indiana, particularly in the southern part of that state (including Lane's hometown of Lawrenceburg) which had seen a strong influx of Southerners throughout the nineteenth century. Historian Nicole Etcheson explains that "Upland South migrants brought with them as well the aggressive masculinity of their native region and injected it into the political culture of their new home." This injection included elements of "southern honor," "which condemned effeminacy and expected men to be ferocious and aggressive."[36]

---

32. *New York Times*, May 5, 1858.

33. Sara Robinson, *Kansas: Its Interior and Exterior Life*, 60.

34. Kristen Tegtmeier Oertel, "'The Free Sons of the North' versus 'The Myrmidons of Border-Ruffianism': What Makes a Man in Bleeding Kansas?" 178.

35. Charles Robinson, *The Kansas Conflict*, 179.

36. Historian Nicole Etcheson writes, "The migration of southerners began after the Revolution, as upland southerners from such states as Kentucky, Tennessee, Virginia, and North Carolina moved down and across the Ohio River and settled communities in

Bertram Wyatt-Brown, a leading historian of Southern perceptions of honor, argued that dueling was accepted as a defense of personal honor. In the South and much of the lower Midwest, honor was based on public perception. Wyatt-Brown depicts two very different forms of honor in nineteenth-century America: "primal honor" and "gentility." "Primal honor," which placed significance on public perceptions of the individual, found a firm footing in Southern culture, and shaped how both men and women perceived each other. "Gentility" was a more internal or intrinsic form of honor, embraced more by religious and intellectual circles, particularly in the North. "Gentility" did play a role in Southern honor, but in a far different manner than that found in northern areas. Wyatt-Brown explains: "Northern gentlemen also assumed these graces, but the order of their priority was quite different, and therefore to them Southern gentility appeared in a curious refraction."[37] Charles Robinson and George W. Brown, two of Lane's most powerful critics, both came from northeastern communities that placed greater emphasis on Northern assumptions of "gentility." They not only rejected but failed to understand the "primal honor" of the South and Old Northwest. So, when Lane aggressively defended his public image with talk of dueling and violence in accordance with Southern and western perceptions of honor, these critics saw fault in the man.

Lane's upbringing in Indiana under the tutelage of a New England–born mother helps explain his apparently contradictory handling of religion and honor. His rearing in southern Indiana, with its cultural emphasis on "primal honor," instilled an aggressive defense of his public image. Yet, his attachment to "gentility" through his mother established a reverence for conservative faith, even if often overshadowed by his rough, western code of conduct. Thus, Lane's religious and moral code was a product of his environment. Critics during his lifetime, and historians who have characterized the man's apparent contradictions as simple opportunism, have all failed to appreciate these environmental factors.

Lane's return to the public stage in Kansas in 1859 could not happen without some handling of the still-lingering Jenkins affair and his bruised reputation. Not only did his sense of honor demand it, but his political

---

southern and central Illinois and Indiana and portions of southeastern and south-central Ohio. Cultural geographers still recognize these areas as southern cultural regions, extensions of the Upland South distinguishable from other areas of the same states by housing types, crops and livestock, food, religion, and dialect." Nicole Etcheson, "Manliness and the Political Culture of the Old Northwest, 1790–1860," 59–60, 61, 62.

37. Bertram Wyatt-Brown, *Honor and Violence in the Old South*, 25–31, 40–41, 142.

future depended upon standing up to his critics. On February 21, with the prompting of proslavery militant Captain Charles Hamilton (who apparently had a run-in with Lane and other free-staters a short time before), a meeting of Kansans in Bourbon County resolved that "Jim Lane, the murderer of Jenkins, was a fit leader for the mob in Lawrence, and the act of his firing upon me and robbing my command was a more ridiculous act of cowardice, and but adds one more infamous passage to a life of 'treason, stratagem and spoils.'"[38] Irate, Lane wrote a lengthy personal explanation, his first public discussion of the Jenkins killing since the previous summer. Prefacing his address by stating that he usually avoided responding to personal attacks, he nonetheless felt compelled to call attention to this particular resolution. He blamed "Democratic wire-pullers" for initiating the meeting and suggested that the Democratic Party, "and those under pay of that party, entertain the opinion that its very existence in Kansas is dependent on crushing out the writer."[39]

As for the killing of Jenkins, Lane expressed remorse, stating that "no one has more deeply felt or more grievously mourned that misfortune, than myself." But such mourning did not demonstrate guilt. He justified the act, arguing that "the fatal trigger was not drawn until the preservation of my own life and that of my family seemed to me to imperiously demand it." Finally, Lane again denied receiving or taking money from Northern donors to the Kansas cause. This accusation, nearly two years old, still haunted Lane.[40]

After carefully refuting the various charges, including criticizing Hamilton and the proslavery "posse" that had attempted to detain some Lawrence residents, Lane turned his attention to the negative press he received. He was "at a loss to understand why it is that I am the subject of so much denunciation." Generally Lane thrived on controversy. But the Jenkins episode had affected him personally and politically. Lane's explanation for the denunciation: Democratic Party opposition. He believed

38. Quoted in Lane's address "To The People of Kansas," *Lawrence Republican,* March 17, 1859. Charles Hamilton was a proslavery settler from Georgia. After he was chased out of Kansas by free-staters, Hamilton led a group of thirty men back into the territory on May 19, 1858, and rounded up nearly a dozen random antislavery settlers. The free-state men were lined up next to a ravine near and shot. Five men were killed, five were wounded, and one man was not hit but feigned death. The event made national news and is known as the "Marais des Cygnes Massacre." See Harvey R. Hougen, "The Marais des Cygnes Massacre and the Execution of William Griffith," 74–94.
39. Lane's address "To The People of Kansas," *Lawrence Republican,* March 17, 1859.
40. Ibid.

that Democrats viewed him as a threat to their success in Kansas. Lane denied that he was seeking political office, but portrayed himself as a regular member of the growing Republican Party. "The writer seeks no leadership—asks no office," he declared, "but simply desires to enjoy the right of free speech, and permission to labor as a private in the ranks of the great Jefferson Republican party of freedom."[41]

Lane closed his address with a modest, yet disingenuous, explanation of his intentions. "I would not be understood as complaining of these assaults," he wrote. "So long as it affords those indulging in them either pleasure or profit, let them howl, until their very throats crack. My history is before the people of Kansas, and to their judgment will I cheerfully submit."[42] Of course he was complaining about the criticism; throughout the address he portrayed himself as a victim. Thus, his closing words were simply gratuitous. And his stated intention to "labor as a private" in the Republican Party was untrue. Lane was actively working to help establish and eventually lead the new political movement.

Still, Lane had to tread lightly. Kansas Republicans scheduled a convention in Osawatomie in May. Following Lane's increased public appearances and association among Republicans, rumors circulated that he would dominate the upcoming assembly. The *Lawrence Republican,* which was friendly toward Lane, tried to dispel this fear by reiterating his stated intention to retire to private life. In fact, the editors agreed that the killing of Jenkins, whether justified or not, was an act that "inevitably drives a man from the 'political scene' to private life." The *Republican* went even further, stating that, "Having announced his intention to retire from public life, Gen. Lane cannot consistently appear at that Convention, in any character whatever."[43] Though some assumed Lane was a prime mover in planning the Osawatomie Republican convention, and would thus be a leading figure there, he apparently did not attend—if he did, there is no record of it.[44] His name is not listed among the numerous delegates who served in the various leadership positions or committees.[45]

41. Ibid.
42. Ibid.
43. Ibid.
44. *Herald of Freedom,* May 21, 1859. Editor George Brown repeatedly associated Lane with the convention, but admitted that "This article is written while that body is probably in session, hence we are wholly ignorant of its action, other than as indicated by county conventions."
45. Wilder, *Annals of Kansas,* 201–3.

While Lane may not have been an active leader in Republican or political activities in the territory, he continued to exert his influence. In June, he wrote a letter to Republicans in Leavenworth discussing their struggle against a strong Democratic presence. He advocated organization, urging them to "treat kindly those who have strayed from the great army of freedom. Win them back to the ranks." He closed by advising them to "[i]gnore personal considerations—heal your dissensions—stand by your guns, and all will yet be well." This call for party unity echoed his attempts to unify the Leavenworth convention a year before. Yet, critics ignored Lane's message. George Brown blasted Lane for the hypocrisy of claiming retirement from public life while actively engaging in political affairs.[46] For men who had come to loathe Lane, any activity by the man was intolerable.

In July, delegates from the territory met in Wyandotte to draw up a constitution once again. Lane did not attend. The convention was nonetheless marked by some controversy, as delegates from some districts were denied admittance.[47] Still, the Wyandotte effort marked the first time that distinct political party rivalry—Republicans versus Democrats—punctuated a constitutional convention in the territory.[48] The bipartisan efforts within the Free State Party were no more. The only debate over slavery focused on whether the institution would be outlawed upon admission into the Union, or if slave owners would have a set time by which they had to remove their property from the new state. Despite efforts by some Democrats to provide a temporary protection of slavery, the Wyandotte Constitution, completed on July 29, contained no recognition of slaveholding rights.[49]

Kansas voters ratified the document in October with 10,421 votes, while 5,530 ballots rejected it.[50] Historian Gary Cheatham credited pro-Southern sympathies and a conservative resistance to the radical features of the Wyandotte Constitution for much the opposition. Further, the referendum tally failed to include a number of communities.[51] Regardless of the dissension and complications surrounding this new constitutional effort, the Wyandotte Constitution moved forward and the upcoming elections stirred an anxious Lane back to action. By the fall, Lane abandoned his

46. *Herald of Freedom,* July 9, 1859.
47. See Wilder, *Annals of Kansas,* 208.
48. Gary Cheatham, "'Slavery All the Time or Not at All': The Wyandotte Constitution Debate, 1859–1861," 172.
49. Ibid., 172–73.
50. Wilder, *Annals of Kansas,* 227.
51. Cheatham, "'Slavery All the Time or Not at All,'" 180.

professed intention to remain a private citizen. In October, he attended a Republican convention in Topeka. His attempts to fight the nomination of Charles Robinson for governor failed and, the *Kansas Press* reported, Lane left "terribly defeated."[52] Nonetheless, his supporters shortly thereafter held an assembly in Lawrence and passed a series of resolutions praising Lane and endorsing his bid for the U.S. Senate. It further resolved that "any attempt by political intriguers to defeat the well-understood wish of the people on this subject, will inevitably react upon them, and may result most disastrously to the integrity and success of the Republican party itself."[53]

With an effective end to the slavery debate in Kansas, divisions within the Free State Party grew in the new Republican movement. Democrats in Kansas identified the opposing factions as "White" and "Black" Republicans. "White" Republicans were said to be conservative, largely consisting of those free-state men who had urged participation in the elections under the Lecompton Constitution. "Black" Republicans, on the other hand, "opposed the voting policy, and under the management of Col. Jim Lane as Commander-in-Chief, they organized armed bodies of men, commissioned and put them into the field, to prevent the so-called Free-State men from voting."[54] This simplistic characterization may have described the basic division with free-state ranks in late 1857, but the Republican infighting in 1860 became more substantial. Economic issues, race issues, and leading personalities now led to various cliques within party ranks. And these factions were somewhat fluid as new conventions met and opportunities arose.

Further, Kansas Republicans had no problem uniting in their opposition to slavery. In early 1860 the territorial legislature considered a bill to abolish slavery. A Democratic minority in the body sternly resisted the legislation. G. M. Beebe declared that "between one-fourth and one-half a million of dollars' worth of property in slaves" could be found in Kansas and argued that "the immediate prohibition of an existing right of property in any given article is beyond either the legislative power of the States or Territories." He recommended immediate postponement of the legislation.[55] His words went unheeded; the Republican-dominated legislature easily passed the bill. In response the governor, Samuel Medary, vetoed the bill on

---

52. *Kansas Press*, November 7, 1859.
53. Resolutions printed in the *Herald of Freedom*, November 5, 1859.
54. *National Democrat*, March 8, 1860.
55. Wilder, *Annals of Kansas*, 240.

February 20. The legislature promptly overrode the veto. Democrats in Kansas denounced the action as dangerous to the future of the Union and passed resolutions at their March convention in Atchison declaring that "the law prohibiting Slavery in this Territory, recently passed by the Republican party in the Territorial Legislature, is in disregard of the Supreme Court of the United States, in contravention of the Constitutional rights of fifteen of the States of this Union, and calculated to weaken the bonds of the Union." The convention further celebrated Medary's attempted veto and the Democratic legislators who voted to sustain it.[56]

Lane's comeback was due in large measure to his legendary speaking abilities. But his ability to influence conventions involved expert political instincts. His friend John Speer recalled an incident in which, at a small assembly, Lane approached an outspoken critic. After engaging the man in some pleasant conversation, Lane rose before the meeting and said: "Mr. President—I move you, if I can meet with a second, [at least a dozen men seconded the motion before they heard it,] that our distinguished fellow-citizen, Mr J O, be made chairman of this meeting." The motion easily carried, and his "enemy" took the chair. Before leaving, Lane handed the new convention president a list of men he recommended to prepare resolutions. Further, he provided the committee chairman his recommended resolutions. Thus, the convention unanimously supported his nomination for the Senate.[57]

Lane also used the power of patronage to gain support. In November, he wrote to Charles Foster about his anticipated selection for the Senate. He stated, "I trust the labor will be cheerfully performed as you know that the time is not far distant when Senator Lane will be able to serve all and will his true friends."[58] A writer to the *Kansas Press* lambasted Lane's political promises, stating that "with his usual recklessness he had promised the same office to a dozen different aspirants."[59] While political opponents generally leveled this criticism, in fact evidence exists of Lane failing to fulfill some promises during his political career. In 1864, D. B. Emmert wrote to Lane listing a series of promised positions he had failed to receive. "First, I was to have an appointment at Washington; then the Land Office at Humboldt, and finally pretty positive assurances of the position of U. S. Assessor

56. Ibid., 242.
57. Speer, *Life of Lane*, 223.
58. Lane to Charles Foster, November 18, 1859, Charles A. Foster Collection, Kansas State Historical Society, Topeka.
59. *Kansas Press*, November 7, 1859.

for this State," Emmert complained. "These were voluntary promises; and yet, they were not only all broken; but when I have written to you, I have been passed by without even an answer to my letters."[60] Part of this problem may have stemmed from Lane's interest in appeasing powerful critics. In 1863, a Kansan wrote to Lane's associate Sidney Clarke complaining that "I know several who done all they could to defeat him, when he needed friends, [and] are reaping a rich harvest at his hands, while those who made the sacrifice to save him, and done it are treated with contempt."[61]

Finally, his effort to secure a Senate seat included the purchase of a newspaper to serve as his official political organ. John Speer had purchased the *Lawrence Republican*. When the printing was in danger of shutting down due to a lack of funds, Lane traveled through a snowstorm to Mark Delahay's home in Leavenworth on Christmas night to raise money. Soon after, the necessary funds were acquired and the pro-Lane newspaper began operations. His political interests enjoyed another boost with the purchase of the *Leavenworth Daily Conservative* by two pro-Lane men.[62]

During this period Lane also became involved in the national Republican ticket. His candidate of choice was Abraham Lincoln. How the Kansan chose the Illinoisan remains a mystery, particularly since Senator William H. Seward of New York not only enjoyed a great deal of Kansas support but also held the highest expectations for the Republican nomination. Yet, Lane did not jump on the very popular Seward bandwagon. Lane did have a direct link to Lincoln through his friendship with Mark Delahay. Delahay was a former Democrat who, like Lane, joined the free-state cause in Kansas. He had known Lincoln in Illinois, and the two maintained their friendship after the former moved to the territory. Like Lane, Delahay has been described as a political opportunist who switched parties to achieve personal advancement.[63] Nonetheless, Delahay was a strong supporter of Lincoln during the 1860 Republican campaign and kept in regular contact with the candidate.

Beyond a mutual friend, other possible reasons for Lane's choice of Lincoln should be considered. For instance, perhaps Lincoln's political rivalry

60. D. B. Emmert to Hon. James H. Lane, February 9, 1864, Sidney Clarke Collection, Carl Albert Congressional Research and Studies Center, University of Oklahoma, Norman.

61. A. Ellis to Hon. Sidney Clark, August 16, 1863, Sidney Clarke Collection, Carl Albert Congressional Research and Studies Center, University of Oklahoma, Norman.

62. Speer, *Life of Lane*, 224–25.

63. John G. Clark, "Mark W. Delahay: Peripatetic Politician," 304, 306.

with Stephen Douglas appealed to Lane. Lincoln sought Douglas's Senate seat in 1858 and had achieved national fame by squaring off against the "Little Giant" in a series of debates that year. Certainly Lane could appreciate someone who had stood up to Douglas. How much this common antipathy for Douglas drew the two men together is unknown, for Lane left no evidence of his reasoning for backing Lincoln. Historian Craig Miner identified other similarities between Lane and Lincoln that also may have contributed to their political bond. They were close in age and both were not only westerners, but former residents of Indiana. Both men had served in the House of Representatives and both were successful orators, capable of reading the mood of an audience. Miner also pointed to a mutual interest in story-telling and a shared appreciation for risqué humor.[64] However, their political backgrounds were quite different. Unlike Lane, Lincoln was an ardent opponent of popular sovereignty as a means to settle the slavery dispute. His opposition to slavery took on a philosophical and humanitarian tone absent from Lane's antislavery position. Lincoln had been a Whig and had long opposed Lane's old Democratic Party and policies, including the war with Mexico that Lane and his fellow Democrats had supported so strongly. Despite their personal similarities, their traditional politics gave little foreshadowing of a partnership.

Yet, the American political scene in 1859 was far from what Lane or Lincoln had known in years past. The sectional conflict and the struggle over slavery had carved large chunks out of the Democratic Party and helped destroy the Whigs altogether. Neither Lane nor Lincoln had chosen to end their traditional political affiliations. Events had restructured the political climate by crushing old party bonds with substantial questions about slavery, the organization of territories, and even the future of the Union. Men like Lincoln and Lane gravitated toward people with similar interests, largely irrespective of former political titles or identities. They found common ground. Lincoln spoke out against slavery as immoral, but he was not an abolitionist. He wanted to keep slavery out of the territories, but accepted its place in the Southern states. While Lane had not voiced a moral opposition to slavery, he had expressed an interest in keeping slavery out of the territories for white settlers since his days as a Democrat in Congress and he too was willing to let slavery remain untouched in the South. Lincoln had never embraced the Democratic principle of popular sovereignty, and suggested that Douglas's efforts with the Kansas-Nebraska Act were

64. Miner, "Lane and Lincoln," 187.

part of a larger conspiracy to make slavery legal everywhere.[65] Lane retained his faith in the principle of popular sovereignty, but saw its application as a failure due to proslavery aggression and traitors within the Democratic Party. Thus, both men came to see and oppose a larger effort to push slavery upon antislavery Americans. Overall, while we do not know exactly how or why Lane embraced Lincoln as a candidate before the Republican national convention, the basic principles and interests these men held, which had seemed at odds before the collapse of the two-party system, ultimately came together.

When Lane first met Lincoln is equally puzzling. On October 17, 1859, Lincoln wrote to his friend Delahay in Kansas about communicating with Lane. Apparently worried that Lane's reputation might harm both Delahay's and his own interests, Lincoln explained that "I have thought it over, and concluded it is not the best way. . . . I never saw him, or corresponded with him; so that a letter directly from me to him would run a great hazard of doing harm to both you and me." However, not intending to lose Lane's support, Lincoln stated that "if the object merely be to assure General Lane of my friendship for you, show him the letter herewith inclosed."[66]

Two months later, in December 1859, Lincoln traveled to Kansas, according to one historian, to practice some ideas in front of an audience without critique from the eastern press. He spoke at Elwood, Troy, Doniphan, Atchison, and Leavenworth. According to Mary E. Delahay, Lane was among guests invited by her father to a dinner party with Lincoln during this trip. Yet, her memory may not have served her well, for on February 17, 1860, Lane attached a note to a letter from Delahay to Lincoln concerning political matters, and wrote, "I have never met you and yet I feel that you are an old acquaintance and I may add friend." In any case, there is no doubt that Lane firmly backed Lincoln for president before the national

---

65. David Zarefsky, *Lincoln, Douglas and Slavery: In the Crucible of Public Debate,* 80–84. Lincoln explained his conspiracy theory during his debates with Douglas in 1858. The passage of Douglas's bill in 1854, the Roger Taney's Supreme Court ruling regarding Dred Scott in 1857, and James Buchanan's support of the Lecompton Constitution in 1858 all seemed too convenient. Creating the analogy of workmen (who shared the first names of notable Democratic figures) constructing a wooden structure, Lincoln told an audience in Springfield, Illinois, during his debate with Douglas that "we find it impossible not to believe that Stephen and Franklin and Roger and James all understood one another from the beginning, and all worked upon a common plan or draft drawn up before the first blow was struck." Robert W. Johannsen, ed., *The Lincoln-Douglas Debates of 1858,* 18.

66. A. Lincoln to Mark W. Delahay, October 17, 1859, quoted in Stephenson, *Political Career of Lane,* 98n.

Republican nomination. Delahay's letter to Lincoln in February 1860 described the obstacles he and Lane faced in preparation for the upcoming Kansas Republican convention. Friends of Seward were working hard to secure the Kansas delegation in his favor. Delahay asked Lincoln, "cant you get of your friends a small loan of money and loan it to me or Genl Lane, and let us do as we please with it; We both have property and are responcible [sic] & for it will give a joint note with interest for its return next fall; see Hatch, Bissell, or such friends as can afford to spare us a small sum of money to be used by us between now and the day our Delegates are appointed." Delahay and Lane failed to secure a pro-Lincoln delegation from Kansas for the Republican National Convention in Chicago, because support for Seward proved too strong.[67] Still, Lincoln won the party nomination there in May 1860 and Delahay and Lincoln broadened the campaign.

Lane's endorsement of the Republican platform in 1860 should not be seen as an abandonment of the Democratic principles he had always championed. In fact, the Republican Party had been shaped by its vastly different membership. "The product of the interaction of a wide variety of political, cultural, socio-economic, and ideological considerations," writes historian William Gienapp, "the Republican party was an amazingly heterogeneous coalition."[68] While Gienapp described the party in 1856, the number of disgruntled Democrats, Know-Nothings, and other former political rivals joining the party had only increased over the following four years. The 1860 platform reflected the common interests of Republicans, even those with Democratic backgrounds. The first plank described the political transition men like Lane had undergone. It stated that "the history of the nation, during the last four years, has fully established the propriety and necessity of the organization and perpetuation of the Republican party, and that the causes which called it into existence are permanent in their nature, and now, more than ever before, demand its peaceful and constitutional triumph."[69] Lane's migration into the Republican

67. Fred Brinkerhoff, "The Kansas Tour of Lincoln the Candidate," 296, 307; Wilder, *Annals of Kansas,* 231; Mary E. Delahay, "Judge Mark W. Delahay," 640; Note from James H. Lane, appended to Mark Delahay to Abraham Lincoln, February 17, 1860, Abraham Lincoln Papers at the Library of Congress; Mark Delahay to Abraham Lincoln, February 17, 1860, Abraham Lincoln Papers at the Library of Congress.

68. Gienapp, *Origins of the Republican Party,* 439.

69. Republican National Platform, 1860, printed in James A. Rawley, *Secession: The Disruption of the American Republic, 1844–1861,* 227.

Party had been a journey of necessity. Not only had Stephen Douglas unceremoniously denied Lane's Democratic loyalty, but the party's abandonment of free-state settlers had led Lane, and countless other Democrats, to find a new political home. Other parts of the Republican platform echoed Lane's position further. The fifth plank condemned the Democratic administration with "measureless subserviency to the exactions of a sectional interest," particularly in regard to Lecompton, and for "its general and unvarying abuse of the power intrusted to it by a confiding people." The tenth and eleventh planks criticized the denial of Kansas residents, by administrative appointees, to the right of self-government and called for the immediate admission of Kansas under its free Wyandotte Constitution. The fourteenth plank was consistent with Lane's interest in protecting naturalization and immigrant rights.[70]

Lane's previous positions on three other important sections of the Republican platform are a little less clear. Planks seven, eight, and nine criticized the expansion of slavery throughout the territories as protected by the Constitution according to the Dred Scott decision, endorsed the belief that the "normal condition of all the territory of the United States is that of freedom," and condemned the reopening of the African slave trade, respectively. While Lane claimed, as an Indiana congressman, that he was "no friend of slavery," there is little information regarding his view about its status in the territories as a whole. His reluctant support of the Kansas-Nebraska Bill demonstrated that he cared about protecting free-soil interests, but did not absolutely object to the possible introduction of slavery into *any* of the territories. Yet, the Republican position of 1860 was a response to the problems brought about by the Kansas-Nebraska Act. The Missouri Compromise had, for thirty years, only outlawed slavery in some of the territories. Initial opposition to the Kansas-Nebraska Bill among Northern Whigs and some Northern Democrats focused on the repeal of that compromise—many opponents did not demand that all territory be off-limits, but that the boundary between free and slave territory be protected.[71] Thus, Lane and the Republican Party as a whole had adopted a tougher line against slavery extension in response to Southern-endorsed, proslavery policy changes.

70. Ibid., 230.
71. Michael Holt, *The Rise and Fall of the American Whig Party: Jacksonian Politics and the Onset of the Civil War,* 807. Eric Foner explains that during the Kansas-Nebraska debates "conservatives and many moderates were content merely to call for the restoration of the Missouri Compromise or a prohibition of slavery extension." Foner, *Free Soil, Free Labor, Free Men,* 127.

Lane paid particularly close attention to the figure that had become his greatest political enemy—Stephen Douglas. Delahay wrote to Lincoln in June about the Democratic Party's choice for president, stating that "Genl Lane is here waiting to learn the result at Balto [Baltimore], he says he wants to spend the remainder of his life on the Stump if Douglas is a candidate he will be a thorn in his side, he will brand him with cowardice [*sic*] and tell of his challenge which he now carries in his Pocket."[72] Still bitter from his treatment at the hands of Douglas during the Kansas Memorial debate four years earlier, Lane chomped at the bit to defeat the "Little Giant" and, according to one Kansan, "howl frightfully against Democracy in favor of 'Old Abe.'"[73] After Douglas secured the Democratic presidential nomination that summer, Delahay and Lane traveled to hotly contested districts in Illinois and Indiana to stump for a Lincoln victory.[74]

Though Douglas secured the Democratic nomination, sectionalism within that party had effectively destroyed its power. A large number of Southern Democrats, determined to protect slaveholding interests beyond what was acceptable to their Northern counterparts, held a separate convention and put John C. Breckinridge on the ballot. A fourth presidential candidate emerged when a group of moderates nominated John Bell of Tennessee under the new Constitutional Unionist Party.[75] Thus, the presidential election of 1860 saw one of the greatest divisions in American political history. Competing interests over slavery, which had torn Kansas Territory apart—sealing the political fate of numerous public officials and ending the lives of dozens of settlers—had finally become a serious threat to the future of the nation as a whole.

Talk of disunion circulated throughout the South in anticipation of the November presidential election. Many Southerners saw Lincoln as a

72. Mark W. Delahay to Abraham Lincoln, June 24, 1860, Abraham Lincoln Papers at the Library of Congress. The Democratic National Convention originally took place in Charleston, South Carolina, in April 1860. Sectional conflict caused the convention to fall apart after fifty delegates from the Deep South walked out once pro-Douglas delegates passed a Northern Democratic platform. A second convention took place in Baltimore six weeks later. See McPherson, *Battle Cry of Freedom*, 213–16, for a brief review of the convention affair, and for a more thorough account see Nevins, *The Emergence of Lincoln*, vol. 2, 207–23 and James L. Abrahamson, *The Men of Secession and Civil War, 1859–1861*, 49–62.

73. George W. Deitzler to Samuel N. Wood, August 18, 1860, Samuel N. Wood Collection, Kansas State Historical Society, Topeka. Deitzler did not support Lane's or Delahay's efforts, and felt that they were counterproductive to Lincoln's success.

74. Clark, "Mark Delahay: Peripatetic Politician," 311.

75. William C. Davis, *"A Government of Our Own": The Making of the Confederacy*, 6.

purely sectional candidate, openly hostile to slaveholding interests. Despite his attempts to reassure Southerners that he posed no threat to slavery where it existed in the states, the sectional conflict had escalated to a fever pitch. His election, purely through Northern votes, sent shock waves through the South. Secessionist Thomas Cobb warned Georgians that the election of Lincoln was simply the culmination of decades of agitation and friction between slaveholding and free states. "Mark me, my friends!" Cobb cried out during Georgia's debate over secession. "The only tie which binds together this party at the North is the Slavery issue. Bank and anti-Bank, Protection and Free Trade, Old Whig and Old Democrat, have all come together. The old issues are ignored, forgotten. Abolitionism and Agrarianism are the only specialties in their platform."[76] While Cobb's description exaggerated Northern sentiments—the strong antislavery interests in the Northern states were largely not abolitionist in nature—he did fairly accurately describe the growing trend in Northern politics. The Free State Party in Kansas in 1855 had been created by antislavery settlers putting aside old political rivalries and issues to unite, temporarily, under the cause of free statehood. The Kansas struggle was a microcosm of the impending Civil War. And people on both sides of this great national conflict began adjusting their political and military attitudes to the radical developments, just as Lane and countless Kansas settlers had adjusted during the previous five years.

On December 20, South Carolina took the radical step of secession. Mississippi, Florida, Alabama, Georgia, Louisiana, and Texas followed over the next month and a half.[77] Senators and representatives from these states formally walked out of the capitol—the national crisis had begun. In the meantime, Kansas finally achieved statehood. On January 29, 1861, President James Buchanan signed the bill admitting Kansas into the Union as a free state under the Wyandotte Constitution. Charles Robinson, Lane's chief political rival in Kansas, who had been elected governor under this constitution, was sworn into office on February 9. Robinson requested the state legislature—which elected the state's senators—to convene on March 26. Lane had become a front-runner in the Kansas Senate race.[78] Yet, he feared that his political opponents in the young state would sabotage his selection.

76. Thomas R. R. Cobb, "Secessionist Speech before the Georgia Secession Convention, November 12, 1860," in William W. Freehling and Craig M. Simpson, eds., *Secession Debated: Georgia's Showdown in 1860*, 22.

77. McPherson, *Battle Cry of Freedom*, 234–35.

78. *White Cloud Kansas Chief*, January 24, 1861.

Lane wrote to Lincoln accusing the new governor of postponing the date in order to weaken his success in the senatorial race.[79] Whether that was Robinson's intent or not, the governor kept a sharp eye on Lane's political interests. "Lane has undertaken a personal fight on me for the purpose of destroying my influence at W," the governor wrote his wife. He bragged, "I can by paying a little attention to the matter make him smell worse than ever. He & his friends are already beginning to falter in their course for fear that I will turn the tables on them which I can do with ease."[80]

Though geographical sectionalism within Kansas had not played a significant role in territorial politics to this time, legislators arranged to choose one candidate from north of the Kansas River and one from south of the river.[81] Rumors began circulating that Lane had arranged a secret campaign partnership with Marcus Parrott—that their respective supporters would help Lane secure the "Southern" seat while Parrot took the "Northern" seat.[82] The *Leavenworth Daily Conservative* ridiculed the rumor, citing Parrott's published criticisms of Lane: "That must be a queer partnership wherein the partners are vilifying one another!"[83] "The truth is simply this," the *Conservative* stated, "The majority of the Republicans in the Kansas Legislature were elected with the understanding that Messrs. Lane and Parrott were the choice of the people for U. S. Senators."[84] In fact, an agreement of some kind may have been made. John Speer, Lane's friend, later spoke of an "understanding" between Lane and Parrott. Yet, as the election approached the candidates jockeyed for position and a number of different factions appear to have developed.[85]

---

79. James H. Lane to Abraham Lincoln, February 21, 1861, Abraham Lincoln Papers at the Library of Congress. Lane may have been justified in fearing a delay in the Senate selection, as some Kansans acknowledged that his popularity was beginning to wane. Peter Bryant wrote to his brother: "There is considerable excitement just now in regard to who will be our U.S. Senators. There are a good many applicants, and it is very hard telling who is ahead. Jim Lane stock was very high, but it seems to be falling." Peter Bryant to his brother, March 10, 1861, in "The Letters of Peter Bryant, Jackson County Pioneer," 344.

80. Charles Robinson to Sara Robinson, January 11, 1861, Charles Robinson Collection, Kansas State Historical Society, Topeka.

81. Stephenson, *Political Career of Lane,* 100.

82. *Leavenworth Daily Conservative,* March 26, 1861.

83. Ibid.

84. Ibid.

85. Speer, *Life of Lane,* 228–29. Historian Wendell Stephenson describes a meeting between Lane and Samuel Pomeroy to defeat Lane's chief opponent in the southern Kansas Senate seat, Frederick Stanton. The agreement between the men helped both secure the Senate seats. Stephenson, *Political Career of Lane,* 102.

Beyond backroom partnerships, Lane worked feverishly for a Senate seat. In addition to his plan to have his friend John Speer take charge of the *Lawrence Republican*, Lane set out to raise more money than all of his opponents combined. He believed that he was the true popular choice, despite the machinations of his political rivals, and told Mark Delahay that "the people are for me the members are for me & by god they shall not defraud me out of my election."[86]

Lane's efforts paid off. On April 4, after a long and arduous series of ballots, the state legislature selected Lane for one Senate seat and Samuel Pomeroy for the other.[87] Though a number of men objected to the voting procedure, the election stood.[88] During the voting process, Lane sat outside the legislative chamber, nearly hysterical. Suffering from another bout of despondency, he cradled a pistol in his hands, determined to kill himself if his Senate bid failed.[89] It was his second recorded time to threaten suicide.

Five days after the selection, Lane supporters held a meeting in Leavenworth. The assembly passed resolutions declaring that the citizens of Kansas "owe a debt of gratitude to Gen. James H. Lane for his unceasing efforts in behalf of Freedom and Republicanism, in Kansas and elsewhere, during the last six years."[90] Lane had fulfilled a goal he had labored to achieve for half a decade. However, he would be greeted in Washington by a national emergency. The seven states of the Deep South had seceded, while secessionists labored to draw the Upper South into the Confederacy. A standoff in the harbor outside Charleston, South Carolina, threatened to escalate the political standoff into war. Washington was rife with tension— a perfect environment for the energy of the fiery James Lane.

Few people in Kansas had imagined that Lane could reemerge politically from the ashes of the Jenkins shooting. Yet, in less than three years

86. James H. Lane to Mark W. Delahay, December 18, 1860, Delahay Family Collection, Kansas State Historical Society, Topeka.

87. After the election of senators, Kansas settler Peter Bryant wrote to his brother that "It is said there was any amount of wireworking and 'skulduggery' performed. Pomeroy moved to Topeka and fitted up an elegant mansion and boarded free gratis all the representatives that voted for him. Whether he fed them 'Aid' [funds sent to the Kansas Territorial Relief Committee for the Kansas cause] or not, deponent knoweth not." Peter Bryant to his brother, April 7, 1861, in "The Letters of Peter Bryant, Jackson County Pioneer," 346.

88. Stephenson, *Political Career of Lane*, 103.

89. Castel, *Civil War Kansas*, 33.

90. *Leavenworth Daily Conservative*, April 10, 1861.

Lane had not only returned to the public stage but also secured a seat in the U.S. Senate. Critics have seen Lane's return as little more than evidence of an insatiable ambition. Lane certainly was an extremely ambitious man, who, like most politicians, thrived in the political world of wheeling and dealing. However, Lane's endorsement of the Republican Party was a natural progression. The Republican 1860 national platform overwhelmingly echoed principles he had held as a Democrat and reflected his experiences in Kansas which had turned him away from that party.

8

Lane and the Beginning
of the Civil War, 1861–1862

"Our motto is the union & nothing less than the union."

Southern secession threatened James Lane's beloved Union and drove him to a new extreme. Enraged at what he saw as the ultimate extension of proslavery aggression, the new senator advocated immediate military action with himself in the lead. His boldness inspired Northerners who wanted to punish secessionists and the South, yet alarmed those who urged a cautious, conservative approach to war. Lane's embrace of total war foreshadowed the bloody 1864 campaigns in Virginia and Georgia, and earned him enmity in Missouri.

South Carolina's secession in December 1860 set off celebrations in Southern towns. Militias drilled, bands played, and fireworks exploded as conventions across the Deep South voted for secession.[1] Shortly before the New Year, Major Robert Anderson, commanding officer of federal forces in Charleston Harbor, moved his men from the vulnerable military positions near the city into Fort Sumter—a fortress constructed on a man-made

1. McPherson, *Battle Cry of Freedom*, 235.

island in the center of the harbor. Southerners erupted in anger at the defensive move, pushing the political conflict closer to war. South Carolinian Mary Chesnut wrote in her diary after Anderson's relocation, "The row is fast and furious now. State after State is taking its forts and fortresses." She credited the military maneuver with giving new life to South Carolina's secession movement. "They say if we had been left out in the cold alone, we might have sulked a while, but back we would have had to go, and would merely have fretted and fumed and quarreled among ourselves. We needed a little wholesome neglect. Anderson has blocked that game, but now our sister States have joined us, and we are strong."[2]

Northerners did not remain idle during talk of Southern secession. Irritated by Southern threats of disunion, many Northerners expressed an eagerness to settle the matter. William Seward told an audience in Auburn, New York, that it was "high time, that we know whether this is a constitutional government under which we live It is high time that we know, since the Union is threatened, who are its friends and who are its enemies."[3] Lane certainly saw himself as a friend, and in the midst of the secession wave, wrote to President-elect Lincoln on January 2, 1861, to offer Kansas's support. "Our motto is the union & nothing less than the union—To accomplish this you can command every true heart in Kansas." For Lane, the men of Kansas had resisted slaveholding aggression for six years, and they were willing to keep up the fight. In fact, Lane offered Lincoln a personal bodyguard: "You are to judge of the necessity & policy of having 1000 true Kansans armed & organized to protect your inaugeration [sic]."[4] Lincoln did not accept the offer, but at the behest of security advisers slipped into Washington in disguise—an action that ignited ridicule across the nation for the incoming leader.[5]

The standoff at Fort Sumter finally exploded on April 12 as Confederate artillery batteries lining the Charleston shore fired upon the federal garrison. For nearly two days the bombardment raged, sending thousands of cannon shot and shell into the fort. Federal guns fired a thousand rounds in reply. The fort received extensive damage, yet only one man died—by an accidental explosion after the fight. Nevertheless, with an exhausted

2. Mary Chesnut, *A Diary from Dixie*, 5.

3. William H. Seward, quoted in Nevins, *The Emergence of Lincoln*, vol. 2, 309.

4. James H. Lane to Abraham Lincoln, January 2, 1861, Abraham Lincoln Papers at the Library of Congress.

5. David Herbert Donald, *Lincoln*, 278–79.

garrison and fire threatening the installation, Anderson surrendered.[6] Southerners, ecstatic with their success, rang church bells and fired cannons in celebration.[7] The forcible capture of a federal fort shocked the North. Lincoln immediately issued a call for seventy-five thousand soldiers—for a ninety-day term—to put down the rebellion. Northern communities eagerly answered the call.[8] In short order, four states in the Upper South passed ordinances of secession and joined the Confederacy.[9] The American Civil War had begun.

As Lane prepared to travel to Washington to take his Senate seat, his supporters championed his cause in Kansas and for the Union. The *Lawrence Republican* praised him, stating that he "goes into the Senate, as a radical Republican, a lover of the Union, with the . . . energy and courage to utter his views with truthful eloquence in behalf of the great principles of Republican Freedom."[10] Lane wasted no time responding to the possible threat to the capital. With Virginia's secession, and Maryland's strong secessionist element, Washington stood in a precarious position. On April 14, Lane organized and took command of the "Frontier Guard."[11] The group consisted of nearly sixty westerners—primarily Kansans—including fellow Kansas Senator Samuel Pomeroy as a private.[12] Senator Cassius Clay of Kentucky raised a similar force, and Major David Hunter took command of the two volunteer companies. Clay's volunteers camped at the Willard Hotel, while Lane, named second in command by Hunter, and his men were assigned to guard the Executive Mansion and given the East Room as their impromptu barracks.[13] John Nicolay and John Hay, Lin-

6. McPherson, *Battle Cry of Freedom*, 273–74.

7. Maury Klein, *Days of Defiance: Sumter, Secession, and the Coming of the Civil War*, 418–19.

8. McPherson, *Battle Cry of Freedom*, 274.

9. The four states that seceded after Lincoln's call for troops were: Virginia (April 17), Arkansas (May 6), North Carolina (May 20), and Tennessee (June 8). The Upper South states of Missouri, Kentucky, and Maryland were split on the issue of secession, but did not formally secede. These states became known as the Border States, and fielded men for both sides of the conflict. Margaret E. Wagner, Gary W. Gallagher, and Paul Finkelman, eds., *The Library of Congress Civil War Desk Reference* (New York: Simon and Schuster, 2002), 6, 8–9.

10. *Lawrence Republican*, April 11, 1861.

11. William C. Davis, *Lincoln's Men: How President Lincoln Became Father to an Army and a Nation*, 28; Speer, *Life of Lane*, 234–36.

12. For a partial roster of the Frontier Guard, see *Lawrence Republican*, May 2, 1861.

13. Edward A. Miller, Jr., *Lincoln's Abolitionist General: The Biography of David Hunter*, 56.

coln's personal secretaries, gave a dramatic account of the rough group of volunteers at their post:

> At dusk they filed into the famous East Room, clad in citizens' dress, but carrying very new, untarnished muskets, and following Lane, brandishing a sword of irreproachable rightness. Here ammunition boxes were opened and cartridges dealt out; and after spending the evening in an exceedingly rudimentary squad drill, under the light of the gorgeous gas chandeliers, they disposed themselves in picturesque bivouac on the brilliant-patterned velvet carpet—perhaps the most luxurious cantonment which American soldiers have ever enjoyed. Their motley composition, their anomalous surroundings, the extraordinary emergency, their mingled awkwardness and earnestness, rendered the scene a medley of bizarre contradictions.[14]

The Frontier Guard's bivouac in the East Room lasted only a short time, but the moral influence these men brought to the president and other officials in Washington was extremely valuable. In April, the small Frontier Guard stood as nearly the only military force protecting the capital as secessionist units amassed on the western side of the Potomac River only a few miles away. Nonetheless, Lane wanted action, and he wanted to lead it. On April 20, he wrote to President Lincoln, "Now, in my opinion is the time for a *Coup de etats*—Could ever one as humble as myself have authority I believe I could precipitate upon this city from the North *through Maryland* such a force as would secure Washington & the Country." Nothing came from this offer, but Lane reportedly "made several scouting expeditions into Virginia, during one of which he captured a secession flag." As Union reinforcements entered the capital, the Frontier Guard was reassigned to the U.S. Navy Yard on April 24. Shortly thereafter the unit was honorably discharged and Lane returned to Kansas to engage in state affairs before the congressional session in July.[15]

Lane continued to involve himself in military matters. He spoke in Lawrence urging the recruitment of troops to resist possible aggression from Missouri. The *Lawrence Republican* reported that Lane "gave as his opinion, that whenever the State of Missouri shall attempt to blockade the

14. John G. Nicolay and John Hay, *Abraham Lincoln: A History,* vol. 4, 106–7.
15. Davis, *Lincoln's Men,* 28; James H. Lane to Abraham Lincoln, April 20, 1861, Abraham Lincoln Papers at the Library of Congress; *Leavenworth Daily Conservative,* April 30, 1861; *Official Records of the War of the Rebellion,* ser. 1, vol. 51, 335 (this will hereafter be referred to as *O.R.*); Stephenson, *Political Career of Lane,* 105.

Missouri river or stop the Hannibal and St. Joe Railroad, troops would be thrown into Missouri." Further, Lane "ridiculed the idea that we were bound to wait for Missouri to secede—saying that if we took that position, all Missouri had to do was refuse to secede herself while she sent men and money and provisions and munitions of war constantly to the enemy." The senator wanted action: "His position was, that our only safety was in eternal vigilance, being not only ready to repel attacks, but to march into the enemy's country at a moment's warning."[16] Lane's focus on Missouri may have been motivated by memories of the territorial struggle, but his concern was legitimate. Secessionists in Missouri were, in fact, a threat to Union interests. They seized a small arsenal in Liberty, Missouri, and distributed its weapons among pro-Southern men. The state's governor, Claiborne Jackson, opposed Lincoln's call for troops and, after support from secessionist legislators, took control of the St. Louis police force and the local militia.[17]

Rumors circulated that Lane would personally lead forces into Indian Territory, Arkansas, and even Missouri. But his mingling in state military affairs irritated political opponents. Governor Charles Robinson had already organized two regiments in Kansas when Lane set about recruiting more. Part of this rivalry focused on patronage, as Robinson overlooked Lane's friends while commissioning officers.[18] The *Kansas State Journal* charged Lane with disrupting the state's military structure in order to steal a regiment.[19] Nonetheless, some earlier critics acknowledged his military value. The *White Cloud Kansas Chief* professed that the Kansas people had great faith in his soldiering ability.[20]

Lane traveled to Washington in June and corresponded with the president and Secretary of War Simon Cameron about military affairs. His determination and his devotion to the Union caught Lincoln's eye. The Frontier Guard's protection of the Executive Mansion and Lane's eagerness to take action in the West was not lost upon the president or his cabinet. On June 20, Lincoln wrote to Cameron saying that "we need the services of such a man out there at once; that we better appoint him a brigadier-general of volunteers to-day, and send him off with such authority to raise a force . . . as you think will get him into actual work quickest."

16. *Lawrence Republican,* May 16, 1861.
17. Allan Nevins, *The War for the Union, Vol. 1: The Impoverished War,* 120–22.
18. Stephenson, *Political Career of Lane,* 106.
19. *Kansas State Journal,* June 6, 1861.
20. *White Cloud Kansas Chief,* May 16, 1861.

Lincoln closed with instructions unnecessary for a man like Lane: "Tell him when he starts to put it through. Not be writing or telegraphing back here, but put it through."[21]

The very same day, Lane asked Lincoln to accept two additional regiments from Kansas.[22] The administration quickly agreed, and Lane eagerly jumped into Kansas military affairs with his new assignment. He was not interested in simply raising regiments for combat—he wanted service in the field. With Lincoln's appointment in hand, Lane's role in Kansas military affairs gained legitimacy, and within a week Lane announced to Kansas residents that he had been given authority not only to recruit five new regiments, but to lead them into battle. "An insurrectionary war, commenced by rebels, in defiance of patriotism and duty, has now approached our border," he explained. "[The President] has been pleased to place in my hands the honor of leading the gallant sons of the youngest State of the Union, to victory in defense of the Union of which it has so lately become a part."[23] Lane remained in Washington for the congressional session, and therefore appointed William Weer the task of organizing the brigade.[24]

He returned to Kansas in August, anxious to carry out a military campaign against secessionists. He faced resistance from political opponents. Some believed that his military actions disqualified him from a Senate seat. Governor Robinson sent Frederick Stanton to Washington in July in an effort to replace Lane. Lane's supporters in Kansas saw this as an underhanded attempt to depose him. The *Lawrence Republican* assured readers that "Gen. Lane will be in the field of battle in good time, and understands himself well enough to know when to get out of his seat in Congress without any man being sent to contest it." Still, Lane found his seat in real jeopardy as the Judiciary Committee favored Stanton's claim. The matter was not settled until January 1862, when the Senate finally voted in favor of Lane. In the meantime, Lane also battled criticism at home. Lane's friends, hoping to silence talk of duplicity in Kansas affairs, reported that the senator had accepted a commission from the governor of Indiana. Despite continued criticism, Lane took control of three new regiments—the Third and Fourth Kansas Volunteers and the Fifth Kansas Cavalry—which made

21. *O.R.*, ser. 3, vol. 1, 280–81.
22. Ibid., 282.
23. *Lawrence Republican,* June 27, 1861.
24. See Weer's call for troops under Lane's authority in *Lawrence Republican,* June 27, 1861.

up the "Kansas Brigade," and prepared for action. His first order of business was to prepare military fortifications and defenses in Kansas. Believing that Fort Scott, a military installation near the Missouri border, was vulnerable, Lane pulled his men and equipment out of that installation and constructed Fort Lincoln, near the Little Osage River. He also struggled to arm and outfit his new brigade, whose soldiers, he complained to Major General John C. Fremont, lacked uniforms, blankets, and shoes promised by the government.[25]

Lane's military preparations worried some in Kansas. Governor Robinson forewarned Fremont that the Kansas Brigade would "get up a war by going over the line, committing depredations, and then returning into our State." Only this action, the governor explained, would generate a threat from Missouri. He boldly stated, "If you remove the supplies at Fort Scott to the interior, and relieve us of the Lane brigade, I will guarantee Kansas from invasion from Missouri until Jackson shall drive you out of Saint Louis." Yet, Confederate success in Missouri in August, particularly the Battle of Wilson's Creek, seemed to justify Lane's excited actions. Confederate General Sterling Price moved north through Missouri with more than six thousand soldiers. Lane went into action. A detachment of his men skirmished with Price's soldiers but fell back. Lane's battle report commended the behavior of his men, but carried an apocalyptic warning. "I am compelled to make a stand here," he wrote, "or give up Kansas to disgrace and destruction."[26]

In fact, Price had no intention of invading Kansas at the time. Instead, Lane received word from a deserter that Price had targeted Lexington, Missouri, and the federal garrison there. Lane still saw the threat to Kansas

---

25. *Lawrence Republican,* July 18, 1861; *Congressional Globe,* 37th Cong., 1st sess., 406; *Congressional Globe,* 37th Cong., 2nd sess., pt. 1, 363–64; *Lawrence Republican,* August 22, 1861. Biographer Wendell Stephenson questioned the accuracy of the Indiana commission, writing: "The Indiana archives have been searched in vain for a record of such an appointment." Stephenson, *Political Career of Lane,* 134. James G. Blunt, "General Blunt's Account of His Civil War Experiences," 213–14; Wiley Britton, *The Civil War on the Border. Vol. I, 1861–1862,* 130; *O.R.,* ser. 1, vol. 3, 446.

26. *O.R.,* ser. 1, vol. 3, 469. The Battle of Wilson's Creek was the first large engagement of the Civil War west of the Mississippi River. Union forces under General Nathaniel Lyon met General Sterling Price and his Confederates ten miles southwest of Springfield, Missouri, on August 10, 1861. Lyon was killed during the battle. Though a tactical victory for the Confederates, Price was not able to pursue the federal soldiers. See Britton, *Civil War on the Border,* vol. 1, 69–107 and William Garret Piston and Richard W. Hatcher, III, *Wilson's Creek: The Second Battle of the Civil War and the Men Who Fought It* (Chapel Hill: University of North Carolina Press, 2000). *O.R.,* ser. 1, vol. 3, 465, 163.

soil as legitimate and awaited the Confederate advance. Nonetheless, he kept an eye on Price. If the Confederates made any move toward Lexington, he planned to "annoy them as far as my forces and the protection of Kansas will admit of." When Price's army did break camp and marched north in early September, Lane started out in pursuit. A small Confederate raid on the town of Humboldt prompted him to leave a defensive force in the area. With the rest of his men, numbering about fifteen hundred, Lane swept through Butler and Parkville in Missouri. The senator failed to interfere with Price's general maneuver against Lexington, but his small force skirmished with Confederates on September 16 at Morristown and captured a load of supplies in Papinsville on September 21.[27]

Reports of depredations tarnished Lane's military success in Missouri during the month of September. Though he had issued his "General Order No. 4" on September 1, declaring that private property of Kansans and other loyal citizens was to be protected, theft became a problem. On September 9, Captain William Prince wrote to Lane asking him to "adopt early and active measures to crush out this marauding which is enacted in Captain [Charles] Jennison's name, as also yours, by a band of men representing themselves as belonging to your command."[28] Wasting no time, on September 19 Lane stood before his brigade and exploded with rage over a recent incident:

> You sneaking thieves, what did you think of yourselves when you were invading the premises of that widow in the north part of town, and stealing her nightdress, her skillets, and her chickens? Were you acting the part of soldiers then? Did you think we were at war with widows? Did you think we were at war with chickens and skillets? That widow had a safeguard from me, which should have been an ample protection against

27. O.R., ser. 1, vol. 3, 164, 490, 196; Stephenson, Political Career of Lane, 111.

28. O.R., ser. 1, vol. 3, 482. Lane's General Order No. 4 included these protections of property: "1st. The rights, persons and property of the people of Kansas must be sacredly observed—not an article of property however trifling must be taken without payment in ready money for the same, or a receipt given by an authorized officer. 2nd. The rights, persons, and property of the loyal citizens of other States must be sacredly observed, and every assistance and protection extended to them. 3rd. Such property of those in arms against the Government as can be made useful in the army, may be seized, but when so seized, must at the very earliest moment be turned over to the quartermaster or Commissary's Departments, the Heads of such Departments giving receipts therefore. He who fails in this, and appropriates or attempts to appropriate any portion of the enemy's property so seized to his own use, is a base robber and shall be punished as such." Printed in Leavenworth Daily Conservative, September 21, 1861.

all intruders. . . . The injury you have done the widow has been repaired as far as possible, but not even your blood could wash out the stain you have brought upon the army.[29]

Author Donald Gilmore scorned this speech, stating: "All of this, of course, was just shoptalk from a fellow who had just stolen a nice piano, carriage, and silk dresses in Osceola, and the men likely chuckled and sneered at Lane's insincere, fatuous ranting behind his back."[30] Gilmore stands as one of the most recent critics of Lane. His book is also filled with numerous historical errors—including the fact that Lane's raid on Osceola referred to above was conducted *after* the September 19 speech. Nonetheless, Gilmore's work demonstrates the popular negative perception of Lane.

In fact, Lane had drawn up rules for his men two days earlier, which were read to the brigade.[31] And many of his men seem to have taken these orders to heart. A newspaper correspondent in the Kansas Brigade described the behavior of the soldiers while passing by a secessionist farm in Missouri. "She was a secessionist, and had one son in the rebel army; but, as Gen. Lane told his men, his army was not at war with widows. This sort of discipline was observed all along the march. Not an apple or peach, or anything else, was touched only by the permission of the owner or the officer in command."[32]

Lane further responded to the matter of theft with a proclamation, issued the same day, to the citizens of Missouri. He explained that he had learned "with deep regret that unwarranted excesses have been committed upon your property, by persons professing to belong to the United States army." Responsibility for those actions, he wrote, must be laid upon others. "We are *soldiers*, not thieves, or plunderers, or jay hawkers. We have entered the army to fight for a peace, to put down a rebellion, to cause the stars and stripes—your flag as well as ours, once more to float over every foot of American soil. This is our sole purpose, and when this has been accomplished in your section, we will take up our departure for fresh scenes, when the vigor of our arms may be seen and felt; until then we remain."[33] But Lane wanted to prevent accounts of federal pillaging from spurring otherwise loyal Missourians into Confederate ranks.

29. *Leavenworth Daily Conservative*, October 5, 1861.
30. Gilmore, *Civil War on the Missouri-Kansas Border*, 137.
31. *Leavenworth Daily Conservative*, October 5, 1861.
32. *Lawrence Republican*, October 3, 1861.
33. Ibid., September 26, 1861; *Liberty Weekly Tribune*, October 4, 1861.

Let every man now in arms return to his home and resume his business. Let your scattered and terified [sic] population return. Reopen your courts, your schools, your churches. Restore the arts of peace. In short act the part of good, loyal, peace-loving American citizens; and the better to prove your claims as such, run up the American Flag before your doors. Let this be done by a concerted movement of each neighborhood, and here in the face of the world and before High Heaven I promise you that the flag which has protected American citizens on every sea, shall be your protection; that this patriotic army of mine, which you so much fear, shall be to you what the strong hearted man is to the delicate woman by his side, a shield and a support. I will protect you against lawless plunderers and marauders from your own State, from Kansas, from anywhere.—We will take you to our bosoms as we do our brethren everywhere, who are loyal as we.[34]

The alternative was destruction:

Should you, however, disregard my advice, the stern visitations of war will be meted out to the rebels and their allies. I shall then be convinced that your arming for protection is a sham; and rest assured that the traitor, when caught, shall receive a traitor's doom. The cup of mercy has been exhausted. Treason, hereafter, will be treated as treason. The massacre of innocent women and children, by black-hearted traitors lately burning a bridge on the Hannibal & St. Joseph Railroad, has satisfied us that a traitor will perpetrate crimes which devils would shudder to commit; they shall be blotted from existence, and sent to that hell which yawns for their reception.[35]

Lane was serious with his threats of destruction. On September 22, upon reaching the Missouri town of Osceola, Lane's men were fired upon by a company of Confederates. The Kansas Brigade shelled the town and chased the defenders away. Much of Osceola was burned. Initial reports credited the artillery barrage for the fire, but Lane admitted that a significant amount of supplies had been destroyed—suggesting that some of the destruction was intentional. Joseph Trego of the Third Kansas Regiment wrote to his wife that after chasing off the rebels and rounding up the horses, mules, wagons, and local slaves, Lane's men "loaded the wagons with valuebles [sic] from the numerous well supplied stores, and then set fire to the infernal town." A correspondent to the *Lawrence Republican* in

34. *Liberty Weekly Tribune,* October 4, 1861.
35. Ibid.

Lane's ranks corroborated Trego's account, explaining that after loading up goods from local buildings, the Kansas Brigade's officers decided to burn the town. Osceola stood as an important distribution center in Missouri, and was thought to be a hotbed of secessionist sentiment. The brigade's officers concluded that the town should be destroyed, rather than allowed to serve as a winter military post for Confederates. Lane's supporters celebrated its destruction as a blow to the Confederate cause. His critics in Kansas, however, bemoaned the action. On October 9, Governor Robinson wrote to the *Leavenworth Times* with a series of complaints in the ongoing feud with Lane. He specifically criticized Lane's boast of destroying secessionist property in Osceola. "What kind of property was this?" Robinson demanded. "Was it contraband of war—arms, ammunition, shot, shell, or cannon? No, it was the clothing, bedding, food and shelter of women and children, every dollar of which will have to be paid back by the General Government as soon as peace is restored."[36]

Adding to the controversy over the brigade's actions in Osceola were accounts of widespread drunkenness. A large supply of liquor was found in the town. H. E. Palmer, of the First Kansas Battery, was among the officers and men ordered to break open and destroy the alcohol before the rest of the brigade could indulge. The effort was only partially successful. He recalled that "the 'mixed drinks' filled the side-hill cellar and ran out of a rear door down a ravine, where the boys filled their canteens and 'tanks' with the stuff, more deadly for a while than rebel bullets."[37] Some of the alcohol was set on fire as it was poured onto the ground to aid in its destruction and prevent its consumption, and witnesses described seeing a stream of flames running down the hill to the Osage River.[38] Despite

---

36. Hildegarde Rose Herklotz, "Jayhawkers in Missouri, 1858–1863," Third Article, Chapter IV, 68. See Lane's report on the "Skirmish at, and destruction of, Osceola, Mo," *O.R.*, ser. 1, vol. 3, 196. See B. Rush Plumly's reports in *O.R.*, ser. 1, vol. 3, 516, 517; also see Lane's report to John C. Fremont, *O.R.*, ser. 1, vol. 3, 505–6. During a speech in Leavenworth two weeks later, Lane briefly described the action (with some embellishment on the size of the opposing force): ". . . go to Osceola, one of the strongest natural points in southern Missouri, where after eighty miles march through the enemy's country we met a greatly superior force, beat it and took and destroyed more than a million dollars worth of property," *Liberty Weekly Tribune*, October 11, 1861. "The Letters of Joseph H. Trego, 1857–1864, Linn County Pioneer," 295; *Lawrence Republican*, October 3, 1861; Herklotz, "Jayhawkers in Missouri," 68. Robinson's letter reprinted in *Liberty Weekly Tribune*, October 18, 1861.

37. H. E. Palmer, "The Black-Flag Character of War on the Border," 457.

38. John Speer, "The Burning of Osceola, Mo., by Lane, and the Quantrill Massacre Contrasted," 306, 309.

these efforts, Palmer explained that "nearly 300 of our men had to be hauled from town in wagons and carriages impressed into service for that purpose."[39]

Historians have disagreed on the merit of Lane's actions in Osceola. Albert Castel rejected contemporary accounts that defended actions against Osceola as "specious and beside the point," arguing that reasons given "could have applied just as well to nearly every town in that section of Missouri."[40] However, former Union soldier Wiley Britton outlined the town's logistic and political importance in his postwar historical work, including its role as county seat and as shipping point for goods on the Osage River.[41] Some Osceola residents later corroborated their town's logistical importance to John Speer during his postwar investigation of the event. Dr. J. Wade Gardner described the lead, salt, and other supplies transferred to and from Osceola and stored in warehouses. He explained that "it was well known that in 1861 said wholesale houses had immense stocks of groceries, whiskies, boots, shoes, clothing, etc., on hand." He believed that Lane had destroyed the supplies, and town, to prevent Confederate forces from using them. Other residents agreed with Gardner.[42] Osceola was not a typical Missouri town. Nonetheless, for Castel, the "truth of the matter is that Lane's Brigade was an irresponsible mob which looted and burned Osceola out of a wanton lust for plunder and a self-righteous desire to injure the Missourians."[43] In many ways, Castel is right. Lane's men were more disorganized than most military units during the Civil War and did carry out shocking acts of destruction. However, Lane and his men foreshadowed William Tecumseh Sherman's later march through the South and his systematic devastation of Southern property. While Lane's campaign was unauthorized by higher military authorities, both his and Sherman's actions served as a form of revenge. Both leaders believed their campaigns served important psychological and logistical purposes in defeating secession.

The conflicting reports of Lane's actions in Missouri are difficult to decipher. No doubt some plundering took place. However, as during the territorial struggle, Lane's reputation for excess probably outran his actions. Biographer Wendell Stephenson explains that although Lane and his men

39. Palmer, "The Black-Flag Character of War on the Border," 457.
40. Castel, *Civil War Kansas*, 54–55.
41. Britton, *Civil War on the Border*, vol. 1, 147–48.
42. Speer, "The Burning of Osceola," 306–7.
43. Castel, *Civil War Kansas*, 55.

"actually committed many depredations in western Missouri, he accepted the responsibility for others to intimidate the enemy." Lane understood the psychological effect of his actions in Missouri. But he possibly underestimated the opposition from many Kansans and Unionists in Missouri. The *Liberty* (Missouri) *Weekly Tribune* declared that Lane's campaigns "are no better than the raids of lawless bands, who spread themselves over a defenseless country to pillage and harry it." Such threat, real or perceived, drove a number of Missouri guerrillas into the saddle against the Union. This prompted some military officers outside of Kansas to denounce Lane, including Major General Henry Halleck, commander of the military department over Missouri. In December, Halleck complained to General George B. McClellan that the "conduct of the forces under Lane and Jennison has done more for the enemy in this State than could be accomplished by 20,000 of his own army." He mentioned rumors of Lane's appointment as brigadier general, announcing, "I cannot conceive a more injudicious appointment. It will take 20,000 men to counteract its effect in this State, and moreover, is offering a premium for rascality and robbing generally."[44]

Price and his Confederates moved south through Missouri and the threat to Kansas appeared to recede. As military operations on the Kansas-Missouri border eased, Lane more actively engaged in the political battle with Robinson. In Leavenworth, he complained that the governor and his friends had "publicly declared their intention to destroy" the Army of Kansas and its efforts to crush out treason.[45] "I have commanded seven armies," he boomed, "and have found that officers succeed best when they treat their men as if they had souls and were human. Be kind to them, and they will obey and fight for you to the last. I would like to see that creature down among the Kansas boys! Let him go among them and inquire about Jim Lane, and he would find they loved him as they do their mother. They would go where he commanded, even if it was to storm the gates of hell.

44. Stephenson, *Political Career of Lane*, 162. Wiley Britton wrote, "General Lane destroyed and appropriated [Unionist] property with the same recklessness that he did the property of the secessionists. He was incapable of seeing that the loyal people of Missouri were entitled to the protection of the Federal Government, even if they were fighting its battles." Britton, *Civil War on the Border*, vol. 1, 148. *Liberty Weekly Tribune*, October 25, 1861. See Herklotz, "Jayhawkers in Missouri," 70–73. Though Donald Gilmore's *Civil War on the Missouri-Kansas Border* has many faults, his discussion of the psychological effect Kansas jayhawking had on Missouri residents is important, especially chapter 10, "The Guerillas' Identity, Extermination, and Trauma," 209–24. *O.R.*, ser. 1, vol. 8, 449.

45. *Lawrence Republican*, October 17, 1861.

And if he wanted to capture the *Old Fellow* [the devil] himself, though aided by Robinson and Prince, he could rely upon the Kansas Brigade."[46]

Lane was not satisfied with verbally denouncing Robinson's handling of military affairs in Kansas. He set about circumventing the governor. On October 9, the day after his Leavenworth speech, Lane wrote to Lincoln accusing Robinson of exerting "his utmost endeavor to prevent the enlistment of men," and having constantly "vilified myself, and abused the men under my command as marauders and thieves."[47] The senator requested the creation of a new military department, consisting of Kansas, much of Arkansas, Indian Territory (modern-day Oklahoma), and other parts of the territories deemed suitable. He volunteered to command the department, and explained that he would resign his Senate seat and "devote all my thoughts and energies to the prosecution of the war."[48]

Lincoln accepted Lane's advice and created the new department. But he placed David Hunter in command. The new provisional governor of Missouri, Hamilton Gamble, had asked Lincoln that Lane not be put in command.[49] Lane's reputation as an undiscriminating raider cost him the job. His supporters were disappointed, but some did try to find a positive spin to it. The *Leavenworth Daily Conservative* pointed out the friendship between Lane and Hunter and their combined efforts to defend the capital in April.[50] However, Wendell Stephenson explains, "It is clear that all of this was to save Lane's face."[51]

When Hunter took command of the new department, he found military matters in Kansas, and the Kansas Brigade in particular, in poor shape. Though a lieutenant under Lane wrote that the senator "is having his whole Brigade rigged out in as good style as any soldiers that I have seen since this war was begun, the Regulars at Fort Leavenworth not excepted," Hunter disagreed.[52] A report of his findings explained, "Nothing could exceed the demoralized condition in which General Hunter found the Third and Fourth Kansas Infantry and Fifth and Sixth Kansas Cavalry,

46. Ibid.
47. *O.R.*, ser. 1, vol. 3, 529.
48. Ibid., 530.
49. Ibid., ser. 1, vol. 17, pt. 2, 92.
50. Hunter had given Lane a sword for his role in commanding the Frontier Guard. Miller, *Lincoln's Abolitionist General*, 56; *Leavenworth Daily Conservative*, November 13, 1861.
51. Stephenson, *Political Career of Lane*, 113.
52. Joseph H. Trego to his wife, October 2, 1861, in "The Letters of Joseph H. Trego," 297.

formerly known as 'Lane's brigade,' on his arrival in this department."
The men were described as "a mere ragged, half-armed, diseased, and
mutinous rabble, taking votes as to whether any troublesome or distasteful order should be obeyed or defied." Further, Lane's men reportedly
stole federal property: "Vast amounts of public property had been taken
from the depots at Fort Scott and Fort Lincoln without requisition or any
form of responsibility, and horses in great quantities and at extravagant
prices had been purchased under irregular orders and paid for by the
United States; these horses being turned over to men and officers who
were then drawing 40 cents per day for them as private property."[53]
Hunter brought soldiers from other states to stabilize the Kansas department and sent seasoned officers to help reorganize the Kansas regiments.

Still, Lane and his men had supporters. The rag-tag and mob-like personality of the Kansas Brigade appalled some military officers, but the
brigade resembled the free-state militias during the territorial struggle. To
some in Kansas, and in other parts of the Union as well, the Kansas
Brigade's appearance was less important than its ability to fight—and
punish—secessionists. A correspondent to the *Lawrence Republican* discussed the burning of Osceola and admitted, "Until this visit, I was not
fully satisfied that the deed was righteous and a necessity. In this as in
many other things, I see evidence of the far-seeing sagacity of Lane and
Montgomery." The *St. Louis Democrat* reported Lane's actions in Pleasant
Hill, Missouri, during his military maneuvers in October, describing the
posting of a large Union flag in the town. Lane called the residents to look
upon it, reportedly saying, "That flag has been your protection, and shall
be still. So long as it remains here you are safe, but if it is cut down, by the
Eternal I will return and burn your town!" The newspaper explained that
the episode "occurred two weeks ago, and although the denizens of Pleasant Hill are said to be about all secessionists, *that flag is still waving over the
town!*" The *Cincinnati Gazette* also approved, stating: "There is no mistake
about it, Lane has done more, and is doing more, to put down this rebellion, in a way that it will stay down, than all the other armies together in
this state [Missouri]. He conquers as he goes."[54]

53. *O.R.*, ser. I, vol. 8, 615, 616.
54. *Lawrence Republican*, November 7, 1861; *St. Louis Democrat*, in *Lawrence Republican*, November 14, 1861. The *Leavenworth Conservator* ran a similar account of Lane's
actions in Pleasant Hill: "The brigade met with no enemy on the march to Osceola.
General Lane plants Union flags in nearly every town he passes, and his object in doing
so is clearly revealed in a speech recently made at Pleasant Hill. He said: "I am here

Lane's plans for suppressing the rebellion went far beyond small raids into Missouri. He had advocated an aggressive campaign through Maryland shortly before Lincoln's inauguration. As the year 1861 closed, he bemoaned the cautious nature of many Union generals. On the Senate floor, Lane asked, "Why is our army inactive?" He could find no legitimate answer:

> Will it be answered that it is still deficient in discipline? That reply would be as unjust as it is illogical. Ours is an army of volunteers, who must not be judged by the rules applied to regulars. You cannot drill it into that mere machine which martinets consider the perfection of efficiency. The citizen-soldier is an individual; no amount of discipline can destroy his individuality. Four months of industrious drill is ample time to prepare such troops for effective service. Prolonged inactivity will finally discourage his zeal. The prospect of action must be ever present as an incentive. Inaction is the bane of the volunteer.[55]

As in Kansas, Lane embraced the differences between volunteers and professional soldiers, relying upon the enthusiasm of the former rather than the professionalism of the latter. Further, he questioned the cautious strategy of some of the Union's top commanders. He believed the time for compromise had long passed—his years in Kansas had made that brutally clear. Lane wanted action:

> The occupation of the rebel States by our army is a military necessity. I laugh to scorn the policy of wooing back the traitors to their allegiance by seizing and holding unimportant points in those States. Every invitation extended to them in kindness is an encouragement to stronger resistance. The exhausting policy is a failure. So long as they have four million of slaves to feed them, so long will this rebellion be sustained. My word for it, sir, long before they reach the point of exhaustion the people of this country will lose confidence in their rulers. And it is unreasonable to expect the loyal citizens of the rebel States to manifest their desire to their allegiance, while their homes and families are in the power of their oppressors. . . . So with the people of the disloyal States: march your

---

once more and this time I raise the Stars and Stripes. So long as that flag waves here your citizens shall receive protection. But let it be torn down by secession hands, and Pleasant Hill comes down as sure as hell." *Leavenworth Conservator,* in *Liberty Weekly Tribune,* November 8, 1861. *Cincinnati Gazette,* quoted in Stephenson, *Political Career of Lane,* 117.

55. *Congressional Globe,* 37th Cong., 2nd sess., pt. 1, 111.

armies there; engage and scatter the forces of the enemy; whip some-
body; evidence your ability to protect the loyal citizens, their homes, and
families; and then, and not till then, will they rally to your standard by
thousands and tens of thousands.[56]

While he advocated action across the whole military front, Lane
planned his own grand campaign. In early 1862, he spoke with War Secretary Simon Cameron about his plan, supposedly supported by General
Hunter, to lead thirty thousand men south from Kansas, possibly through
Indian Territory, and into Arkansas. A couple of weeks later, he reportedly
discussed the matter with Lincoln, General George B. McClellan, and
Edwin M. Stanton (who replaced Cameron in January). The leadership
supported his ideas, though McClellan questioned Unionist sentiments in
the South. Lane replied, "I will take good care to leave no rebel sentiment
behind me. If Missouri, Arkansas and the Indian country will not come
peaceably under the laws of the government, my plan is to make them a
wilderness. I will give the traitors twenty-four hours to choose between
exile and death." He closed with the ominous warning that "if I can't do
better I will kill off the white traitors and give their lands to the loyal black
men." News of his plan circulated across the North, and drew a great deal
of support. The *Lawrence Republican* excitedly anticipated Lane's return to
Kansas to lead twenty thousand men. The *National Republican* announced
that Lane enjoyed full support from the Lincoln administration for his
aggressive plans. "No announcement could be more gratifying to the
country," the editors exclaimed. "It is the *beginning of the end of this war.*"
And the *Kansas State Journal,* generally unfriendly to Lane, agreed that
"General Lane acting vigorously, earnestly and consistently . . . is entitled
to and will, no doubt, receive the aid, influence and best wishes of the people of the whole country. The honor and the character of the people of
Kansas are peculiarly involved in its success."[57]

Lane returned to Kansas in late January, ready to take command. Unfortunately, he found competition from General Hunter. On January 27, Hunter
declared his intention to lead the expedition, "unless otherwise expressly
ordered by the Government."[58] Lane immediately telegraphed his friend

---

56. Ibid.
57. *O.R.,* ser. I, vol. 53, 512. An account of Lane's meeting with Lincoln, McClellan, and
Stanton was published in the *New York Daily Tribune,* January 18, 1862; quoted in Stephenson, *Political Career of Lane,* 119. *Lawrence Republican,* January 9, 1862; *National Republican,*
in *Lawrence Republican,* January 9, 1862; *Kansas State Journal,* January 16, 1862.
58. *O.R.,* ser. 1, vol. 8, 529.

Congressman John Covode with the news and requested that he confer with "the President, Secretary of war, and General McClellan, and answer what I shall do."[59] Lane was largely to blame for the confusion, for he had exaggerated Hunter's support for his role in the campaign.[60] In December the senator told Secretary Cameron that he [Lane] was "to go to Kansas to act entirely under [Hunter's] direction."[61] Yet, Hunter—who supported an aggressive move into the Confederacy—had been unaware of Lane's specific plans to lead the campaign. After Lane returned to Kansas and set about preparing for the expedition, Hunter wrote to new Secretary of War Edwin Stanton in February to clarify the senator's position. "Previous to his arrival here, the fact of his appointment [as brigadier general] and the belief that he had accepted it, were so widely current and credited, that many regard him as if in the service; and I am held responsible (in the belief that he has reported to me for duty and is under my control,) for much that I cannot endorse or approve in his line of conduct," he complained. "[W]hile the fact that he has not accepted, but is here as a Senator and member of the Military Committee places him beyond any supervision of mine, and his acts are independent of my judgment."[62] Hunter wanted to know whether Lane was acting as senator or as a commissioned officer in the upcoming campaign.

The dispute over the expedition's command generated excitement in Kansas and within military circles. William P. Dole, U.S. Commissioner of Indian Affairs, wrote to Lincoln on February 3 in support of Lane. He explained that "I could not have been mistaken, in the fact, that it was contemplated at Washington, that Genl Lane, should command the expedition, fitting out here, for a southern campaign. I am at the same time aware that it was expected, that Genl Hunter, would willingly acquiesce, in this arrangement, he retaining the superior command, and superintending, the entire organization, of the expedition, and controlling all its movements, untill [sic] it entered the field." He described the relationship between the two men as friendly, but told the president "the public are very much excited on the subject, and will be more than disapointed [sic], if Genl Lane, is not suffered in some way to command the expedition."[63]

59. Ibid., 529, 530.
60. Miller, *Lincoln's Abolitionist General*, 80–81.
61. *O.R.*, ser. 1, vol. 53, 512.
62. David Hunter to Edwin M. Stanton, February 1, 1862, Abraham Lincoln Papers at the Library of Congress.
63. William P. Dole to Abraham Lincoln, February 3, 1862, Abraham Lincoln Papers at the Library of Congress.

Although many believed Hunter would allow Lane to command the campaign, the department commander did not agree. He expressed surprise and dismay at Lane's behavior. In a letter to Lincoln, Hunter wrote, "It is clear that he either is, or assumes to be, bitterly disappointed at not receiving practical control of the department, with liberty to place members of his own staff and personal retinue in charge of the Quartermaster and Commissary departments at this Post." Further, Hunter attributed Lane's motives to financial interests: "His disappointment in these respects may possibly be accounted for by the swarm of Contractors who have accompanied his return to Kansas and the great number of schemes involving large expenditures which are said to have received his sanction."[64]

Hunter became increasingly agitated with Lane's actions, and continued to defend himself before administration and federal officials. On February 8, in a letter to Major General Halleck, the general accused Lane of using his reputation to gain influence and power: "It seems, from all the evidence before me, that Senator J. H. Lane has been trading at Washington on a capital partly made up of his own Senatorial position and partly of such scraps of influence as I may have possessed in the confidence or esteem of the President, said scraps having been 'jayhawked' by the Kansas Senator without due consent of the proper owner." Though Lane had portrayed the campaign as a joint effort between the two men, Hunter declared that "so little was I personally consulted, that to this hour I am in ignorance what were the terms or striking points of Senator Lane's programme."[65] Lane had not consulted with Hunter, directly or indirectly, about the campaign.

It is not clear that Lane's plans were entirely mischievous—that he intended to ignore or disregard Hunter's authority. Lane understood that Hunter would ultimately have to approve his command. Instead, the senator likely assumed that Hunter would not object to him leading the campaign, and worked accordingly. But Lane was not willing to bet his Senate career on this assumption. While publicly touting his appointment as brigadier general, Lane never actually accepted it. He waited to secure his chosen military command before cutting his legislative ties.[66] Hunter found evidence of this in a telegram to Lane from Congressman Covode

64. David Hunter to Abraham Lincoln, February 4, 1862, Abraham Lincoln Papers at the Library of Congress.
65. *O.R.*, ser. 1, vol. 8, 830.
66. In a February 13 letter to Hunter, Lane admitted that he retained his Senate seat until his chosen military assignment was confirmed: "But it is all-important before I resign my seat in the United States Senate to accept the office of Brigadier General, so

in Washington, which warned the senator that "Hunter will not get the money or men he requires. His command cannot go forward. Hold on. Don't resign your seat."[67] Hunter thus requested Lincoln and Stanton to force Lane to accept the commission or give up the matter.[68]

Lane did not give up the command opportunity yet. He obtained support from the Kansas legislature; both houses sent Lincoln resolutions endorsing his promotion to major general and his command of the Southern expedition. He even elicited support from leaders of two Indian nations. Ho-po-eith-le-yo-ho-la, "Head Chief of the Creek Nation," and A-luk-tus-te-nu-ke, "Head Chief of the Seminole Nation," endorsed a petition to Lincoln requesting that Lane lead the Southern expedition. Lincoln stood firm. He had always understood that Lane was under Hunter's command. On February 10, the president officially settled the dispute. He wished to retain the services of both men, but in this matter, "General Hunter is the senior officer and must command when they serve together. . . . If they cannot come to an amicable understanding, General Lane must report to General Hunter for duty, according to the rules, or decline the service."[69]

Hunter believed that Lane would sabotage the expedition, or at least his own role in it, if he could not control it. "He is bestirring himself in a thousand little irritating processes," Hunter told Halleck on February 8, "trying to make a quarrel or 'disagreement' with me his pretext for backing out of an employment which he never intended to accept."[70] A letter from Lane to Hunter on February 13 indicated that he intended to challenge Hunter's decision, and perhaps justify his own actions, but did not appear quarrelsome. Lane wrote, "I shall consider neither personally offensive, nor shall anything that shall arise, beget a misunderstanding between us. I have said

kindly tendered to me by the President and so cordially confirmed by the Senate, that our understanding should be full thorough." Lane to Hunter, February 13, 1862, Abraham Lincoln Papers at the Library of Congress.

67. John Covode to General Lane, quoted in letter from David Hunter to Henry Halleck, February 8, 1862, *O.R.*, ser. 1, vol. 8, 831.

68. David Hunter to Abraham Lincoln, February 4, 1862, and David Hunter to Edwin M. Stanton, February 1, 1862, both in Abraham Lincoln Papers at the Library of Congress.

69. Stephenson, *Political Career of Lane*, 121; *O.R.*, ser. 1, vol. 8, 534. Lincoln wrote to the secretary of war on January 31 clarifying his support of the expedition. He stated: "General Lane has been told by me many times that he is under the command of General Hunter, and assented to it as often as told. It was the distinct agreement between him and me when I appointed him that he was to be under Hunter." *O.R.*, ser. 1, vol. 8, 538, 551.

70. Ibid., 830, 831.

to you several times, and I repeat the remark here that I would accept no military command in your department unless such command was satisfactory to you or unless we could work harmoniously together." But Lane wanted to know why Hunter did not agree to what the government had come to believe and support, that he [Lane] should lead the expedition. He bluntly asked in a letter to Hunter, "Is it consistent with the public service, and your own honour,—and to oblige the President of the United States to give me the command of that expedition with you alone as my senior officer, and commander when serving together?"[71]

Hunter would not be swayed. He wrote to Lincoln the following day complaining of Lane's behavior. "Had he reported for duty I would gladly have assigned him to a command not merely commensurate with his rank, in the strict military sense." But, Hunter argued, Lane had not returned to Kansas as a man under his command, for "never once did he talk or even hint of reporting for duty, but on all occasions used the phrase that he wished to 'cooperate' with me in conducting the Expedition,—his idea of 'cooperation' clearly being that he was to command the column while I remained in Fort Leavenworth approving of his requisitions on the Quartermaster, Commissariat, and Ordnance Departments." And the irate general was not through with his condemnation of Lane:

> I know no man in Kansas to-night, Mr. Lincoln,—not even those very adherents of his who are gazing hungrily on the Quartermaster & Commissariat patronage they expect him to bestow,—who feels, or in ordinary conversation would even profess to feel the least confidence in the veracity of Senator James H. Lane. By friend as enemy he is regarded as an unscrupulous trickster,—a demagogue in all the worst senses of that word,—whose promises are to be relied upon just as it may suit his convenience to keep or break them. This, in so far as I have had any, has been my own experience of his character; and it was in view of his gross misstatements of former conversations,—misstatements of which I have documentary evidence,—that I was obliged to insist upon having our official intercourse reduced to writing on both sides.[72]

Hunter closed his letter by apologizing for such blunt talk, and agreed to whatever punishment was due if he had overstepped his authority. But, he

71. Lane to Hunter, February 13, 1862, Abraham Lincoln Papers at the Library of Congress.
72. Hunter to Lincoln, February 14, 1862, Abraham Lincoln Papers at the Library of Congress.

announced, "I am not willing that the cause of the Union should be imperiled and its flag disgraced by the appointment to supreme command of one whose only claim to consideration must be based on a total misapprehension of his true character."[73] Hunter leveled serious charges against Lane, and his characterization of Lane echoed sentiments voiced by other critics during previous years. Yet, Lane was not deemed a demagogue by all, as shown by the steadfast support for his leadership during the Southern Expedition controversy.

Lane realized that his plan to command the Southern Expedition had failed. He wrote to Lincoln on February 16, reporting that his efforts to "harmonize" with Hunter were unsuccessful and that he would decline the brigadier general commission.[74] Though he no longer labored to gain a battlefield command, Lane's interests in Kansas military affairs continued throughout the war.

Lane's actions during the first year of the war highlight the energy and enthusiasm that won him support from many in Kansas and even the president—as well as the condemnation of his political opponents and other military officers. His marches into Missouri have been portrayed as valuable strikes against secession as well as lawless raids bent on revenge and plunder. Yet, Lane worked for the same interest he had always embraced: the stability of the Union. Lane championed an aggressive war that would punish those who had dared threaten the future of the Union, and, he believed, enforce the law under the present circumstances. Southerners brought on the war, he maintained, and must be ready to feel its consequences. His attempts at compromise in the sectional conflict had been destroyed during his tenure in Kansas, and thus he rejected talk of moderation. His raids into Missouri were not careless, nor were they random acts of plunder, though they may have been shocking. And they foreshadowed Sherman's total warfare in Georgia and South Carolina. Historian Charles Royster described Sherman's view of war as such: "In war the power of some people over others was no longer confined by precedent, compromises, and documents. Instead, it consisted of direct violence in many forms, ranging from killing thousands of men to taking some food—violence cumulatively demonstrating the subjugation of the weaker to the stronger."[75] In 1861, few people believed that the growing

73. Ibid.
74. Stephenson, *Political Career of Lane*, 122.
75. Charles Royster, *The Destructive War: William Tecumseh Sherman, Stonewall Jackson, and the Americans*, 353.

conflict would, or could, see widespread destruction of towns, homes, and property. But Lane not only believed that such actions were necessary but also was ready to lead the charge. A military veteran of the Mexican War and militia leader in Kansas, Lane's passion for action drove him into military affairs in 1861. As a motivated leader, Lane wanted to be in command. He wanted to be at the center. His eagerness to get into the fight led him to blur the lines of political and military authority. He certainly tried to secure his chosen command in the army before relinquishing his legislative seat. However, he did not lustfully grab for power solely for his own sake. Lane's efforts, at least in his own mind, were sincere. He wanted to lead troops into the South because he truly believed it would help win the war.

Lane was his own worst enemy. His poor relations with Hunter denied him his coveted command, and drew accusations of demagoguery and corruption. Hunter portrayed the Kansan as a megalomaniac. Though confident to the point of arrogance, Lane always recognized Lincoln's authority, and understood the system in which he worked. His failed attempt to command the Southern Expedition does demonstrate a level of opportunism, but one that arguably compares to the push for military and political advancement many Americans engaged in during the war.

Ultimately, Lane's actions and words during the first part of the Civil War must be compared to his past. Since his days as an Indiana congressman, Lane had announced his love of the Union and dedication to protecting it from dangers outside and within. As the sectional conflict turned bloody, and as the traditional party system crumbled, he adapted his tactics to protect those interests. He met radical threats to the Union, as he saw it, with an extreme response.

9

Lane and His Enemies, 1862–1863

"It has been said that Lane never sleeps, and he does not when there is danger."

James Lane continued to be the center of controversy during the first half of the war. Two particular events, one in 1862 and the other in 1863, have been cited by Lane's critics as further evidence of opportunism and fanaticism. The first centered on his rivalry with Charles Robinson. The political infighting in Kansas came to a boiling point in 1862, and signaled a victory of the pro-Lane faction over the governor, helping lead to the latter's postwar excoriation of the senator. The second involved one of the worst atrocities of the Civil War, as a large band of Missouri guerrillas under the command of William C. Quantrill destroyed the town of Lawrence and killed more than 150 citizens in the process. Both of these events highlight the controversial image of Lane. Yet, neither of these episodes distracted Lane from his larger goals and principles. In fact, his words and actions in both cases followed, in their own extreme way, Lane's constant drive to protect Kansas and the Union. While he no doubt realized political opportunities in his battle with Robinson and the war against Missouri guerrillas, he truly believed his actions were necessary for the success of his state, his party, and his country.

While the feud between Governor Robinson and Lane had simmered since before the war, it reached new heights during the latter part of 1861. The pro-Lane faction in Kansas had unsuccessfully tried to oust Robinson through a constitutional technicality. The Republican State Central Committee, dominated by Lane's friends, nominated George A. Crawford to replace Robinson on grounds that the governor's term actually expired in January 1862, rather than 1863. The state legislature had tried to remedy this problem by extending the state offices for another year, but Crawford's supporters rejected this act as unconstitutional. Crawford's name was placed on ballots in the November 1861 state election, but he was the only candidate for governor. Many Kansans rejected Crawford's bid, including the State Election Board, which refused to count votes submitted for him. Crawford appealed to the State Supreme Court. Robinson feared that he might in fact be forced out of the executive position. The Chief Justice was Thomas Ewing, Jr., a former colleague of Robinson's who had shifted his loyalty to Lane. Despite Ewing's political allegiances, he approached the case on strict legal grounds. Writing for the majority decision, Ewing concluded that the legislative act extending state offices was legitimate. Robinson remained the state's governor.[1]

The dispute over the governorship had barely settled when a new scandal rocked Kansas politics and brought an impeachment case against Robinson. The issue revolved around the sale of bonds. In 1861, the state legislature had approved the sale of two types of bonds—"war bonds" and "seven per cent bonds"—to help raise money for the state's military effort. The legislature approved the sale of war bonds to the sum of $20,000, though there was some question later as to whether that total meant the par value or the amount of real money acquired. Robinson and State Treasurer H. R. Dutton decided to issue $40,000 worth of bonds to receive an anticipated $20,000 in real cash. Robinson's friend and banking partner Robert S. Stevens then purchased $31,000 of these war bonds and promptly sold them to the Interior Department for ninety-five cents on the dollar—pocketing some $14,300 profit.[2]

As for the "seven per cent" bonds, an initial effort by the Kansas legislature to have two Leavenworth businessmen, Austin M. Clark and James C. Stone, handle the sale of $150,000 of these bonds failed when the men

1. Castel, *Civil War Kansas*, 69–70; Collins, *Jim Lane*, 203.
2. Cortez A. M. Ewing, "Early Kansas Impeachments," 310–11; Castel, *Civil War Kansas*, 71.

reported that they could not sell them at a respectable price.[3] The legislature then authorized Governor Robinson, Secretary of State John W. Robinson (not related), and Auditor George S. Hillyer to sell the bonds with the restriction that they were to be sold for at least seventy cents on the dollar.[4] As with Clark and Stone, the state officials had little luck finding buyers. That was until Robert Stevens once again stepped into the picture. He reported to Hillyer and John Robinson that the U.S. Interior Department would purchase the seven percent bonds. Stevens then presented a contract that allowed him to pocket any proceeds over sixty cents on the dollar of bonds sold. Historian Cortez Ewing argued that had Stevens not included this contract, the forthcoming impeachment proceedings may not have materialized.[5] But Secretary Robinson and Auditor Hillyer were desperate enough to sell the bonds that they agreed to Stevens's terms. Fifty thousand dollars' worth of bonds were delivered to Stevens at forty cents on the dollar, while another $37,000 worth was delivered at seventy cents. Governor Charles Robinson recognized the legal problems with the arrangement and refused to approve it.[6]

Despite the governor's hesitancy, J. Robinson and Hillyer agreed to give Stevens full authority over the sale of Kansas seven percent bonds. Governor Robinson had authorized the two men to make any arrangement that followed the directions outlined by the state legislature, but the two men signed their names and attached the governor's name without his approval. Stevens then offered the Interior Department $150,000 par value bonds at eighty-five cents on the dollar. Secretary of the Interior Caleb B. Smith accepted the sale pending President Abraham Lincoln's approval. Lincoln, in turn, agreed to back the arrangement as long as the Kansas congressional delegation signed off on it. Senator Samuel Pomeroy and Congressman Martin Conway quickly approved, but Lane withheld his signature, likely because he knew the close relationship between Stevens and his political rival Charles Robinson. This threatened the whole arrangement.[7]

The following events have never been fully revealed, but somehow Lane's signature—or a close copy—soon appeared on the approval letter to Lincoln. On December 17, 1861, the president then authorized the sale and the Kansas seven percent bonds were sold to the Interior Department. Lane

3. Castel, *Civil War Kansas,* 71.
4. Ibid., 72.
5. Ewing, "Early Kansas Impeachments," 312.
6. Castel, *Civil War Kansas,* 72.
7. Ibid., 72–73.

argued that he had not knowingly signed the letter, and stated that the signature was either a forgery or signed by mistake. Stevens and Thomas Corwin, who had helped broker the deal with the Interior Department, later testified that Lane's private secretary, George A. Reynolds, had been paid $1,000 to procure the senator's signature. Both Reynolds and Lane denied being bribed. Had money changed hands in this episode, it likely did not go to Lane, for he was famously unconcerned with acquiring personal wealth (reflected by his ragged clothing and poor finances).[8] Regardless of how the signature appeared, the deal was done. Stevens sold $150,000 of seven percent bonds to the Interior Department for eighty-five cents on the dollar. Because of the terms of his contract, he pocketed $37,500.[9]

Lane was back in Kansas following the sale, mostly working to take control of the Southern Expedition. Yet, he reportedly set about discrediting Charles Robinson. In late January 1862, the Kansas legislature adopted a resolution investigating the sale of bonds. The committee in charge of the matter consisted entirely of pro-Lane men, and by mid-February it presented a resolution impeaching Governor Robinson, Secretary of State Robinson, and Auditor Hillyer. The resolution passed without a dissenting vote, and the legislature appointed an impeachment committee. Eight impeachment articles were leveled against J. Robinson, seven against Hillyer, while Charles Robinson faced five.[10] The impeachment court itself did not convene until June. The subsequent trial cleared J. Robinson and Hillyer of all but one charge—violating Kansas laws through the sale of bonds at only sixty cents on the dollar. The court removed both men from their positions, but it did not restrict either man from holding office in the future. By the time of Charles Robinson's trial, the steam seems to have been let out of the impeachment process. His entire trial lasted one day, with the prosecution and defense statements lasting less than fifteen minutes each. Because the governor had not been actively involved in the sale

8. Lane only expressed an interest in money to cover living costs and to aid his political rise. Even Lane's critics acknowledge his general apathy toward material goods. Leverett Spring wrote, "In addition to all other burdens and disabilities he had no money. The wolf was often at his door. 'I have been refused credit for a loaf of bread in Lawrence,' he said on one occasion, 'and my family have not even the necessaries of life.' When the senatorial contest opened, Lane succeeded in borrowing twenty dollars, proceeded to the capital and opened headquarters in one of the hotels. Efforts were made to induce his landlord to turn him out of doors on the ground that he could never pay his bills, but the plot failed." Spring, "The Career of a Kansas Politician," 96.

9. Castel, *Civil War Kansas*, 73–74.

10. Ewing, "Early Kansas Impeachments," 314–15.

of bonds in Washington, and because his name had been attached to the contract without his formal approval, the court overwhelmingly cleared Robinson.[11] Nonetheless, the event damaged his reputation in Kansas. Historian Albert Castel argues that "the impeachment trial marked the final and nearly total victory of Lane in his long and bitter rivalry with Robinson."[12] Robinson finished his term as governor in early 1863 and lost nearly all of his political power. He was an influential figure in some circles, but Lane had clearly come to dominate Kansas politics.

The bond issue marks a particularly important point in the history of early Kansas and in the relations between Lane and Robinson. It was largely a matter of internal or state politics, carried out by factions within Kansas. Lane's actual role in the affair was relatively minor. Nonetheless, it has been used by some of Lane's critics to reflect upon his character. More important, it illustrates the heights of animosity between Lane and Charles Robinson, whose writings in the later decades of the nineteenth century have done much to cement Lane's image as a dangerous radical.

Lane's efforts to dominate Kansas politics have helped boost his reputation as an opportunist and politician void of principles. The nature of American politics—particularly during a time when elevated tensions and distrust helped lead to a national war—with its rumors of backdoor deals and smear tactics, feeds the image of corruption and absolute selfishness. No one can deny that Lane eagerly and successfully labored to secure a dominant political influence, or perhaps even control, in Kansas. It was primarily because of his success against equally ambitious men that Lane's reputation has taken such a beating. Yet, one should not suppose that political infighting is inherently unprincipled. Efforts to establish political hegemony have been carried out by some of America's most famous and respected statesmen. This action reflects ambition, and Lane certainly was ambitious. But ambition is not void of principle. Discussing America's odd mentality toward politicians, John F. Kennedy wrote that "in private life, as in industry, we expect the individual to advance his own enlightened self-interest—within the limitations of the law—in order to achieve overall progress. But in public life we expect individuals to sacrifice their private interests to permit the national good to progress."[13] While Lane's self-promotion and struggle for political hegemony in the state certainly

11. Ibid., Castel, *Civil War Kansas,* 76–77; Wilder, *Annals of Kansas,* 317–19.
12. Castel, *Civil War Kansas,* 77.
13. Kennedy, *Profiles in Courage,* 7.

cannot be classified as selfless, he saw himself as a champion of demo-cratic principles and the interests of Kansas. This is not to argue that Lane's actions were good or right, and in no way should this be interpreted as a justification or defense for what he said or did during his political career. Instead, Lane must be seen as a believer in the deeper principles and objec-tives he proved loyal to—the interests of free white Northerners and the stability of his party and the Union.

As the war dragged on, Lane found himself in the middle of one of the most famous and controversial episodes in Civil War history. On August 20, 1863, Confederate guerrilla leader William Quantrill led a force of nearly 450 men on a daring venture into Kansas. Their target was Lawrence. The town had already suffered two previous raids by Mis-sourians over the past eight years: the standoff known as the Wakarusa War in December 1855 and the Sack of Lawrence in the spring of 1856. The two years of brutal, unconventional warfare on the Kansas-Missouri bor-der during the Civil War further inflamed the animosity of Missourians toward their Kansas neighbors. Lawrence not only remained the center of antislavery (or even abolitionist) sentiment in Kansas but also was the home of despised Jayhawkers—like James Lane.

Shortly before 5 a.m. on August 21, after avoiding federal scouts, Quantrill's raiders rode up to the outskirts of the sleepy town. John McCorkle, a guerrilla in the ranks, recalled that his commander turned to the men and said, "Boys, this is the home of Jim Lane and [Charles] Jenni-son; remember that in hunting us they gave no quarter. Shoot every soldier you see, but in no way harm a woman or a child."[14] With those words, they swept into Lawrence, killing nearly every man they saw. The guerrillas were heard shouting "Osceola! Kansas City! Remember the girls!"[15] The cry of "Osceola," of course, referred to the destruction of that town in Mis-souri by Lane and his brigade in September 1861. The other calls referred to the recent collapse of a dilapidated jail in Kansas City that housed female relatives of some notorious Bushwhackers, such as Bloody Bill Anderson.[16] For many in Quantrill's ranks, the raid was a form of vengeance.

The only military force in town consisted of fewer than two dozen unarmed enlistees of the Fourteenth Kansas and a separate camp of equally unprepared black recruits. The guerrillas charged through the white

14. John McCorkle and O. S. Barton, *Three Years with Quantrill: A True Story Told by His Scout John McCorkle*, 125.
15. Thomas Goodrich, *Bloody Dawn: The Story of the Lawrence Massacre*, 87.
16. McCorkle, *Three Years with Quantrill*, 120–23.

encampment, firing at the panic-stricken men. An eyewitness later wrote that "one little fellow, about fifteen years old, after being shot at a dozen or more times, succeeded in reaching a point close to my house. Then a bullet struck him and he fell to his knees. As they came on he held up both hands and said:—'For God's sake don't murder me, don't murder me.'" A guerrilla shouted back, "No quarter for you federal sons of bitches."[17] Former slave Andrew Williams was among the black recruits, and later wrote that when Quantrill's men entered Lawrence, "wee thought they was union men until one in the crowd Said Brake Ranks." The black soldiers scattered. Williams remembered, "wee left home and went down Kaw River a Bout 4 miles and hide in the Brush." Williams did not return to Lawrence until the next day.[18] Seventeen of the twenty-two white soldiers were killed in the attack; most of the black men managed to escape.[19]

Quantrill and his men rode down Massachusetts Street, into the center of town. One of their first targets was the Eldridge House, the large hotel reconstructed on the site of the old Free State Hotel destroyed during the Sack of Lawrence in 1856. It retained its reputation as a formidable defensive structure, and the raiders wanted to capture it quickly. Completely surprised, the hotel guests surrendered after Quantrill offered them leniency—something the rest of Lawrence's male population did not enjoy. Houses and businesses were raided and nearly every man the guerrillas found was killed. Around this time, groups of raiders broke away to raid other parts of the town. Some Kansans reported that Quantrill's men had a map of the area marked with the locations of certain homes or businesses to be destroyed. Others noted that the guerrillas carried "death lists," which included the names of the town's most wanted men. James Lane was certainly a prime target. A black informant for Quantrill reported that Lane was out of town. In fact, while Lane had been away from Lawrence for a short time, he had returned and was in bed at home that morning. A small detachment of the raiders forced local resident Arthur Spicer to lead them to the home, warning that "if you veer to the right or left, you are a dead man!" Lane's house was located west of town, and it took a few minutes for the guerrillas to arrive. In the meantime, Lane had

17. Account of Henry Clarke, quoted in Thomas Goodrich, *Black Flag: Guerrilla Warfare on the Western Border, 1861–1865*, 78.

18. "Civil War on the Kansas-Missouri Border: The Narrative of Former Slave Andrew Williams," edited by William A. Dobak, 240.

19. Castel, *Civil War Kansas*, 129; Duane Schultz, *Quantrill's War: The Life and Times of William Clarke Quantrill, 1837–1865*, 169–70.

heard the sound of gunfire, but first dismissed it as fireworks. When a black man, racing past the house, shouted that guerrillas were attacking Lawrence, Lane jumped out of bed and ran to the window while his wife and children scrambled in panic. He called upon them to find two guns stashed somewhere in the house. The guns could not be found in time, so Lane grabbed the ceremonial sword the men of the Fifth Indiana Regiment had presented him at the end of the Mexican War in hopes of putting up some sort of defense. When Spicer and the guerrillas arrived at the gate, Lane's family begged him to leave. He realized that making a stand was hopeless, dropped the sword, and scrambled out a back window. As the raiders approached the front door, Lane, clad only in his nightshirt, ran into a cornfield behind the house.[20]

As the guerrillas walked to the front door, Mary Lane greeted them and explained that her husband was not at home. As Quantrill had ordered, Mary and the children were not harmed, but the Bushwhackers destroyed furniture, scattered the senator's papers, and even stole the jewelry on the hands of Mary and her daughter. Even when young James, Jr., found one of the shotguns in the house and held it in defiance, a guerrilla fired a warning shot to convince the boy to hand it over. Young James did, and the house was then set on fire. Although Mary and the children tried to extinguish the flames, the raiders were ultimately successful in burning the house down. Before leaving, the men confiscated Lane's sword and the black and yellow banner he had received while serving as provost marshal in Mexico City. The guerrillas mistakenly believed that the banner was a "black flag," a real example of the symbol for no mercy, rumored to have been given to Lane by ladies in Leavenworth earlier in the war.[21]

Lane did not stay in the cornfield long. Carefully he made his way to a pasture. At one point he saw three guerrillas ride in his direction. Scrambling behind a log, he waited for them to pass. Armed with only a small penknife, Lane planned to kill himself rather than be captured. "That was the only weapon I had," he told John Speer later, "and as I knew, if they captured me, they would torture me to death, I intended to thrust that little blade up into my brain to escape torture."[22] The guerrillas rode by unaware

20. Fisher, *The Gun and the Gospel,* 175, 178; Burton J. Williams, "Quantrill's Raid on Lawrence: A Question of Complicity," 146–47; Goodrich, *Black Flag,* 83; Castel, *Civil War Kansas,* 132; Speer, *Life of Lane,* 265–66; *New York Times,* September 4, 1863.

21. *New York Times,* September 4, 1863; see note by William E. Connelley in Stephenson, *Political Career of Lane,* 27.

22. Speer, *Life of Lane,* 316.

of his presence, and Lane traveled to outlying farmhouses where he procured a plow horse and an ill-fitting pair of pants. Dozens of other men, half-clad and terribly frightened, also came scrambling out of the woods and gullies, frantically trying to escape the carnage in Lawrence. Lane set about organizing an armed resistance to Quantrill's men, but little could be done.[23]

The destruction of Lawrence continued until around 9 a.m., when Quantrill led his force out of town and back toward Missouri, still plundering and destroying Kansas farms they passed. More than 150 people were killed in the raid. Quantrill lost only one man, who had become so drunk that he had lagged behind his fellow Bushwhackers after they left and was killed by angered residents. More than two hundred homes were destroyed and the city suffered around $2.5 million in damage.[24] Much of Lawrence was a charred ruin. Lane's friend John Speer lost two sons during the attack. One was killed while running from Quantrill's men; the other died when his father's newspaper office was torched with him inside. That evening, the distraught father was seen combing through the ashes of the building looking for the body. It was never found.[25] As the residents slowly surveyed the damage of their town, looking over the charred buildings and scattered bodies of their husbands, brothers, and fathers, Lane came charging down the street awkwardly mounted on the workhorse, screaming out, "Follow them boys, let us follow them!" Behind him rode a handful of farmers and townsmen, armed with everything from shotguns to corn knives. A few more townspeople grabbed horses and joined the pursuit, but many others stood in shock or helplessly watched the motley group of citizen-soldiers ride by, unable to find a horse among the destruction.[26]

Lane and his band of around thirty-five men followed the Confederate trail for some miles until linking up with Major Preston Plumb and a combined force of nearly two hundred Union cavalrymen from various regiments. The unit had been following reports of a guerrilla incursion into Kansas since 1 a.m. that morning. By midday, they were close on the guerrilla trail. Lane reportedly tried to take control of the combined force, but Plumb resisted and a brief argument ensued. Finally, Plumb turned away from Lane and led his men down the road toward the guerrilla body. Lane and his rag-tag militia followed. Within a short distance, the rear of Quantrill's force could be seen. Captain Charles Coleman, of the Ninth

23. Schultz, *Quantrill's War,* 186.
24. Goodrich, *Black Flag,* 94.
25. Goodrich, *Bloody Dawn,* 122; Speer, *Life of Lane,* 266.
26. Goodrich, *Bloody Dawn,* 119.

Kansas Cavalry, charged a portion of the command against the raiders. Plumb and Lane, with the rest of the men, headed south to block a ford at Ottawa Creek a mile away. Coleman's detachment clashed with a sixty-man rearguard led by guerrilla George Todd, and a brief firefight ensued. Todd and his men fell back and reestablished their line. The Kansans pursued until they came to a fence. Across the field on the other side stood the guerrilla force watching and waiting. The two sides stared at each other.

In the meantime, Plumb and Lane heard the sound of gunfire, and abandoned their plan to cut off Quantrill at the creek. They wheeled their horses around and led their men toward the sound of fighting. Lane charged his plow horse ahead of Plumb and arrived among the tired Kansas soldiers. He ordered the fence to be torn down and an attack made. When no one moved, Lane shouted at the men, dismounted, and began pulling at the fence with his own hands. Finally, Coleman ordered the Kansans to dismount and fire a volley at the distant Confederates.[27]

The federal volley had an unintended consequence. A number of their horses, startled by the crack of muskets and carbines, bolted across the field toward the guerrillas. Some Kansans ran after them. Seeing an opportunity, Todd and his men charged. The Union men panicked. Back through the corn they ran, with Confederate bullets whizzing over their heads. The stubborn Lane, still pulling at the fence rails, turned and watched the entire Union command melt away in the face of the bold guerrilla charge. He quickly scrambled back into the cornfield, narrowly escaping the raiders. The Confederates reeled their horses at the fence line, and laughed and jeered at the retreating Kansans before returning to Quantrill's main force. The Union cavalry horses and men were exhausted from the previous hours of riding and skirmishing. A fraction of them reorganized and continued the pursuit. Kansas soldiers continued to skirmish with Quantrill's men until the guerrillas, also exhausted, slipped back into Missouri and scattered.[28]

Quantrill's raid against Lawrence shocked and enraged people across the North. Historian Albert Castel called it "the most atrocious act of the war" and "the outstanding single event of the Civil War in Kansas, the bloody climax of the border strife with Missouri."[29] Kansans struggled to

27. See various reports from Union officers regarding the raid on Lawrence and subsequent chase in *O.R.*, ser. 1, vol. 22, 572–93. Goodrich, *Bloody Dawn*, 136–38; Castel, *Civil War Kansas*, 133–34; Schultz, *Quantrill's War*, 216–19.

28. Schultz, *Quantrill's War*, 219; *O.R.*, ser. 1, vol. 22, 590. Also see Albert R. Greene, "What I Saw of the Quantrill Raid," 430–45.

29. Castel, *Civil War Kansas*, 136.

understand and respond to the destruction. Missouri guerrillas had raided Kansas towns before, and Lawrence residents had feared that they might become the victims of such an attack. However, the size of Lawrence and its distance from the Missouri border (some fifty miles) seemed to make it an unlikely target, even if it had strategic and moral value. Quantrill's success in making the journey with a considerable force, carrying out a surprise attack against the town, and then riding back to Missouri not only destroyed those assumptions but also led some to form conspiracy theories. A couple of months after the attack, Charles Robinson (who had been in town but also escaped capture or death) wrote that he believed "Genl. Lane and his elements were in collusion through third persons with Quantrel [sic]." He admitted that he had "no proof of it and no one out of Kansas would believe such a thing possible and hence I am not disposed to say anything about it publicly." But, he added, "the world never will know nor believe the insanity, or deep depravity of some of our politicians, especially of one [James H. Lane]."[30] Robinson had previously argued that Lane's actions in Missouri brought violent retaliation, and in many ways he was right. The destruction of Osceola had been called out by the guerrillas, and the exploits of Lane's men had become infamous. Yet, now the former governor privately accused the senator of conspiring with the enemy. Robinson likely did not believe that Lane knew about the raid on Lawrence. Instead, he shared a view with others in the area that Kansas Jayhawkers had made an agreement with Missouri Bushwhackers not to interfere in each other's plundering operations.[31]

There is no evidence that Lane had made any arrangements or agreements with guerrillas. The fact that he had been named as a possible conspirator or colleague by Robinson only highlights the level of animosity between the two men and foreshadows how Robinson's writing would color Lane's image in later years.

Lane was heavily involved in the political firestorm following the destruction of Lawrence. After the attack on Lawrence, he had a hand in one of the most controversial military actions taken against American citizens in the country's history. The commander of the District of the Border, Brigadier General Thomas Ewing, Jr. (former Chief Justice of the Kansas Supreme Court), issued Order No. 11 on August 25, 1863, which required all inhabitants of Missouri's Jackson, Cass, and Bates counties (except those

30. Charles Robinson to Amos A. Lawrence, October 6, 1863, Charles Robinson Collection, Kansas State Historical Society, Topeka.
31. See Williams, "Quantrill's Raid on Lawrence," 144–45.

living within one mile of certain military posts) to leave their homes by September 9. Unionists affected by this order were allowed to relocate to specified areas once they had proved their loyalty to military authorities. Those who did not demonstrate their loyalty to the Union, at least to the satisfaction of the local military commander, were commanded to move away from the district entirely. In short, the Union military set out to depopulate at least three counties. The act was not simple revenge against Missouri for Quantrill's raid. Albert Castel argues that the roots of the order stretch back as far as the Bleeding Kansas era. It was, in many ways, part of the escalating animosity and violence between Missourians and Kansans that had begun in 1854. The destruction of Lawrence spurred this particular order, although discussion of relocating some Missouri families had taken place earlier in the summer. Union officials had struggled to deal with Missouri guerrillas for nearly two years. Facing the difficulty of defeating unconventional warriors on their own territory, officers like Ewing believed that denying Bushwhackers safety and support from local inhabitants would reduce their effectiveness. Thus, the order had real strategic objectives, even if its effectiveness was questionable.[32]

The enforcement of Order No. 11 was severe, as thousands of people were removed from their homes and forcibly relocated. Indeed, Castel says that, with the exception of the internment of Japanese Americans during World War II, this order was "the harshest treatment ever imposed on United States citizens under the plea of military necessity in our nation's history." Yet, Castel also believes that Ewing's order may have prevented even worse destruction at the hands of Lane and vengeful Kansans. According to a correspondent of the *New York Times*, Lane met with Ewing two days after the raid and urged him to clear out the border counties of all people. "He declared his intention," the writer continued, "unless this was done by the military authorities, of rousing the citizens and doing it himself." On August 27, Lane spoke before a crowd in Leavenworth and urged his fellow Kansans to grab their guns and equipment and meet at Paola on September 8 (the last day before Ewing's Order No. 11 went into

32. *O.R.*, ser. 1, vol. 22, pt. 2, 473; Albert Castel, "Order No. 11 and the Civil War on the Border," 358, 366–67; Charles R. Mink, "General Orders, No. 11: The Forced Evacuation of Civilians during the Civil War," 132; *O.R.*, ser. I, vol. 22, pt. 2, 428–29. Historian Hildegarde Rose Herklotz also argues that the order was ineffective, but in the sense that it did not stop Kansans from raiding into Missouri. She writes little of its result on Missouri guerrillas. Herklotz, "Jayhawkers in Missouri," Third Article, Chapter IV, 97.

effect) for a great raid into Missouri. They would retrieve property stolen by Quantrill's men and exact vengeance. "Let them carry widespread devastation to every house and barn," Lane cried out, "to every field of corn, every hog and head of stock, which, if not destroyed, will be used by those who are prepared to murder us. I take the ground here of vengeance for blood and devastation for safety."[33]

Lane also turned full-force against the commander of the Department of Missouri, Major General John M. Schofield. The senator had already voiced his opposition to Schofield earlier in the summer, when the latter replaced Samuel Curtis—a man friendly to Lane and his military and political interests. Lane believed Schofield was too conservative, a perception shared by other hard-line Unionists and radicals in Kansas and Missouri.[34] Lane was further frustrated when Schofield's reorganization of the department disrupted his previous influence, and the senator labored to restore Kansas military command to his preferred leaders. Now, following the destruction of Lawrence, Lane saw it as a vindication of his earlier warnings. "It has been said that Lane never sleeps, and he does not when there is danger," he told the Leavenworth audience; "but we depended upon the military authorities for protection, and were surprised, or we would have protected ourselves and whipped the rebels like h—l." He noted that veterans of the territorial conflict could vouch for his claim. "What was Schofield dong?" Lane cried out. "Administering oaths to bushwhackers, and trying to woo them back to their allegiance instead of killing them!"[35] This policy, he continued, had not worked in 1861 and certainly would not work now. He asked the crowd in Leavenworth to adopt a resolution calling for Schofield's dismissal.

Lane also turned to Abraham Lincoln to get rid of Schofield. "The result of the massacre at Lawrence has excited feelings amongst our people which make a collision between them and the military probable," Lane and A. C. Wilder wrote the president. "The imbecility and incapacity of Schofield is most deplorable. Our people unanimously demand the removal of Schofield, whose policy has opened Kansas to invasion and butchery." Lincoln had long struggled to balance the volatile Missouri situation. He acknowledged the receipt of Lane and Wilder's message, and,

33. Castel, "Order No. 11 and the Civil War on the Border," 357, 363; *New York Times,* September 4, 6, 1863.

34. See Castel, *Civil War Kansas,* 110.

35. *New York Times,* September 6, 1863.

without naming the authors of the complaint, asked Schofield to "do your utmost to give them future security and to punish their invaders."[36]

Schofield knew who his critics were, and notified Lincoln that "those who so deplore my 'imbecility and incapacity' are the very men who are endeavoring to bring about a collision between the people of Kansas and the troops under General Ewing's command."[37] He was not about to let Lane lead an unauthorized raid into Missouri. While Order No. 11 was harsh enough to let out some of the steam behind the Paola gathering, Schofield did not want to take any chances. On September 4 he issued General Order No. 92, which declared that "the militia of Kansas and Missouri not in the service of the United States will be used only for the defense of their respective States" and would not be allowed to cross into other states without specific orders from a district commander. "No armed bodies of men not belonging to the United States troops," Schofield reiterated, "or to those portions of Kansas and Missouri which have been placed under the orders of the department commander by the Governors of the respective States, will be permitted, under any pretext whatever, to pass from one State to the other."[38] To make sure this order was carried out, a military contingent headed to Paola on September 8 to block any attempt by regular Kansas citizens to raid Missouri.

Albert Greene, of the Ninth Kansas Cavalry, was among the seventy-five soldiers ordered to Paola. While riding to the town, the officer in command of the force, Colonel William Weer of the Tenth Kansas Infantry, halted the men and announced that their assignment was "to head off that d—d fool Lane." "The epithet was not relished," Greene remembered, "since we were all 'Lane men,' if for no other reason than that our officers were unanimously and bitterly 'anti-Lane.'"[39] Nonetheless, the enlisted men accepted their orders—although they agreed that there were not enough soldiers in the region, let alone among their group, to stop Lane if he and his followers were so determined.

The gathering in Paola was smaller than expected. Bad weather dampened the mood somewhat. Thus, only a few hundred Kansans assembled near a roughly built platform, surrounded by rows of plank seats. The soldiers filed to the front of the audience and commandeered the front row. Shortly afterwards, Lane walked on stage and immediately went into

36. O.R., ser. 1, vol. 22, pt. 2, 475, 479.
37. Ibid., 484.
38. Ibid., 511–12.
39. Greene, "What I Saw of the Quantrill Raid," 446.

action. Greene recalled that the speech "was on a high, tense key, and was wild, incoherent and bloodthirsty; a Niagara torrent of invective, profanity and bad grammar." As usual, Lane punctuated his verbal frenzy with a partial undressing. He pulled off his long linen coat, while complaining of the incompetence of local military leaders; his cravat came off when he announced his wish to make Missouri a "burning hell." With his arms upraised, Lane screeched, "Missourians are wolves, snakes, devils, and d—n their souls, I want to see them cast into a burning hell!" and ripped open his shirt front to expose "a wide expanse of hairy jungle," Greene wrote. The crowd exploded with cheers, as the soldiers groaned. Colonel Weer rose and looked over the audience for a short time, then turned and stared Lane in the face. According to Greene, Lane looked at the soldiers and saw the row of shining carbines, and quickly changed his tone. "But," he told the crowd, "General Schofield says all these people must go back to their desolate homes empty-handed and with broken hearts." Some in the crowd laughed, but apparently the mood had been spoiled, at least for a time. Later that evening, the former commander of the Seventh Kansas Cavalry and notable Jayhawker Charles Jennison spoke before the Paola crowd, and in the ensuing excitement Lane was called to the stage for another effort. He continued with his pronounced desire to see Missouri destroyed. Despite the excitement, no raiding expedition came together. Greene believed that had there not been a military presence to stop the proposed raid, "they would have started for Missouri that night."[40]

Because the proposed invasion never materialized, the event in Paola was largely seen as a bust for Lane.[41] Yet the actual raid may not have been Lane's only goal. While he would have eagerly led a group of Kansans into Missouri, he likely saw value in intimidating Missourians and pressing Ewing and Schofield—two men he had criticized as too soft on Missouri secessionists—into more aggressive action. No actual invasion would be necessary for that objective, only a viable threat. On August 28, the day after his speech in Leavenworth proposing the raid, Lane telegraphed Ewing that those who gathered in Paola on September 8 "would place themselves under [Ewing's] orders." Lane had little intention of carrying out an extralegal invasion of Missouri, although he would have taken part in the official depopulation effort. Ewing admitted to

40. Ibid., 447–48.
41. For instance, see *Leavenworth Daily Conservative*, September 10, 11, 13, 1863; *Leavenworth Daily Times*, September 10, 11, 12, 1863.

Schofield that the Paola episode was "intended partly, I think, to scare the people in the border counties into prompt compliance with my order, and partly for political capital." He assured Schofield that he had "but little doubt I will be able to control matters so as to prevent any considerable acts of retaliation."[42]

Lane biographer Robert Collins also questions Lane's intentions with the Paola gathering. He notes that Paola seems an odd place to assemble Kansans for a raid, as it was not well located to draw large numbers of enraged citizens. Yet, Collins admits that Paola is close to the Missouri border (only around ten miles away), a fact that suggests the raid was not completely a bluff. Furthermore, the two Missouri counties directly across the Missouri line are Cass and Bates, both of which were affected by Order No. 11. Since the Paola gathering was intentionally coordinated with the implementation of that order, the location is not surprising at all, but a logical stepping-off point for an incursion. Nor is the chosen gathering day, September 8, mysterious. Collins points out that the date fell on a Tuesday, and was two and a half weeks after Quantrill's raid. "Why not choose September 5, a Saturday, or September 4, a Friday, exactly two weeks after Lawrence?" he asks.[43] Again, one must consider Order No. 11, which went into effect on September 9. The Paola gathering met the evening before three Missouri counties were to be forcefully depopulated. To lead an invasion before that time—during the grace period set out by Order No. 11—would have brought condemnation from even his military and political allies. But Lane's effort could take on an air of legitimacy if the rag-tag invasion force corresponded, even aided, with the enforcement of the order. Overall, Collins suggests that Lane constructed the Paola raid to fail; that he ultimately saw the event as an opportunity to lead Kansans in venting their frustrations and thus gain political capital without actually carrying out the expedition against the wishes of the established military authorities or Lincoln. While Collins believes this explanation reflects well upon Lane, by showing his political genius, it also portrays the senator as a complete opportunist.[44]

The truth is likely somewhere in the middle. Lane had been involved in the border war for almost a decade. There is no doubt that he would have gladly led another expedition into Missouri—he was proud of his earlier military exploits and his time in the field had only ended when his attempt

42. O.R., ser. 1, vol. 22, pt. 2, 490.
43. Collins, Jim Lane, 234.
44. Ibid., 233–34.

to command the Southern Expedition failed. He probably was disappointed that Schofield and Ewing rejected the proposed raid, although he should not have been surprised. But he also believed that the Paola gathering would pressure them into making a more aggressive response to Quantrill. In short, Lane was serious about the raid going forth, but also understood its strength as a political tool. Finally, he wanted to take a leadership role in the wake of the destruction of Lawrence. He had been in that town during the attack, had lost his home, and had barely escaped with his life. A man of action and high emotion, he had immediately led a pursuit. Lane had been involved in the Lawrence episode from the beginning and he was not one to turn over command or sit on the sidelines, especially when he distrusted local military authorities. The proposed raid was a natural response from a man like Lane—it was a gathering of the people to vent their frustrations, to put pressure on the military establishment, and even to help enforce a military order.

While the Missouri raid fizzled out, Lane's desire to oust Schofield still lingered. A group of radicals in Missouri shared his disdain for the general and put together a delegation to press Lincoln for Schofield's reassignment. The group, standing seventy strong, arrived at the White House on September 29 and presented its complaints. Lincoln handled the group calmly, and asked for evidence that Schofield had harmed the Union cause. Simply disagreeing with them politically, the president explained, was not sufficient ground for his removal. The following day, Lane and a small group of Kansans joined the Missouri delegation and returned to the White House. Lane led the formidable gathering into the East Room. Lincoln's secretaries John Hay and John Nicolay later described the assembled westerners as remarkable "more for sincere earnestness, and a bearing evincing stubborn determination to get what they considered their rights, than for either high average intelligence or adroitness." Nonetheless, the secretaries acknowledged, the group was "officered by a few leaders of great ability."[45]

Lincoln met with the group for two hours. Again they leveled their complaints against Schofield. But the president persisted in his demand for some evidence of wrongdoing. "I cannot act on vague impressions," Lincoln said. "Show me that he has disobeyed orders; show me that he has done something wrong, and I will take your request for his removal into serious consideration." Lincoln addressed the delegation's points one at a time, picking apart many of the radicals' complaints. He concluded the

45. Nicolay and Hay, *Abraham Lincoln,* vol. 8, 214–15.

meeting by telling his guests, "I have no right to act the tyrant to mere political opponents. If a man votes for supplies of men and money, encourages enlistments, discourages desertions, does all in his power to carry the war on to a successful issue, I have no right to question him for his abstract political opinions." The Missourians and Kansans filed out of the White House with a promise from the president to give them his answer after a few days of consideration.[46]

On October 5, Lincoln replied to the westerners. He told them he was unconvinced by their complaint that Missouri Unionists had suffered under Schofield's command: "the whole case as presented fails to convince me that General Schofield . . . is responsible for that suffering and wrong."[47] The district commander would remain in place, at least for the time being. While Lincoln had shot down their effort to oust Schofield, the president afterwards admitted that the Missouri Radicals (and perhaps the Kansans too) "are nearer to me than the other side in thought and sentiment, though bitterly hostile personally. They are the unhandiest fellows in the world to deal with; but after all their faces are set Zionward."[48]

Schofield wrote in his journal that Lane and the radical delegation left Washington "very much crestfallen." Lane notified the general that he had given up the feud and would not oppose Schofield unless new circumstances made it necessary. Lincoln supposedly told Lane that "whoever made war on General Schofield, under the present state of affairs, made war on him—the President."[49] Unwilling to stand against Lincoln, or lose his support, the senator acquiesced. Yet, only a few months later, Lane turned against Schofield after the general removed Lane's ally Major General James G. Blunt. The senator requested that Lincoln create a separate department for Kansas under the command of a different general. At this point, the president agreed and divided Kansas and Missouri into two departments. Schofield was transferred to Sherman's army in Tennessee, where he proved an able battlefield leader.[50]

From 1862 through 1863, Lane's political influence in Kansas was at its highest. This would change, though, in 1864 as political rivalries and increasing factionalism wore down his popularity. His enemies rebounded in the state legislature, and competing interests in Kansas railroad devel-

46. Ibid., 216–19.
47. John M. Schofield, *Forty-Six Years in the Army*, 94.
48. Nicolay and Hay, *Abraham Lincoln*, vol. 8, 218–20.
49. Schofield, *Forty-Six Years in the Army*, 99.
50. Castel, *Civil War Kansas*, 161–63.

opment virtually assured that he would make enemies when supporting one route over another.[51] Even when Lane and his supporters were successful in their struggle for political control, such as with their rivalry with Robinson, the victories seemed to create new enemies. These local political matters took up quite a bit of Lane's time, and naturally have been a prime focus for many of his critics as well as for Kansas historians.

The internal political struggles in Kansas are important. But a strong focus on Republican infighting in the state often fails to appreciate the nation's larger political situation. Such focus, intentionally or unintentionally, portrays Kansas political events as unique. The rivalries and factionalism in Kansas may be seen as almost an anomaly, and someone like James Lane comes across as particularly opportunistic and ambitious. It is easy to forget that the whole nation was in the midst of the greatest factionalism in its history. The political party system had crumbled under sectionalism. And the election of a president led to a political divide that sent millions of men into armed combat. Border states saw their people so at odds that brothers and neighbors literally fought each other. They did not exchange merely harsh words, but bullets, cannon shells, and bayonets. Missouri had two separate governments, one loyal to the Union and one dedicated to the Confederacy. At no other point in U.S. history was society so divided, were people so hostile to each other, and were rivalries so pronounced as during Lane's political career.

This does not mean that Lane's actions are excused. But Lane must be seen in his time and in his place. As a man concerned with his state, his party, and his country, his story extends beyond the boundaries of Kansas. He was a product of nineteenth-century American society and politics, an eager participant in the political rivalries that punctuated the culture. He came to power in an era when men and women were willing to defend their political ideologies to the point of physical confrontation, first in Kansas and then across the country. Lane thrived in this environment. Political battles drove his energy. His success in this type of climate not only showed his abilities but also created an army of enemies. Overall, political rivalries, as those seen between Lane and Robinson or Lane and Schofield, were not unusual.

So what do Lane's political and military battles in 1862 and 1863 tell us about his principles? Lane's role in the bond issue and Robinson's subsequent impeachment trial offer little information about his larger goals.

51. Ibid., 167.

Instead, the episode was the pinnacle of a long-running dispute between Robinson and Lane, grounded in their different political tactics. Both men had the same general interest in keeping slavery out of Kansas (although Robinson's antislavery credentials were based on firm humanitarian grounds) and in protecting the Union. But Robinson rejected Lane's increasingly radical rhetoric and tactics for these purposes. In turn, Lane opposed Robinson's conservative approach. The divide between the men became so great that their differences rather than their commonalities have dominated the historical scene. Robinson's postwar speeches and writings portrayed Lane as a fanatic, whose unstable mind threatened the state and the Union. Robinson did not see, or refused to accept, Lane's dedication to democratic principles and the integrity of the Union and his party. Many historians have followed in Robinson's wake.

Quantrill's attack on Lawrence, and its fallout, has contributed to Lane's image as a demagogue and fanatic. Its role as revenge for the burning of Osceola, and other Jayhawking actions in Missouri, was accepted by Missourians and many Kansans alike. It seemed to confirm Robinson's 1861 statement that Kansas was in greater danger because of Lane's military exploits.[52] There is little doubt that Lane's actions and reputation contributed to Quantrill's decision to attack Lawrence. But, as with other intrastate disputes and events, too few historians or writers discuss Lane's interests or goals outside of the specific Missouri-Kansas conflict. His campaign into Missouri in 1861 has been perceived as primarily a plundering operation, and his response to Quantrill's attack on Lawrence is portrayed as a rabid call for revenge or a lustful grab for power. While there is truth to all of these perceptions, they do not provide a complete picture. Lane's actions before and after the Lawrence raid were consistent with his belief that secessionists in Missouri were the real threat, and that only bloody and bitter warfare—only total war—could protect Kansas and the Union. He took the Union cause personally, and saw its opponents as his own enemies. His actions were shocking, and they arguably caused more problems for himself, his friends, and perhaps even his cherished nation and party. But, as Lincoln said of the western radicals, Lane had his face "set Zionward."[53]

52. *O.R.*, ser. 1, vol. 3, 469.
53. Nicolay and Hay, *Abraham Lincoln,* vol. 8, 218–20.

10

Lane and Slavery, 1861–1865

"We march to crush out Treason, and if Slavery does not take care of itself, the fault is not mine."

In this chapter, we will backtrack a bit to investigate James Lane's policies regarding slavery during the Civil War. Early in the war, his hard-line stance against secession struck at the institution. His words and actions in 1861 not only stand as some of the first and most vehement attacks against slavery by a prominent government official but also provide a remarkable look into his mind. As before, his actions seemed to reveal a wild, unpredictable personality. It was no surprise that Lane at this time was called, and sometimes called himself, a radical.[1] Yet, as before, a close examination of his actions against slavery uncovers a consistency of principle and goals. It may be difficult to find a natural progression between the support of the Kansas-Nebraska Act and the forcible freeing of slaves. But the uniformity is there. Lane adapted to overcome the obstacles he believed the nation faced.

Lane, like other Republicans, embraced a hard line against the expansion of slavery into the territories. However, few embraced emancipation as an immediate war goal in 1861. Lincoln's inaugural address repeated

1. See *Lawrence Republican*, April 11, 1861.

his steady claim that he had "no purpose, directly or indirectly, to interfere with slavery in the States where it exists."[2] The Union war effort specifically focused on crushing secession. Still, loyal representatives and senators from slaveholding areas feared for the safety of the institution during the conflict. On July 18, Senator Lazarus Powell of Kentucky proposed an amendment, to the army organization bill, to prevent Union forces from interfering with slavery. Lane immediately rose and introduced the clause, "except to crush out rebellion and hang traitors."[3] During the ensuing debate of the institution's role in the brewing conflict, Lane stated that he represented "a constituency whose rights have been trampled on by the slave oligarchy of this country. Fraud, cruelty, barbarism were inflicted upon them by that power." Yet, he declared, Kansans had been willing to leave the past behind and accept slavery where it existed, had not slavery been forced upon them and led to disunion:

> An attempt is now made, and by that power, to overthrow the Government—to destroy the Union. They have brought upon us this conflict. If, in that conflict, the institution of slavery perish, we will thank God that he has brought upon us this war. We wish not be misunderstood. We would have stood by the compromises of the Constitution, and permitted slavery to exist in the States where it was planted; would not, by word or act, have disturbed it; but they have forced upon us this struggle, and I, for one am willing that it shall be followed to its logical conclusion.[4]

Lane's "logical conclusion" was an end to slavery in the United States. As with his migration into the Republican Party, Lane's position on slavery in 1861 was reactive to larger events.

Lane's statements appeared radical, but he was not yet an abolitionist. While he maintained that "the institution of slavery will not survive, in any State of this Union, the march of the Union Armies," he did not embrace the destruction of slavery as a specific war aim. He clarified that his interests regarding slave property specifically related to an owner's loyalty to the Union. When senators talked of protecting the right of property, Lane stated: "While I think that policy might be a correct one, so far as returning slaves to the Union men is concerned, I should think it highly impolitic, and in a military sense highly improper, so far as the traitors are concerned." Still,

2. Abraham Lincoln First Inaugural, printed in Rawley, *Secession*, 239.
3. *Congressional Globe*, 37th Cong., 1st sess., 186.
4. Ibid., 187.

Powell believed Lane was "for emancipating slavery now." Lane made his position clear: "I disavow any intent upon the part of the Government or its army to war against the institution of slavery. I said that the effect of marching an army on the soil of any slave State will be to instill into the slaves a determined purpose to free themselves; and, in my opinion, they will crush out everything that stands in the way of acquiring that freedom." He took a middle ground between those who wished to forcefully end slavery and those who wished to protect it. He as yet refused to officially fight to end slavery, but he would not labor to protect the institution. "So far as I am concerned," he told his colleagues, "I do not propose to make myself a slave catcher for traitors and return them to their masters."[5]

If Lane did not want to return slaves to their masters, then he had to find something to do with them. He proposed a colonization effort, like that advocated by some abolitionists and antislavery Northerners over the previous five decades.[6] He wanted to "digest a plan to colonize the slaves thus liberated by their own act at some point outside of the Union convenient thereto. Sir, I want to see, so soon as it can be done constitutionally, these two races separated, an ocean between; that—South America—the elysium of the colored man; this the elysium of the white."[7] This was hardly surprising from a man who had supported the exclusion of blacks from Kansas Territory.

Only one week after his comments on the floor, the Senate voted on a resolution from John J. Crittenden of Kentucky and Andrew Johnson of Tennessee that outlined the object of the war. It resolved that the current military effort to suppress the rebellion "is not prosecuted upon our part in any spirit of oppression, nor for any purpose of conquest or subjugation, nor for the purpose of overthrowing or interfering with the rights or established institutions of those States."[8] Three radicals voted against the resolution and

---

5. Ibid., 187, 189, 190.

6. Colonization—the sending of former slaves to colonies outside the United States—took root in the 1810s and 1820s. In 1817 the American Colonization Society was founded. Though between 1817 and 1867 the society helped send around six thousand black individuals to Liberia, colonization never became as successful as its supporters hoped. Many white and black Americans opposed colonization. Peter Kolchin, *American Slavery, 1619–1877*, 185. For more information on support and opposition to black colonization, see Henry Mayer, *All on Fire: William Lloyd Garrison and the Abolition of Slavery*, 61–63, 72–73, 77–78; Eric Foner, *Forever Free: The Story of Emancipation and Reconstruction*, 25–26, 189–90.

7. *Congressional Globe*, 37th Cong., 1st sess., 190.

8. Ibid., 257.

more than twenty senators withheld their vote.[9] Yet Lane voted in favor, and the resolution passed.[10] His goal was to preserve the Union, not to abolish slavery. Its disruption or even destruction, he believed, was inevitable during the upcoming conflict and he welcomed its end. But the formality of fighting against it was not necessary. First and foremost, Lane wanted to save the Union, let slavery stand or fall as it might.

Not everyone in the Union took such a casual approach to slavery. On August 30, 1861, General John C. Fremont, the Republican Party's 1856 presidential candidate who now served as Union commander of forces in Missouri, declared martial law in that state and authorized the confiscation of secessionist property and slaves. The general's next step was even more controversial. Without consulting superiors, Fremont issued a local military emancipation proclamation. Slaves confiscated from rebels were to be freed. While abolitionists and Radical Republicans celebrated the move, moderates and conservatives in the Northern states, including Lincoln, were shocked. The move threatened to send the tenuous border states of Kentucky, Maryland, and Missouri into the Confederacy.[11] Lincoln privately asked Fremont to adjust his order to match the more conservative Confiscation Act. When the general refused to do so, Lincoln publicly rescinded Fremont's order.[12] Lincoln did not want to interfere officially with the nation's domestic institutions because such a move had not yet, in his mind, become "an indispensable necessity."[13]

Lane was in Kansas during the excitement over Fremont's actions, and he initially maintained his proclaimed neutral position. During his October 8 speech in Leavenworth, he answered complaints that his Kansas Brigade threatened slavery in Missouri by explaining that slaves freed themselves. Property, including slaves, of loyal Missourians could be recovered. But he would do nothing to protect the slave property of those who were for disunion. "We march to crush out Treason, and if Slavery does not take care of itself, the fault is not mine," he announced. "It can never be made my duty to defend it for the benefit of Traitors." He directly linked the institution to the interests and well-being of those in rebellion,

9. McPherson, *Battle Cry of Freedom*, 312.

10. *Congressional Globe*, 37th Cong., 1st sess., 265.

11. William K. Klingaman, *Abraham Lincoln and the Road to Emancipation, 1861–1865*, 72–74.

12. Doris Kearns Goodwin, *Team of Rivals: The Political Genius of Abraham Lincoln*, 392.

13. Abraham Lincoln to A. G. Hodges, April 4, 1864, in Paul M. Angle and Earl Schenck Miers, eds., *The Living Lincoln*, 601.

clarifying, "If they do not want to lose their slaves, let the Traitors lay down their arms, and our troops will be glad to leave their borders. . . . A rebellious province or State must be visited by the severe chastisement of war; Traitors must suffer the loss of property, and desolation must overwhelm them before they will acknowledge the Government against which they have revolted."[14]

Nonetheless, Lane's understanding of slavery began to change with experience in the field. A month after his Leavenworth speech, Lane repeated his view before a group of Indiana and Kansas soldiers in Springfield, Missouri, but elaborated on the nature of slavery and its role in bringing war to the Union. "An oligarchy, more cruel and proscriptive than ever scourged and cursed a nation, ancient or modern, has brought on this war *for* slavery," he asserted, "and if we are required to protect, defend, or in any way help slavery, then we are required to cooperate with the enemy to help him, to defend him, and to work for the same end." He questioned the idea that Union men could "place ourselves thus in alliance with our deadly and barbarous foes, and at the same time conquer them, subdue them, crush them!" Lane foreshadowed the Union's changing war effort and described his own progress in opposing slavery. He understood that it was at the heart of the conflict; the Kansas Brigade's march into Missouri had revealed to him the value of disrupting the institution in the war against secession:

Astonishing as it may seem to you, gentlemen of Indiana, yet the fact we have repeatedly demonstrated that a heavier blow is dealt out of the realm of Secessia in the abduction or freedom of a slave, than in the killing of a soldier in arms. I may put this truth in a stronger light still: abduct from the same family a slave and kill in arms a son, and the loss of the slave will be regarded as the greater misfortune—the calamity for which there is no healing balm. I could bring forward more than one thousand witnesses whose observation and experience qualify them to speak of the truthful candor of these remarks. If, then, by allowing the slave to fall into the wake of the army, and find the priceless boon of freedom, we void bloodshed, save property from destruction, and strike

14. *Lawrence Republican,* October 17, 1861. The *Liberty Weekly Tribune,* October 11, 1861, carried a slightly different version of the speech. It records Lane's words as: "We march to crush out treason and let slavery take care of itself. If they don't want slavery to perish let them lay down their arms—or do the other thing—keep Lane's Brigade out of Missouri. . . . When you march through a State you must destroy the property of the men in arms against the Government—destroy, devastate, desolate. This is a war."

death dealing blows upon the head and front of this rebellion, does not every consideration that is just and good, require that this policy be adopted. This war is *for* slavery—let us make it the mighty engine for slavery's destruction, and the rebels will soon cry, enough. . . . Every guarantee that is given to slavery by the Government strengthens the rebels in their course.[15]

Lane held a unique position. Other Union military officers had been politicians. But because Lane managed to hold both roles simultaneously, he influenced policy and practice in the field. His willingness to engage in the aggressive campaigns he advocated provided a remarkable opportunity to test his ideas. And, because of his experience in the field, he could adapt his policy ideas accordingly. "The policy, inaugurated by the Kansas Brigade which I have the honor to command, was not adopted in a moment, but it is the result of experience," he told the crowd.[16] He saw firsthand the effect of disrupting slavery in Missouri with his Kansas Brigade, and it thrilled him. It weakened secessionist morale and strength by depriving rebels of their property, their investments, and their labor force. Though this disruption would burden Southern Unionists, Lane considered that to be an acceptable cost. He supported compensating loyal slave owners for property lost.[17] Compensation was easier to handle than protecting the institution. "Preserving slavery will cost the Government ten times as much as crushing the rebellion," he announced.

Lane's speech in Springfield differed from his previous discussions of slavery. Though he had declared earlier in the speech that his creed was *"Let slavery take care of itself,"* he acknowledged that the institution could not be ignored or pushed aside. Secessionists had waged war to preserve slavery, and thus Union men must take a stand:

Since the rebels have failed to nationalize slavery, their battle cry is, "Down with the Union—let slavery lift up its crest in the air," and here I solemnly vow, that if Jim Lane is compelled to add a note to such an

15. *Lawrence Republican,* November 21, 1861.

16. Ibid.

17. In Springfield, Lane stated: "I would cheerfully give my consent to have them paid out of the national treasury for any loss they might sustain." *Lawrence Republican,* November 21, 1861. In July 1862, Lane proposed the following provision to a military bill: "Provided, That in all cases where such man, boy, mother, child, or children shall owe service or labor to any loyal citizen by any law, usage, or custom, such loyal citizen shall be entitled to receive just compensation for the loss of the same." *Congressional Globe,* 37th Cong., 2nd sess., pt. 4, 3337.

infernal chorus, he breaks his sword and quits the field. (Tremendous applause.) Let us be bold—inscribe "Freedom to all" on our banners—and appear that we are the opponents of slavery. It is certain as if written in the book of fate, that this point must be reached before the war is over. Take this stand and enthusiasm will be inspired in the ranks. In steadiness of purpose and courage, each soldier will be a Spartan hero. The spirit of the Crusader will be united with the iron will of the Roman, and an army of such soldiers is invincible.

He directly credited his position to the Kansas conflict. Turning to the Indianans, Lane admitted that his stance likely seemed strange to those not baptized by the territorial struggle. He assured them, "when your military education has received that peculiar cast which experience is sure to give it, and which now characterizes the Kansas soldier, then will we march shoulder to shoulder, and victoriously, too, against the enslavers of men, and against the traitors to the best Government on earth."[18]

Lane's Springfield speech showed his progression in tackling slavery in the war. Only months earlier he had supported a resolution that separated the institution from the war effort. Now, after spending time in the field, Lane adopted a broader vision for the Union cause. He advocated pressing Lincoln for an emancipation proclamation:

It should be the business of Congress at its coming session to pass a law directing the President of the United States by proclamation to order the rebel States, within thirty or sixty days, to lay down their arms and return to their allegiance, or in default thereof, declare all men free throughout their domains, and so far as I am concerned, I hope the Almighty will so direct the hearts of the rebels, that like Pharaoh they will persist in their crime and then will we invade them and strike the shackles from every limb.[19]

Freedom, Lane believed, should be the new watchword of the Union.

Lane's Springfield speech shows a man in transition. He began the speech with a professed desire to leave slavery alone, yet closed with a call for its forcible end. This apparent contradiction may have been an oratorical plan, as Lane soothed his audience with more moderate language at first, so as to not turn them off immediately to his more radical idea of emancipation. As the crowd responded to his magnetism, and his heroic

18. *Lawrence Republican*, November 21, 1861.
19. Ibid.

imagery, Lane made his case against slavery more forceful. Lane's call for an emancipation proclamation was a radical tactic for a conservative principle. He had found what Lincoln had not accepted at the time of Fremont's proclamation, and would not embrace for another year: that an official move against slavery was "an indispensable necessity" for preserving the Union. Lane believed that emancipation would end the biggest threat to national unity overall. In Boston, three weeks after his Springfield speech, Lane called for a permanent peace by crushing out the "disease" of slavery. By this, he did not mean an affliction against humanity or black Americans, but a curse upon the Union. Should the war end with slavery intact, another sectional war would remain inevitable. And Lane chastised the coward "who wants a peace patched up with the knowledge that our children will have this battle to fight over again."[20]

Lane continued his campaign by speaking in cities across the nation. Before a crowd in Washington, D.C., he reviewed his former Democratic embrace of the institution, announcing that he "was taught to reverence slavery beyond the bible or any of the ordinances of God." He claimed that it was "a crime to discuss the question" and that "Northern reverence compelled two great political parties to engraft on their platforms that the righteousness of slavery, being above even the government of God, should be no more discussed, 'either in or out of Congress.'" Lane may have exaggerated his previous feelings toward slavery for effect, but his description of Democratic tiptoeing around slavery was sincere.[21] He told his audience how his experiences in Kansas and in the ongoing war had opened his eyes. "I saw it stuff the ballot-boxes of my own State," he roared; "I saw it raise the black flag, and inscribe on it 'no quarter'; I saw the most exalted officers of the government, debauched by it, prostitute the Government itself to its own destruction!" The slaveholding power, Lane argued, caused a national war and raised an army "within six miles of here, and hence along two thousand miles of border, seeking the destruction of the

20. "Extracts from Speech of General Lane, at Tremont Temple, Boston, November 31, 1861," *Kansas Collected Speeches*, 6.
21. See also Lane's Leavenworth speech in *Freedom's Champion*, February 1, 1862. He said: "Even in 1852 I was still a Democrat, when our party at Baltimore declared that all other subjects might be agitated, but Slavery was sacred. We might 'agitate' the Word of God, 'agitate' His law, 'agitate' the golden streets of the golden city—but before Slavery we must bow our faces in silence—it was too sacred to be talked about. I have lost that reverence, and so much progress have I made that I would not give one drop of the blood of the humblest soldier within the sound of my voice to save Slavery from eternal perdition."

mildest and best Government on earth."[22] Forced black labor, he continued, strengthened the rebel cause. Slaves raised crops, made clothes, and generally provided vital resources for the Confederate war effort. Striking against slavery as a whole meant victory in arms.

By late December 1861, Lane advocated his new policy in the Senate. The secessionists fought to keep their slaves, he reasoned, so take away those slaves and you deprive them of their ability and motivation to fight. "In my opinion, obtaining possession of these slaves by the Government would be more effective in crushing out rebellion, than the seizure, if it could be made, of every ounce of ammunition they possess. As the fear of losing their slaves is now the incentive to war, so would then the desire for their recovery be the inducement for peace."[23] Lane explained how easily such a move could be undertaken, since slaves flocked to Union armies. He had seen it in Missouri. So many slaves fled their homes to follow the Kansas Brigade in Missouri that newspapers called the band Lane's "Black Brigade." The *Leavenworth Daily Conservative* reported that the group numbering 256 contrabands followed H. D. Fisher, chaplain of the Fifth Kansas, and H. H. Moore, chaplain of the Third Kansas, out of Missouri and into Kansas.[24]

Emancipation meant four million freed slaves, a far grander issue than a trickle of self-liberated black men and women fleeing into Union lines. Lane continued to champion colonization of freed blacks. "The good of both races require their separation," he stated during his Springfield speech. "Ages of oppression, ignorance and wrong, have made the African a being inferior in intellect, and social attainments to the Caucassian [*sic*], and whilst together, we shall always have low, cringing servility on the one hand, and lordly domination on the other, it is better for both parties that each enjoy the honors and responsibilities of a nationality of his own." Personal prejudices against blacks would interfere with harmony among the

---

22. "Speech of Gen. Lane, in Washington, on the evening of Dec. 2d, 1861, on the occasion of a serenade in his honor," *Kansas Collected Speeches*, 8.

23. *Congressional Globe*, 37th Cong., 2nd sess., pt. 1, 111.

24. Escaped or freed slaves in Union lines came to be called "contraband," largely due to Union General Benjamin Butler's handling of escaped slaves in Virginia. After three slaves fled to Union lines in May 1861, a Confederate officer arrived and demanded their return. Butler refused on the grounds that the slaves had been property used against federal forces, and were thus legitimate contraband for confiscation. Noah Trudeau, *Like Men of War: Black Troops in the Civil War, 1862–1865*, 10. See also Fred A. Shannon, "The Federal Government and the Negro Soldier, 1861–1865," 567; *Leavenworth Daily Conservative*, printed in *Lawrence Republican*, November 21, 1861.

races. Lane admitted his own prejudice, voicing his opposition to complete social integration. "Now, for the good of us both," he told a crowd in Washington, "let us give them the discipline that attends freedom and free labor, then let us kindly separate them from us, and all will be well." Africa was an obvious choice, but Lane recognized the impossibility of transporting four million people across the ocean. He saw Central or South America as possibilities, and he joked with one audience that South Carolina would be a suitable place as well. But such plans were for the future, and during his campaign in Missouri, Lane had faced the real problem of finding a place for the slaves coming into his lines. Chaplain Fisher of the Fifth Kansas later recalled that "the second day out Lane sent for me on the march, and explaining our imminent danger of attack and the helpless condition of the great multitude of blacks, said: 'What shall I do with them?'" Fisher reminded Lane that the war had severely limited the labor force in Kansas, and that "the women and children in Kansas needed help to save the crop and provide fuel for winter." He advised Lane "to send the negroes to Kansas to help the women and children." Lane curtly replied, "I'll do it." Lane ordered Fisher and two other chaplains to lead the refugees to Kansas, and there distribute their property and find them homes. Fisher described the trek as harrowing, the group always wary of attack, moving day and night to reach Kansas and freedom. Upon making the border, Fisher stopped the procession, raised himself up on his horse and, he later recalled, "there under the open heavens, on the sacred soil of freedom, in the name of the Constitution of the United States, the Declaration of Independence, and by authority of General James H. Lane, I proclaimed that they were 'forever free.'" The slaves adopted new names to help prevent identification and a return to slavery, and many of them took up laboring jobs or farming in Kansas.[25]

25. The *Lawrence Republican,* November 21, 1861, reported that "Gen. Lane proposes to establish a colony in some Southern clime. Hayti has enlisted attention, and has demonstrated the fact that the negro race is capable of self-government. It will become a question whether the government should not provide some place of refuge for this oppressed people, not to coerce them to any particular locality, but hold out inducements which can be found no place else." "Speech of Gen. Lane, in Washington, on the evening of Dec. 2d, 1861, on the occasion of a serenade in his honor," *Kansas Collected Speeches,* 12. A report of Lane's impromptu speech before a Washington audience on December 2, 1861, recorded Lane discussing the matter: "Then, suppose we take another policy: obtain a country contiguous to this—a portion of South America, for instance—[Voice—"South Carolina."] Well, now, that idea of South Carolina strikes me very favorably. [Laughter.] I desire, first, to see the shackles stricken off in a legitimate manner, so that our stars and stripes may, in truth, wave over a country of

Many more blacks fled from Missouri into Kansas without military aid. In May 1862 Lane claimed that Kansas supported four thousand Arkansas and Missouri fugitive slaves, and by mid-July reported that the number had increased to sixty-four hundred. White Kansans had to adjust to this large influx of blacks. Like Lane, some in the new state accepted black migration for its effect on the war. Sol Miller, editor of the *White Cloud Kansas Chief,* explained that Kansans "never fancied the idea of having free Negroes colonized among us; but wherever our armies march, we trust they will leave the traitors niggerless."[26]

As the war progressed into 1862, Lane's anger with secessionists only increased. He told a crowd in Leavenworth in January, "When I think who caused this war, I feel like a fiend. When I think that the men who have been the Cabinet officers, the Senators, the Congressmen, the Generals, the Colonels; when I think that the very men who, for twenty years, have fattened on this Government, are now raising their hands to strike it down—I feel like taking them all by the throat—like throttling and strangling them all."[27] To end this war, Lane repeated, drastic measures would be needed. Though critics often lambasted Lane for irrational ranting in his speeches, his logic was sound. Slavery must be disrupted in order to win the war, he told the crowd. To keep a slave in bondage would require a bloodless war, "[f]or if you kill a master the slaves will escape." Lane proposed to kill those masters serving in the Confederate Army. And he now embraced a more radical means of warfare—arming blacks. To the audience, Lane prefaced this plan with a vivid story from his service in the Mexican War. During a scouting expedition he had come across the bodies of Mexican men, women, and children, killed and mutilated by Comanches. Upon hearing the news, General Zachary Taylor stated, "The Comanches seem to be fighting on the same side we are. We won't interfere with them." Lane looked at his audience, let the story sink in and

---

freemen." *Lawrence Republican,* January 2, 1862. The *Lawrence Republican,* November 21, 1861, also suggested reserving some Southern states for black colonization: "If the Government shall be compelled to subdue the South, and colonization is necessary, why not give them a few of the States of the South for a heritage, rather than the traitor masters? The guilty should suffer rather than the innocent. Let the oppressor seek a new home rather than the oppressed." Fisher, *The Gun and the Gospel,* 42, 156, 157.

26. Richard Sheridan, "From Slavery in Missouri to Freedom in Kansas: The Influx of Black Fugitives and Contrabands into Kansas, 1854–1865," 36–37; *Congressional Globe,* 37th Cong., 2nd sess., pt. 3, 2149, and pt. 4, 3337; *White Cloud Kansas Chief,* November 28, 1861.

27. *Freedom's Champion,* February 1, 1862.

announced, "I don't say I would call the Comanches but I do say that it would not pain me to see the negro handling a gun, and I believe the negro may, just as well become food for powder as my son."[28]

Though he preferred white men to fight the war, and freed slaves to serve as laborers for the Union cause, Lane remarked he didn't "propose to punish the negro if he kills a traitor." The idea of former slaves brandishing weapons against whites struck a long-standing fear in American, and particularly Southern, minds.[29] Lane understood that this proposition would shock some in his audience, and admitted, "I may lose my standing in the Church, but I tell you I take stock in every negro insurrection, and I don't care how many there are." It all came down to winning the war: "If [rebels] don't want to be killed by negroes let them lay down their arms."[30]

Lane's proposal was not an idle threat. At this early date in the war (almost a year before black regiments were formally mustered into federal service), he seriously considered the active role former slaves could play in defeating the Confederacy. Many in the North had no problem using escaped slaves in labor roles. Daniel Wilder, of the *Leavenworth Daily Conservative*, explained that many black men who had flocked to Lane's brigade were "employed as teamsters and cooks" and aided in gathering information for white Union soldiers. Yet, Wilder noted with an air of sarcasm, "It is a curious fact that white men and black men can live in the most intimate relationship so long as the latter are slaves; but as soon as the black man becomes free the 'odor' and 'inferiority' are so insufferable that contact is contagious."[31] Elevating blacks to soldiers would require support, or at least acceptance, from not only Union officials but also a large section of

28. Ibid.
29. The South did experience a few legitimate slave revolts, such as that led by Nat Turner in Virginia in 1831. However, white fears of slave revolt often led to massive retaliation against suspected threats. Bertram Wyatt-Brown explains that white Southerners were not obsessed with fear of revolt on a daily basis. Instead, there were short bursts of panic and anger as threats or perceived threats arose. See Wyatt-Brown, *Honor and Violence in the Old South*, 154–86. John Brown's raid on Harper's Ferry in 1859 and Lincoln's Emancipation Proclamation issued in 1863 were both denounced as evidence of Northern attempts to incite slave insurrection. For more information on Southern attitudes toward slave insurrection as related to the war, see J. L. M. Curry, "The Perils and Duty of the South, . . . Speech Delivered in Talladega, Alabama, November 26, 1860," in John L. Wakelyn, ed., *Southern Pamphlets on Secession, November 1860–April 1861*, 40; Mark M. Krug, "The Republican Party and the Emancipation Proclamation," 109; William J. Cooper, Jr., *Jefferson Davis, American*, 408–9; Kolchin, *American Slavery*, 155–60.
30. *Freedom's Champion*, February 1, 1862.
31. *Leavenworth Daily Conservative*, October 8, 1861.

a large anti-black public. Before the crowd in Leavenworth he defended the integrity and abilities of black men and women he had seen in Missouri. "The negroes are much more intelligent than I had ever supposed," Lane admitted. "I have seen them come into camp (occasionally) looking down as though slaves. By and by they begin to straighten themselves, throw back their shoulders, stand erect, and soon look God straight in the face. They are the most affectionate, impulsive, domestic beings in the world." Taking another shot at his old political party, Lane declared, "No one loves mother, wife, children, more than the negro, and they are an altogether smarter people than we give them credit for—I mean, we Democrats!"[32] And, he continued, black men would make fine soldiers.

> After a long day's march, after getting supper for the men, after feeding and cleaning the horses, I have seen them out, just back of the tents drilling. And they take to drill as a child takes to its mother's milk. They soon learn the step, soon learn the position of the soldier and the manual of arms. You even see that in the innermost recesses of their souls the "devil is in them." Gen. Washington did not lie when he said his negroes fought as well as white men. Gen. Jackson did not lie when he paid that noble compliment to his black soldiers at New Orleans. Give them a fair chance, put arms in their hands and they will do the balance of the fighting in this war.[33]

Throughout 1862 Lane proclaimed the abilities of freed slaves. He began to sound like an abolitionist, particularly in his denunciation of slavery. In New York, speaking before an audience at the Cooper Institute, Lane asked, "Did you ever notice a darkey baby? Why, they favorably compare with white babies when infants—why then do they sink below when grown? Because they are stupified [sic] by the master's lash."[34] Blacks were not natural savages, as leading Southern figures had proclaimed.[35] Instead, the violence and oppression from slavery broke them down. But, Lane argued, they could be redeemed and made into a valuable Union asset. In

---

32. Ibid.
33. Ibid.
34. *Lawrence Republican,* June 26, 1862.
35. For instance, Confederate President Jefferson Davis defended slavery as beneficial to blacks in a message to the Confederate Congress on April 29, 1861: "In moral and social condition [African slaves] had been elevated from brutal savages into docile, intelligent, and civilized agricultural laborers, and supplied not only with bodily comforts but with careful religious instruction." Quoted in Kenneth Stampp, ed., *The Causes of the Civil War,* 118.

New York, he admitted that he had already taken the step of arming former slaves. "In drill, after marching an entire day, when the whites sought
repose, the slaves in whose hands I had placed arms to slay traitors to their
country with—went to work learning the drill of the soldier—and I say
they learned the drill as rapidly as we—they have the capability." Again,
his actions had purpose. The Kansas warrior recognized the difficulty in
squashing resistance to the government and saw that black men could be
used to aid, perhaps even replace, white men in defeating secessionists. He
warned his audience that as the Confederate armies lost on the battlefield,
guerrilla warfare would commence and rebels would seek refuge in the
hills and swamps of the South. "I propose to meet it by setting the slaves
of those men free, and setting them to hunt them out," Lane proposed.
"Let [the rebels] seek shelter in the swamps of Florida; send your regiments of emancipated slaves after them, and they'll outlive them two to
one." This strategy would not only effectively end the rebellion, he
believed, but also save countless white Union soldiers.[36]

Not surprisingly, Lane's plan found criticism from conservatives, who
labeled him a radical and abolitionist. In July 1862, on the Senate floor, he
defended his stance. "We radicals, abolitionists if you please, have asked
that the white soldier shall be kept for battle, and that the loyal black men
of the Confederate States may be permitted to do necessary work, and be
armed for the perpetuating of this Union." Historian Albert Castel writes
that Lane was motivated by presidential ambition; that he advocated and
worked for black military service "to become the hero of the Northern radicals and so ride the abolitionist horse into the White House." This seems
unlikely, for Lane remained a consistent supporter of Lincoln as president.
Further, as Lane's friend John Speer (Castel calls him one of Lane's "hench-
men") later wrote, prejudice against blacks at this time limited the success
and popularity of black military units, a fact Lane corroborated on the Senate floor before the next presidential election. Castel even admits this fact.
The "abolitionist horse" was quite small in the Union when Lane pushed
the arming of freed slaves, and would not provide any strong base for a
presidential bid, even if Lane did have that intention—a fact that the politically adept Lane could not have missed.[37]

36. *Lawrence Republican,* June 26, 1862.
37. *Washington Republican,* printed in *Lawrence Republican,* July 24, 1862; Albert Castel, "Civil War Kansas and the Negro," 132; Speer, *Life of Lane,* 261. On the Senate floor
in February 1864, Lane praised Lincoln's cautious approach to emancipation and black
military service, stating: "In my opinion, when the history of this Administration comes

In truth, Lane was only an abolitionist in the fact that ending the institution and freeing slaves would save the Union and protect the interests and lives of loyal white Americans. His concern for the rights or well-being of the slaves themselves was secondary to, and a product of, those objectives. To his critics, Lane compared his actions to those of England and its colonies in Asia. "The native troops were called to the field, armed, and employed to put down the insurrection against English authority." Without that native help, he continued, Britain would have lost India. As for how that reflected radicalism, Lane declared:

> If to oppose the using of American volunteers for the protection of rebel property; if to favor the confiscation of rebel property constitutes radicalism, then, Mr. President, I am a radical. If opposing the use of American soldiers for the return of fugitive slaves to rebel masters; if opposition to the policy of driving from our lines the loyal men of the rebellious States because of their color renders me an abolitionist, then, Mr. President, I am one. Radical and abolitionist, Mr. President, I say crush out this rebellion, even if human slavery should perish in the land.[38]

Lane may have been labeled a radical and may have even embraced that label. But he did so to contrast the conservative element of the Republican Party. He did not see his ideas or actions as extreme—only as necessary.

Ever a man of action, Lane put his plan to arm blacks into operation. In July 1862 the *Missouri Democrat* received word of Lane's authority to recruit

---

to be written, the proudest page therein will be the record of the fact that Mr. Lincoln had the self-possession, the wisdom, the sagacity to restrain himself and friends from issuing the emancipation proclamation and arming the blacks until public sentiment was well-nigh ripe to sustain him. To have acted thus before the 22d of September would have been to have acted too soon. It would have imperiled the political power of the Government, a matter we could not afford to lose then any more than now." *Congressional Globe*, 38th Cong., 1st sess., pt. 1, 672. Castel, *Civil War Kansas*, 91. Historian William D. Mallam described the resistance to abolitionism throughout the North: "Fort Sumter and Lincoln's call to arms aroused a people to defend the Union, but it did not make abolitionists of a generation that had grown up hating abolitionists perhaps as much as it loathed the institution of slavery. And it was not just Democrats or the neutralists of the Border States who felt a deep distaste for the possibility of the war's developing into an antislavery crusade. There were many conservative Republicans who felt the same. In New York the powerful Weed-Seward machine never reconciled itself to emancipation as a war aim. In New Jersey, abolitionism failed to arouse any enthusiasm throughout the entire course of the war. There were strong conservative Republican factions in Connecticut and in Pennsylvania, and, as one would expect, in Ohio, Indiana, and Illinois as well." William D. Mallam, "Lincoln and the Conservatives," 34.

38. *Washington Republican*, printed in *Lawrence Republican*, July 24, 1862.

more soldiers for Kansas units and the expectation that black regiments would be formed—"the first to be fully equiped [sic] and in the field." The reports proved true, as Lane wrote to Secretary of War Edwin Stanton on August 5 announcing that he expected two regiments of black soldiers. The very next day, perhaps realizing the need for administrative approval, he telegraphed Stanton that he was "receiving negroes under the late act of Congress," and asked, "Is there any objection?" Stanton did not immediately reply, and Lane continued his work fielding a black infantry unit. Word of black soldiers in Kansas excited many in the region, particularly after August 6 when Lane publicly issued General Order Number 2 outlining black Union service. The orders rewarded any former slave of a rebel master with freedom. Lane based his authority upon two pieces of congressional legislation passed in July 1862: an amendment to the Militia Act, which authorized the president to accept black men into "any war service they may be found competent," and the Second Confiscation Act, which deemed those slaves captured from rebel masters as forever free.[39]

Many in Kansas came to accept the necessity of arming blacks to defeat secession, and defended Lane's policy. The *Lawrence Republican* acknowledged that critics charged Lane with "being ambitious," but pronounced that "it is a just ambition; an ambition that attains to higher and nobler ends than that of mere wanton destruction for the purpose of gaining fame for himself."[40] The *Republican* correctly recognized Lane's actions as something beyond self-promotion. Historian Dudley Taylor Cornish explained that the recruitment of black soldiers in Kansas had a legitimate, strategic motive. Military activities in the region placed an extensive burden on available white regiments. Cornish states, "The demands were so great that practicality ruled out prejudice, slowly at first, and then with gathering speed."[41] Lane had simply recognized this practicality earlier than most others. While the senator surely reveled in his role as recruiter, his push for black soldiers was initially quite controversial. He did not follow public opinion on this issue; rather he led public opinion to a necessary political and military policy.

39. *Missouri Democrat*, printed in *Lawrence Republican*, July 31, 1862; *O.R.*, ser. 3, vol. 2, 294, 311, 312. No reply from Stanton has been found, and Lincoln's secretaries John Hay and John Nicolay surmise that the war secretary intentionally allowed Lane to proceed uninterrupted in raising black troops. Nicolay and Hay, *Abraham Lincoln*, vol. 6, 445. Hans L. Trefousse, *The Radical Republicans: Lincoln's Vanguard for Racial Justice*, 217; Allen C. Guelzo, *Lincoln's Emancipation Proclamation: The End of Slavery in America*, 125.

40. *Lawrence Republican*, August 14, 1862.

41. Dudley Taylor Cornish, "Kansas Negro Regiments in the Civil War," 419.

Well after Lane had commenced building the black unit, administration officials began to voice concern. On August 23, three weeks after Lane had first telegraphed Stanton about raising a black regiment, the secretary of war finally offered a slight objection. While he was pleased that Kansas recruiting progressed so well, Stanton clarified that black regiments could only be raised with special authority from the president. "He has not given authority to raise such troops in Kansas, and it is not comprehended in the authority issued to you." Stanton closed his message with the assertion that Lane's black regiments "cannot be accepted into the service."[42] The secretary did not order Lane to stop the enlistment of blacks or disband those in the ranks, only reminded him that such action was unauthorized. Undaunted, Lane continued his recruitment of blacks, perhaps from a combination of personal stubbornness and a confidence in Lincoln's support. John Speer later wrote of Lane's assurances from Lincoln on the matter. The senator described to Speer a verbal promise from the president that Kansas black regiments would be "clothed and subsisted until such time as they could be brought into line armed and equipped for battle."[43] Whether Lane actually received this promise from Lincoln may never be known. In any case, the senator pushed ahead with the project.

Various Kansas officers fought for leadership of the First Kansas Colored Volunteer Infantry—the first black regiment from a Northern state. James Montgomery, who had gained a violent reputation during his military excursions against proslavery settlers and Missourians during the territorial struggle, wrote to Governor Charles Robinson requesting command of the black regiment over equally notorious Charles Jennison. The feud between the two men became so great that Jennison tried to break up the regiment rather than let it succeed without him. Lane wisely ignored both men and gave the command to Captain James Williams from the Fifth Kansas Cavalry, who had recruited soldiers for the regiment along with Captain Henry Seaman. Although historian Albert Castel charged Lane with selecting Williams because he was "a man the Senator could easily control," Williams proved to be an extremely capable and independent military leader who strongly advocated for the rights and abilities of his men.[44]

42. *O.R.*, ser. 3, vol. 2, 445.
43. Speer, *Life of Lane*, 261–62.
44. James Montgomery to Charles Robinson, August 3, 1862, Charles Robinson Collection, Kansas State Historical Society, Topeka; Castel, "Civil War Kansas and the Negro," 133; *Leavenworth Daily Conservative*, August 6, 1862. Williams was highly

Recruiting men and finding officers for the rest of the regiment proved difficult as well. The *New York Times* in late August reported that Lane enjoyed immense popularity among blacks in the Kansas area, and that black men were "enthusiastic to enlist and fight. Already about a hundred stalwart fellows are enrolled in Lawrence in two companies, both expected to be filled." Yet, Benjamin Van Horn, the white captain of Company I, First Kansas Colored Regiment, later described problems Lane experienced in filling the ranks. Lane and Williams "had great difficulty in getting the niggers to enlist, the secessionists had run all of the loyal Indians out of the Indian Territory and the Government had located them at the Sac and Fox Agency and was feeding them there," Van Horn wrote in 1909. When asked by Lane to go to the agency to entice the black men to join the service, Van Horn "made all the excuses I could, [but] finally I told them I would try it." Other sources suggest that some of the men serving in the Kansas black regiment may not have been volunteers at all. Lane told a Leavenworth audience that "the negroes are mistaken if they think white men can fight for them while they stay at home." To the delight of the white crowd, he told blacks "we have been saying that you would fight, and if you won't fight we will make you." Lane saw black soldiers as a resource, not as a demonstration of human equality. Reports of Kansans raiding Missouri counties for black "recruits" filtered back to Lincoln. Edward M. Samuel, a Union man in Clay County, Missouri, wrote to the president in September that fifteen Kansans had forcibly taken around twenty-five black men from neighboring communities for "General Lane's negro brigade." Members of the Missouri State Militia caught up with the group on its way back to Kansas, captured eight of the "jayhawkers," and recovered all of the blacks and a number of stolen horses.[45]

By October 1862 portions of the First Kansas Colored Volunteer Infantry were in the field. Five companies marched into Bates County, Missouri, on October 26. Three days later, part of the unit engaged a Confederate force in a brief firefight. Eventually the Confederates fell back and the black sol-

---

regarded by soldiers of the First Kansas Colored Infantry. In the 1880s he successfully petitioned Congress for recognition of the bravery and accomplishments of Kansas black soldiers. His popularity was demonstrated on October 7, 1890, when he attended a regimental reunion in Leavenworth. The *Leavenworth Times* reported the event, and declared that "his brilliant war record and achievements make him beloved by all who were under his command." *Leavenworth Times*, October 8, 1890.

45. *New York Times*, August 17, 1862; Benjamin Van Horn Autobiographical Letter, January 4, 1909, Benjamin Van Horn Collection, Kansas State Historical Society, Topeka; *Leavenworth Daily Conservative*, August 6, 1862; *O.R.*, ser. 1, vol. 13, 619.

diers counted eight dead and eleven wounded. The skirmish between a few dozen men—which by October 1862 barely warranted attention in comparison to the massive campaigns in the war—has become known as the Battle of Island Mound. It might have been forgotten, except that it was the first engagement of an organized black unit during the Civil War.[46]

Lane championed black military service for the remainder of the war. In December 1862 he proposed a bill to "call into the field two hundred regiments of infantry composed of persons of African descent" to help end the war. His reasons still focused on necessity, and white interests, rather than advancing human rights or equality. In 1864 he told a colleague on the Senate floor that he would prefer to send all white Union soldiers home to their families, while black soldiers took the burden of combat. "I am not so devoted to, so much the lover of the negro race that I would permit them to remain at home enjoying its luxuries while white men are called upon to defend them." He supported putting one million black men in uniform so "that white troops may be relieved from the dangers and fatigues of the Army." Yet Lane genuinely came to recognize the abilities and interests of black soldiers. When Senator Anthony Kennedy questioned the potential of black men in combat, Lane referred to the battle at Island Mound as a glorious example of a small unit fighting off a much larger band of "black-hearted traitors." He declared that "they showed as much pluck, as much steadiness, as much skill in the use of their weapons as any troops that ever fought." And he criticized the prejudice leveled toward these men by the federal government, arguing that "we have lost a great deal by discriminating against the colored soldier." By classifying them differently than whites in uniform, he maintained, the Confederate government was invited to treat them as less than legitimate federal soldiers. "When we put the uniform of the United States upon a person," he told the Senate, "he should be the peer of any one who wears the same uniform, without reference to complexion." In 1864 Lane supported legislation to retroactively pay men of the First Kansas Colored Infantry for service rendered before the unit's federal muster. He also critiqued legislation that threatened to discriminate against black soldiers who had previously been slaves.[47]

46. Trudeau, *Like Men of War*, 3–7; Dudley Taylor Cornish, *The Sable Arm: Black Troops in the Union Army, 1861–1865*, 77; Castel, "Civil War Kansas and the Negro," 134; "Report of Maj. Richard G. Ward, First Kansas Colored Infantry," *O.R.*, ser. 1, vol. 53, 455–58.

47. *Congressional Globe*, 37th Cong., 3rd sess., pt. 1, 171; 38th Cong., 1st sess, pt. 4, 3487; and 37th Cong., 3rd sess., pt. 2, 1442. Black soldiers were initially paid less than

Lane continued to offer suggestions for the future of former slaves. Throughout the war years, colonization remained his favorite option, and it was a popular idea with the president and other officials as well. In February 1864 Lane eloquently argued that a section of Texas be set aside for the black population.[48] He still harbored prejudice against blacks, though it was now based more on the belief that they were only unprepared for, not incapable of, self-government.[49] But, he argued, blacks faced nearly insurmountable hardships if they remained in the Southern states, where the white population remained hostile to black advancement. "Extend to them that substantial freedom to which they are so justly entitled," he said, "grant them power; the privilege of selecting their own rulers; of framing their own laws, and I venture the opinion that the day will soon come when we will be proud of our protégés."[50]

Lane's colonization proposal did not come to fruition, for it did not offer a practical solution to America's race problem. Nonetheless, the senator continued to defend the basic interests of former slaves. He did not embrace universal suffrage, but in May 1864 objected to the denial of suffrage to black men who had served the Union. "I am unwilling to say by any vote of mine," Lane proclaimed, "that a man defending his country and this city shall be excluded from the ballotbox of the city, while copperheads, traitors . . . have the right of suffrage." Though Kansans had recently voted against black suffrage, Lane voiced his hope that "the time may come, and soon come, when we can safely extend to the colored men of our country all the political rights that we enjoy ourselves."[51]

Lane's early and energetic assault against slavery during the war is noteworthy, but cannot be seen as any extraordinary change of principle

---

white soldiers, and often were assigned to more labor-intensive duties. See James M. McPherson, *The Negro's Civil War: How American Blacks Felt and Acted during the War for the Union*, 197–207; Cornish, *The Sable Arm*, 181–96; Edwin S. Redkey, ed., *A Grand Army of Black Men: Letters from African-American Soldiers in the Union Army, 1861–1865*, 229–48. *Congressional Globe*, 38th Cong., 1st sess., pt. 1, 481–83, 640. The unit first organized in August 1862 but was not officially mustered into federal service until January 1863. Lane questioned the word "free" in a bill to pay black soldiers. Ibid., 869–73. For a good description of Lane's part in raising black soldiers in Kansas, see his comments on pages 872 and 873.

48. Luveta W. Gresham, "Colonization Proposals for Free Negroes and Contrabands during the Civil War," 31–32.

49. Lane stated, "Uneducated, dependent, they look to us as helpless infancy, requiring direction, protection, and to a great extent subsistence, and at this time instructions how to obtain it." *Congressional Globe*, 38th Cong., 1st sess., pt. 1, 673.

50. Ibid., 675.

51. Ibid., pt. 3, 2244.

on his part. His approach to slavery during this period was practical—a tactical approach to help his nation. Even his eventual embrace of abolition as a moral and principled boost for the Union was not incompatible with his earlier opposition to slavery. Admittedly, his opposition to human bondage progressed, but Lane had never backed the institution. As long as national and party peace required recognition of slaveholding interests, Lane acquiesced. But when slavery and its advocates defied the democratic process and then made war against the Union, he no longer tolerated the institution. Though radical in appearance, Lane's main campaign against slavery, like his actions in Kansas, were consistent to his principle of preserving the Union.

Lane arguably underwent some transformation with his attitude toward race. The man who had reportedly compared blacks to mules, who had labored to incorporate the exclusionary laws against blacks in Kansas, and who had argued against black citizenship in the wake of the Wyandotte Constitution, came to be a chief proponent for black military service and a notable defender of black abilities. He saw a war against the institution of slavery as a blow to the Confederacy and armed black men as a great tool for the Union. To put black soldiers successfully into federal service, he had to convince others that the step was necessary, as well as feasible. He came to believe in the humanity, intelligence, and bravery of former slaves. And his denunciation of racial prejudice within the military, in regard to pay and classification, was a particularly enlightened measure considering his previous apathy toward blacks. Though Lane championed black rights and interests far beyond that of many Americans in the 1860s, his motivation was pragmatic, rather than truly humanitarian or opportunistic.

Still, historians should not assume too much about Lane's racial attitudes. He was not among the most radical of Republicans on the issue of race relations. To the end of the war, Lane admitted that he and other white Americans harbored certain prejudices against blacks that would complicate integration. He repeatedly advocated plans for colonization. As will be seen in the following chapter, the Radical Republican contingent in Congress adopted the mantra of universal suffrage, an idea that Lane never endorsed. He came to believe that blacks were capable of self-government, but deemed them unprepared. Thus, his discussions of race by the end of the Civil War provide a snapshot of old and new perceptions. For instance, when Lane participated in a debate on race relations in February 1864, particularly the right of blacks to testify in court, he proudly proclaimed that Kansans had "long since eradicated this much of their prejudices toward the oppressed African." Yet, when integration was discussed, Lane stated that "I was then and am now opposed to the amalgamation of the two races, believing, as I do, that the product is inferior to either race."[52] Blacks were no longer comparable to mules—but they were not equal to whites.

This transformation of attitude toward blacks was an important and positive step in Lane's social and personal views. But it was somewhat separate and even secondary to his primary goals and interests. What mattered to James Lane was the integrity of his party and the preservation of the Union for white Americans.

52. Ibid., pt. 1, 837, 841.

11

Lane and the End of the Civil War, 1864–1866

"I propose to-day and hereafter to take my position alongside the President of the Republican party and stand there unflinchingly so long as he remains faithful to the principles of that party."

During the last two years of the Civil War, James Lane struggled against political attacks in Kansas and even took to the field one more time—as an aide to a commanding officer—when Confederate Sterling Price threatened federal forces in Missouri and Kansas one last time, in 1864. But his role in Abraham Lincoln's reelection and his handling of Reconstruction politics provide more important clues to his political and personal principles. Because he was labeled a radical during the first half of the war, Lane's moderate approach to Reconstruction brought further accusations of inconsistency. Yet, as before, his consistent goals were the stability of the Union and his political party. His attempts to protect both (as he saw them) ultimately led to his political downfall and contributed to his death.

Lane had been a steadfast supporter of Lincoln since the 1860 election. During the uncertain presidential election of 1864, the Kansas senator maintained his loyalty. Lincoln's secretaries John Nicolay and John Hay later described Lane's support of the president as opportunistic, arguing that the senator had turned against the administration until he found supporting the president advantageous for his own political career. Then, the two men believed, Lane "instantly trimmed his sails to catch the favoring breeze." As Lane biographer Wendell Stephenson explains, though, the secretaries must have "had access to information not now extant, for although Lane differed with the President, his numerous speeches reveal a consistent support of the administration." Available evidence shows that Lane defended the president vehemently against critics throughout the war. William Stoddard, another Lincoln aide, claimed—also years later— that at the Grand Council of the Union League in the summer of 1863, Lane "had been a severe critic of Mr. Lincoln at the beginning of the evening's oratory," but had been persuaded to support Lincoln after one delegate made a particularly emotional defense. In any case, by late 1863, there was no doubt that Lane fully endorsed Lincoln's reelection. "I declare the administration to be a success," Lane announced in December 1863. "I supported Honest Old Abe for the position he now holds, and still stand by him. He is a radical and as such I am with him."[1]

As early as December 1863 Lane stumped for Lincoln's reelection and labored to protect the integrity of the party under the president's leadership. He and Lincoln faced particularly stubborn opposition from his Kansas colleague in the Senate, Samuel Pomeroy. Pomeroy preferred Secretary of the Treasury Salmon Chase for the presidency. Some believed that Pomeroy may have been jealous of Lane's relationship with Lincoln. Whatever his motivation, Pomeroy took part in a secret campaign to boost Chase's chances of election while limiting Lincoln's. In February 1864, after a pamphlet entitled "The Next Presidential Election" circulated through the Northern states declaring Lincoln's reelection to be unwise, Pomeroy signed a second pamphlet naming Chase as the proper replacement. Though marked private, this second document was published in public journals and became known as the "Pomeroy Circular." Far from hurting Lincoln's image, the two documents backfired. Northerners denounced the pamphlets and the men whose names were attached to them. In March 1864, Lane challenged Pomeroy's loyalty to the party and called himself a "member of the original radical Union party of this country." He declared that "when I see an effort made to divide the loyal party of the country against him who, in my opinion, is the consistent, stern, and proper leader of that party, Abraham Lincoln, President of the United

---

1. Nicolay and Hay, *Abraham Lincoln,* vol. 9, 61; Stephenson, *Political Career of Lane,* 141; William Osborn Stoddard, "The Story of a Nomination," 268–69; *Washington Chronicle,* quoted in the *Kansas Daily Tribune,* December 25, 1863.

States, I will here or elsewhere endeavor to expose the effort, let it come from whom it may."[2]

Though Lane called himself a radical, his positions differed from the Radical Republicans. This group included figures such as Benjamin Wade, Charles Sumner, and Thaddeus Stevens. These Radical Republicans opposed Lincoln's cautious and moderate approach to emancipation and Reconstruction. While Lane had earlier called for an emancipation proclamation and the arming of black soldiers, he came to champion the president's tactful handling of the war. Lane may have taken a much more aggressive approach in the prosecution of the war than Lincoln, but he realized that the president shared exactly the same priority—the defense of the Union. Lane's embrace of the radical image focused on his early opposition to conservatives, including those in the Republican Party, who supported a limited war. His bulldog tactics and total war mentality generated criticism as extremist and radical. Yet, when political leaders who held more progressive social and racial ideas came to construct a "Radical" clique in Congress, Lane did not follow.

In 1864, Lane became an instrumental part of the Lincoln reelection campaign. Leverett Spring wrote that Lincoln personally chose the master stump speaker to open the campaign in New York at the end of March. At the Cooper Institute, Lane praised the president's leadership and abilities, and bemoaned the calamities that would fall upon the nation if another candidate was selected.[3] He pushed his friends in Kansas to make Lincoln's reelection their priority in the upcoming election cycle. "So important do I consider the Presidential fight," Lane wrote to Kansan Sidney Clarke, "that I think I have the right to ask every friend of mine to forego his own promotion in the selection of delegates to the national convention and in the nomination of candidates for state offices. In both cases I deem it absolutely necessary to regard only the success of Mr. Lincoln."[4] In Kansas, John Speer worked under Lincoln's personal request to secure support for the president's Republican nomination. The newspaperman helped elect Lane as a delegate to the Republican (or Union Party) national

2. William Frank Zornow, "The Kansas Senators and the Reelection of Lincoln," 141, 136–37; Nicolay and Hay, *Abraham Lincoln*, vol. 8, 318–19; *Congressional Globe*, 38th Cong., 1st sess., pt. 2, 1028.

3. Spring, "The Career of a Kansas Politician," 102. John Speer confirms Spring's account, Speer, *Life of Lane*, 279.

4. Lane to Sidney Clarke, March 6, 1864, Sidney Clarke Collection, Carl Albert Congressional Research and Studies Center, University of Oklahoma.

convention scheduled in Baltimore on June 7, 1864.[5] Kansas also elected Lane a delegate to the Grand Council of the Union League set to be held in Baltimore the day before.

The Grand Council was particularly important as a preview to the Republican meeting, for nearly two-thirds of the Union League members present were delegates to the convention. The Union League consisted of leading Republicans and war Democrats who strongly supported the war against secession. It also included a number of men hostile to the president who planned to use the Grand Council as a platform to slam the administration. Lincoln supporters hoped that the meeting would serve as a harmless venting session—or as Stoddard explained, "the place where all the anti-Lincoln steam [would] . . . be let off"—thus allowing the actual convention to proceed constructively and with a more moderate tone. Still, some radicals believed that even if Lincoln's nomination was unavoidable, the Union League could push a more radical platform for the Republican Party.[6]

A few days before the Grand Council and the convention, Lane visited Lincoln at the White House for a private meeting. Though no record of the discussion exists, Stoddard believed the two men discussed the strong anti-Lincoln force within the Union League and the impending Republican nomination.[7] As a delegate to both events, Lane prepared to support the president against all opponents.

On Monday, June 6, 1864, the Grand Council of the Union League met in Baltimore, closing its doors to all those but legitimate delegates. As expected, the large assembly swiftly turned into an anti-Lincoln rally. As soon as Samuel Miller of Pennsylvania made a motion to recommend the nomination of Lincoln for reelection, the radicals unleashed their fury. Across the hall delegates rose in succession to denounce Lincoln with charges so appalling, Stoddard claimed, that had they been uttered at the party convention, "that body could afterward have reached no peaceful agreement by ballot, nor could it have adopted any platform of resolu-

5. John Speer places the date of the National Convention as June 7, 1864, while William O. Stoddard labels the date as June 8, 1864. Both men were present at the convention. Historian William Zornow agrees with Speer on the date: Speer, *Life of Lane*, 279; Stoddard, "The Story of a Nomination," 270; Zornow, "The Kansas Senators and the Reelection of Lincoln," 142. Historian John Waugh also places the National Convention on June 7: John C. Waugh, *Reelecting Lincoln: The Battle for the 1864 Presidency*, 188.
6. Stoddard, "The Story of a Nomination," 271; Waugh, *Reelecting Lincoln*, 185, 184; Stoddard quoted in Zornow, "The Kansas Senators and the Reelection of Lincoln," 142.
7. Stoddard, "The Story of a Nomination," 270.

tions upon which it could have placed Abraham Lincoln before the people as a candidate for presidency." While Lincoln supporters had expected the president's opponents to vent their frustration, the voracity of the assault caught them off-guard. Charges of tyranny, corruption, favoritism, and a host of other abominable accusations were leveled against Lincoln. No person stood to defend the president. One observer believed that the grand president of the council, a purportedly pro-Lincoln man, only recognized those delegates who opposed the administration. Supporters of Lincoln sat in silence, some wondering, "Has Lincoln no friends left?"[8]

Finally, as the radicals had expended most of their fury, Lane's slender frame rose. The chairman promptly recognized him. The Kansan drew upon all of his mastery of western stump speaking, using his eyes and his body to take command of the crowd. Silently he stood, turning to stare over the room and the delegates for a long moment. "For a man to produce pain in another man by pressing upon a wounded spot requires no great degree of strength," he boomed, "and he who presses is not entitled to any emotion of triumph at the agony expressed by the sufferer." The delegates who had joined in the assault upon Lincoln had won no great victory, Lane believed, nor had demonstrated any amount of skill. "For a man to take such a crowd as this now is, so sore and sick at heart and now so stung and aroused to passionate folly . . . for a man to address himself to such an assembly and turn the tide of its passion and its excitement in the opposite direction; that were a task worthy of the highest, greatest effort of human oratory." Though he disingenuously claimed to be "no orator at all," Lane had absolute confidence in his ability to take over the session. "All that is needful is that the truth should be set forth plainly, now that the false has done its worst."[9]

Lane picked apart the radical accusations against Lincoln. Turning to the vast throng of men assembled, he demanded to know "one man whom you could or would trust, before God, that he would have done better in this matter than Abraham Lincoln has done, and to whom you would be more willing to intrust [sic] the unforeseen emergency or peril which is next to come?" If someone had an alternate, Lane called out, "Name your other man!" He lectured the assembly that Republicans "shall come together to be watched, in breathless listening, by all this country,—by all the civilized world,—and if we shall seem to waver as to our set purpose,

8. Zornow, "The Kansas Senators and the Reelection of Lincoln," 143; Stoddard, "The Story of a Nomination," 271–72; Waugh, *Reelecting Lincoln*, 185.
9. Lane quoted in Stoddard, "The Story of a Nomination," 272.

we destroy hope; and if we permit private feeling, as tonight, to break forth into discussion, we discuss defeat; and if we nominate any other man than Abraham Lincoln we nominate ruin!"[10]

The audience sat captivated by Lane's defense of Lincoln. Stoddard described the scene of delegates leaning forward "while they more or less rapidly are swept into the tide of conviction and are made to believe, with him, that any other nomination than that of Lincoln to-morrow is equivalent to the nomination of [Democratic candidate George B.] McClellan by the Republican Convention and his election by the Republican party; that it would sunder the Union, make permanent the Confederacy, reshackle the slaves, dishonor the dead and disgrace the living."[11] Lane took his seat. No one stood to reply. The assembly then voted on a resolution approving the Lincoln administration. Few dissented, though many did not vote. Then the council endorsed Lincoln's bid for reelection.[12] The critics' steam had been let out and the notorious Kansan had cooled its effect.

The following day the Union national convention met at the Front Street Theatre, a large but inadequate site for a political rally.[13] Filled to capacity as the convention opened, the theater echoed with cheers as various speakers championed the war against the Confederacy. The resolutions provided by the platform committee won unanimous approval. With that finished, former war secretary Simon Cameron moved that Lincoln and his vice president Hannibal Hamlin be nominated by acclamation. The move was designed by Cameron to throw the convention into an uproar, and it worked. Delegates shouted their disapproval, the noise almost deafening. Some tried to bring order, including Thaddeus Stevens, who demanded a roll call and vote by the states. The chaos drowned his words. Governor William Stone of Iowa rose and called for Cameron's motion to be tabled. Lane's powerful voice pierced through the assembly, "Stand your ground, Stone! Stand your ground! Great God, Stone, Kansas will stand by you!" Both Lane and Stone strongly supported Lincoln. Yet, by tabling Cameron's motion, the convention could proceed with order and secure Lincoln's nomination through a dignified vote of the states. Further, while Lincoln's nomination seemed likely, a change of vice presidential candidates was in the works.[14]

10. Ibid., 272–73.
11. William Stoddard, *Inside the White House in War Times*, 242.
12. Stoddard, "The Story of a Nomination," 273; Waugh, *Reelecting Lincoln*, 187.
13. Waugh, *Reelecting Lincoln*, 188.
14. Ibid., 194; also see *New York Times*, June 9, 1864, for an account of the convention.

As the roll call commenced, each state's delegation cast unanimous votes for the president, until Missouri was called. John Hume, chairman of Missouri's new radical delegation, announced that his colleagues could not vote for Lincoln on the first ballot. After a pause of disbelief, the convention erupted into chaos once again. Lane's voice for a second time rose above the din, calling on the convention to hear the Missouri delegation. Hume explained that while the Missouri Republicans would stand behind whoever the convention nominated, they had been instructed to cast their first ballot for Ulysses S. Grant, the Union general and hero currently slugging it out against Robert E. Lee in Virginia. The Missouri delegation faced a hostile crowd, as others shouted for them to change their vote. One Missourian feared that he and his colleagues would be picked up and physically thrown out of the convention by their fellow Republicans.[15] Yet Lane, the tireless champion of Lincoln and the man whose name struck fear and hatred in the State of Missouri, backed Hume and the Missouri delegation. The men were his neighbors and had come as Republicans and legitimate delegates to the convention, Lane argued. To deny them their voice and right to vote as they pleased countered the principles that the party embraced. Stone joined Lane, and eventually the assembly quieted enough to continue with the roll call. Finally, as the last delegation, Nevada, endorsed Lincoln, Hume rose and switched Missouri's votes to Lincoln. The theater erupted in chaos once again, although this time in popular celebration.[16]

With Lincoln's nomination secured, the convention turned to the vice presidential question. Hannibal Hamlin from Maine had held the position for the previous four years, and some expected him to retain the seat. Yet, Lincoln and other Republicans considered the value of someone who could draw in Democrats and Southerners as the task of Reconstruction loomed. Andrew Johnson, the appointed military governor of his home state of Tennessee, was offered as a possibility. Some historians have given Lane credit for playing a pivotal role in Johnson's nomination as well. Leverett Spring quoted Lane as claiming to have "originally selected [Johnson]" and to have "urged him on the convention at Baltimore." Lane's friend John Speer confirmed that the senator endorsed Johnson and wrote of a conversation early in 1864 among some Kansas leaders on the upcoming election. Hamlin, most there concluded, would be the party's choice.

15. Ibid., 195–96.
16. Ibid., 196.

"No—Andrew Johnson," Lane announced. "Mr. Lincoln does not want to interfere; but he feels that we must recognize the South in kindness. The nominee will be Andy Johnson." Whether or not Lane was instrumental in the initial selection of Johnson for the role, the senator did back the Tennessean and helped make Kansas one of the first state delegations to endorse him at the convention.[17]

Overall, some writers have emphasized Lane's role in Lincoln's reelection. According to Lincoln's secretary William Stoddard, Lane helped silence the president's critics leading up to the convention and believed that as a result of Lane's impressive Union League speech, "the greatest political peril then threatening the United States had disappeared."[18] While historians Spring and William Zornow also spoke of Lane's magic in securing the Grand Convention for Lincoln, they did not particularly question the president's overall chances of nomination. Two more recent works on Lincoln give entirely different descriptions of the president's nomination. John Waugh in his book *Reelecting Lincoln* stressed the power of the radical opposition to the president and discussed Lane's defense of Lincoln. When the convention unanimously endorsed the incumbent, the author portrayed Lincoln as surprised upon hearing news from Baltimore, exclaiming "What! Am I renominated?" According to Waugh, Lincoln expressed relief when assured the news was correct and requested that a message be sent to him at the White House as soon as the vice presidential candidate had been selected.[19] Doris Kearns Goodwin, in her popular study of Lincoln, *Team of Rivals*, provides an almost completely opposite account of Lincoln's attitude. She quotes Noah Brooks's description of meeting with Lincoln the night before the Baltimore convention. When Brooks told the president that his nomination was certain, Lincoln "cheerfully conceded that point without any false modesty." Goodwin gives no detailed description of the Grand Council or national convention, and Lane is not mentioned. Further, in a complete contradiction to Waugh, Goodwin explains that the president learned of the convention's selection of Andrew Johnson as vice president before receiving word of his own nomination.[20]

As with the selection of Johnson, Lane's actual role in securing Lincoln's nomination may be questionable. What is not open for debate, though,

17. Spring, "The Career of a Kansas Politician," 103; Speer, *Life of Lane,* 284; Waugh, *Reelecting Lincoln,* 201.

18. Stoddard, "The Story of a Nomination," 273.

19. Waugh, *Reelecting Lincoln,* 196.

20. Goodwin, *Team of Rivals,* 624, 626.

was the senator's notable stand against the president's critics during the 1864 election cycle. At the Baltimore convention, Lane proposed an advisory group headquartered in St. Louis to take charge of the Republican campaign in the West. Party leaders enthusiastically endorsed the plan and placed Lane as chairman and treasurer of the committee. With typical enthusiasm, Lane championed the Republican cause in Indiana, Missouri, and Kansas. His work benefited not only Lincoln but also his own reelection. Finding a strong opposition movement—largely opposed to him personally—in his home state, Lane labored to retain his seat. Some Kansas Republicans complained of Lane's power and conduct in state politics. He had become a political powerhouse, much to the dismay of his opponents. Edward Russell, chairman of the state's Republican executive committee, wrote to Lincoln in September of the senator's "faction" abusing federal patronage and ignoring the honest interests of Kansas "at the expense of principles, party and Country." Lane did in fact look to Lincoln for political help, including asking the president to replace certain Kansas officials hostile to his Senate reelection. Lane's Senate campaign found an unlikely ally in Confederate General Sterling Price. When the Confederate force moved through Missouri, eventually turning toward Westport near the northeastern Kansas border, Lane rushed home to bang the war drum. He and his Senate colleague Pomeroy temporarily shelved their political rivalry to serve as aides-de-camp to Union General S. R. Curtis in the field. Pro-Lane newspapers covered the senator's actions, boosting his popularity and ensuring his reelection.[21]

Though Lane's tie with Lincoln helped boost his political future, any portrayal of his support of the president as simply opportunistic or expedient ignores the senator's tireless endorsement of the administration's policies. While Lane called himself a radical, he fully stood behind Lincoln in the face of radical opponents and endorsed the moderate policies and interests of the executive, including the softer approach to Reconstruction. At the national convention in Baltimore, Lane not only backed the Missouri delegation's balloting but also advocated the representation of Unionist delegates from seceded states. The *Washington Chronicle* specifically noted Lane's determination "in demanding the recognition by the convention of

21. Stephenson, *Political Career of Lane,* 145; Zornow, "The Kansas Senators and the Reelection of Lincoln," 144; Edward Russell to Lincoln, September 22, 1864, and Lane to Lincoln, December 20, 1864, both in Abraham Lincoln Papers, Library of Congress. John Speer gives an elaborate account of Lane's reactions to the Price raid, including reports from the field. Speer, *Life of Lane,* 285–301.

the gallant Unionists of such States as Louisiana, Tennessee and Arkansas," and other western territories. Even before the Baltimore convention, Lane had defended Southern Unionist representation in Congress. On May 21, Lane presented the credentials of William Fishback as a legally elected senator from the Unionist population of Arkansas, and days later defended that state's right of representation according to Lincoln's Proclamation of Amnesty and Reconstruction issued in December 1863. Lincoln advocated a lenient policy toward the Southern states. When 10 percent of a state's voting population supported the Union, that minority could establish a new state government. Lincoln's plan, historian Eric Foner argues, was not "a hard and fast policy from which Lincoln was determined never to deviate." Instead, it was designed to shorten the war and establish white support for emancipation. Lane endorsed this policy and continued to support Arkansas Unionist recognition in Congress. Radicals in Congress opposed Lincoln's plans for Reconstruction, disputing even the executive authority to handle it. In June, after Lane introduced a joint resolution "for the recognition of the free State government of the State of Arkansas," Senator Charles Sumner of Massachusetts argued that the time had not yet arrived to recognize Arkansas officials since that state did not retain its regular place in the Union. "The power to admit States into this Union," he argued, "and, by consequence, the power to *readmit* them, are vested in Congress, to be exerted by joint resolution or bill, to which the concurrence of both Chambers and the approval of the President are necessary."[22]

Lane labored over the course of the following year to induce the Senate to decide upon the status of the Unionist Arkansas government and its elected officials. The assembly repeatedly dismissed the matter. Lane remembered the frustrations he and his fellow free-state Kansans experienced with the federal response to their statehood movement, and stood at the plate for Arkansas. "Here is a State government that has been recognized by the executive department of this Government," he told the Senate, "and although I have not determined for myself whether to vote for the admission of these two gentlemen or not, I am exceedingly desirous that the question shall not be settled at this session against the loyal people of Arkansas."[23] The loyal people of that state had created an organized

22. *Washington Chronicle*, quoted in Stephenson, *Political Career of Lane*, 145; *Congressional Globe*, 38th Cong., 1st sess., pt. 3, 2458–59, 2842, 2897. For a discussion of the proclamation, see Eric Foner, *Reconstruction: America's Unfinished Revolution, 1863–1877*, 35–37.
23. *Congressional Globe*, 38th Cong., 1st sess., pt. 3, 3362.

government, he argued, had held a legal election according to federal law, and now asked for recognition in Congress. In many ways, it was similar to the Free State movement in Kansas Territory. In March 1865, when Senator John Conness of California complained of Lane's persistence in pushing the Arkansas senators' admission, the Kansan directly compared his own experience to that of the Southern Unionist officials.

> I was an applicant here as a Senator-elect nine years ago under just such circumstances as Mr. Snow, Mr. Fishback, and Mr. Baxter present themselves. I came here as the representative of a State organization of the free-State men of Kansas against the slave oligarchy of the Union backed by the Administration. I heard on that occasion from the lips of Bayard and Hunter and Mason, and that class of men, now traitors, just such speeches against that organization as are now made against the loyal people of Arkansas; and just such denunciations against me fell from the lips of those men as have fallen from the lips of the Senator from California against Mr. Fishback.[24]

He saw Radical Republican opposition to the Arkansas loyalists as a betrayal of the Republican Party's earlier support of Kansas, and chastised Charles Sumner of Massachusetts and Benjamin Wade of Ohio for their resistance. "I take this opportunity to say to the Senator from Massachusetts and to the Senator from Ohio that those speeches in denunciation of that [Kansas] State organization were answered by those two Senators who are now here repeating the very speeches that they then answered," Lane said. "I invite those Senators to look into the Congressional Globe of 1856. . . . [for] that Congressional Globe shows that the Senator from Ohio and the Senator from Massachusetts are trampling upon their own record, and repeating the speeches that they had then answered." Finally, turning to Conness, Lane defiantly announced that he "must remember that I have traveled the same road that these men [from Arkansas] traveled; that the people I represent have traveled the same road that their constituents are traveling."[25]

Overall, Lane's efforts to secure seats for the Arkansas Unionists during the war failed. Nonetheless, he continued to press the Senate to recognize the Unionist Southern governments of Arkansas, Louisiana, and Tennessee. He told his colleagues that the state organizations were "indispensable to the protection of the Union men in those States." Lane wanted

24. Ibid., 2nd sess., pt. 2, 1428.
25. Ibid.

to help the Unionist men in the fight against the Confederacy. Further, as with the abolition of slavery, Lane believed that federal support of Unionist Southerners hurt the Confederacy. "I am one of those who believe that the bringing back of any of the seceded States into the Union does more to demoralize our opponents and to close out this rebellion than any other act that we can accomplish," he confidently stated. "It is worth more than all the victories which can be gained in the field."[26]

Radical Republicans attempted to enforce a Reconstruction policy more stringent than the president's in July 1864. This alternative, in the form of a bill sponsored by Senator Benjamin Wade of Ohio and Congressman Henry Winter Davis of Maryland, proposed a delay in Reconstruction until a majority of a Southern state's white male population backed the federal Constitution. Only those men who could take the Ironclad Oath— a pledge that one had never voluntarily supported the Confederacy— would be granted voting rights. It also protected freed black rights to a larger extent than Lincoln's plan.[27] The Wade-Davis Bill passed the Senate by a slim margin, with Lane voting in support.[28]

Lane's handling of the bill is confusing. The Senate spent relatively little time in debate, and Lane's remarks on the Senate floor were brief and generally focused on proposed amendments. Though he voted with Radicals who did and would continue to push for more aggressive policies for Reconstruction, possible reasons for Lane's affirmative vote are apparent. While defending the bill, Wade made two important points that echoed Lane's persistent concerns. First, Congress would soon adjourn; if this bill was not passed, it would do so without providing any legislative plan for reconstructing the South and the nation. The public would demand to know upon what principles and grounds Southerners would be readmitted, Wade argued, "and we must be prepared to give an answer to it."[29] Lane had been frustrated, and would continue to be frustrated, by the Senate's resistance to recognize Southern Unionists. Not only did the Senate not seat Arkansas' senators-elect, but it declined to decide the status of the loyal Southern governments. This led to Wade's second point, an answer to the American public of why Southern Unionist officials had not been

26. Ibid., pt. 1, 594.
27. Foner, *Reconstruction*, 60, 61; Allan G. Bogue, *The Earnest Men: Republicans of the Civil War Senate*, 240–42.
28. Eighteen senators voted in the affirmative, fourteen opposed. Seventeen members were absent. *Congressional Globe*, 38th Cong., 1st sess., pt. 4, 3491.
29. *Congressional Globe*, 38th Cong., 1st sess., pt. 4, 3449.

recognized. Wade predicted that his fellow senators would face criticism of tyranny and despotism. "That would be wrong," Wade announced. "We ought to be able to answer authoritatively everybody that demands to know upon what principle they shall be admitted."[30] Perhaps the idea of providing some type of congressional plan appealed to Lane, even if some details stood in opposition to his interests. Unfortunately, Lane's specific reasons for voting for the Wade-Davis Bill remain a mystery. In any case, Lane found himself in a tug-of-war between the power and plans of the Republican executive and the Republican Congress.

The president exercised a little-known executive power with the Wade-Davis plan, the pocket veto. By not signing the bill, Lincoln allowed the plan to die a silent death. Lane later bragged of advising "Mr. Lincoln to withhold his signature to that bill because it disfranchised the loyal men in those States."[31] In fact, Lane had voted for an amendment to remove a racial classification from the bill, but the proposal was defeated.[32] Further evidence that he did not adopt the principles of the Wade-Davis Bill may be found in his persistent endorsements of the loyalist Arkansas government on grounds completely rejected by the Radical Republicans. Though Lane's exact reasons for voting for the bill may never be known, there is no doubt that his actions were driven in part by a concern for Republican unity. The bill serves as one of the first major divides between what was shaping up as the Radical Republican contingent in Congress and the presidency, and Lane may have been motivated to make a public display of support for the Republican Congress.

Biographer Wendell Stephenson believed Lane's late-war conservative approach to Reconstruction and support of Southern Unionists was at odds with his early wartime thoughts. Stephenson points to remarks made on the Senate floor in June 1862, in which Lane arrogantly boasted "I laugh to scorn the idea of extending constitutional rights over a State and people who trample under foot that Constitution. . . . The idea of those states being in the Union is, to me, ridiculous."[33] True, Lane had taken a more nonchalant approach toward Unionists before, particularly with his apparent apathy toward Missouri Unionists who suffered from his

30. Ibid., 3450.

31. Ibid., 39th Cong., 1st sess., pt. 2, 1802.

32. Only Lane and four other senators voted for the amendment. *Congressional Globe,* 38th Cong., 1st sess., pt. 4, 3449.

33. Stephenson, *Political Career of Lane,* 152; *Congressional Globe,* 37th Cong., 2nd sess., pt. 4, 3236.

military campaigns in 1861. Early in the war, public officials spent little time actively pursuing Reconstruction policies, as the Union's military efforts still foundered. At that time, Lane focused more energy on foiling secession than trying to construct loyal governments in the seceded states. But even in 1861 and 1862 Lane did not completely ignore Southern Unionists. Stephenson fails to acknowledge Lane's comments regarding loyalists during that same June 1862 Senate debate. When Senator Orville Browning of Illinois asked the Kansan how he perceived the strong Unionist population in Tennessee, Lane replied that "a portion of the people of Tennessee deny that they are out of the Union; and I am willing to say . . . that Tennessee is in the Union. The question of going out of the Union is with the people. The people of Tennessee deny that they are out of the Union; and I would be as far as the Senator from Illinois from disturbing the institutions of the State of Tennessee."[34]

Lane made it clear that he opposed only secessionists. As before, Lane's excited rhetoric and actions caused observers and historians to miss the logic and principles behind them. Far from demonstrating a "remarkable change in attitude toward the status of the seceded states," as Stephenson argues, Lane's priorities remained constant.[35] Secession had to be defeated. The loyal people of the South who repudiated the Confederacy and supported the Union, and, after 1862, agreed to emancipation, would be welcomed with open arms.

Still, Lane had to find a balance between his and Lincoln's wish to recognize loyalist Southern governments and Radical Republican efforts to enforce a stricter policy upon the whole South. Lincoln's assassination in April 1865 only complicated the matter. Radicals initially celebrated their future under the apparently more aggressive Johnson. The vice president had repeatedly voiced his hatred of secessionists, stating, "Treason must be made infamous and traitors punished."[36] Radical Republicans welcomed this message, including Benjamin Wade who wrote, "By the gods, there will be no trouble now in running the government."[37] Yet, Eric Foner explains that "neither vindictiveness toward the South nor a carefully worked-out plan of Reconstruction distinguished Radicalism in the spring of 1865." Instead, black suffrage stood as the single most identifiable fea-

34. *Congressional Globe,* 37th Cong., 2nd sess., pt. 4, 3236.

35. Stephenson, *Political Career of Lane,* 152.

36. Johnson quoted in Howard Means, *The Avenger Takes His Place: Andrew Johnson and the 45 Days That Changed the Nation,* 117.

37. Benjamin Wade quoted in Brooks D. Simpson, *The Reconstruction Presidents,* 68.

ture among this group.[38] Lane supported limited black suffrage, but, like many moderate Republicans, never embraced the measure as a defining feature of Reconstruction. And while he certainly had voiced calls for punishing secessionists, Lane's support of pro-Union Southern governments clashed with Radical interests. Nonetheless, Johnson's first few weeks in power gave little indication of the complications between Radicals and more conservative Republicans that would come.

In late May 1865, Johnson initiated his own plans for Reconstruction. While he claimed to follow in Lincoln's footsteps, the new president's plan set in motion policies far outside the previous executive's interests. First, while Lincoln had approached Reconstruction moderately and intended to readmit the states as quickly and smoothly as possible, Johnson incorporated an amnesty policy for Confederates far more sweeping than anything proposed by Lincoln. Moreover, Johnson gave himself massive authority in the amnesty plan, requiring wealthy Southerners to petition him personally for a pardon. His initial goal had been to dethrone the established Southern elite, whom he blamed for dragging the South into the war. Though initially used cautiously, by September 1865 the president issued dozens, even hundreds, of pardons a day. Lane still supported Johnson, but complained of the president's liberal handling of pardons for former Confederates. For Radical Republicans, Johnson's actions were even more disturbing, as the reestablishment of traditional white authority in the South began to undermine the interests and freedoms of former slaves. Far from controlling Reconstruction, Johnson was overwhelmed. By fall of 1865 the elections in the South had confirmed the Radicals' fears. Benjamin Humphreys, a former planter and Confederate general, campaigned for the Mississippi governorship in October 1865, proudly wearing his old field jacket that sported three holes from Yankee bullets. Humphreys won the election easily, and three days afterward was pardoned by Johnson. Humphreys and the Mississippi state government quickly began to implement stringent laws against freed slaves. Known as the "Black Codes," these laws limited the political and social rights of blacks. Other Southern states quickly followed with similar codes.[39]

38. Foner, *Reconstruction*, 178; also see David Warren Bowen, *Andrew Johnson and the Negro*, 149–50.

39. Simpson, *The Reconstruction Presidents*, 72; Foner, *Reconstruction*, 183; Jonathan Dorris, *Pardon and Amnesty under Lincoln and Johnson: The Restoration of the Confederates to Their Rights and Privileges, 1861–1898*, 140; Stephenson, *Political Career of Lane*, 155; David M. Oshinsky, *"Worse than Slavery": Parchman Farm and the Ordeal of Jim Crow Justice*, 20–21.

Many Republicans exploded with rage at this flagrant violation of black rights. Radicals organized their opposition to Johnson, and campaigned across the Northern states for black suffrage. Though very vocal, Radicals did not make up a majority of the Republican Party, and referendums on black voting rights went against the Radicals in many Northern states, including Kansas.[40] Lane again found himself in a trying situation. His two priorities, the Union and his party, were again on unsteady ground. As Radical Republican pressure mounted against the president, Lane labored to protect party unity. In February 1866, while urging the Senate to recognize the Unionist Arkansas government, Lane warned of "dark clouds in the horizon of the great Union party of this country and of the country itself." He admitted to the Radicals that the Arkansas government did not recognize black suffrage, but defended their qualifications on every other ground. He demanded that the Arkansas senators be received, and he threatened to resist every Senate motion, bill, or action that postponed their admission.[41] Lane very clearly stood against the Radicals.

In the growing contest between Radical Republicans and Johnson, Lane further established his place in the president's camp in January 1866. In Kansas he championed Lincoln's moderate Reconstruction policies and provided an able defense of Johnson's efforts to promote "reconciliation and harmony" among the sections after the bitter war.[42] Sol Miller of the *White Cloud Kansas Chief* called Lane's effort "most moderate" and "devoid of the blood and thunder" typical of his speeches.[43] But Lane's defense of Reconstruction policies relied upon legislation that would soon fracture the Republican Party. Illinois Senator Lyman Trumbull, himself a moderate, crafted a bill extending the life of the Freedmen's Bureau, a federal organization dating back to 1863 that handled concerns for freed slaves in the South. The bill did not make the bureau permanent, but did boost its authority, including over the judiciary in the South.[44] Lane supported this bill in Kansas and encouraged his audiences in the state to pass resolutions endorsing it. Despite Lane's and Trumbull's expectations of executive support, Johnson vetoed the bill. Lane was placed in an embarrassing situation.

On February 19 the Senate received Johnson's veto message. Recognizing the volatility of the veto, Lane moved to have the Senate adjourn and handle the matter at a later time. Finding some resistance, Lane explained

40. Foner, *Reconstruction*, 222–23.
41. *Congressional Globe*, 39th Cong., 1st sess., pt. 2, 1026.
42. *Topeka Weekly Leader*, January 18, 1866.
43. *White Cloud Kansas Chief*, January 25, 1866.
44. Rembert W. Patrick, *The Reconstruction of the Nation*, 67.

his concern, announcing that he was "very anxious . . . to preserve the unanimity, the union of the loyal party of the United States, the Republican
Union party." When others pressed the matter, Lane began a filibuster and
forced a postponement of the veto issue until the following day.[45] On February 20 the Senate took up the veto and, though drawing a majority, failed
(by only two votes) to enlist the necessary two-thirds majority to override
the president.[46] Lane voted with most of his Republican colleagues in support of the bill, although some Kansas papers reported that he would have
sustained the veto had his vote been necessary.[47] He was desperately trying to work with both sides to keep the party united.

Trumbull's Civil Rights Bill, however, created an even more serious rift
among Republicans, and would prove to be the most significant problem
of Lane's Senate career. This legislation adopted a course far more radical
than the Freedmen's Bureau Bill. It better protected black rights across the
nation and gave weight to the Thirteenth Amendment. According to historian Eric Foner, Radicals and moderates held slightly different interpretations of the bill. For Radicals, the bill was expansive, protecting equality
in virtually every aspect of public life. Moderates took a more narrow
view, primarily by protecting black labor and contract rights. Both sides
agreed in equalizing black access to courts and punishment of crime. Lane
voted for the bill. His only comments during discussion of the legislation
focused on the status of Indians.[48]

Johnson vetoed the Civil Rights Bill, sending much of the Republican
Party—not only Radicals—into a frenzy. As a supporter of the president,
Lane faced the toughest political decision of his life, not excepting the
Kansas-Nebraska issue. As a young congressman from Indiana, Lane had
struggled to balance party and personal issues with Stephen Douglas's
legislation. Yet, while controversial, that measure had enjoyed the support
of the administration and the Democratic Party's leaders. Here, in 1866,
Lane stood at the edge of a frightening gorge between the president and
the Republican-dominated Congress. Other senators recognized Lane's
precarious position in the upcoming veto debate and worked to garner his
support against the president. A correspondent to the *Atchison Daily Free
Press* wrote of watching various Radical senators conversing with Lane on

45. *Congressional Globe*, 39th Cong., 1st sess., pt. 1, 917, 918.
46. Ibid., 943.
47. *Atchison Champion*, quoted in the *White Cloud Kansas Chief*, March 18, 1866;
Stephenson, *Political Career of Lane*, 156.
48. Foner, *Reconstruction*, 244; *Congressional Globe*, 39th Cong., 1st sess., pt. 1, 606–7,
498, 499, 504, 506, 522, 523.

the Senate floor. The writer explained that according to Senator Henry Wilson of Massachusetts, "General Lane promised to vote for the bill."[49]

On April 6, Lane introduced a compromise Reconstruction resolution. With this plan, Congress would admit senators and representatives of former Confederate states after governments there had annulled their ordinances of secession, ratified the Thirteenth Amendment, and repudiated rebel debts and recognized debts of the United States. Further, Southern states were required to grant limited suffrage to freed slaves: black men over twenty-one, who could read the Constitution in English, sign their names, and who owned property of $250 or more would have the right to vote.[50] When Senator Benjamin Brown of Missouri demanded to know if Johnson approved of this plan, Lane admitted that he had "no assurance from the President of the United States on that or any other subject." But, he continued, "this I do know; that the Republican party of which I am a member is crumbling to pieces, and that every day we postpone the reception of these States tends to insure the destruction of that party. I know further, that if both branches of the Congress of the United States pass this joint resolution and the President signs it, it will bring the Republican party together in harmony, and continue the political power of this country in the hands of that party."[51]

Lane declared his shock at the treatment of the president by members of the Senate, specifically Benjamin Wade. Johnson had been called a despot and dictator, Lane explained, for continuing the Reconstruction policies marked out by Lincoln. Turning to the Radical endorsement of universal black suffrage, Lane told his colleagues, "You cannot carry before the people of this country suffrage to the unqualified black man." Only by granting limited suffrage, as he had endorsed, and as laid out by Johnson, would the Republican Party find unanimity across the North.[52] More significantly, though, Lane defiantly defended the president and his constitutional right of the veto. Johnson's rejection of the bill amounted "merely to a vote to reconsider, with the lights given in his reasons for the veto." Rather than accept this presidential "vote" to rework the legislation, the president's critics had denounced him as a despot. This reaction, Lane believed, threatened the party and the Union far more than the veto itself. He looked across the Senate floor and said, "so far as I am concerned, I pro-

49. *Atchison Daily Free Press*, April 17, 1866.
50. *Congressional Globe*, 39th Cong., 1st sess., pt. 2, 1799.
51. Ibid.
52. Ibid.

pose to-day and hereafter to take my position alongside the President of the Republican party and stand there unflinchingly so long as he remains faithful to the principles of that party, defending him against the Senator from Ohio as I defended his predecessor against the same Senator."[53]

For the next two hours Lane and Wade argued on the Senate floor, debating Johnson's policies and the congressional response. Though Lane at first offered no assurance of Johnson's endorsement of his resolution, he steadfastly argued that the plan was entirely consistent with, and was even a version of, Johnson's Reconstruction policy. The Kansan read an August 15, 1865, letter from Johnson to Mississippi Governor William Sharkey, which listed in detail the expectations of that state's new government. Undeniably, Lane's resolution copied much of Johnson's letter. Senator Trumbull was not impressed, and asked for further evidence that Johnson would back the resolution. Lane ignored the question, stating that the president had been compelled to veto the Civil Rights Bill.[54]

Trumbull found a problem with Lane's logic, pointing out that the Kansan had voted for the Civil Rights Bill. How could he now argue that the president was bound to veto it? Lane's explanation illustrated his conflicting position as a supporter of the president in an increasingly radical Senate, and in the face of Reconstruction woes. It may also shed light on his handling of the Wade-Davis Bill. He claimed to "feel the absorbing and overwhelming danger that is upon our country, and was willing to waive my objections to the bill, and permit it to pass."[55] The Southern state governments were forming, and Lane desperately wanted Congress to act, even if the legislation was imperfect. Thus, as with the Wade-Davis Bill, Lane voted with Congress but accepted a veto. In his drive to protect party integrity, maintain moderate Reconstruction policies, bring order to the Union, and support his party's executive leader, Lane struggled to defend himself against apparent contradictions.

When the Senate voted on whether to pass the Civil Rights Bill over the president's veto, Lane backed the president. After the roll call, he reportedly received a telegram from friends pleading with him to support the bill and warning him that a failure to do so would be the end of his political career. Upon reading the telegram, Lane purportedly said, "The mistake has been made. I would give all I possess if it were undone."[56] The

53. Ibid.
54. Ibid., 1803.
55. Ibid.
56. Quoted in Stephenson, *Political Career of Lane*, 157.

accuracy of this account is questionable. Shortly after Lane's death in the summer of 1866, his wife, Mary, responded to a report that her husband regretted his vote against the Civil Rights Bill. "This statement I know to be without a shadow of foundation," she wrote; "as the Senator on all occasions in speaking of that vote said time would vindicate the correctness of that vote, and that he fully appreciated the importance of the good opinion of his party and friends, but that he regarded the Civil Rights Bill objectionable on Constitutional grounds."[57] Further evidence of his belief in his vote may be found in a letter to John Speer. On April 11 Lane wrote to Speer concerning the criticism he received. "It seems to me that I am entitled to be heard before condemnation." He continued, "I think I can show that the civil rights bill is mischievous and injurious to the best interests of the black man, but if I cannot the legislature shall fill my place."[58]

Despite any confidence Lane had in supporting the president, the public came down hard on him, condemning his vote against the bill. Newspapers across the state criticized him for abandoning his "radical" position. According to the *Leavenworth Daily Conservative*, nineteen prominent Kansas papers supported Congress, while only nine backed Lane and Johnson. In Lawrence, residents passed a resolution that declared "we feel humiliated by the recent vote in the United States senate, of our senator, James H. Lane, in opposition to the civil rights bill, and in indorsement of pernicious doctrines with which the President returned and endeavored to defeat that eminently just and proper measure." Many of Lane's friends tried to support him, but warned him to regain the radical reputation he had previously established. In fact, for the rest of the spring Lane voted with the majority in the Senate. Still, his reputation in Kansas sank so low that Republicans there decided to keep him out of the public eye during the upcoming elections. For the first time in his life, Lane succumbed to defeat. John Speer later recorded that Lane talked of his efforts to unite the president and Republican Congress. The senator had remarked, "with a very sad expression of countenance, that he had exhausted every resource of his nature, and could not move [Johnson]." Compounding his unpopularity in the Senate and at home, Lane faced charges of financial improprieties. A congressional investigation backed his claims of innocence, but

57. Mary Lane to unknown, July 25, 1866, James H. Lane Papers, Kansas Collection, Spencer Research Library, University of Kansas Libraries. The letter is unsigned, but references "my deceased husband" in the first line.

58. J. H. Lane to J. Speer, April 11, 1866, quoted in Stephenson, *Political Career of Lane*, 158.

the blow to his already damaged reputation and mental state could not be overcome so easily.[59]

For some months in 1866, Lane's health had been declining. The actual cause was unclear, although it was likely due to a combination of stress, fatigue, and an episode of depression. Despite a doctor's warning to stay and rest in Washington, Lane returned to Lawrence in the spring for some unspecified business. His reception in Kansas was cold. The *Emporia News* reported that while at home, "no demonstration was made over him, and he made no speech. Many of his old friends did not even call upon him." Broken in spirit and in health, Lane set out for Washington later that month. By the time he reached St. Louis, around June 22, his health had declined markedly. A local physician, Dr. T. G. Comstock, attended to Lane and found that he suffered from "dizziness, extreme depression of spirits, sinking sensations, numbness of the limbs after sleeping, intense ner vousness and loss of sleep." Lane refused to be left alone, complaining that his despondency was unbearable. After a few days of rest, his symptoms improved, but he was in no shape to continue the journey back to Washington. The physician telegraphed the Senate reporting Lane's illness, and notified his wife in Lawrence. Mary replied by telegraph that she could not meet her husband in St. Louis due to her own illness. Thus, Lane determined to travel back to Lawrence, with Dr. Comstock by his side.[60]

The physician and others with Lane noted that despite his ailment, his physical strength remained. The illness he suffered from seemed primarily mental and emotional. During the journey toward Kansas City, Lane became increasingly flustered and exclaimed that he was losing his mind. At one point he declared his wish to admit himself to an insane asylum, and asked for the nearest one. His companions managed to calm him down, and within a short time Lane began conversing cheerfully. He explained his political motivations regarding his most recent and controversial vote, noting his concern for party unity. The *St. Louis Democrat* reported that "he said in substance that he had felt compelled, in order to preserve, if possible, the harmony of the Republican party, to take a course which had brought down upon him bitter denunciations from former friends, and that wrong motives had been unjustly imputed to him."[61]

59. *Leavenworth Daily Conservative,* April 17, 20, 1866; Stephenson, *Political Career of Lane,* 159; Speer, *Life of Lane,* 313; *Congressional Globe,* 39th Cong., 1st sess., pt. 5, 3904–5.
60. *St. Louis Democrat,* reprinted in the *New York Times,* July 8, 1866; *Emporia News,* June 30, 1866.
61. *St. Louis Democrat,* reprinted in the *New York Times,* July 8, 1866.

By the time Lane arrived in Kansas City, his spirits had risen noticeably. Mary met him there and the couple relaxed, even doing some sightseeing. The Lanes and some friends decided to attend the theater in the evening, but Lane panicked slightly when he saw that the performance was the "Maniac's Daughter," and warned his physician that he feared the effect of watching such a play. Nonetheless, he sat through the first half before retiring for the night. In the morning, Lane and his wife took a steamer to Leavenworth and then traveled to his brother-in-law's house outside of that city. He once again fell into a depression. At this point, Dr. Comstock, who had accompanied the senator during the previous few days, started back for St. Louis. Before he left, he consulted with the new attending physician over their patient's health. The men agreed that Lane suffered from a "softening of the brain."[62] John Speer visited Lane at the home and after joking with the senator that he seemed in better health than reports had claimed, heard Lane reply, "The pitcher is broken at the fountain. My life is ended; I want you to do my memory justice; I ask nothing more."[63] Despite attempts to cheer Lane up, Speer resolved that nothing else could be done.

On July 1, Lane and two other gentlemen were riding in a carriage on the farm. As they stopped to open a gate, Lane hopped out, said good-bye to his surprised companions, walked a little way from the vehicle, placed a revolver into his mouth, and pulled the trigger. The bullet passed through the roof of his mouth and out the top of his head.[64] Amazingly he did not die instantly, but lingered another ten days, finally succumbing to his wound on July 11.

Why Lane broke down after the Civil Rights vote and committed suicide remains a bit of a mystery. Clearly he suffered some mental malady, almost certainly depression. An analysis of available information regarding Lane's mental health by a trained psychologist may offer a diagnosis. Lane had contemplated or threatened suicide at least three times before, although the reasons and the seriousness of intent behind the episodes vary. Ten years earlier, when warned by his friend Samuel Walker on the Kansas border about leading his "army" of Northern emigrants into the territory, Lane tearfully replied, "if you say the people of Kansas don't want me, it's all right; and I'll blow my brains out. I can never go back to the states and look the people in the face and tell them that as soon as I had

62. Ibid.
63. Speer, *Life of Lane,* 315.
64. Ibid.

got these Kansas friends of mine fairly into danger I had to abandon them."[65] Whether or not this was a valid threat, it still stands as a documented example of previous talk of suicide—and foreshadowed his actual means of suicide in 1866. The second incident took place during the Kansas legislature's vote for U.S. senator. As the legislators left the room, Lane was found outside the assembly, gun in hand, describing his plan to shoot himself had the election not gone his way.[66] The final example was during William Quantrill's raid on Lawrence. While hiding from the guerrillas, Lane resolved to end his life by stabbing himself in the eye with a penknife rather than be captured. However, because he believed that the guerrillas would torture and kill him (a fear that was justified given the wanton killing that day), this incident had little to do with mental illness or depression.[67]

In any case, Lane probably suffered from some long-term psychological issue. Perhaps he was bipolar, which might help explain his notorious episodes of extreme energy and radical behavior as well as his bouts of despondency. His friends and some historians have noted a family history of suicide. An older brother, Colonel John F. Lane, killed himself during a campaign against the Creek and Cherokee Indians in the Florida Everglades in the 1830s. Although James Lane believed his brother had committed suicide, a third brother, George W. Lane, was convinced that John's death had been an accident. Following James's suicide, George wrote to the *Atchison Champion* regarding the claim that John Lane had intentionally ended his life. Based on accounts George had obtained, he believed that John had accidentally collapsed on his own sword during a headache-induced fainting spell, from which he had been known to suffer.[68] The manner of John's death was fairly gruesome, as he fell down upon his upraised sword, thrusting the blade through his eye and into his brain. This manner of death may have inspired James Lane's plan in case of being discovered by Quantrill's men.

The reason for his death, like his actions during life, has been portrayed in various ways. His political enemy, Charles Robinson, believed that Lane

65. Quoted in Gleed, "Samuel Walker," vol. 6, 267.

66. Craig Miner, *Kansas: A History of the Sunflower State*, 85.

67. Quantrill's raiders killed most of the men they found in Lawrence, and they made a specific effort to find Lane. When Quantrill was shot and captured by Union soldiers later in the war, he spoke with his captors for a time before dying. "You want to know what would have been done with Jim Lane had he been captured?" he reportedly asked the soldiers. "I would have burned him at the stake." Schultz, *Quantrill's War*, 187.

68. *Atchison Champion*, reprinted in the *New York Times*, August 11, 1866.

had failed to cover up evidence of improprieties which threatened his Senate seat, and, heading back to Kansas after learning of new scandals in Washington, killed himself. "Thus ended the career of a man without principles or convictions of any kind," Robinson wrote, "who was comparatively weak and harmless when alone, but with the support of the Administration at Washington, with unlimited patronage and irresponsible power, was an instrument of untold evil."[69]

Historian Lloyd Lewis interpreted Lane's suicide in a radically different way. Lewis refuted Robinson's belief that Lane fell to the criticism and threat of public censure: "He had always thrived on accusations against himself, and had climbed by turning them to his own account." Even the political fallout following the Civil Rights vote, Lewis believed, would not discourage the man who "had met political midnight many times before, and with a whirlwind campaign had turned it once more into dawn." Instead, Lewis saw Lane's death as the romantic end of a tragic play. Consistent with the idealism of the Defender-Contemporary school of thought, which championed Lane as a heroic yet tragic figure, Lewis declared that "as I read the record of his life, Jim Lane shot himself because with the end of the Civil War, he saw his whole world gone, his era dead, his age vanished. He was the pioneer, the adventurer, the restless hunter for new horizons, and the glories of that time had vanished. He was a revolutionist, and the revolution had been won and was thenceforth to be in the hands of the corporation lawyers. He was a fighter, and the war was over."[70]

Both extreme interpretations of Lane's death leave much unexplained. Lane likely did suffer from the stress of his political fallout in Kansas and of the charges of corruption. Why he broke down and chose suicide instead of going on the political offensive, or even taking time off to rebound as he had before, might be explained by his poor emotional or mental health. Whatever combination of factors led to Lane's death, his suicide has only made the controversy surrounding this man more significant and more interesting.

Lane's final years in the Senate appear to show a man who embodied Radical Republicanism, yet who abandoned the mantra for a conservative—even "Democratic"—position.[71] Really, there was no contradiction. Lane appeared radical, and in a sense was radical in how he sought to

69. Robinson, *The Kansas Conflict*, 460.
70. Lewis, "The Man the Historians Forgot," 101, 102.
71. E. A. Smith of the National Bank in Kansas wrote to Congressman Sidney Clarke in January 1866: "Lane came back this time a full fledged Johnson Democrat as he terms

prosecute the war. Yet, beyond his relatively early turn against slavery and his progressive approach to blacks, Lane never became a true Radical Republican. In short, he did not change or abandon any positions that he had held. All of his actions—before, during, and after the Civil War—must be viewed as reactions to events and to his environment. He had faced similar complaints in Kansas in 1857 when, for a short time, he had worked with notorious proslavery advocate Dr. J. H. Stringfellow in land speculation. Antislavery settlers at that time wondered how the fiery free-state leader could so easily and quickly settle down with the "enemy." They accused him of abandoning the cause. In reality, in early 1857 the struggle in Kansas had temporarily subsided. Free-state worries, while still present, took a back seat to normal affairs. Thus, facing no direct threat from Stringfellow or many other proslavery Kansans, Lane had no problem focusing on peaceful concerns.

The ability to stir up popular emotion was Lane's greatest gift as well as his greatest enemy. While he believed what he said, his rhetoric was designed to inspire and generate support. But his audiences, and many authors and historians since, have had a hard time seeing his real objective. Some saw a demagogue, barking to a crowd what they wanted to hear. And even those who supported Lane often failed to see the logic beneath. Like a coach stirring up his team at halftime, Lane cheered on free-state Kansans in the 1850s and Unionists in the 1860s. His talk and tactics were all designed to help his party, his state, and the nation. And as time and events progressed, he adjusted to meet the new challenges. Unfortunately, those he spoke to often failed to understand the limitations of his vision. Excited by his enthusiasm and rhetoric, they kept the momentum going and as the war came to a successful end, they carried their expectations further than Lane had ever intended. When he saw fervor threaten to split the party, he called for moderation. In the end, he had a front-row seat as the party crumbled.

---

it and tells his constituents that he discovered when he went on to Washington that it would not be politic for him to fight a Democratic Administration for four years to come and he accordingly set about trimming his sails and made his accustomed general visit to the Legislature with a view to get that August body to indorse this 'Democratic-Anti-Suffrage-policy' in which he succeeded so far as to get a resolution introduced and referred to that effect." It is highly doubtful that Lane called himself a Democrat or voiced support for the Democratic Party, given his die-hard defense and celebration of the Republican Party throughout the war. Instead, Smith may have been adding his own view of Lane's position. E. A. Smith to Sidney Clarke, January 18, 1866, Sidney Clarke Collection, Carl Albert Congressional Research and Studies Center, University of Oklahoma.

Conclusion

During a public address on territorial Kansas in 2007, a prominent Kansas historian referred to James Lane's political transition from a pro-Douglas Democrat into a pro-Lincoln Republican as either an intense conversion or a hypocritical façade, depending upon one's own views. The assessment accurately describes the two main interpretations of Lane. But neither perception truly explains his political odyssey. The last twelve years of Lane's life may best be called an odyssey, for his migration from Democrat to Republican was a dramatic, and often chaotic, journey. Lane weathered the political storms of the Kansas-Nebraska Act, the Wakarusa War, the Kansas Memorial, "Bleeding Kansas," Southern secession, and Reconstruction, always keeping his eye on the Union and its democratic principles. He saw the political party as a vessel to reach those goals. When the vessel steered off course, Lane strove to set it back in line. Only when he saw the Democratic Party as hopelessly lost did he truly "abandon ship" and board another, keeping the same objectives in mind. In this he was not alone. Countless other Democrats broke from their party in the 1850s to help form the Republican Party. In that sense, Lane was only one of many.

Following his vote for the Kansas-Nebraska Act and his move to Kansas, Lane learned that popular sovereignty in practice did not resemble what had been promoted in theory. He always embraced the democratic principle of self-government, convinced that popular sovereignty could work if proslavery abuses were resisted. His leadership within the free-state ranks was based on the belief that democratic principles superseded oppressive local laws. Thus, he and his free-state colleagues saw their resistance to territorial officials, and even federal officials, as true to the Constitution, true to the nation, and true to democracy. The failure of the Kansas Memorial in the Senate proved to Lane that his beloved Democratic Party had been corrupted by proslavery interests. The sack of Lawrence and caning of Charles Sumner in 1856 convinced many others of this same belief. It proved to Lane and many people across the North that the Democratic Party now threatened the future of not only a free Kansas but also democracy itself.

Why have writers and historians seen Lane's political transition as opportunistic or unprincipled, when so many other Americans made a similar political shift? The answer appears to be threefold. First, and foremost, Lane's reputation for wild rhetoric and radical action often obscured his objectives and principles, particularly among his critics. Second, the habit of historians to focus almost solely on Lane in Kansas places a disproportionate amount of attention on the nasty political infighting of the Republican Party there and the bitter rivalries. His time in Indiana and his work in Washington on national matters are too often ignored. Finally, no historian until now has tried to interpret Lane's actions in the broader context of the collapse of the second-party system and the sectional conflict.

Lane's transition from the Democratic Party to the Republican Party was not unusual. Like others of the time, he adjusted his affiliations and tactics to protect his interests and objectives. It was only in these tactics that he really differed from most other former Democrats. He lambasted Democrats, condemned territorial and federal officials, and led military attacks against proslavery opponents. No one can deny that Lane was a master politician. He was full of ambition and used subtle tactics and tricks to promote himself and his cause. Yet, even self-promotion does not exclude principle. Lane linked his political party with the future of the nation. He linked himself with that future too, believing that he knew what to do and how it should be done. Such arrogance understandably generated disdain among both contemporaries and some later observers. But that disdain has unfairly led to a disregard for Lane's consistent objectives.

Lane's ability to make political alliances and stir up support with his legendary oratory could take him only so far. His mastery of political theater excited passions, but often failed to transmit the weight and logic of his mind. Many did not appreciate his rough western demeanor; others looked upon him with suspicion as a dangerous rabble-rouser. Yet, perhaps the greatest irony of Lane's life was that his odyssey did not take him as far as he helped carry others. He proved capable of cooling down as quickly as he heated up—far more capable in this manner than many of his constituents and colleagues. Because his intensity burned so quickly and because he could carry a crowd with him, Lane helped generate a radicalism in Kansas that actually outran his own sentiments. He advocated, and even led, violent attacks against proslavery forces in Kansas in 1856—yet did business with notable proslavery leaders during the quiet months of 1857. He carried out total war in Missouri and declared that Southern secessionists should be wiped out in 1861—yet fervently backed Southern representation in Congress as early as 1863. He armed black men and supported their interests in 1862—yet backed Andrew Johnson's veto of the Civil Rights Bill in 1866. All of these actions, and others, were condemned by contemporaries and historians alike as inconsistent, unprincipled, and unpredictable. Standing alone, with no background or context, these examples do indeed appear contradictory. But when studied in a timeline, with consideration of the deeper points of his speeches and letters, and with a careful note of the limits he set on his own radical actions, consistency appears.

John F. Kennedy wrote, "Perhaps if the American people more fully comprehended the terrible pressures which discourage acts of political courage, which drive a Senator to abandon or subdue his conscience, then they might be less critical of those who take the easier road—and more appreciative of those still able to follow the path of courage."[1] Historians who carefully research Lane's background and rely upon contextual analysis will find that Lane did have principles, that he maintained those principles more than previously believed, and that his larger actions can be explained, if not excused. Lane did not always take the easier road.

1. Kennedy, *Profiles in Courage*, 3–4.

Bibliography

Manuscript Collections

Indiana Historical Society, Indianapolis
       John G. Davis Collection
       William H. English Collection
Indiana State Library, Indianapolis
       Allen Hamilton Collection
       Richard L. Dawson Collection
Kansas State Historical Society, Topeka
       Benjamin Van Horn Collection
       Charles Foster Collection
       Charles Robinson Collection
       Cyrus Kurtz Holliday Collection
       Delahay Family Collection
       George Washington Brown Papers, 1855–1914
       Isaac Goodnow Collection
       J. A. Hallderman Collection
       James Abbott Collection
       James H. Lane Collection
       James Monroe Williams Papers
       James Montgomery Collection
       James Rodgers Collection
       James Stanley Emery Collection
       James W. Denver Collection
       John Brown Collection

Journal, Leavenworth Constitutional Convention
Kansas Biographical Scrapbook
Kansas Collected Speeches and Pamphlets, Vol. 9
Oscar Learnard Collection
Samuel N. Wood Collection
Thaddeus Hyatt Collection
Webb Scrapbook
William Connelley Collection
Library of Congress, Washington, D.C.
Abraham Lincoln Papers
University of Kansas: Spencer Research Library, Lawrence, Kansas
James H. Lane Papers
Lane Scrapbook
University of Oklahoma: Carl Albert Congressional Research and Studies
Center Congressional Archives, Norman, Oklahoma
Sidney Clarke Collection

Newspapers

Atchison Daily Free Press
Emporia News
Freedom's Champion (Atchison, Kans.)
Detroit Free Press
Herald of Freedom (Lawrence, Kans.)
Indianapolis Daily Journal
Indianapolis Daily State Sentinel
Indianapolis Morning Journal
Kansas Daily Tribune (Lawrence and Topeka)
Kansas Free State (Delaware, Kans.)
Kansas Freeman (Topeka)
Kansas National Democrat (Lecompton)
Kansas Weekly Herald (Leavenworth)
Lawrence Republican
Leavenworth Daily Conservative
Leavenworth Times
Lecompton Union
Liberty Weekly Tribune (Liberty, Mo.)
Missouri Republican (St. Louis)
New York Times

New York Tribune
Topeka Weekly Leader
Weekly Indiana State Sentinel (Indianapolis)
White Cloud Kansas Chief

Published Primary Sources

"Administration of Governor Shannon." In *Transactions of the Kansas State Historical Society,* vol. 5 (Topeka: Kansas State Historical Society, 1896), 234–64.

Angle, Paul M., and Earl Schenck Miers, eds. *The Living Lincoln.* Trustees of Rutgers College in New Jersey: Marboro Books Corp., 1992.

Berneking, Carolyn, ed. "A Look at Early Lawrence: Letters from Robert Gaston Elliott." *Kansas Historical Quarterly* 43, no. 3 (Autumn 1977): 282–96.

Blunt, James G. "General Blunt's Account of His Civil War Experiences." *Kansas Historical Quarterly* 1, no. 3 (May 1932): 211–65.

Bryant, William Cullen. *Power for Sanity: Selected Editorials of William Cullen Bryant, 1829–1861.* Compiled and Annotated by William Cullen Bryant II. New York: Fordham University Press, 1994.

Butler, Pardee. *Personal Recollections of Pardee Butler with Reminiscences by His Daughter Mrs. Rosetta B. Hastings.* Cincinnati: Standard Publishing Co., 1889.

Chesnut, Mary. *A Diary from Dixie.* Edited by Isabella D. Martin and Myrta Lockett Avary. New York: Gramercy Books, 1997.

"Civil War on the Kansas-Missouri Border: The Narrative of Former Slave Andrew Williams." Edited by William A. Dobak. *Kansas History* 6, no. 4 (Winter 1983): 237–42.

Congressional Globe. Washington, D.C.: Blair and Rives, 1834–1873.

Dickson, C. H. "The 'Boy's' Story: Reminiscences of 1855." *Transactions of the Kansas State Historical Society.* Vol. 5. Topeka: J. K. Hudson, 1896, 76–87.

Eldridge, Shalor Winchell. *Recollections of Early Days in Kansas.* Topeka: Kansas State Printing Plant, 1920.

Freehling, William W., and Craig M. Simpson, eds. *Secession Debated: Georgia's Showdown in 1860.* New York: Oxford University Press, 1992.

"Governor Denver's Administration." *Transactions of the Kansas State Historical Society.* Vol. 5. Topeka: Kansas State Historical Society, 1896, 464–561.

"Governor Geary's Administration." *Transactions of the Kansas State Historical Society.* Vol. 5. Topeka: Kansas State Historical Society, 1896, 264–69.

"Governor Medary's Administration." *Transactions of the Kansas State Historical Society.* Vol. 5. Topeka: Kansas State Historical Society, 1896, 561–633.

"Governor Reeder's Administration." *Transactions of the Kansas State Historical Society.* Vol. 5. Topeka: Kansas State Historical Society, 1896, 163–234.

"Governor Reeder's Escape from Kansas." *Transactions of the Kansas State Historical Society.* Vol. 3. Topeka: Kansas State Historical Society, 1886, 205–23.

"Governor Walker's Administration." *Transactions of the Kansas State Historical Society.* Vol. 5. Topeka: Kansas State Historical Society, 1896, 290–464.

"Letter from John Brown, Jr., to the Committee of Quarter-Centennial Celebration, January 25, 1886." In *Transactions of the Kansas State Historical Society,* "Embracing the Third and Fourth Biennial Reports, 1883–1885." Vol. 3. Topeka: Kansas State Historical Society, 1886, 463–66.

"Letters of George Caleb Bingham to James S. Rollins." Pt. V, January 22, 1862–November 21, 1871. Edited by C. B. Rollins. *Missouri Historical Review* 33, no. 1 (October 1938): 45–78.

"Letters of Joseph H. Trego, 1857–1864, Linn County Pioneer, The." Pt. 1, 1857, 1858. Edited by Edgar Langsdorf. *Kansas Historical Quarterly* 19, no. 2 (May 1951): 113–32.

"Letters of Joseph H. Trego, 1857–1864, Linn County Pioneer, The." Pt. 2, 1861, 1862. Edited by Edgar Langsdorf. *Kansas Historical Quarterly* 19, no. 3 (August 1951): 287–309.

"Letters of Julia Louisa Lovejoy, 1856–1865." Pt. 1, 1856. *Kansas Historical Quarterly* 15, no. 2 (May 1947): 127–42.

"Letters of Julia Louisa Lovejoy, 1856–1865." Pt. 5, 1860–1864—Concluded. *Kansas Historical Quarterly* 16, no. 2 (May 1948): 175–211.

"Letters of Peter Bryant, Jackson County Pioneer, The." Pt. 1. Edited by Donald M. Murray and Robert M. Rodney. *Kansas Historical Quarterly* 27, no. 3 (Autumn 1961): 320–52.

McClure, James. "Taking the Census and other Incidents in 1855." In *Transactions of the Kansas State Historical Society,* vol. 8 (Topeka: Geo. A. Clark, 1904), 227–50.

McCorkle, John, and O. S. Barton. *Three Years with Quantrill: A True Story Told by His Scout John McCorkle.* Norman: University of Oklahoma Press, 1992.

National Party Platforms. Vol. 1, 1840–1956. Compiled by Donald Bruce Johnson. Chicago: University of Illinois Press, 1978.

Official Records of the War of the Rebellion, The. (Also known as *The War of the Rebellion: a Compilation of the Official Records of the Union and Confederate Armies.)* Washington, D.C.: Government Printing Office, 1880.

Reader, Samuel James. "The First Day's Battle at Hickory Point, From the Diary and Reminiscenses [*sic*] of Samuel James Reader." Edited by George A. Root. *Kansas Historical Quarterly* 1, no. 1 (November 1931): 28–49.

Redkey, Edwin S., ed. *A Grand Army of Black Men: Letters from African-American Soldiers in the Union Army, 1861–1865.* Cambridge: Cambridge University Press, 1992.

Robinson, Sara. *Kansas: Its Interior and Exterior Life.* Boston: Crosby, Nichols and Co., 1856.

Ropes, Hannah. *Six Months in Kansas: By a Lady.* Boston: John P. Jewett and Co., 1856.

Schofield, John M. *Forty-Six Years in the Army.* New York: Century Co., 1897.

Sumner, Charles. *Charles Sumner: His Complete Works.* With Introduction by George Frisbie Hoar. Boston: Lee and Shepard, 1900.

"Topeka Movement, The." *Collections of Kansas State Historical Society.* Vol. 13. Topeka: W. R. Smith, 1915, 125–249.

Wakelyn, John L., ed. *Southern Pamphlets on Secession, November 1860–April 1861.* Chapel Hill: University of North Carolina Press, 1996.

"When Kansas Became a State." *Kansas Historical Quarterly* 27, no. 1 (Spring 1961): 1–21.

Secondary Sources

Abing, Kevin. "Before Bleeding Kansas: Christian Missionaries, Slavery, and the Shawnee Indians in Pre-territorial Kansas 1844–1854." *Kansas History* 24, no. 1 (Spring 2001): 54–70.

Abrahamson, James L. *The Men of Secession and Civil War, 1859–1861.* Wilmington, Del.: Scholarly Resources Inc., 2000.

Berwanger, Eugene H. *The Frontier against Slavery: Western Anti-Negro Prejudice and the Slavery Extension Controversy.* Urbana: University of Illinois Press, 1967.

———. "Negrophobia in Northern Proslavery and Antislavery Thought." *Phylon* 33, no. 3 (1972): 266–75.

Blackmar, Frank W. *The Life of Charles Robinson: The First State Governor of Kansas.* Topeka: Crane and Company, 1902.

Bogue, Allan G. *The Earnest Men: Republicans of the Civil War Senate.* Ithaca, N.Y.: Cornell University Press, 1981.

Bowen, David Warren. *Andrew Johnson and the Negro.* Knoxville: University of Tennessee Press, 1989.

Breisach, Ernst. *Historiography: Ancient, Medieval, and Modern.* 2nd ed. Chicago: University of Chicago Press, 1994.

Brigham, Johnson. *James Harlan.* Iowa City: Iowa State Historical Society, 1913.

Bright, John D., ed. *Kansas: The First Century.* New York: Lewis Historical Publishing Company, Inc., 1956.

Brinkerhoff, Fred W. "The Kansas Tour of Lincoln the Candidate." *Kansas Historical Quarterly* 13, no. 1 (February 1944): 294–307.

Britton, Wiley. *The Civil War on the Border.* Vol. 1, *1861–1862.* New York: G. P. Putnam's Sons, 1899.

Brown, George W. *False Claims of Kansas Historians Truthfully Corrected.* Rockford, Ill.: George Brown, 1902.

Carnes, Mark C., and John A. Garraty, eds. *American National Biography.* Oxford: Oxford University Press, 1999.

Castel, Albert. "Civil War Kansas and the Negro." *Journal of Negro History* 51, no. 2 (April 1966): 125–38.

———. *Civil War Kansas: Reaping the Whirlwind.* Lawrence: University Press of Kansas, 1997. Originally published as *A Frontier State at War: Kansas, 1861–1865.* Ithaca, N.Y.: Cornell University Press, 1958.

———. "Jim Lane of Kansas." *Civil War Times Illustrated* 12, no. 1 (April 1973): 22–28.

———. "Order No. 11 and the Civil War on the Border." *Missouri Historical Review* 57, no. 4 (July 1963): 357–68.

Cecil-Fronsman, Bill. "'Advocate the Freedom of White Men, As Well As, That of Negros': *The Kansas Free State* and Anti-Slavery Westerners in Territorial Kansas." *Kansas History* 20, no. 2 (Summer 1997): 102–15.

Cheatham, Gary L. "'Slavery All the Time or Not at All': The Wyandotte Constitution Debate 1859–1861." *Kansas History* 21, no. 3 (Autumn 1998): 168–87.

Clark, John G. "Mark W. Delahay: Peripatetic Politician." *Kansas Historical Quarterly* 25, no. 3 (Autumn 1959): 301–13.

Clugston, W. G. *Rascals in Democracy.* New York: Richard R. Smith, 1940.

Collins, Robert. *Jim Lane: Scoundrel, Statesman, Kansan.* Gretna, La.: Pelican Publishing Company, 2007.

Connelley, William Elsey. *An Appeal to the Record.* Topeka: William Connelley, 1903.

———. *James Henry Lane: The "Grim Chieftain" of Kansas.* Topeka: Crane and Co., 1899.

———. "The Lane Trail." *Collections of Kansas State Historical Society.* Vol. 13. Topeka: W. R. Smith, 1915, 268–79.

———. *The Life of Preston B. Plumb.* Chicago: Browne and Howell Company, 1913.

———. *A Standard History of Kansas and Kansans.* Vol. 1. Chicago: Lewis Publishing Co., 1918.

Corder, Eric. *Prelude to Civil War: Kansas-Missouri, 1854–1861.* London: Crowell-Collier Press, 1970.

Cornish, Dudley Taylor. "Kansas Negro Regiments in the Civil War." *Kansas Historical Quarterly* 20 (May 1953): 417–29.

———. *The Sable Arm: Black Troops in the Union Army, 1861–1865.* Lawrence: University Press of Kansas, 1987.

Cunningham, Roger D. "Welcoming 'Pa' on the Kaw: Kansas's 'Colored' Militia and the 1864 Price Raid." *Kansas History* 25, no. 2 (Summer 2002): 87–101.

Davis, Kenneth S. *Kansas: A History.* New York: W. W. Norton and Co., 1984.

Davis, William C. *"A Government of Our Own": The Making of the Confederacy.* New York: Free Press, 1994.

———. *Lincoln's Men: How President Lincoln Became Father to an Army and a Nation.* New York: Free Press, 1999.

Donald, David Herbert. *Lincoln.* New York: Simon and Schuster, 1995.

Dorris, Jonathan Truman. *Pardon and Amnesty under Lincoln and Johnson: The Restoration of the Confederates to Their Rights and Privileges, 1861–1898.* Chapel Hill: University of North Carolina Press, 1953.

Etcheson, Nicole. *Bleeding Kansas: Contested Liberty in the Civil War Era.* Lawrence: University Press of Kansas, 2004.

———. "James H. Lane: Radical Conservative, Conservative Radical." In Virgil W. Dean, ed., *John Brown to Bob Dole: Movers and Shakers in Kansas History* (Lawrence: University Press of Kansas, 2006), 33–45.

———. "Manliness and the Political Culture of the Old Northwest, 1790–1860." *Journal of the Early Republic* 15, no. 1 (Spring 1995): 59–77.

Ewing, Cortez A. M. "Early Kansas Impeachments." *Kansas Historical Quarterly* 1, no. 4 (August 1932): 307–25.

Ewy, Marvin. "The United States Army in the Kansas Border Troubles, 1855–1856." *Kansas Historical Quarterly* 32, no. 4 (Winter 1966): 385–400.

Fehrenbacher, Don E. *The Dred Scott Case: Its Significance in American Law and Politics.* New York: Oxford University Press, 2001.

Fisher, H. D. *The Gun and the Gospel: Early Kansas and Chaplain Fisher.* Chicago: Kenwood Press, 1896.

Foner, Eric. *Forever Free: The Story of Emancipation and Reconstruction.* New York: Alfred A. Knopf, 1995.

———. *Free Soil, Free Labor, Free Men: The Ideology of the Republican Party before the Civil War.* New York: Oxford University Press, 1970.

———. *Reconstruction: America's Unfinished Revolution, 1863–1877.* New York: Harper and Row, 1988.

Franklin, John Hope. *Reconstruction after the Civil War.* Chicago: University of Chicago Press, 1961.

Gara, Larry. *The Presidency of Franklin Pierce.* Lawrence: University Press of Kansas, 1991.

Gienapp, William E. *The Origins of the Republican Party, 1852–1856.* New York: Oxford University Press, 1987.

Gihon, John H. *Geary and Kansas: Governor Geary's Administration in Kansas with a Complete History of the Territory. Until June 1857.* New York: Books for Libraries Press, 1971.

Gilmore, Donald. *Civil War on the Missouri-Kansas Border.* Gretna, La.: Pelican Publishing Company, 2006.

Gleed, Charles S., ed. *The Kansas Memorial: A Report of the Old Settlers' Meeting Held at Bismarck Grove, Kansas, September 15th and 16th, 1879.* Kansas City: Press of Ramsey, Millett and Hudson, 1880.

Goodrich, Thomas. *Black Flag: Guerrilla Warfare on the Western Border, 1861–1865.* Indianapolis: Indiana University Press, 1995.

———. *Bloody Dawn: The Story of the Lawrence Massacre.* Kent, Ohio: Kent State University Press, 1991.

———. *War to the Knife: Bleeding Kansas, 1854–1861.* Mechanicsburg, Pa.: Stackpole Books, 1998.

Goodwin, Doris Kearns. *Team of Rivals: The Political Genius of Abraham Lincoln.* New York: Simon and Schuster, 2005.

Gower, Calvin W. "Gold Fever in Kansas Territory: Migration to the Pike's Peak Gold Fields, 1858–1860." *Kansas Historical Quarterly* 39, no. 1 (Spring 1973): 58–74.

Graber, Mark. *Dred Scott and the Problem of Constitutional Evil.* Cambridge: Cambridge University Press, 2006.

Greene, Albert R. "What I Saw of the Quantrill Raid." *Collections of the Kansas State Historical Society.* Vol. 13. Topeka: W. R. Smith, 1915, 430–51.

Gresham, Luveta W. "Colonization Proposals for Free Negroes and Contrabands during the Civil War." *Journal of Negro Education* 16, no. 1 (Winter 1947): 28–33.

Guelzo, Allen C. *Lincoln's Emancipation Proclamation: The End of Slavery in America.* New York: Simon and Schuster, 2004.

Harrell, David Edwin, Jr. "Pardee Butler: Kansas Crusader." *Kansas Historical Quarterly* 34, no. 4 (Winter 1968): 386–408.

Hart, Charles Desmond. "The Natural Limits of Slavery Expansion: Kansas-Nebraska, 1854." *Kansas Historical Quarterly* 35, no. 1 (Spring 1968): 32–50.

Heidler, David S., and Jeanne T. Heidler, eds. *Encyclopedia of the American Civil War: A Political, Social, and Military History.* Santa Barbara: ABC-CLIO, 2000.

Herklotz, Hildegarde Rose. "Jayhawkers in Missouri, 1858–1863." First Article, Chapter I. *Missouri Historical Review* 17, no. 3 (April 1923): 266–84.

———. "Jayhawkers in Missouri, 1858–1863." Third Article, Chapter IV. *Missouri Historical Review* 28, no. 1 (October 1923): 64–101.

Holt, Michael F. *The Fate of Their Country: Politicians, Slavery Extension, and the Coming of the Civil War.* New York: Hill and Wang, 2004.

———. *The Political Crisis of the 1850s.* New York: John Wiley and Sons, 1978.

———. *Political Parties and American Political Development from the Age of Jackson to the Age of Lincoln.* Baton Rouge: Louisiana State University Press, 1992.

———. *The Rise and Fall of the American Whig Party: Jacksonian Politics and the Onset of the Civil War.* New York: Oxford University Press, 1999.

Hougen, Harvey R. "The Marais des Cygnes Massacre and the Execution of William Griffith." *Kansas History* 8 (Summer 1985): 74–94.

Ingalls, John James. "John Brown's Place in History." *North American Review* 138 (February 1884): 138–50.

———. "Kansas 1541–1891." *Harper's Magazine* 86, no. 515 (April 1893): 697–713.

Isely, W. H. "The Sharp's Rifle Episode in Kansas History." *American Historical Review* 12, no. 3 (April 1907): 546–66.

Jaffa, Harry V. *Crisis of the House Divided: An Interpretation of the Issues in the Lincoln-Douglas Debates.* Chicago: University of Chicago Press, 1982, 1959.

Johannsen, Robert W. "A Footnote to the Pottawatomie Massacre, 1856." *Kansas Historical Quarterly* 22, no. 3 (Autumn 1956): 236–41.

———. "The Lecompton Constitutional Convention: An Analysis of Its Membership." *Kansas Historical Quarterly* 23, no. 3 (Autumn 1957): 225–43.

————, ed. *The Lincoln-Douglas Debates of 1858.* New York: Oxford University Press, 1965.

————. *Stephen A. Douglas.* New York: Oxford University Press, 1973.

Johnson, Samuel A. *The Battle Cry of Freedom: The New England Emigrant Aid Company in the Kansas Crusade.* Westport, Conn.: Greenwood Press, 1977.

Josephy, Alvin M., Jr. *The Civil War in the American West.* New York: Alfred A. Knopf, Inc., 1991.

Kennedy, John F. *Profiles in Courage.* New York: HarperPerennial, 2000.

Klein, Maury. *Days of Defiance: Sumter, Secession, and the Coming of the Civil War.* New York: Vintage Books, 1997.

Klingaman, William K. *Abraham Lincoln and the Road to Emancipation, 1861–1865.* New York: Viking, 2001.

Knupfer, Peter B. *The Union As It Is: Constitutional Unionism and Sectional Compromise, 1787–1861.* Chapel Hill: University of North Carolina Press, 1991.

Kolchin, Peter. *American Slavery, 1619–1877.* New York: Hill and Wang, 1993.

Krug, Mark M. "The Republican Party and the Emancipation Proclamation." *Journal of Negro History* 48, no. 2 (April 1963): 98–114.

Lavender, David. *Climax at Buena Vista: The American Campaigns in Northeastern Mexico, 1846–47.* Philadelphia: J. B. Lippincott Company, 1966.

Lewis, Lloyd. "The Man the Historians Forgot." *Kansas Historical Quarterly* 8, no. 1 (February 1939): 85–103.

Lisowski, Lori A. "The Future of West Point: Senate Debates on the Military Academy during the Civil War." *Civil War History* 34, no. 1 (March 1988): 5–21.

Luthin, Reinhard H. "Some Demagogues in American History." *American Historical Review* 57, no. 1 (October 1951): 22–46.

Malin, James C. "Judge Lecompte and the 'Sack of Lawrence,' May 21, 1856, Part 1: The Contemporary Phase." *Kansas Historical Quarterly* 20, no. 7 (August 1952): 465–94.

————. "The Motives of Stephen A. Douglas in the Organization of Nebraska Territory: A Letter Dated December 17, 1853." *Kansas Historical Quarterly* 24, no. 4 (November 1951): 321–53.

Mallam, William D. "Lincoln and the Conservatives." *Journal of Southern History* 28, no. 1 (February 1969): 31–45.

Malone, Dumas, ed. *Dictionary of American Biography.* New York: Charles Scribner's Sons, 1933.

Martin, George. "The First Two Years of Kansas." *Transactions of the Kansas State Historical Society, 1907–1908.* Vol. 10. Topeka: Kansas State Historical Society, 120–48.

Mayer, Henry. *All on Fire: William Lloyd Garrison and the Abolition of Slavery.* New York: St. Martin's Press, 1998.

McPherson, James M. *Battle Cry of Freedom.* New York: Oxford University Press, 1988.

———. *The Negro's Civil War: How American Blacks Felt and Acted during the War for the Union.* New York: Ballantine Books, 1991.

Means, Howard. *The Avenger Takes His Place: Andrew Johnson and the 45 Days That Changed the Nation.* Orlando, Fla.: Harcourt, Inc., 2006.

Mildfelt, Todd. *The Secret Danites: Kansas' First Jayhawkers.* Richmond, Kans.: Todd Mildfelt Publishing, 2003.

Miller, Edward A., Jr. *Lincoln's Abolitionist General: The Biography of David Hunter.* Columbia: University of South Carolina Press, 1997.

Miner, Craig. *Kansas. A History of the Sunflower State, 1854–2000.* Lawrence: University Press of Kansas, 2002.

———. "Lane and Lincoln: A Mysterious Connection." *Kansas History* 24, no. 3 (Autumn 2001): 186–99.

Mink, Charles R. "General Orders, No. 11: The Forced Evacuation of Civilians during the Civil War." *Military Affairs* 34, no. 4 (December 1970): 132–37.

Monaghan, Jay. *Civil War on the Western Border, 1854–1865.* Lincoln: University of Nebraska Press, 1955.

Mullis, Tony R. *Peacekeeping on the Plains: Army Operations in Bleeding Kansas.* Columbia: University of Missouri Press, 2004.

Nevins, Allan. *The Emergence of Lincoln.* Vol. 1: *Douglas, Buchanan, and Party Chaos, 1857–1859.* New York: Charles Scribner's Sons, 1950.

———. *The Emergence of Lincoln.* Vol. 2: *Prologue to Civil War, 1859–1861.* New York: Charles Scribner's Sons, 1950.

———. *Ordeal of the Union.* Vol. 1: *Fruits of Manifest Destiny, 1847–1852.* New York: Charles Scribner's Sons, 1947.

———. *Ordeal of the Union.* Vol. 2: *A House Dividing, 1852–1857.* New York: Charles Scribner's Sons, 1947.

———. *The War for the Union.* Vol. 1: *The Improvised War, 1861–1862.* New York: Charles Scribner's Sons, 1959.

Nicolay, John G. *The Outbreak of Rebellion.* New York: DeCapo Press, 1995. Originally published New York: Scribner's Sons, 1881.

———, and John Hay. *Abraham Lincoln: A History.* Vols. 1–10. New York: Century Co., 1890.

Oates, Stephen B. *To Purge This Land with Blood: A Biography of John Brown.* New York: Harper and Row, 1970.

Oertel, Kristen Tegtmeier. "'The Free Sons of the North' versus 'The Myrmidons of Border-Ruffianism': What Makes a Man in Bleeding Kansas?" *Kansas History* 25, no. 3 (Autumn 2002): 174–89.

Oshinsky, David M. *"Worse than Slavery": Parchman Farm and the Ordeal of Jim Crow Justice.* New York: Free Press Paperbacks, 1997.

Palmer, H. E. "The Black-Flag Character of War on the Border." *Transactions of the Kansas State Historical Society.* Vol. 9. Topeka: Kansas State Historical Society, 1905–1906, 455–66.

Patrick, Rembert W. *The Reconstruction of the Nation.* London: Oxford University Press, 1967.

Pease, Jane H., and William H. Pease. "Confrontation and Abolition in the 1850s." *Journal of American History* 58, no. 4 (March 1972): 923–37.

Phillips, William. *The Conquest of Kansas by Missouri and Her Allies: A History of the Troubles in Kansas, from the Passage of the Organic Act until the Close of July, 1856.* Boston: Phillips, Sampson and Co., 1856.

Plummer, Mark A. *Frontier Governor: Samuel J. Crawford of Kansas.* Lawrence: University Press of Kansas, 1971.

———. "Governor Crawford's Appointment of Edmond G. Ross to the United States Senate." *Kansas Historical Quarterly* 28, no. 2 (Summer 1962): 145–53.

Rawley, James A. *Race and Politics: "Bleeding Kansas" and the Coming of the Civil War.* Philadelphia: J. B. Lippincott Company, 1969.

———. *Secession: The Disruption of the American Republic, 1844–1861.* Malabar, Fla.: Robert E. Krieger Publishing Company, 1990.

Redpath, James. *The Public Life of Capt. John Brown.* Boston: Thayer and Eldridge, 1860.

Robinson, Charles. *The Kansas Conflict.* Lawrence: Journal Publishing Company, 1898.

———. "Topeka and Her Constitution." *Transactions of the Kansas State Historical Society.* Vol. 6. Topeka: Kansas State Historical Society, 1897–1900, 291–316.

Royster, Charles. *The Destructive War: William Tecumseh Sherman, Stonewall Jackson, and the Americans.* New York: Alfred A. Knopf, 1991.

Russel, Robert R. "The Issues in the Congressional Struggle over the Kansas-Nebraska Bill, 1854." *Journal of Southern History* 29, no. 2 (May 1963): 187–210.

Sanborn, Franklin B., ed. *The Life and Letters of John Brown, Liberator of Kansas and Martyr of Virginia.* New York: Negro University's Press, 1969.

————. "Some Notes on the Territorial History of Kansas." *Collections of the Kansas State Historical Society.* Vol. 13. Topeka: W. R. Smith, 1915, 249–65.

Schultz, Duane. *Quantrill's War: The Life and Times of William Clarke Quantrill, 1837–1865.* New York: St. Martin's Press, 1996.

Scott, Otto J. *The Secret Six: John Brown and the Abolitionist Movement.* New York: Times Books, 1979.

Shannon, Fred A. "The Federal Government and the Negro Soldier, 1861–1865." *Journal of Negro History* 11, no. 4 (October 1926): 563–83.

Sheridan, Richard. "From Slavery in Missouri to Freedom in Kansas: The Influx of Black Fugitives and Contrabands into Kansas, 1854–1865." *Kansas History* 12 (Spring 1989): 28–47.

Simons, W. C. "Lawrence Newspapers in Territorial Days." *Collections of the Kansas State Historical Society.* Vol. 17. Topeka: Kansas State Historical Society, 1928, 325–38.

Simpson, Brooks D. *The Reconstruction Presidents.* Lawrence: University Press of Kansas, 1998.

Smith, Elbert B. *The Presidency of James Buchanan.* Lawrence: University Press of Kansas, 1975.

Speer, John. "The Burning of Osceola, Mo., by Lane, and the Quantrill Massacre Contrasted." *Transactions of the Kansas State Historical Society.* Vol. 6. Topeka: Kansas State Historical Society, 1900, 305–12.

————. *Life of Gen. James H. Lane, 'The Liberator of Kansas.'* Garden City, Kans.: John Speer, 1897.

Spring, Leverett W. "The Career of a Kansas Politician." *American Historical Review* 4, no. 1 (October 1898): 80–104.

————. *Kansas: The Prelude to the War for the Union.* Boston: Houghton, Mifflin and Co., 1885.

Stampp, Kenneth M. *America in 1857.* New York: Oxford University Press, 1990.

————. *And The War Came: The North and the Secession Crisis, 1860–1861.* Baton Rouge: Louisiana State University Press, 1990.

————, ed. *The Causes of the Civil War.* Englewood Cliffs, N.J.: Prentice-Hall, Inc., 1974.

————. *The Imperiled Union: Essays on the Background of the Civil War.* New York: Oxford University Press, 1990.

Stephenson, Wendell Holmes. *The Political Career of General James H. Lane.* Topeka: B. P. Walker, 1930.

————. "The Transitional Period in the Career of General James H. Lane." *Indiana Magazine of History* 25, no. 2 (June 1929): 75–91.

Stoddard, William Osborn. *Inside the White House in War Times.* New York: C. L. Webster and Co., 1890.

———. "The Story of a Nomination." *North American Review* 138 (March 1884): 263–73.

Sumner, Charles. *Charles Sumner: His Complete Works. With introduction by Hon. George Frisbie Hoar.* Vol. 2. Boston: Lee and Shepard, 1900.

Thornbrough, Emma Lou. *Indiana in the Civil War Era, 1850–1880.* Indianapolis: Indiana Historical Society, 1966.

Trefousse, Hans L. *The Radical Republicans: Lincoln's Vanguard for Racial Justice.* New York: Alfred A. Knopf, 1969.

Trudeau, Noah Andre. *Like Men of War: Black Troops in the Civil War, 1862–1865.* New York: Little, Brown and Company, 1998.

Villard, Oswald Garrison. *John Brown, 1800–1859.* Boston: Houghton Mifflin Company, 1910.

Watts, Dale E. "How Bloody Was Bleeding Kansas: Political Killings in Kansas Territory 1854–1861." *Kansas History* 18, no. 2 (Summer 1995): 116–29.

Waugh, John C. *Reelecting Lincoln: The Battle for the 1864 Presidency.* New York: Crown Publishers, Inc., 1997.

Welch, G. Murlin. *Border Warfare in Southeastern Kansas, 1856–1859.* Pleasanton, Kans.: Linn County Publishers, 1977.

Wells, Damon. *Stephen Douglas: The Last Years, 1857–1861.* Austin: University of Texas Press, 1971.

Wilder, Daniel C. *The Annals of Kansas.* Topeka: Geo. W. Martin, Kansas Publishing House, 1875.

Williams, Burton J. "Quantrill's Raid on Lawrence: A Question of Complicity." *Kansas Historical Quarterly* 34, no. 2 (Summer 1968): 143–49.

Wyatt-Brown, Bertram. *Honor and Violence in the Old South.* New York: Oxford University Press, 1986.

Zarefsky, David. *Lincoln, Douglas and Slavery: In the Crucible of Public Debate.* Chicago: University of Chicago Press, 1990.

Zimmerman, Charles. "The Origin and Rise of the Republican Party in Indiana from 1854 to 1860." *Indiana Magazine of History* 13, no. 3 (September 1917): 211–69.

Zornow, William Frank. *Kansas: A History of the Jayhawk State.* Norman: University of Oklahoma Press, 1957.

———. "The Kansas Senators and the Reelection of Lincoln." *Kansas Historical Quarterly* 19, no. 2 (May 1951): 133–44.

Index

Lane Trail, 94
Lawrence, Kans., 4, 39, 49–50, 54, 85; and "Anti-Kidnapping Meeting" in 1859, 156–60; Quantrill's attack on, 204–7, 209; and Wakarusa War, 55–58. *See also* Sack of Lawrence
Lawrence Republican: and "Anti-Kidnapping Meeting," 156–57; and destruction of Osceola, 185–86, 190; on Lane's ambition, 234; on Lane and rebellion in Missouri, 179–80; on Lane's criticism of Lecompton convention, 124; and Lane's return to public life, 162; purchased by John Speer, 166, 174; and Senate election of 1861, 174; and the Southern Expedition, 192; supports Lane in Washington, 178, 181

Lawrenceburg, Ind., 18
Learnard, Oscar, 102
Leavenworth, Kans., 188, 210, 213, 222
Leavenworth Constitution: as alternative, 142; and black suffrage controversy, 143, 147–48; failure of, 148, 149; origins, 142–43
Leavenworth Daily Conservative: on black refugees from Missouri, 227; on Lane and Hunter, 189; on Lane's support of Johnson, 260; purchased by Lane supporters, 166; on racial prejudice, 230; on Senate race in 1861, 173
Leavenworth Herald, 50, 129
Leavenworth Journal, 129
Leavenworth Times, 186
Lecompte, Samuel, 50, 85
Lecompton, Kans., 122–23
Lecompton Constitution: before Congress, 140–42; drafted, 124; and English compromise, 149; free-state debate on, 131–32; rejected by free-state voters, 134, 149; rigged ratification plan, 124, 132; supported by Buchanan, 124
Lecompton convention, 113, 122, 124
Lee, Robert E., 247
Legate, James, 36, 140
Lewis, Lloyd, 9–10, 264
Lexington, Mo., 182, 183
Lexington Express, 123
Liberty, Mo., 180
Liberty Weekly Tribune, 188

Lincoln, Abraham, 1, 226; appoints Lane recruiting commissioner, 180–81; approves Kansas bond sale, 201; assassinated, 254; and black recruitment, 235, 236; calls for 75,000 volunteers, 178; compared to Lane, 19, 166–67; creates new military department in Kansas, 189; election of, 172; inaugural address, 219–20; inauguration of, 177; in Kansas, 168; and Kansas-Nebraska Act, 167–68; meets Lane, 168; and nomination in 1864, 248; as presidential candidate in 1860, 166, 171–72; pressed by radicals to remove Schofield, 215–16; presses Schofield to defend Kansas, 211–12; and Reconstruction, 250; reelection of, 241; and reelection opposition, 242, 245; rescinds Fremont's proclamation, 222; rivalry with Stephen Douglas, 166–67; and slavery, 167; and Southern Expedition, 192–95 *passim;* supported by Lane, 166; vetoes Wade-Davis Bill, 253
Louisiana, 172, 251

Maine, 247
Maryland, 178, 222
Mason, James, 72
May, Caleb, 148
McClellan, George B., 188, 192, 246
McClure, James, 40
McCorkle, John, 204
McLean, John, 73, 81
Medary, Samuel, 164–65
Mexico City, 20
Militia Act, 234
Miller, Samuel, 244
Miller, Smith, 29
Miller, Sol, 155, 229, 256
Minneola, Kans., 142–43
Mississippi, 172, 255
Missouri: and animosity toward Kansas, 204; early Confederate success in, 182; delegation at 1864 Republican convention, 247; and Fremont's emancipation proclamation, 222; and Kansas Brigade raids, 184, 185–88; and Lane's "Army of the North," 99–100; Lane's destructive war in, 187–88, 197; Lane's proclamation to, 184–85; and Lane's Southern Expedition, 192;

rejects fraudulent votes, 122; requests federal reinforcements, 118; resigns, 124

Walker, Samuel, 96, 98, 154, 262

Washington, D.C., 146, 174, 226

Washington Chronicle, 249–50

Washington Union, 135

Watson, C. R., 77, 78, 79

Weekly Indiana State Sentinel, 32–33, 90

Weekly Mississippian, 99

Weer, William, 181, 212

Weller, John, 77

Westport, Mo., 249

Whig Party, 3, 21, 28, 35, 46, 102, 167, 170

Whitcomb, James, 19

White Cloud Kansas Chief: on freed slaves in Kansas, 229; on Lane's

inconsistency, 144, 147; on Lane's killing of Jenkins, 155; on Lane and Reconstruction, 256; supports Lane as military leader, 180

Whitfield, J. W., 44

Wilder, A. C., 211

Wilder, Daniel, 230

Willard Hotel, 178

Williams, James, 235

Wilson, Henry, 76, 258

Wilson's Creek, battle of, 182

Wood, Samuel N., 85

Woodson, Daniel, 99, 100

Wright, Joseph, 35

Wyandotte Constitution, 163, 172, 239

Wyandotte constitutional convention, 163